Mastering IBM WebSphere Portal

Ron Ben-Natan
Richard Gornitsky
Ori Sasson
Tim Hanis

WILEY

Wiley Publishing, Inc.

Published by
Wiley Publishing, Inc.
10475 Crosspoint Boulevard
Indianapolis, IN 46256
www.wiley.com

Copyright © 2004 by Wiley Publishing, Inc., Indianapolis, Indiana

Published simultaneously in Canada

ISBN: 0-7645-3991-4

Manufactured in the United States of America

10 9 8 7 6 5 4 3 2

For general information on our other products and services or to obtain technical support, please contact our Customer Care Department within the U.S. at (800) 762-2974, outside the U.S. at (317) 572-3993 or fax (317) 572-4002.

Wiley also publishes its books in a variety of electronic formats. Some content that appears in print may not be available in electronic books.

Library of Congress Cataloging-in-Publication Data

Credits

Acquisitions Editor
Jim Minatel

Development Editor
Scott Amerman

Project Editor
Pamela Hanley

Copy Editors
TechBooks

Editorial Manager
Kathryn A. Malm

**Vice President and Executive
Group Publisher**
Richard Swadley

**Vice President and Executive
Publisher**
Robert Ipsen

Vice President and Publisher
Joseph B. Wikert

Executive Editorial Director
Mary Bednarek

Project Coordinator
Sandy Joshi

Proofreading and Indexing
TECHBOOKS Production Services

*I would like to dedicate this book to Ruthy,
who is thankfully still a wonderful part of our life.*

—Ron Ben-Natan

*I would like to dedicate this book to the loves of my life,
my wife Marcelle and my sons, Joshua and David.*

—Richard Gornitsky

*I would like to dedicate this book to Yael,
for her love and support*

—Ori Sasson

*I would like to dedicate this to my wife, Susan, for her generosity, love,
and understanding; my parents and older sister for contributions too
numerous to mention and too vague to articulate; the constant
company of Kismet and Skates; and in loving memory of Tux.*

—Tim Hanis

Contents

Foreword

The explosion of access to information and applications, made possible by the Internet and the World Wide Web, has given rise to a new set of challenges for information technology professionals. Portal frameworks such as WebSphere Portal Server provide capabilities and services needed to meet requirements for consistent administration, look and feel, and navigation across all of these sources of content. In addition, portals enable productivity-enhancing services such as single sign-on and role-dependent personalization that bring the right tools and information to the right people in an organization. When combined with tools such as WebSphere Studio Application Developer, used for the development of specialty components (portlets), a portal becomes not only an essential element of any system integration strategy but also a fundamental tool for the development and deployment of new applications.

Software development frameworks evolve out of the observation of programming patterns that frequently recur throughout the industry. Uses of programming techniques such as CGI–bin .exe's, Pearl scripts, and the like have required programmers to re-create or recode basic services such as memory and thread management, security, authentication, connections to database and back-end data sources, and markup generation libraries. Frustration with these repetitive tasks and initiatives like the Java Community Process gave rise to formalized frameworks of services such as J2EE application servers. J2EE application servers are now commonplace and widely deployed in many enterprises.

As enterprises require more and more integration among their application systems and as Web-based user interfaces have become the hub of application access, the J2EE model has been stretched and adapted. As before, we can observe patterns of use in many enterprises centered around the *aggregation* of content, applications, and services, which makes it easy to create navigational models over the aggregation. Techniques such as JSP-includes were used to assemble larger applications out of pieces. However, these pieces lacked formal specifications for life cycle management and a contract between the components and their container. From these reuse patterns, IBM and others developed the specifications for a reusable component model, *portlets*. Formalization of portlets led directly to the development of management applications for portlets, or portal frameworks, and to a new breed of products to extend the capabilities of J2EE, such as WebSphere Portal (WP).

Portals and their building blocks, portlets, are quickly becoming "norms" for enterprise class application development and deployment environments. As components, portlets encapsulate Web applications in a life cycle and rendering scheme that makes them manageable and aggregatable by portals. The specifications for portlets are becoming codified by industry standards such as the Java Community JSR 168 and the corresponding Web services standard, WSRP. Portlets can be arbitrarily combined with other portlets to create more complex assemblies and navigational structures. This composition makes possible administrative assembly of applications. As the standards mature, they are being enhanced with capabilities that make it possible for portlets to interact with one another and send data and control signals that make portlets work together. Indeed, portlet composition can be thought of as a generalized component assembly programming model in which individually developed components are wired together to form new, more complex components. This powerful model will fundamentally change the way Enterprise Applications are built. Instead of monolithic application structures, applications will be built of modular, reusable components. Standards will ensure that the development and deployment models are portable and reusable across many environments. In addition, catalogs of prebuilt application pieces will enable business professionals with a keen understanding of the business to construct solutions that today projects require in the IT department.

Looking to the future, we see the continued evolution of the portal-based programming model leading to advanced "workplace" style applications. Workplaces bring an unprecedented level of user and administrator control to the design and deployment of component-based solutions. In a workplace, the role of the individual and the intersection of this role with the work processes that go on in all businesses are paramount. Workplaces, which are fundamentally based on the concepts and technology of portals and portlets, combine advanced notions of community, self-service, business process modeling, and management to form powerful and enterprise productivity-enhancing systems. Mastery of the portal concepts and techniques will help all information technology professionals, not just Java programmers, to solve the future information and application integration challenges of their organizations.

Ron Ben-Natan, Richard Gornitsky, Tim Hanis, and Ori Sasson have authored an authoritative "must-have" guide to the capabilities of WP. *Mastering IBM WebSphere Portal* contains all that one must know to get started and become proficient with the portal application development and delivery environment. Beginning with the basics of installation and configuration, moving through the user interface concepts of skins, themes and tag libraries, and ultimately system administration, you will come to understand all of the essentials for working with WP. In addition, the authors explore the prebuilt capabilities for collaboration among portal users. Finally, you'll learn the ins and outs of the portal and portlet programming models and best practices for developing and debugging your own portlets.

Portals extend Enterprise Application development to the next level. All application developers and system administrators can benefit from a thorough understanding of the power and flexibility offered by this new breed of system framework. I hope you enjoy *Mastering IBM WebSphere Portal*, and find that the next-generation environment of the WP truly enables enhanced productivity and improved business results.

Douglass Wilson
Distinguished Engineer, CTO,
IBM Lotus Software Division

Acknowledgments

The authors would like to thank the following people whose efforts were critical to the success of this book. Specifically we would like to thank Mike Rhodin, Larry Bowden, Douglass Wilson, Hershel Harris, Brandon Smith, and Bill Swatling for their support and encouragement. We would also like to thank Mike Durham, Kathy Sitar, and Uwe Zimmerman for their help in involving us in the WebSphere Portal 5.0 Beta program. Special thanks go to Theresa Smit, Jeffrey Hay, Stefan Hepper, Jim Bonanno, Lisa Tomita, Rob Davis, Ashok Iyengar, George Fridrich, and Venkata Gadepalli for their invaluable help in performing the technical review.

This book would not have come to fruition without the patience and dedication of our editors Jim Minatel and Scott Amerman.

About the Authors

Ron Ben-Natan is Chief Technical Officer at Guardium, a leader in database and data access security. Ron is an expert in the field of portals, portal integration, and portal security. He has developed portal platforms for the telecommunication and energy industries, a security portal, and has been involved in the implementation of numerous enterprise portals. He is also an expert in distributed computing, J2EE applications, application and database security, and Web services. He has published 8 technical books including several best-selling WebSphere Application Server books and over 40 technical articles.

Richard Gornitsky is a Consulting I/T Architect for IBM Software Services for Lotus whose expertise is in integrating WebSphere Portal in Fortune 500 firms from concept to production. He has extensive experience in the full life cycle development of high transaction solutions, which includes simultaneously managing multiple large complex application development and infrastructure projects. His industry experience includes finance, insurance, telecommunications, pharmaceutical, software manufacturing, and retail/distribution. Gornitsky is a requested technical speaker.

Tim Hanis is a Senior Software Engineer at IBM in Research Triangle Park, North Carolina. He holds computer science degrees from Penn State University and North Carolina State University. He is the lead developer for WP business portlets and has extensive experience in helping customers solve business problems using WebSphere products. Tim can be reached at hanistt@us.ibm.com.

Ori Sasson Ori Sasson is an independent software consultant operating out of Singapore. He is an expert in Java Enterprise Development with J2EE, business integration, data mining, and systems security. He has authored fourtechnical books and several technical articles.

Introduction

If you are a user of Web applications you are also most likely a user of portals. If you develop, manage, or administer Web applications, then you are probably already building or managing Web portals or have thought that you should get started with portal technologies. If you fall into any one of these categories and your Web technology of choice is IBM's WebSphere then this book is for you.

Web portals are becoming the de facto standard for packaging Web applications, and Web applications are increasingly being developed as "portal plugins" (often called portlets). Regardless of whether the domain is consumer applications or business applications, portals have become the consensus user interface for Web applications. In the consumer world all major Web sites present a portal look and feel: Yahoo and MyYahoo, MSN, and Amazon are just commonly known examples. If you work for a large corporation you probably have some form of corporate portal—offering you various human resources (HR), finance, and corporate communication applications in a portal-like environment.

Why are Web portals so successful? Because they bring together important functions such as integration, presentation, organization, and customizations—functions that are needed in every complex application environment. Why have they succeeded in Web application environments? Because these application environments tend to be highly complex, provide tens, hundreds, and sometimes thousands of disparate applications and serve huge user populations—sometimes many millions of users.

Given this very real need, companies have been offering portal server technologies since the dawn of Web applications. But like other information technology domains, portals too have gone through a maturation process.

Some of the early leaders in this space are no longer leaders and some have completely disappeared. On the other hand, many of the large players including IBM, Microsoft, Oracle, BEA, and SAP offer portal products—products that are mature, complete, and very functional.

It is no secret that IBM has been very aggressive and extremely successful with the WebSphere family of products. The WebSphere Application Server started with no market share and today dominates the J2EE application server landscape world; according to some market reviews it has passed BEA WebLogic to become the market share leader. What is less well known is that the same has been happening in the portal space with WebSphere Portal quickly becoming a leader in the portal server space. In fact, WebSphere Portal has the highest new adoption rate within large corporations and is being used within more and more projects and across all industry verticals.

If you are among the many people involved in these portal projects, this book is for you. While WebSphere Portal is a mature product, it is also a highly complex and more specialized one, which means that there are less available resources for you to rely on. It supports many functions and you can use it to do a great number of things and in many ways. This complexity has the unfortunate side effect that WebSphere Portal is not easy to master. The goal of this book is to ease this pain, that is help you master WebSphere Portal.

Overview of the Book and Its Goals

This book will teach you how to install, use, administer, manage, and implement a WebSphere Portal V.5 environment. It will also teach you how to develop and deploy portlets (implementing your custom functionality) on a WebSphere Portal V.5 infrastructure. The focus is not only on developers, but also on administrators, architects, and managers involved with WebSphere Portal projects. If you are a developer you will make the most of this book if you have a Java development background. However, because the focus is on portlets and the inner functions of the portal server, even people with less-than-perfect Java skills will benefit from the book.

Because portals are normally found in business applications environments with a high degree of complexity, the book also shows you how to address the interaction between the portal and other elements in the enterprise. Portal applications are not islands of functionality—if anything they are the fabric that forms the bridges. Therefore, you will learn not only about the portal as a server but also how it interacts with components such as LDAP servers, Enterprise Applications, mobile devices, and even other (vertical) portals.

How This Book Is Organized

In order to master WebSphere Portal V.5, the book will take you through a series of topics starting with those focused on the portal itself and culminating with topics that discuss how the portal fits in within enterprise environments.

You will first learn how to install and customize the portal, as well as how to migrate existing environments to version 5. Next you will learn how to administer and manage portals, including defining portlets, pages, and user interface properties. You will also learn how to use personalization, collaboration, search, document management, and content management within WebSphere Portal V.5. The third set of chapters of the book discuss portlets and show you how to use the portlet API, how to develop portlets, and how to use various development frameworks that make this an easy task. Finally, the last part of the book focuses on WebSphere Portal V.5 within the enterprise environment and shows you how to address topics such as high availability, security and single-sign-on, identity management, Web services, Enterprise Applications, and mobility.

The book starts with an introduction to the WebSphere product family and a review of what WebSphere Portal is responsible for within the complete product family. You will learn about the three dimensions of WebSphere Portal (WP) experience: the user experience, the developer experience, and the administrator experience. You will then get an overview of the WP architecture and what's new in WP version 5.0.

Chapters 2 and 3 will take you through the installation procedures for WP 5.0. WP 5.0 greatly improves upon the various WebSphere Portal Server versions 4.x in terms of installations. If you are using a Windows platform turn to Chapter 2, and if you are using Linux, turn to Chapter 3. If you are using other Unix platforms you can start with Chapter 3 and make changes to the installation procedures based on the WP InfoCenter.

Chapter 4 continues with installation by teaching you how to use Oracle, DB2, or Microsoft SQL Server as the back-end database for your WP instances. In addition, Chapter 4 takes you through WP 5.0 customization topics. You will learn how to use WPSconfig and various configuration templates, how to configure the databases used by WP, and how to configure WP when using remote access.

In Chapter 5 you will complete the installation topics by learning how to install and use the WebSphere Portal Toolkit and the WebSphere Portal Test Environment. You will also learn how to install and activate the Lotus Workplace Web Content Management modules and Tivoli's Web Site Analyzer. Finally, you will learn how to diagnose and troubleshoot problems that you may encounter.

Chapter 6 is the last chapter in the first part of the book and covers topics relating to migration to WP 5.0. If you are already using WebSphere Portal Server 4.x, this chapter will teach you how to upgrade your system to WP 5.0 smoothly and easily. If you are starting fresh on WP 5.0 you can skip this chapter.

In Chapter 7 you will learn about defining elements within your portal. You will learn how to create portals and define pages and how to customize your portal's structure.

Chapter 8 continues this theme by teaching you how to tailor the portal's user interface. You will learn what themes and skins are and how to define your own custom style for your portal. You will also learn how to take existing styles and modify them rather than building new styles from scratch.

In Chapter 9 you will learn about one of the most important topics supported by WP: personalization. You will learn about the various personalization features within WP 5.0, how to use rule-based personalization, and how the personalization API can help you with advanced personalization.

Chapter 10 focuses on portal administration and reviews all of the main administration tasks that you will be required to do when maintaining your portal. You will learn about the WP settings, permissions, and access control and in each topic you will see how to perform the main administration tasks.

Chapter 11 reviews document management and content management within WP 5.0. Like personalization, these topics are often synonymous with portals and the chapter will walk you through some of the main tasks you may need to perform, such as setting up workflows, creating content templates, and categorizing content.

Chapter 12 goes on to complete the second part of the book by introducing you to collaboration and to search. You will learn how to use collaboration components—whether they are Lotus components or Microsoft components. You will also learn how to implement search within your portal, manage search taxonomies and categorizations, and set up extended search capabilities.

In Chapter 13 you will learn about portlets and the focus turns to the development of custom functionality to be deployed within your portal. You will learn about the portlet container and the portlet life cycle and will see how to use portlet configuration objects, portlet requests, and portlet responses. Finally, you will learn about the portlet event model.

Chapter 14 continues with portlets and focuses on the portlet API. You will learn about the JSR 168 API and the various portlet APIs at your disposal. You will learn about the portlet processing model, URI addressability, and about services and objects.

In Chapter 15 you will see how easy it is to develop portlets using WebSphere Studio and the embedded Portlet Toolkit. The chapter (along with

Chapter 16) takes you through a complete development cycle using an example poll portlet. Chapter 16 continues with the poll portlet and show you how to implement the controller and action classes, and how to build the view classes and take care of the model classes.

Chapter 17 teaches you how to develop the poll portlet using the JSR 168 API—providing you will a full arsenal of development techniques that you can use in your environment. The chapter also teaches you how to debug your code and how to use trace logging as part of the development life cycle.

Chapter 18 completes the development part of the book by teaching you how to use the struts portlet framework. Struts is the de facto Web application framework in Java server environments and it is very likely that you will develop portlets that make use of struts' Model-View-Controller paradigm. You will learn how to build both the Web deployment descriptor and the portlet deployment descriptor and how to set up the struts configuration file. You will then revisit the poll portlet and see how it would look within a struts environment.

Chapter 19 moves on from a development focus to address authentication issues and how you can integrate an LDAP environment into your WP 5.0 servers. You will learn how to configure your portal to connect to your LDAP servers and how to implement enterprise identity management.

Chapter 20 continues with this theme and addresses the larger issue of single-sign-on and identity management when using WP 5.0 with either Netegrity SiteMinder or Tivoli Access Manager. You will learn how to configure WP 5.0 to use each of these platforms and the issues you need to think about when doing such a deployment.

Chapter 21 goes on to provide you with planning and implementation skills that will help you set up WP 5.0 in a high-availability environment. You will learn about WP clusters and how to build clusters supporting either vertical or horizontal scaling. You will learn how to configure a clustered environment and how to deploy portlets in such an environment.

Chapter 22 is all about Web services in the context of WP 5.0 After a very quick review on Web services you will learn about remote portlets. You will then learn about two methods for using Web services within a WP environment and for each method you will see what configuration tasks and what development tasks you may need to do within your portal.

Chapter 23 is one of the longest chapters in the book and addresses the issue of integrating external applications into WP. In this chapter you will learn what integration options are available and for each category you will learn what needs to be done. You will learn about using adapters to integrate back-end systems with portlets, using middleware connectors, and about the Portal Application Integrator. You will also learn how to set up back-end single-sign-on and about the Credential Vault service. You will then learn about front-end integration techniques such as Web Clipping and Web embedding as an alternate integration strategy.

The last chapter in the book, Chapter 24, shows you how to support users who do not only use PCs and desktop Web browsers but rather use mobile and wireless devices to access functionality deployed through WP. You will learn about Transcoding Technologies and about WebSphere Everyplace Access as an enabler for supporting mobile users.

The following table shows the chapters that will be of most interest to portlet developers, portal administrators, portal implementation specialists and enterprise architects:

ROLE	FOCUS CHAPTERS
Portlet developer	13, 14, 15, 16, 17, 18, 22
Portal administrator	4, 5, 6, 10, 19, 20, 21, 22, 23
Portal implementation specialist	7, 8, 9, 10, 11, 12, 19, 20, 21, 23, 24
Enterprise architect	19, 20, 21, 22, 23, 24

Summary

This book is about mastering WebSphere Portal V.5. If you are just starting with WebSphere Portal, we recommend you read the chapters in sequence, starting with the installation of the portal, through the various tasks you will need to perform, and ending with advanced topics relevant to enterprise deployment. If you are already familiar with WebSphere Portal, feel free to jump directly to the chapter that fancies your interest—we wrote the book in a way that almost all chapters present a topic from start to finish and is almost self-contained. In any case, we hope that you enjoy the book and that the book will help you gain mastery over WebSphere Portal V.5.

WebSphere Portal Primer

CHAPTER

1

Introducing WebSphere Portal

What is a portal and why do I need it? What does WebSphere Portal offer that I can't do with custom code? In this chapter, we will answer these questions and introduce you to the WebSphere brand and more specifically to WebSphere Portal. We will show you how WebSphere Portal can help you rapidly develop and deploy applications that will impact your bottom line by introducing you to its features and architecture. At the end of this chapter you will understand why you need a portal and how WebSphere Portal meets your portal requirements.

What Is a Portal and Why Do We Need Them?

When the Internet was first introduced, applications were simple and text based. Graphics were soon introduced, and programmers found out that much of the development effort was shifting to look and feel rather than implementing business function. Then developers felt it would be cool to integrate various other sites into their own; however, this generated a smorgasbord look and feel. Security soon became an issue and each site then required authentication. If the developer had integrated multiple sites into his or her own site, the user would endure the frustrating experience of having to do multiple logins on a single site, each with a different name and password. By the 1990s the Internet was experiencing a massive boom when numerous software companies and IT departments were developing software; however, most of it provided the same functionality. Many groups were designing search engines and collaboration software and IT managers were questioning why they were constantly redesigning the wheel and why productivity and quality were so low. Then, if there weren't enough headaches, Internet applications were required to be accessible on many different devices with very different attributes such as desktops, mobile phones, and palm pilots. Some devices can handle sophisticated graphics and have lots of visual room while others have limited input and output capabilities (e.g., a mobile phone).

Portals, specifically WebSphere Portal, help today's businesses address the Internet challenges. It helps programmers focus on developing the business functionality by letting the portal manage the look and feel, personalization, content management, and security. It allows users to integrate different applications from disparate locations and enables them to seamlessly exchange information. Each user can create a personalized device-independent "desktop" with a consistent look and feel by using drag and drop components. Much of the functionality that is required for Web experience does not have to be programmed but can be found in the portal library, a collection of "shrink wrap packaged" portlets or portal applications.

The WebSphere Family

WebSphere is a software platform that enables you to develop, deploy, and integrate all types of enterprise-scale e-business applications: from business to business, customer to business, employer to employee, on demand, and even legacy.

WebSphere is made up of three components (Figure 1-1): foundation and tools, reach and user experience or business portals, and business integration.

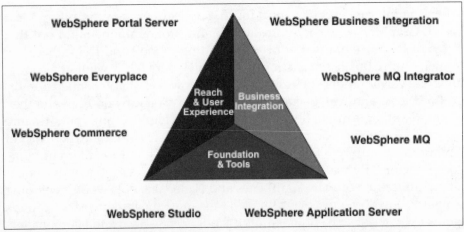

Figure 1-1 IBM WebSphere components.

Foundation and Tools

The "engine" and the "frame" of the WebSphere constitute the WebSphere Application Server (WAS). It is the environment in which you run and manage your Java applications. WAS is a complete, open standard Java 2 Platform, Enterprise Edition (J2EE) 1.4 application server that enables you to perform the following tasks:

1. Integrate easily to other e-business and legacy applications through its support of J2EE Connector Architecture. This gives a consistent way of connecting and communicating to other applications without complex programming.

2. Communicate to other distributed systems using guaranteed and reliable persistent high-performance messaging based on the Java Messaging Service (JMS) and/or Web Services.

3. Deploy and administer applications with ease on a single server. With the optional WebSphere Application Server Network Deployment, you can manage and administer a large number of servers and reduce your administration costs with its automated server management. Installation and administration capabilities are further enhanced through the support of Java Management Extensions, which enables integration with third-party system management products such as Tivoli, Candle, and CA.

4. WAS provides you with performance optimization and reliability by allowing you to control and isolate each application run-time environment. With the WebSphere Application Server Network Deployment option, you get high availability and high transaction support through clustering and caching. Using clustering, it supports load balancing and automatic failover capability. Load balancing can be done at the routers, Web servers, or the application servers. It also provides content-based routing and edge-based caching.

5. Sophisticated and complete security support through

   a. Secure system resources with the Java 2 security model

   b. Standardize authentication with Java Authentication and Authorization Services (JAAS)

   c. Secure communication channels (TLS/SSL) using Java Secure Socket Extension

   d. Security encryption and message authentication using Java Cryptographic Extension

   e. Public Key Infrastructure (PKI) integration based on Java Cryptographic Architecture. PKI manages the issuing, distribution, and authentication of private and public digital keys. Digital keys are used to authenticate an individual or a resource.

   f. Secure interoperability between application servers

   g. Support for registries based on Lightweight Directory Access Protocol (LDAP)

   h. Single sign-on support using Trust Association Interceptor or Lightweight Third Party Authentication (LTPA)

6. Deploy applications independent of hardware and software environments. WAS can be deployed on Intel, Sun, HP, and IBM hardware platforms running AIX, Linux, zOS, OS/400, Solaris, HP-UX, and Windows 2000/2003.

To enable rapid deployment of applications on WAS, IBM provides WebSphere Studio: a suite of integrated application development tools based on the ECLIPSE open standard framework. From a single user to a large team environment, developers can rapidly develop, debug, and test their WebSphere Applications and then seamlessly deploy into a WAS environment. The WebSphere Studio integrates with the Rational product line including modeling to code generation, testing, and version control.

The foundation and tools component also includes WebSphere Host Integration family, which enables you to integrate your legacy assets with your e-business.

Business Integration

WebSphere Business Integration is a suite of 24 products that provides end-to-end integration by performing the following tasks:

1. Using modeling to design, simulate, and plan business processes

2. Providing products that facilitate linking people, processes, applications, system, and data

3. Enabling you to connect to your customers and partners

4. Allowing you to control and track business processes

5. Enabling you to review, analyze, and improve processes and performance

Items 1, 4, and 5 are supported by the WebSphere Business Integration. Item 2 is supported through message brokering and formatting using WebSphere Business Integration Message Broker. IBM WebSphere Business Integration Message Broker transforms and enhances real-time information between applications that use different message structures and formats.

Item 3 is supported by WebSphere MQ. WebSphere MQ allows you to integrate applications using messaging.

WebSphere Business Portals

WebSphere Business Portal suite focuses on the e-business user experience. It consists of WebSphere Commerce, WebSphere Everyplace, WebSphere Voice, and WebSphere Portal.

WebSphere Commerce enables a user to create selling, buying, and channel management solutions for anything from a simple on-line sales channel to a multitier integrated demand chain.

WebSphere Everyplace provides a suite of tools that facilitate the delivery of Web pages and e-business applications to a broad range of mobile devices.

WebSphere Voice supports development and deployment of conversational and voice recognition e-business solutions. It also provides translation services and unified messaging that includes voice mail, e-mail, and faxes.

The last product, but the most important from this book's perspective, is WebSphere Portal, which, according to IBM's Web site (www.ibm.com), provides "a single point of personalized interaction with applications, content, processes, and people." Now we explore this statement and elaborate what it means.

What Is WebSphere Portal?

Previously in this chapter, we discussed what a portal is. WebSphere Portal provides all these capabilities plus the availability and scalability required for large enterprise applications. But to really understand what WebSphere Portal is, you need to look at from the users', programmers', and administrators' perspectives.

The User Experience

WebSphere Portal allows users to create their own virtual desktops that are machine independent. Each user can create his or her own portal pages and customize the content and look and feel of these pages. They can add functionality to their pages through *portlets*, which are portal applications. Portlets are custom made by your sites' programmers, downloaded from the IBM portal catalog, or are available from software vendors. Each portlet has settings that allow users to customize the functionality for their environment. An extensive set of portlets is available from IBM and its partners

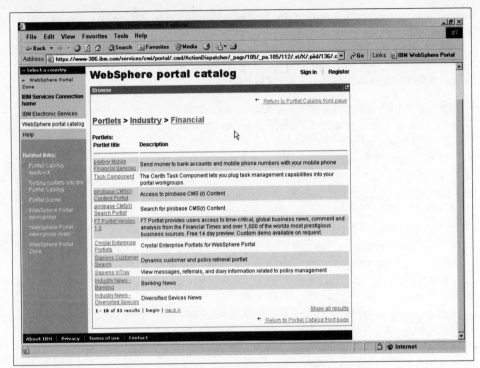

Figure 1-2   Financial portlet section of the WebSphere Portal Catalog.

through the Portal Catalog at `www.ibm.com/software/genservers/portal/portlet/catalog`.

At last count IBM had 531 portlets in its catalog. Figure 1-2 shows some financial portlets available from the catalog. Portlets can be easily added to a page by clicking on the Edit Layout link at the top page you want to customize.

Users can have as many personalized pages as they want. They are arranged in a hierarchical manner with any level of depth starting from their home page. Based on their permissions, users can choose for each page or set of pages their own themes, skins, and layout. Themes define the fonts, colors, spacing, and other look-and-feel components of the page. They are a combination of cascading style sheets, JSP files, and images. Skins comprise title bars, borders, shadows, etc. that surround the portlets. Each page and the pages associated with its tree can have their own theme and skins, thus creating a virtual portal. Each department that enters into the portal will have its own look and feel.

WP Page Navigation supports complex navigation trees and labels that logically group a set of navigation elements.

WebSphere Portal allows users to view content on multiple devices and in multiple languages, including double byte and bidirectional. It also generates markup that complies with the American Disability Act Section 508 Web Accessibility Standards and the guidelines of the W3C Web Accessibility Initiative. If the portal needs automatic translation, users can incorporate WebSphere Translation Server.

Content Management

WP provides the user the ability to syndicate content or to get up-to-date personalized and filtered content and services from multiple subscriber sources such as Financial Times, Hoovers, Factiva, and others. These subscribers support the Rich Site Summary (RSS) format, so their news and entertainment content can be displayed, managed, and edited with WP's built-in RSS portlet.

WebSphere Portal also enables the user to manage the creation, approval, and publishing of Web content through the support of Web Content Management products. Integration kits are provided on how to publish RSS content from Web Content Management vendors such as Documentum and Vignette. WebSphere Portal also provides its own sophisticated Web Content Management system called IBM Lotus Workplace Web Content Management (ILWWCM).

ILWWCM (formally known as Aptrix) is an enhanced Web Content Management System that replaced WebSphere Content Publishing. ILWWCM is a separately installed component that you need to get from your IBM representative. In the next version, it should be totally integrated into WebSphere Portal.

ILWWCM is designed for organizations with users that publish content to a Web site, whether it is marketing updating product information or human resources updating information on benefits. Content can be published through templates or forms and consists of images, Word documents, Excel, HTML, and so forth.

Through the ILWWCM administrator, users can contribute content, have it categorized, and deployed in a controlled manner using a workflow model. ILWWCM manages the task list of each user and through the establishment of role security enables what content can be changed, created, or deleted by a user. With the use of the workflow model, it coordinates the review and publishing process.

To address more sophisticated content manager requirements, use IBM Content Manager.

Document Management

WebSphere Portal Document Manager (PDM) provides users the ability to view, add, edit, and delete documents within a common folder hierarchy that can be user-defined. Documents can be made available immediately or to go through an approval process using a defined workflow model. PDM uses WP's access controls, so users can define who can create, read, update, and/or delete a document based on their roles. Authorizations can be set by folder, which will be inherited to the subfolders. PDM provides a subscription capability that enables users to see in their Update folder, for a specified period, a document when it is changed.

PDM supports multiple different types of documents and provides productivity components that enable users to create and edit rich text, spreadsheets, and presentation documents within their browser.

Search

WebSphere Portal provides the user with a vast range of search capabilities. It is built on a sophisticated search engine that supports free-text queries with query assistance and query word completion. Queries can be performed in any language and can use wildcard, advance query operators, synonyms, stop word lists, and fielded search options. The results of the search can be summarized, clustered, and/or categorized using categories that are predefined (over 2,400 categories) or user-defined. WP can index and then search text and 200 other file formats using built-in document filters over the intranet or Internet. Use of the search capabilities is made through the search portlet, the WP crawler, or the document indexer. Both the crawler and the document indexer have a complete scheduler.

Enhanced search is also provided through IBM Lotus Extended Search and DB2 Information Integrator. Portlets using these technologies can integrate and combine other search engines and indexes. Lotus Extended search also allows seamless searches across a collection of Domino servers, databases, and the Internet where the user perceives that the collection of systems is a single server.

Collaboration

WebSphere Portal provides complete support for collaboration through the Notes, Domino, and Domino Web Access portlets. These portlets provide access to collaboration applications that use Lotus Notes databases on Domino servers such as Mail, Calendar, To Do, Notes View, TeamRoom, and Discussion. Additional portlets are available that integrate Domino.doc, Discovery Server, QuickPlace (Lotus Team Workplaces), and Sametime (Lotus Instant Messaging and Web Conferencing).

WP offers Collaboration Center, which is a framework that integrates People Finder, the Web Conference Center, QuickPlace, and Sametime.

QuickPlace provides workspaces for sharing and organizing ideas while Sametime provides instant messaging, shared white boards, and electronic meeting support.

WebSphere Portal enables integration of Domino, Sametime, QuickPlace, and Discovery Server into your portlet by providing Lotus Collaboration Components that are a suite of APIs and JSP tags.

Personalization

WebSphere Personalization server, which is a component of WebSphere Portal, provides the ability to display specific content to site users based on business rules. A business rule is the representation of a business requirement using a coding language based on English language syntax and semantics. The personalization server works by performing the following tasks:

1. Creating a user profile by collecting user information and classifying it into segments
2. Creating models for the content that defines it by its attributes. For instance, a content model might contain product name, price, and age segment.
3. Matching the user segment to the content on the basis of any combination of filtering, rules, or recommendation engine.

The personalization rules are referenced in the portlets. They are created using Web-based tools. You use the rules to classify site visitors into segments and then match the content to the segment.

Another method provided to match site visitors with content is through the recommendation engine. The recommendation engine uses statistical techniques to identify groups of users with similar interests.

WebSphere Portal also provides implicit profiling services that enable the dynamic creation of personalization business rules based on site visitor data.

WebSphere Portal also provides campaign management tools, which enable a business goal to be reached by defining and executing a set of business rules. For instance, you may have a campaign to increase sales of a particular product. To do this, you define business rules that identify likely customers based on the attributes of site visitors or registered users. Content can be displayed on your Web site or personalized e-mail can be sent. Campaigns have start and stop times; they can be prioritized, and can be run in parallel with other campaigns.

Performance

No matter how sophisticated your portal is, it will not be effective if it does not meet your performance, functional, and personalization requirements. WebSphere Portal creates logs that feed into the IBM Tivoli Web Site Analyzer. The Web Site analyzer will analyze the data and report metric in both graphic and text formats so that you can determine the effectiveness of your Web site and focus on areas to improve it.

The Developer Experience

WebSphere Portal allows the developer to focus on functionality development rather than deal with look-and-feel function. Programmers create portlets that are simple Java applications that are extensions to HTTP servlets. Through portlets, they can access and manipulate Web-based content (such as Web pages, syndicated content feeds) and other Java applications/portlets through messaging and/or Web services and not have to deal with issues relating to look and feel. Figure 1-3 shows the page layout and how portlets fit in.

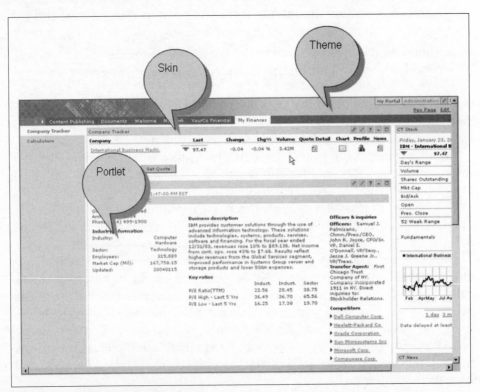

Figure 1-3   The parts of a portal page.

WebSphere Portal also provides a mechanism for portlets to communicate with each other. The developer can send information through a portlet action and a portlet message. For instance, when a portlet displays information on a city, a second portlet can display its weather information by having the city portlet create a portlet action and encode it into the URL that is used for displaying weather. Upon clicking the URL, an action listener is called and then a portlet message is sent to the city portlet for the name of the city.

This method requires an extensive design and coding work. WP provides another method to pass messages independently called cooperative portlets. Cooperative portlets can be "Click-2-Action" or "wired." Portlets express their desire to interact with a broker who at runtime matches data types between the sources of one portlet with the action of another portlet. If a match occurs with a "Click-2-Action portlet," a pop-up menu appears on the page that will enable the user to transfer the data to the connected portlet. If the portlet is wired by an administrator, then the data will be exchanged automatically as opposed to having to wait for the user to click the pop-up menu.

WP gives developers the ability to develop portlets very easily using Web Clipping. This feature enables developers to visually or text select portions of a Web page and create a portlet that displays the information and optionally rewrite the links. Clipping portlet can support other sites' security through the use of WP Credential Vault.

Through the portlet Application Programming Interface (API), WebSphere Portal provides programmers the ability to dynamically discover available services, thus keeping service code independent of the portlet. WP provides discoverable services for managing the portal's content repository, persistent TCP/IP connections, and the Credential Vault. Other services such as mail can be implemented by the portal developer.

WebSphere Portal provides developers with a rich set of security API. Portal server supports the JAAS architecture. JAAS is a component of the standard Java security model that enables authenticating subjects and fine-grain access control. Developers can use the JAAS API to access JAAS-enabled back-end applications and can also use the credential API to authenticate without seeing the credential secret.

WP provides developers with support for Web Services for Remote Portlets (WSRP) 1.0, a new standard that allows "plug-n-play" of Web Services with Portals. WSRP enables remoting the presentation layer as opposed to regular Web services, which focus on remoting application data. WSRP transmits the actual markup rendered by the remote portlet.

WP provides basic support for JSR 168 1.0 portlets. JSR 168 is a Java Specification Request that defines a common set of portlet capabilities and API. This will allow JSR 168 compliant portlets to run in any vendor's portlet container that supports the JSR 168 standard.

If developers need to quickly access Enterprise Application Systems such as SAP, PeopleSoft, Siebel, then they can use WebSphere Portal Application Integrator. This tool allows rapid development of portlets through a GUI. The developer chooses fields and operation that he or she wants enabled in the portlet from objects found by the tool through querying the back-end system. Operations include searching, updating, deleting, and creating records. WPAI can also support integration of relational databases and Domino applications.

Developers can easily develop, test, and debug portlets using WebSphere Studio suite in conjunction with the portal toolkit. Wizards are available to you for creating portlets, building the portlet deployment descriptor, packaging it into a WAR file, and then deploying it into your production or test WP server.

The Administrator Experience

WebSphere Portal enables an administrator to have complete dynamic control over user access right for every portal resource including portlets, pages, and user groups. Control is set by using permissions. The permissions are defined by the user role. WP has defined roles (Administrator, Security Administrator, Delegator, Manager, Editor, Privileged User, and User), which the administrator or user associates with the resource. A role has a set of permissions that determine whether he/she can view, update, delete, or create the resource. If a role is assigned to a page, group, or folder, then resources below the parent inherit the permissions unless they are specifically blocked. A user can also delegate his or her role to other users. Administrators can also lock pages and/or page layout, thus restricting the impact component users can have on the company portal.

WebSphere Portal Member Services provides administration services through portlets for creating, updating, and deleting portal users and for managing their access rights. These services are provided at both the user and group levels. Users can be members of one or more groups and groups can be members of other groups. Users also have the ability to register and manage their own account information in the language of their choice (given that support has been implemented). Portal Administrators can define the information about the user that will be collected. User profile information can be supported in an LDAP and/or a database. Extended information about a user profile that is not supported by the default LDAP schema can be stored in a look-aside database.

Users can administer themselves ("self-care") or a separate administrator can perform the administration. Registration and self-care are done using forms that are easily modified.

WebSphere Portal supports form-based authentication (HTML user prompted form) through WAS or a third-party authentication server such as Tivoli Access Manager or Netegrity Siteminder. Single sign-on is also supported through WAS, and third-party authentication servers are also supported using LTPA tokens. WP also provides a Credential Vault service that allows portlets to store and access securely user IDs and passwords for applications that are accessed on remote systems.

WebSphere Portal gives the administrator the ability to control the portal globally by setting the default language, the cache timeout, handling of new user sessions, taking action when an unauthorized user accesses a portlet, and mapping of URLs.

WP also enables administrators to define new mobile devices and browsers so the portal will know what markup language to use and what the capabilities of the device/browser are.

Of course, WP also provides the standard features that allow users and administrators to easily install, activate, and configure portlets, themes, skins, and pages.

Tools are also provided to ease batch administration, migration, and configuration. Administrators can also enable and control tracing.

WebSphere Portal Architecture

So you now understand what WebSphere Portal does, but you would wonder how it works. WebSphere Portal is basically a suite of J2EE Enterprise Applications running and interacting with each other on the WAS.

In Figure 1-4, you can see the WebSphere Portal Architecture. It consists of three components: the page aggregator, the portlet container and services, and the J2EE engine. It starts with the page aggregator getting an HTTP request from WAS and then performing the following tasks:

1. Determines the device and user information based on the request

2. Collects the pages and portlets requested and then filters them based on the user entitlements

3. The portal dispatches specific Java Server Pages (JSPs), which issue includes for portlet Web modules. These portlet Web modules are invoked as servlets and are then rendered based on their service method (edit vs. view). This process results in the layout of the rows, columns, and graphics of the page.

4. Portlets that perform actions and execute messages such as Click-2-Action are processed first.

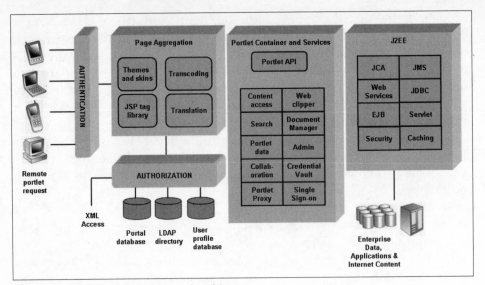

Figure 1-4   The WebSphere Portal Architecture.

5. Portlets that support the target markup are added to the rendering phase.

The second component is the Portlet Container and services. This component controls the portlets and provides services for them to interact with other applications or platforms. Portlets are simple independent HTTP servlets that are reusable and communicate with each other or other resources with well-defined interface. Services, such as Search, collaboration, and Document Manager, extend the functionality of the portlet to support an Enterprise environment.

The standard for the portlet API is JSR 168. JSR 168 is still evolving and as such is still a subset of the functionality of the WP Portlet API. As JSR 168 evolves, the respective WP Portlet API will be deprecated. Presently, both API are very different, have their own containers, and are supported independently.

The last component is the J2EE Engine under which Portal runs. J2EE or Java 2 Platform, Enterprise Edition is an open standard made of components needed to build enterprise applications. J2EE also defines the application and platform model these components run under.

The Java Application Model consists of application components: Java application clients, applets, servlets, JSPs, and Enterprise Java Pages (EJPs). J2EE also defines the Java run-time environment each component runs in. They are called containers and they run on Java 2 Platform, Standard Edition. J2EE also standardizes services which enable applications to integrate with Enterprise Applications. Services comprise JDBC for database connectivity, JMS for messaging, JavaMail, JAAS for JavaMail, Java API for XML Processing (JAXP), Java IDL, and Java Transaction Architecture for persistent transactions. IBM WebSphere Application Server is fully J2EE certified. Certification is obtained executing successfully the compatibility test suite.

In the WebSphere Portal architecture, you can see that security through authorization and authentication is supported by both the portlet container and services component and the J2EE engine.

WebSphere Portal Packaging

IBM WebSphere Portal V5.0 has two types of packages for the enterprise and two additional packages for small business. Table 1-1 describes the packages for the enterprise. IBM WebSphere Portal Enable for Multiplatforms, version 5.0 is the basic package, while IBM WebSphere Portal Extend for Multiplatforms version 5.0 is the full package.

Table 1-1 Packaging for WebSphere Portal Enable and Extend for Multiplatforms, Version 5.0

COMPONENT	DESCRIPTION	ENABLE	EXT-END
Portal server	J2EE application running in WAS. Provides portal framework consisting of presentation, user management, security, connectivity, and other services. Also includes IBM Cloudscape, version 5.1; a Java-based database.	X	X
WebSphere Application Server Enterprise 5.0 Fix Pack 1	Provides J2EE services for WebSphere Portal. Includes IBM HTTP Server and deployment manager	X	X
IBM Directory Server version 5.1	LDAP Directory Server for storing and retrieving user data required for authentication	X	X
IBM DB2 Universal Database Enterprise Server Edition, version 8.1 with Fix Pack 1	Relational database required to store portal data	X	X

(continued)

Table 1-1 *(continued)*

COMPONENT	DESCRIPTION	ENABLE	EXT-END
Portal toolkit 5.0	WebSphere Studio plug-in that aids in the development, testing, and debugging of portlets	X	X
WebSphere Studio Site Developer version 5.0 with Fix Pack 1	Integrating development environment for building, debugging, testing, and deploying J2EE applications with HTML pages, servlets, and JSPs	X	X
Web Content Management	Provides complete Web content management system, document management, and personalization server	X	X
IBM Tivoli Web Site Analyzer, version 4.5	Provides information on site availability and performance		X
IBM WebSphere Translation server 5.0	Translates Web pages, e-mail messages, and chat conversations into multiple languages	X	X
IBM Lotus Collaborative Components	A suite of APIs and JSP tags that enables integration of Domino, Sametime, QuickPlace, and Discovery Server into your portlet	X	X
IBM Lotus Collaboration Center	Framework that integrates People Finder, the Web Conference Center, QuickPlace and Sametime		X
IBM Lotus Extended Search version 4.0	Enables searches across distributed structured and unstructured data through a single point of access		X
Sametime	Instant messaging and online awareness		X
QuickPlace	Virtual teamrooms		X

Table 1-2 describes the packages for the small business. IBM WebSphere Portal-Express for Multiplatforms, version 5.0 is the basic package while IBM WebSphere Portal-Express Plus for Multiplatforms version 5.0 has some additional features. IBM WebSphere Portal-Express packages come with a simpler installation and the option for user or processor-based licensing.

Table 1-2   Packaging for WebSphere Portal—Express and Express Plus for Multiplatforms, Version 5.0

COMPONENT	DESCRIPTION	EXPRESS	EXPRESS PLUS
Portal server	J2EE application running in WAS. Provides Portal framework consisting of presentation, user management, security, connectivity, and other services. Also includes IBM Cloudscape, version 5.1; a Java-based database	X	X
WebSphere Application Server-Express 5.0 Fix Pack 1	Provides J2EE services for WebSphere Portal. Includes IBM HTTP Server and deployment manager	X	X
IBM Directory Server Express version 5.1	LDAP Directory Server for storing and retrieving user data required for authentication	X	X
Portal toolkit 5.0	WebSphere studio plug-in that aids in the development, testing, and debugging of portlets.	X	X
WebSphere Studio Site Developer version 5.0 with Fix Pack 1	Integrating development environment for building, debugging, testing, and deploying J2EE applications with HTML pages, servlets, and JSPs	X	X
Web Content Management	Provides complete Web content management system, document management, and personalization server	X	X
IBM Lotus Collaborative Components	A suite of APIs and JSP tags that enables integration of Domino, Sametime, QuickPlace, and Discovery Server into your portlet	X	X
IBM Lotus Collaboration Center	Framework that integrates People Finder, the Web Conference Center, QuickPlace and Sametime.		X
Sametime	Instant messaging and online awareness		X
QuickPlace	Virtual teamrooms		X

WebSphere Portal Platforms

WebSphere Portal V5.0 supports the platforms shown in Table 1-3.

Table 1-3 WebSphere Portal Platforms

PLATFORM	NAME
Hardware	■ IBM-compatible PC with Windows 2000 Server with Service Pack 2 or Service Pack 3, Windows 2000 Advanced Server with Service Pack 2 or Service Pack 3, Red Hat or SuSE operating environment ■ IBM pSeries with AIX, version 5.1 ML3 or version 5.2 operating environment ■ Sun processor with Solaris operating environment, version 8 ■ IBM zSeries or IBM S/390® Parallel Enterprise Server™ capable of running SuSE Linux Enterprise Server, version 7 (31-bit) operating environment
Software	■ AIX V5.1, 5.2, 5.3 ■ RedHat Enterprise Linux AS for Intel ■ RedHat Linux for Intel (×86) 8.0 2.4 ■ RedHat Linux for zSeries 7.2 2.4 ■ Solaris 9 (Fix level: 9 12/2002) ■ Solaris 8 (July 29, 2002 or later) ■ SuSE Linux for Intel (×86) 7.3 2.4 ■ SuSE SLES for Intel (×86) 7 2.4 ■ SuSE SLES for Intel (×86) 8 2.4 ■ SuSE SLES for S/390 8 2.4 ■ SuSE SLES for S/390 7 2.4 ■ Windows 2003 Standard ■ Windows 2003 Enterprise ■ Windows 2000 Advanced Server SP2+ ■ Windows 2000 Server SP2+
Databases	■ IBM Informix, version 9.3 or version 9.4 ■ Cloudscape, version 5.1 with Fix Pack 13 ■ Microsoft SQL Server Enterprise 2000 Service Pack 3 ■ DB2 Universal Database for z/OS and OS/390, version 7.1 ■ DB2 Universal Database Enterprise Server Edition, version 8 with Fix Pack 1 ■ DB2 Universal Database, version 7.2 with Fix Pack 7 and Fix Pack 8

Table 1-3 *(continued)*

PLATFORM	NAME
	■ Oracle 8i, version 8.1.7
	■ Oracle 9i, version 9.2.0.1
LDAP Servers	■ IBM Directory Server, version 4.1 and version 5.1
	■ Lotus Domino Enterprise Server, version 5.0.12
	■ Lous Domino, Release 6.0
	■ Sun ONE (formerly iPlanet) Directory Server 5.0
	■ Microsoft Active Directory (as included with Windows 2000 Server)
	■ Novell eDirectory 8.6
Web Browsers	Windows platform:
	■ Internet Explorer 5.5 and 6.0
	■ Opera 6.0, 6.1, and 7.0
	Windows, Linux, AIX, Solaris operating environment:
	■ Netscape 6.2 or 7.0
	■ Mozilla 1.0.2, 1.2.1, and 1.3

What's New in WebSphere 5.0 (including 5.0.2)

WebSphere Portal version 5.0 offers significant improvements over Web-Sphere Portal version 4.2.1, among which are the following:

- Installation is now simpler and more reliable.
- Cloudscape, a Java database, is installed automatically. Cloudscape requires no configuration and is maintenance free.
- Configuration utility is provided to easily customize WebSphere Porter to use other databases, LDAP Servers, or Web servers.
- Improved database and LDAP server support
- Basic support for WSRP 1.0
- Basic support for JSR 168
- Web Clipping Portlet has been updated to make clipping portlets simpler to create and perform better.
- Search has been greatly enhanced that enables you to find, index, categorize, summarize, and support more than 200 documents. Search will enable you to define your our own category tree or it will automatically categorize using 2,400 predefined categories.

- Cooperative portlets that enable dynamic portlet interaction on a page

- Portal pages can be arranged in a tree hierarchy. Administration is much easier because the child pages can inherit the parent's permissions.

- Application Portlet builders enable you to rapidly create portlets to access and manipulate data from an enterprise application.

- Improved navigation through Portlet menus. Portlet menus can be created using static XML or dynamically generated.

- Ability to map user-friendly URLs to pages so you don't have to use cryptic portal URLs

- A new document repository and management system called PDM. PDM also provides the ability to author documents such as text, word, spreadsheet, and presentations in the portal.

- The administrative interface has been enhanced with new administrative portlets, improvements in the Navigation, new and improved themes and skins, and context-sensitive links.

- Lotus Collaboration Center has been enhanced with portlets for People Finder, support for QuickPlace in My Lotus Team workplaces, support for Sametime in Lotus Web Conferences, and more.

- The business portlets have been enhanced by adding an Internet Mail Box, single Notes and iNotes portlet, a Newsgroup portlet, and Mylist portlet (simple check-off list).

- XML access, which is the batch processing interface for the portal, has been enhanced in function and documentation.

- Improved handling of error messages by enabling error messages to be localized

- Transcoding can now be used at the portlet level by administrators.

- Portal Toolkit has been updated for version 5 and includes new and improved Wizards.

- Improve performance through WAS cluster support, performance instrumentation, reduced session data, unified caching architecture based on Dynacache, smarter invalidation, and faster login times

Summary

In this chapter we introduced you to portals, which is the WebSphere product family, and more importantly to WebSphere Portal. We gave you grounding on the WP architecture, its packaging, and supported platforms. We showed some great features introduced in this version. Now that we wetted your appetite by telling you at a high level all the great things about the WebSphere Portal, let's we give you some substance. The rest of the book will show you how to install and use the product for an Enterprise environment. We will start with the first steps so you can install the product in various environments and program a simple portlet. After each chapter we will build upon the topic so that by the time you complete reading the book you will be able to deploy WebSphere Portal in an enterprise environment.

In the next chapter we will introduce step 1 to deploying WebSphere Portal: installing a simple portal.

## CHAPTER 2

Installing WebSphere Portal on Windows 2000 Server

Before WebSphere Portal version 5.0 came along, users had to dedicate an inordinate amount of effort to figure out how to successfully install WebSphere Portal Server. Installations were complex, took a long time, and required huge number of parameters to input. The installation process was inflexible and intolerant of incorrect parameters to the point where an incorrect value would cause the installation to stall and the installation would have to be manually backed out and redone. Users would feel great pride at the end of the installation process that they were able to complete it, almost like they got a 1600 on their SATs.

IBM clearly recognized that this situation was unacceptable. The company has made a huge effort to simplify the process. With WebSphere Portal Extend, you need only four disks to get started. (You get 57 disks in all, but the rest are to support different platforms and languages. They also include products that you will need as your use of WebSphere Portal becomes more sophisticated and your sites get larger.)

Getting Going: A Quick Install

So you want to install WebSphere Portal quickly on a clean system. Figure 2-1 shows that WebSphere Portal 5.0.2 is going to be installed on one server, with WebSphere security not enabled. This includes the supporting components WebSphere Application Server Enterprise version 5.0 Fix Pack 2 (with some additional fixes), IBM HTTP Server 1.3.26.1, and Cloudscape V5.1.26. Cloudscape (really DB2 Java) is an install-and-forget database. It is used to store information about user identities, credentials, permissions,

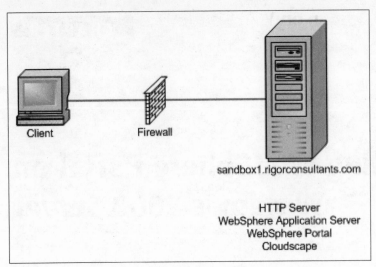

Figure 2-1   A simple installation configuration.

and documents. Designed to be maintenance free and dynamically tuned, it is targeted for sites with less than 2,000 users. It is great for just getting started with small-to-medium-size businesses.

First, you need some hardware, specifically the following:

- Pentium 4 processor at 1.4 GHz or higher

- 1 GB of RAM or more per processor (this is very important)

- At least 3 GB of disk space on an NTFS file system. If you are using Cloudscape, which is the default database, you should have a lot more.

- Network connectivity with a static IP address and a configured fully-qualified host name. WP can work with a dynamic IP configuration if you do not use single sign-on with WAS security enabled. The portal system must be able to resolve an IP address from its fully-qualified host name.

On the software side, you need Windows 2000 Server or Advance Server SP2+. It runs fine on SP4. WP should work with the following browsers:

- Microsoft Internet Explorer 5.5+ on Windows

- Mozilla 1.0.2+ on Windows and Linux with the Java script enabled

- Netscape Communicator 6.2+ on all platforms

- Opera Web Browser 7.11+ on Windows

We really encourage IE 6.0 SP1 to be used for best results.

Getting Information on Your Windows Server

Before you start, you need to perform some tasks on your Windows Server to make it ready for the install. Specifically:

1. Identify your service pack version by typing **winver** in a command prompt. Make sure it is Service Pack 2 or greater.

2. Make sure you have a static IP address by going to Start ⇨ Settings ⇨ Network and Dial-Up connection. Right-click on your network adapter LAN connection and select Properties. Select Internet Protocol (TCP/IP) and click Properties. Ensure that Use the following IP address is selected.

3. Make sure that your server has a fully qualified host name and is properly configured. In a command prompt, ping your server's fully qualified domain name and see if your IP comes up and four successful replies are returned.

4. Make sure that the following ports are not being used by typing **netstat–an** in a command prompt:
   - 443 (standard HTTPS port)
   - 523 (DB2 Administration Server)
   - 8008 (IBM HTTP Server Administration port)
   - 50000 (DB2 instance connection port)
   - 50001 (DB2 instance interrupt port)
   - 50002 (DB2 Control Server)
   - 55555 (WAS database port)
   - 9081 (Default Portal Port)
   - 9090 (WAS Administration port)

5. If you are going to set up WebSphere Application Server or IHS as a service, make sure that the user account you will use to install WebSphere Portal is a local Windows user ID, part of the administrators group, and has the user rights to Act as part of the Operating System and Log on as a service. To add or view User rights select Start ⇨ Programs ⇨ Administrative Tools ⇨ Local Security Policy. Double click Local Policies and then double click User Rights Assignment. Double click on the user right you are interested in and then modify it if required.

6. Make sure Microsoft Internet Information Services is not running since it listens on the same port as IBM HTTP Server. Go into Services under Administrative Tools and stop or disable World Wide Publishing Service.

7. Make sure that PATH environment variable is not set too long. If it is, you may get a message in the `wpsinstalllog.txt` stating the input line is too long or the syntax of the command is incorrect.

8. Disable any firewall products.

Okay, now you are ready to go.

Installing on Your Windows Server

To install WebSphere Portal:

1. Disable any firewall on the server where WP will be installed. After the install, re-enable it and open the appropriate ports and set appropriate rules.

2. Insert the Setup disk in the CD drive. The program should automatically start unless the autostart function is disabled. If it is so, then run `install.bat` from the root directory of the CD.

3. Select the language for the install and click OK.

4. The Welcome panel will then be displayed. You will then be given the option to browse the infocenter if you choose Launch Infocenter. Otherwise click Next.

5. Figure 2-2 will then appear. This is the license agreement. Review the license agreement and if you accept click Next. If you don't then hit Cancel and return the software.

6. The installation then checks the machine for operating system and software prerequisites. If you are installing on Windows XP Professional (yes, you can but it is not supported so users beware!), you will get an error message but just ignore it and hit Next.

7. Figure 2-3 will then appear giving you a choice of a Full or Custom install. Choose Full.

8. In Figure 2-4, you will then be asked to specify the directory to install WebSphere Application Server. If the directory does not exist, it will be created. By default, IBM suggests that you install in `c:\Program Files\WebSphere\AppServer`; however, you may instead want to install in `c:\WebSphere` since the directories are easy to get when you are accessing them in a command prompt. Enter the directory and click Next.

9. The next screen (see Figure 2-5) asks you to specify the directory to install the IBM HTTP Server. Choose the default. If the directory does not exist, it will be created. Click Next.

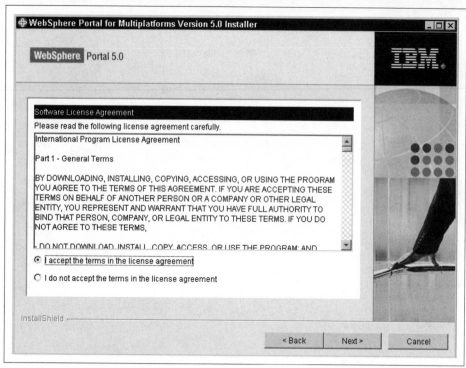

Figure 2-2 WebSphere Portal license agreement.

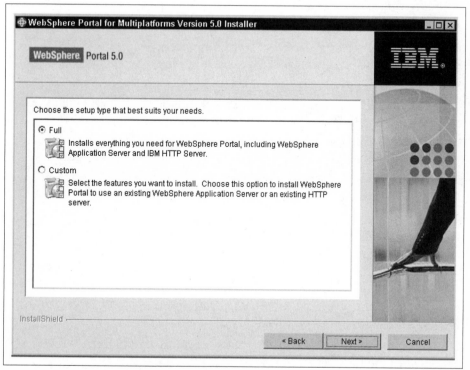

Figure 2-3 Choosing installation type.

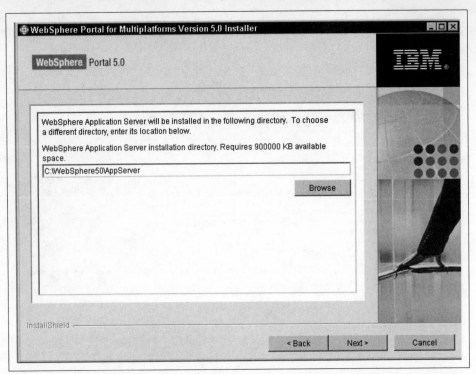

Figure 2-4 Specifying WebSphere Application Server installation directory.

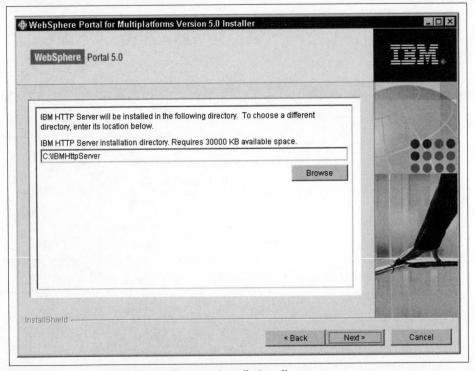

Figure 2-5 Specifying IBM HTTP Server installation directory.

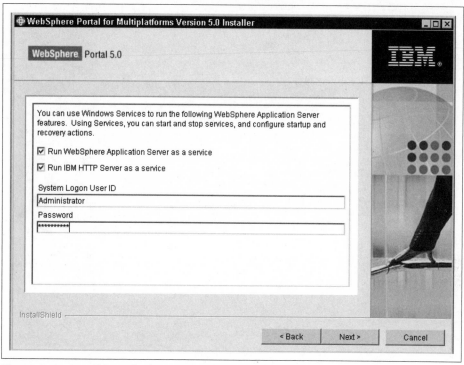

Figure 2-6 Specifying whether you want to run services.

10. Now you are asked (see Figure 2-6) if you want to run WebSphere Application Server and IBM HTTP as services. If you choose this option, specify a user name and password that has administrator privileges. The user ID may have the policy rights to "Log on as a service and Act as port of the operating system." If the user ID does not have them, the installation program will update the user ID and ask you to log out and log back before continuing with the installation. You should install WebSphere Application Server and IBM HTTP as services so they can be run remotely without the administrator logged in.

11. Specify the node name (see Figure 2-7) where you want the WebSphere Portal application to be installed within the WebSphere Application Server cell. This value must be unique and is usually the host name of the computer. Also enter the fully qualified host name or the static IP address of the computer running WebSphere Application Server. Click Next. In Figure 2-6, you choose a node name sandbox1 and a fully qualified host name sandbox1 .rigorconsultants.com.

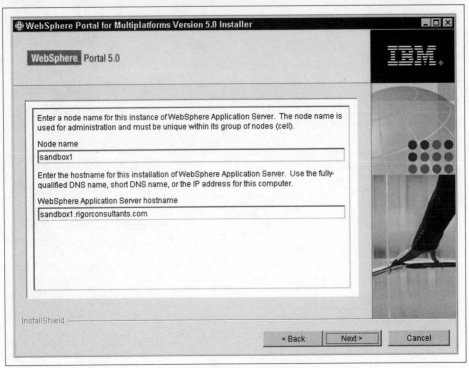

Figure 2-7 Specifying physical location of WebSphere Portal.

12. In the next screen (see Figure 2-8), you will be asked where you want to install WebSphere Portal. Usually it is installed off the WebSphere directory root as a peer to the WebSphere Application Server. Click Next.

13. Enter the user ID and password for the WebSphere Portal Administrator (see Figure 2-9). The password and user ID must be at least five letters long and contain no blanks. This user ID is specific to the WebSphere Portal and does not have to be an Operating System User ID but it must conform to the rules of the LDAP if you are using an LDAP to manage your users.

14. Verify the components to be installed and click Next.

That's all the information you need to give. It's that simple. After you click Next, the program starts installing the selected components. You see the progress indicator moving as the components are installed. It will probably take an hour or two, depending on your system's performance. When the installation is finished, a confirmation panel is displayed with a listing of the components installed. The confirmation panel will also display the port number used to access the portal. The port number is also stored in the

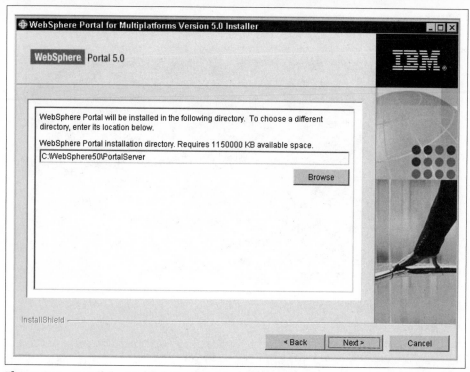

Figure 2-8   Specifying WebSphere Portal installation directory.

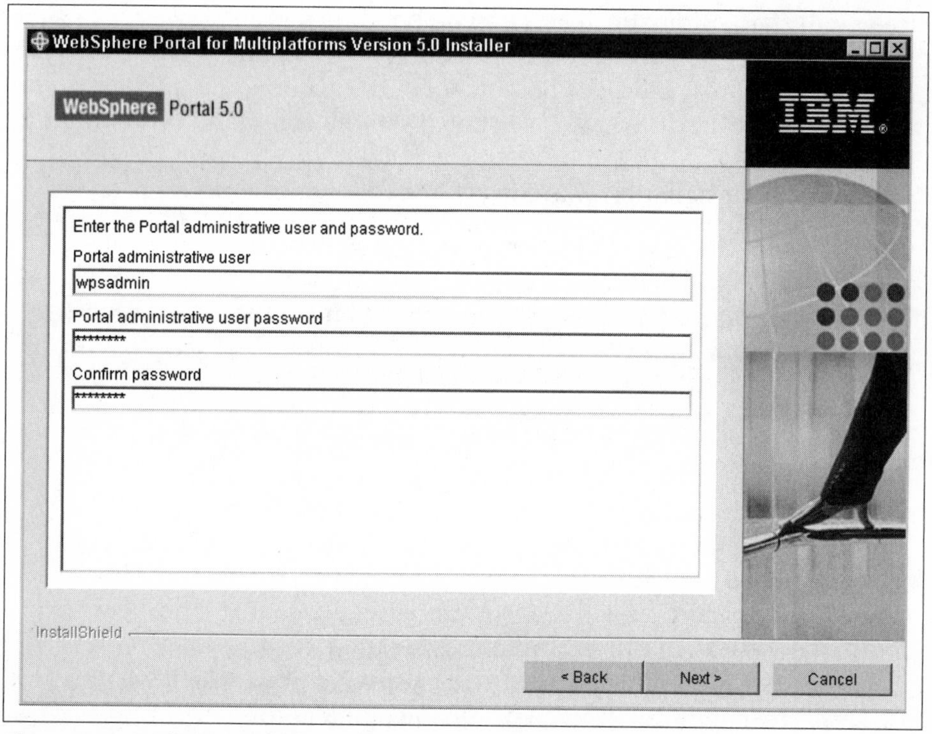

Figure 2-9   Defining WebSphere Portal administrator.

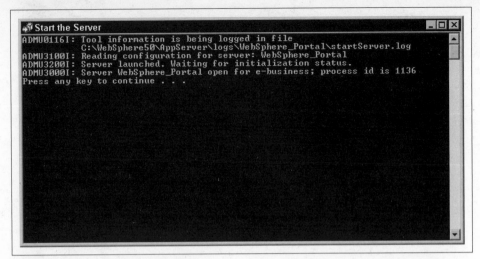

Figure 2-10 Starting the Portal Server.

WpsHostport property <wp_root>/config/wpconfig.properties file. Record the property number and click Finish. Menu entries will be added under Start ⇨ Programs for IBM HTTP Server and WebSphere Application Server and WebSphere Portal. Since IBM HTTP was set up as a service, it will start automatically when you boot the server. However, to start the Portal Server you will need to click Start ⇨ Programs ⇨ WebSphere ⇨ Portal Server V5.0 ⇨ Start the Server. A command box will appear. If you have a successful start, you will see entries in the command box similar to Figure 2-10.

To verify the installation was correct, the following steps are necessary:

1. Make sure the IBM HTTP Server is installed and is not in conflict with another HTTP server such as IIS or Apache. On your Web browser enter your fully-qualified host name in the address bar (e.g., sandbox1.rigorconsultants.com). You should see a page with "Welcome to IBM HTTP Server" (see Figure 2-11).

2. Start the portal server by going to Start menu and clicking Programs ⇨ IBM WebSphere ⇨ Portal Server V5.0 ⇨ Start the Server.

3. Enter in the address bar in your browser the URL http://<hostname.yourco.com>:,port>/wps/portal where hostname.yourco.com is the WebSphere Portal fully-qualified host name and port is the port number in the confirmation panel (usually 9081). In our example. It is http://www.rigorconsultants.com:9081/wps/portal. Click Go and you should see the WebSphere Portal Welcome Page as shown in Figure 2-12. Please note that a full installation does not

Figure 2-11   IBM HTTP Server Welcome screen.

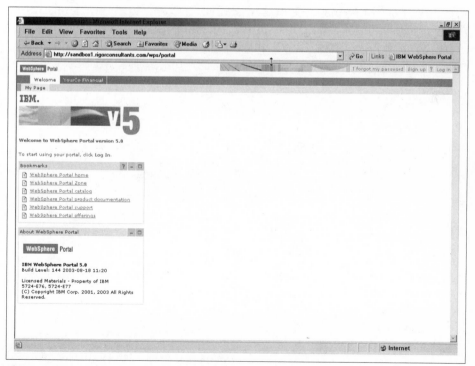

Figure 2-12   WebSphere Portal Server Welcome screen.

configure WebSphere Portal with the IBM HTTP Server even though it is installed with it. This must be done separately. By default, WebSphere Portal uses the WebSphere Application Server internal HTTP server (port 9081).

Installing with an Existing Web Server and an Existing WebSphere Application Server

This installation is relatively easy. Except in the real world, you rarely install with a new instance of the Web server and a new instance of WebSphere Application Server. Here is an example of a more realistic install. Figure 2-13 shows a Web server in the DMZ connected to an existing WebSphere Application Server 5.0 in a secured zone. We are going to install Microsoft IIS plug-ins on a remote Web server and use an existing WebSphere Application Server 5.0 on sandbox1.rigorconsultants.com to install the portal. While there is an option to upgrade the WebSphere Application Server to a new version, the upgrade will not do the migration of security objects, deprecated API, cluster configuration, etc. It will just upgrade the server code.

1. On the Web Server, http.rigorconsultants.com, first check to see if the plug-ins have been installed in the httpd.conf file. If you see the following lines then go to step 12:

```
LoadModule ibm_app_server_http_module
"C:\WebSphere\AppServer/bin/mod_ibm_app_server_http.dll"
WebSpherePluginConfig "C:\WebSphere\AppServer/config/cells/plugin-
cfg.xml"
```

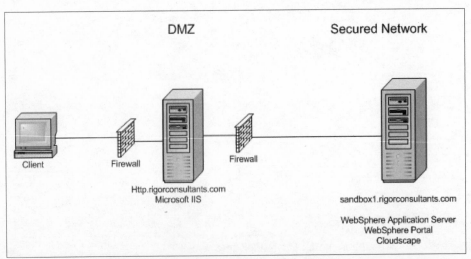

Figure 2-13   Installations on existing Web server and existing Web application server.

2. Stop the Web Server

3. Place the WebSphere Portal CD, which contains the WebSphere Application Server installation program (for Windows it should be CD 1.1 of WebSphere Portal V5.0), in http.rigorconsultants.com CD drive.

4. Launch the WebSphere Application Server installation entering in a command prompt drive:\was\win\WAS50\install.exe, where the drive is your CD drive. If you are installing WebSphere Portal 5.0, then WebSphere Application Server Enterprise Fixpack 1 (base plus frame) must be installed with the additional fixes required by WP. If you are installing WP 5.0.2, then WebSphere Application Server Enterprise Fix Pack 2 (base plus frame) must be installed with the additional fixes required by WP.

5. Select the language you want to use for the installation, and click OK.

6. Click Next on the welcome panel, indicate that you accept the license agreement, and click Next.

7. Select Custom.

8. On the features panel in Figure 2-14, deselect all features except Web Server Plugins and the entry for the specific Web server for which you are installing the plug-in. Click Next.

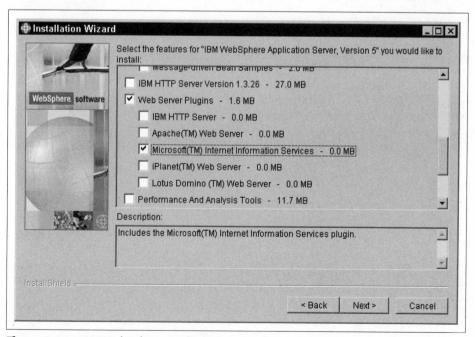

Figure 2-14 IBM WebSphere Application Server features panel.

9. Specify the directory path where you want to install the WebSphere Application Server files. This path must be the same as that used for the WebSphere Application Server installed on the local machine. Click Next.

10. Specify the location of the Web server configuration file, if requested. For IIS, it is not requested. Click Next.

11. Finish the installation.

12. Place CD in `sandbox1.rigorconsultants.com`.

13. Perform steps 1–7 in the previous section. Choose custom installation.

14. Select Configure to an Existing Install of WebSphere Application (see Figure 2-15). Click Next.

15. The installation program will then find the location of your WAS instance (as indicated in Figure 2-16). If it does not find it, click on Browse and locate the directory. Click OK and then Next.

16. The rest of the install is same as steps 11–14 of the quick install.

17. Verify the Web Server is running and create a back-up copy of `<wp_root>/config/wpconfig.properties file`.

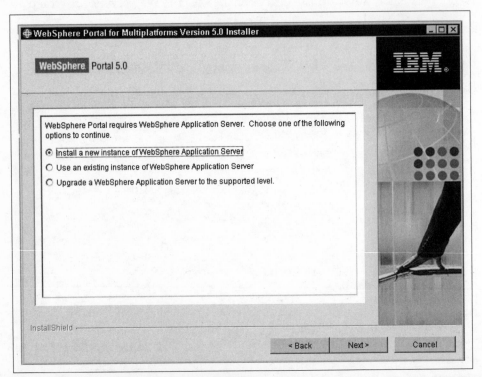

Figure 2-15 Choosing type of WAS installation.

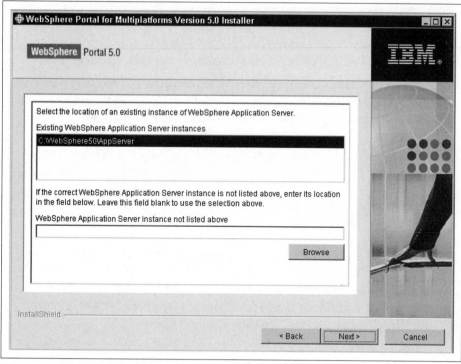

Figure 2-16   Finding the location of the WAS instance.

18. Using a text editor, open `<wp_root>/config/wpconfig`
    `.properties`, uncomment and set

    ```
    WpsHostName=localhost
    WpsHostPort=80
    ```

    WpsHostName is the fully qualified host name of the machine
    running WebSphere Portal while WpsHostPort is the port number
    that your Web Server is listening for HTTP traffic. You may not have
    to change any settings here.

19. Save the file, open a command prompt, and change the directory to
    `<wp_root>/config`.

20. Enter the command `WPSConfig.bat httpserver-config`.

21. Restart the Web Server on http.rigorconsultants.com and then
    restart the WebSphere Portal.

Installing WebSphere Portal Fixpack 2

In order to run WebSphere Portal 5.0.2, you have to install WebSphere Portal
Fixpack 2. Assume that security is not installed and that this is a Windows

installation. Consult the readme files before you update. To do so, perform the following steps:

1. Stop your Web server and all WebSphere servers, including WP.

2. On the IBM site, download the WebSphere Application Server base fixpack 2 for Windows. It should be about 221 MB. Unzip the files and install the fixpack as per the instructions in the readme.

3. On the IBM site, download the WebSphere Application Server Enterprise Fix Pack 2 for Windows. It should be about 105 MB. Unzip the files and install the fixpack as per the instructions in the readme.

4. Restart the servers and ensure they successfully start. Then stop the servers.

5. On the IBM site, download the WebSphere Portal Fix Pack 2 for Windows. You need to download the fixpack 2 file. It should be about 359 MB. On the same download page, also download the WAS 5.0.2 additional fixes file. It should be about 14 MB. Unzip the files into a directory called `<wp_root>\update`.

6. Install the `WP_PTF_502.jar` using the UpdateWizard. Choose all the fixes and apply them. This applies to additional fixes to WebSphere Application Server so you can install WebSphere Portal 5.0.2.

7. Set up the Java environment by running `<was_root>\bin\setupCmdLine.bat`.

8. Open a command prompt and change the directory to `<wproot>\update`.

9. Enter the command, `updatePortal -fixpack -installDir "<wp_root>" -fixpackDir "<wp_root>\update" -install -fixpackID WP_PTF_502`

10. Upon successful completion, change the directory to `<wp_root>\config`.

11. Enter the command **WPSconfig.bat WP-PTF-502-DPortalAdminPWD=portalAdminPassword**, where portalAdminPassword is your WebSphere Portal administrator password. You must perform this step right after you have applied the fixes or the portal will be corrupted. This command must complete successfully. It will take quite a while to execute. If it does not complete successfully, then run `WPSconfig.bat UNINSTALL-WP-PTF-502 DPortalAdminPWD=portalAdminPassword`,

where `portalAdminPassword` is your WebSphere Portal administrator password, correct the problem, and redo this step.

12. Upon successful installation, start the Web Server and WebSphere Portal and log in. Check the version number on the WebSphere Portal Welcome Screen. It should now read IBM WebSphere Portal 5.0.2 in the lower left-hand corner.

13. Log in as an administrator. Click Document Manager and update the search index.

Summary

In this chapter, you have experienced the radically simplified WebSphere Portal installation, which provides a dramatic improvement on the customer experience. But most customer configurations require special installations configurations. The next chapter will explore installations for Linux platforms and examine more complex configurations.

## CHAPTER 3

Installing WebSphere Portal on Linux

In the last chapter we showed how to install WebSphere Portal on a Windows 2000 Server platform. From the WebSphere Portal installation manual, much of the installation process can be extrapolated to the other platforms by making a few adjustments, right? It would be great if this were true, but it is not! The differences are a result of the lack of integration into the Linux user interfaces. The integration is more difficult due to numerous varieties of Linux user interfaces.

In this chapter you are going to learn how to install and uninstall WebSphere Portal on a Linux platform in either a graphics or a text environment. Linux was chosen due to the popularity of the platform and the close similarities to the zLinux, Solaris, and AIX installations.

Installing on Linux

So, you're going to install WebSphere Portal on Linux. First, let's deal with the urban legends. Despite what it says in the installation manual, WebSphere Portal does not work with all versions and permutations of Linux (see Figure 3-1). WebSphere Portal 5.0.2 has been certified with RedHat Enterprise Linux AS for Intel, RedHat Linux for Intel (x86) 8.0 2.4, RedHat Linux for zSeries 7.2 2.4, SuSE Linux for Intel (x86) 7.3 2.4, SuSE SLES for Intel (x86) 7 2.4, SuSE SLES for Intel (x86) 8 2.4, SuSE SLES for S/390 8 2.4, and SuSE SLES for S/390 7 2.4. For installation, you might be considering doing a full install. However, this will install IBM HTTP 1.3.26.1, which is not recommended for Unix systems. IBM HTTP 2.0.42.21 is based

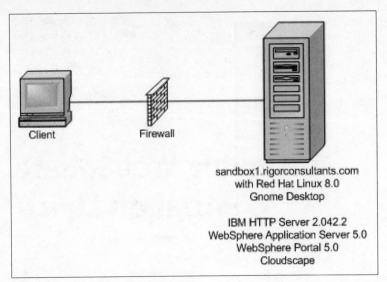

sandbox1.rigorconsultants.com
with Red Hat Linux 8.0
Gnome Desktop

IBM HTTP Server 2.042.2
WebSphere Application Server 5.0
WebSphere Portal 5.0
Cloudscape

Figure 3-1 The Linux configuration.

on Apache 2.0, which enables for Unix threading in hybrid multiprocess, multithreaded mode. Realistically, most installations install the IBM HTTP Server on a separate server.

The installation you should be examining, which we will use as an example, is a custom installation using IBM HTTP 2.0.42.2 as the Web server and an installation of WAS 5.0 with WebSphere Portal 5.0 using Cloudscape on Red Hat 8.0 with the Gnome desktop.

The hardware requirements are as follows:

- A Pentium 4 processor at 1.4 GHz or higher
- 1 GB of RAM or more per processor (this is very important)
- 1.5 GB or more disk space on the root directory, 2.5 GB or more on /opt directory, and 500 MB or more for /home directory
- Network connectivity with a static IP address and a configured, fully qualified host name

Getting Information on Your Linux Server

Before you start, you need to perform some tasks on your Linux server to make it ready for the install. Specifically, perform the following tasks:

1. Identify your version of Linux.
2. Make sure you have a static IP address by going to Gnome Menu ⇨ System Settings and clicking Network Configurations. Highlight

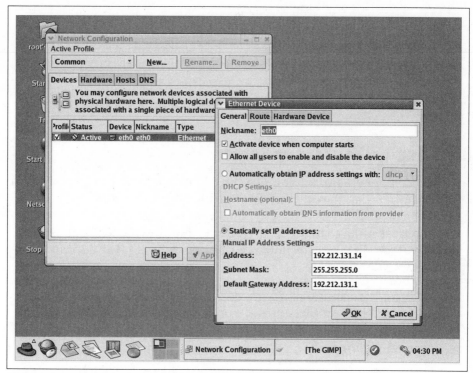

Figure 3-2   Network configuration utility.

Device and click Edit. Verify this is a static IP, as shown in Figure 3-2.

3. Right-click on the desktop and click New Terminal, and ping your server's fully qualified domain name and see if your IP comes up and four successful replies are returned.

4. Make sure that the following ports are not being used by typing **netstat-an** in a command prompt:

- 443 (standard HTTPS port)
- 523 (DB2 Administration Server)
- 8008 (IBM HTTP Server Administration port)
- 50000 (DB2 instance connection port)
- 50001 (DB2 instance interrupt port)
- 50002 (DB2 Control Server)
- 55555 (WAS database port)
- 9081 (Default Portal Port).

5. Make sure that user account has root or root authority.

6. Make sure no other Web server, such as Apache, is running. Remember, Red Hat installs Apache 1.3 even if you choose not to install the Web Server package.

7. Disable the Linux firewall.

You are now ready to install WebSphere Portal on Red Hat Linux 8.0.

Installing on Your Linux Server

To install WebSphere Portal, you first need to install a more current version of HTTP server than the one installed during a typical install:

1. Log in as root, go to the IBM Web site, and download the IBM Developer Kit, Java Technology Edition Version 1.3 and IBM HTTP Server 2.042.2.

2. Uncompress the IBM Developer kit and install it in /opt.

3. Edit your shell profile, append /opt/IBMJava2-131/bin to your PATH variable, export it, and reinitialize your environment (or log out and log in).

4. Uncompress the IBM HTTP install image in /opt/ibmhttp.

5. Open a new terminal, change directory to /opt/ibmhttp, and enter **java–jar setup.jar.**

6. Choose the language in which to run the installation. The Welcome screen appears (see Figure 3-3). Click Next.

7. The license agreement appears. Choose to accept and click Next.

8. Specify the directory name (see Figure 3-4). Choose the default /opt/IBMIHS. Click Next.

9. Select the type of installation (see Figure 3-5). Choose Typical, which installs everything. Click Next.

10. A window will appear summarizing your choices (see Figure 3-6). Click Next.

11. The installation then starts. A progress bar will appear with a message that states Installing IBM HTTP Server. Wait. If the progress bar has reached 100 percent and after five minutes the message has not changed to Updating the RPM database, the process has stalled. Hit Cancel, Reboot, Delete /opt/IBMIHS, and go back to step 5.

12. After the RPM database has been updated, click Finish.

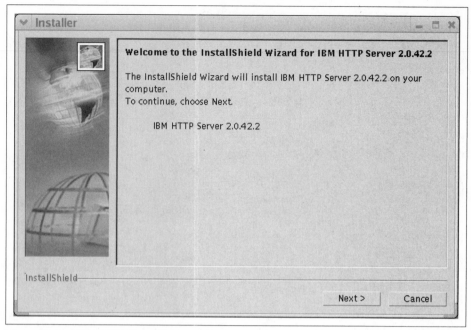

Figure 3-3   IBM HTTP Server 2.0.42.2 Welcome screen.

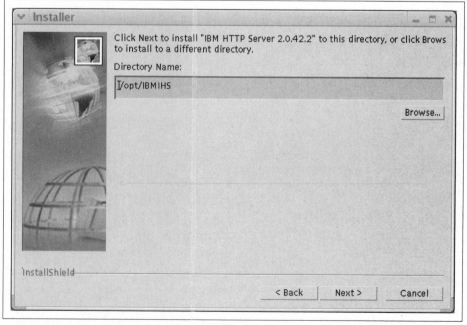

Figure 3-4   IBM HTTP Server directory.

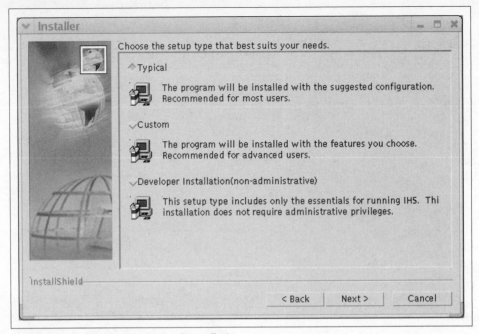

Figure 3-5   Choosing the type of installation.

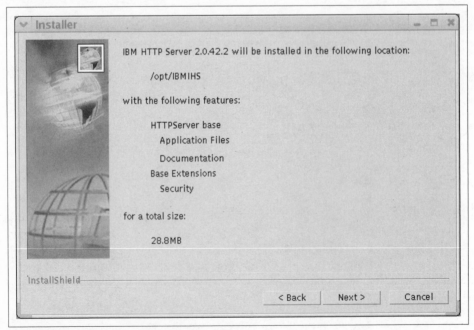

Figure 3-6   Summary of installation options.

Figure 3-7   IBM HTTP Server 2.0 Welcome screen.

13. Start the HTTP server by going into `/opt/IBMIHS/bin` and entering **./apachectl start**. Verify that the Web server is working by starting your Web browser and entering your fully qualified host name in the address bar (for example, `sandbox1.`
`rigorconsultants.com`). You should see a page with **Welcome to IBM HTTP server** (see Figure 3-7).

14. Place the WebSphere Portal setup disc in the CD drive. Start a new terminal session and change the directory to `/mnt/cdrom`. Enter the command **./install.sh**.

15. Select the language for the install and click OK. Also close the terminal session so you will be able to eject the CD when the installation process requests you.

16. The Welcome panel will then be displayed. You will then be given the option to browse the infocenter if you choose Launch Infocenter. Otherwise click Next.

17. The license agreement will appear. Select `I accept the terms in the license agreement` and click Next.

18. The installation then checks the machine for operating system and software prerequisites. Click Next.

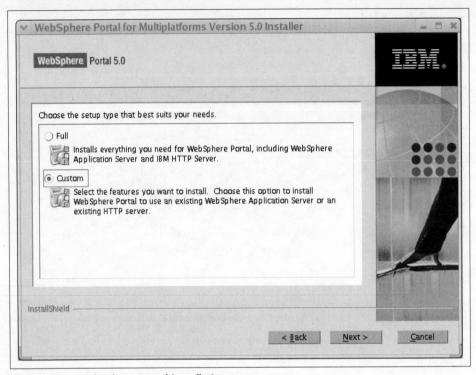

Figure 3-8 WebSphere Portal installation type screen.

19. You will then be asked if you want a Full or Custom install (see Figure 3-8). Choose Custom.

20. You will then be asked if you want to install a new WebSphere Application or configure to an existing install of WebSphere Application. Click on New Install and select Next.

21. You will then be asked to specify the directory to install WebSphere Application Server (see Figure 3-9). If the directory does not exist, it will be created. By default, IBM suggests that you install in `/opt/WebSphere/AppServer`. Enter the directory and click Next.

22. The next screen asks you if you want to install IBM HTTP Server or configure WAS to use an existing Web server (see Figure 3-10). Choose `Install the plug-in for an Existing Http Server`. Click Next.

23. You will then be asked to choose the type of HTTP server to use with WAS (see Figure 3-11). Click IBM HTTP Server. Click Next.

24. The next screen will ask you to specify the location of the http configuration file (see Figure 3-12). Enter **/opt/IBMIHS/conf/httpd .conf** and click Next.

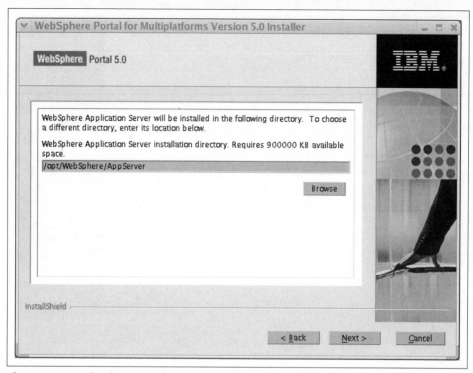

Figure 3-9 WebSphere installation directory screen.

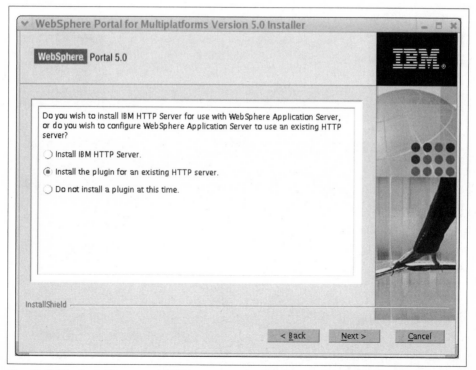

Figure 3-10 Installing a new HTTP server or configuring an existing Web server.

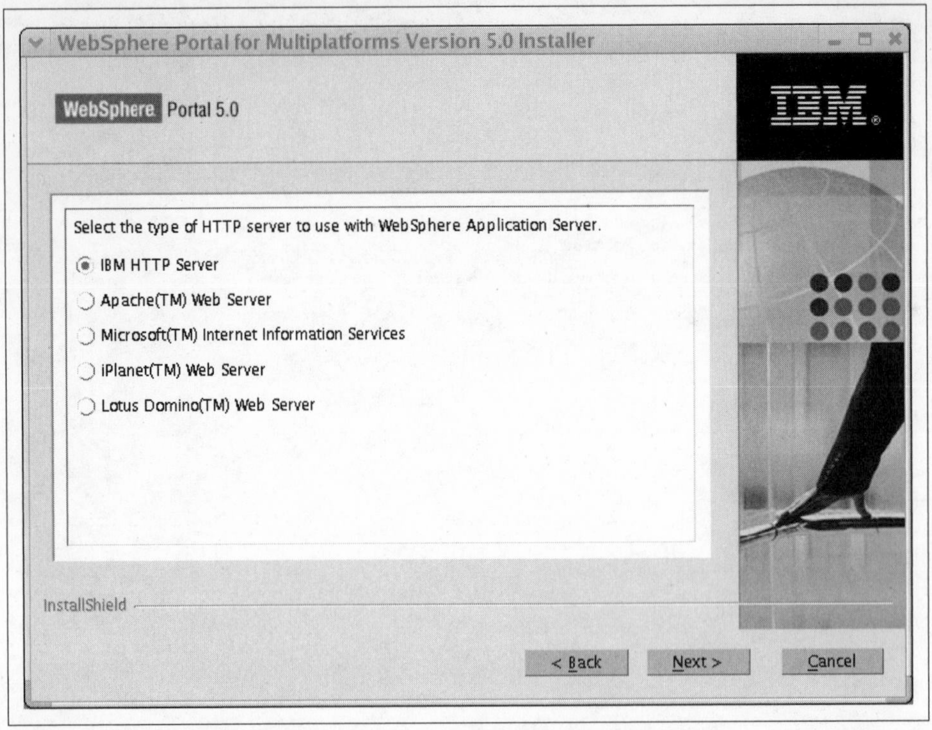

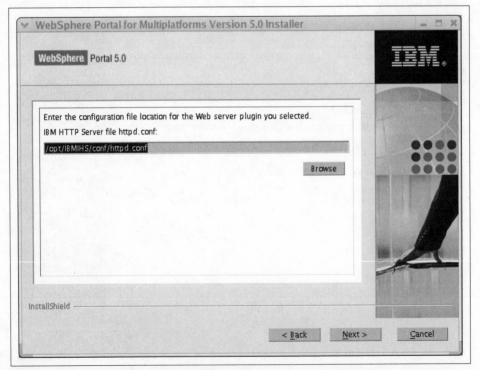

Figure 3-11   Choosing the HTTP server to install the plug-in.

Figure 3-12   Specifying the location of the HTTP server configuration file.

25. You will then be asked where you want to install WebSphere Portal. Usually it is installed off the WebSphere Application Server directory root or `/opt/WebSphere/Portalserver`. Click Next.

26. Enter the user ID and password for the WebSphere Portal Administrator. (see Figure 2-9). The password and user ID must be at least five letters long and contain no blanks. This user ID is specific to the WebSphere Portal and does not have to be an Operating System User ID but it must conform to the rules of the LDAP if you are using an LDAP to manage your users.

27. Verify the components to be installed and click Next.

Next, the program starts installing the selected components. You see the progress indicator moving as the components are installed. When it asks you for a CD, you will have to right-click on the CD icon and click Eject. When the installation is finished, a confirmation panel, such as the one shown in Figure 3-13, is displayed with a listing of the components installed. The confirmation panel will also display the port number used to access the portal. The port number is also stored in the WpsHostport

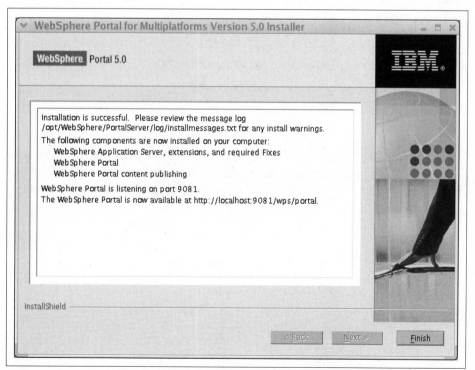

Figure 3-13 Screen after a successful install.

property in `<wp_root>/config/wpconfig.properties` file. Record the port number and click Finish.

In Linux, the installation program does not add menu items to the desktop. You will need to do this manually. You will also need to apply fixpack 2. Use the instructions in Chapter 2 except for downloading the Linux fixpacks and use forward slashes instead of backward slashes for the commands. Remember to replace .bat with .sh for the script commands.

The WebSphere Portal installation modifies the Web server configuration file to support IBM HTTP 1.3.26.1 Web server plug-ins. To correct the entries to support IBM HTTP 2.042.2, go to the `http.conf` file in `/opt/IBMIHS/conf` and change:

```
LoadModule ibm_app_server_http_module
/opt/WebSphere/AppServer/bin/mod_ibm_app_server
```

to

```
LoadModule was_ap20_module
/opt/WebSphere/AppServer/bin/mod_was_ap20_http.so
```

Next you have to configure WP to use the IBM HTTP Web Server instead of the WebSphere Internal HTTP server, which is only to be used for development or to show prototypes. You must do the following steps to configure WP to use IBM HTTP Server:

1. Open a terminal session and go to `<wp_root>/config`.

2. Edit wps.properties and set WpsHostPort=80.

3. Enter **./WPSconfig.sh httpserver-config**.

4. Wait for the Build Successful message.

5. Restart the Web server and WebSphere Portal.

Next create a service for IBM HTTP Server so that it will start at startup. In `/etc/rc.d/init.d`, create a script file called ibmhttp with permissions 755 and insert the following code. The code will support start, stop, restart, and provide status for the IBM HTTP Web Server.

```
#!/bin/bash
#
# Startup script for the IBM Http Web Server
#
# chkconfig: - 86 16
# description: IBM HTTP is a World Wide Web server. It is used to
serve \
#            HTML files and CGI.
# processname: ibmhttpd
# config: /opt/IBMIHS/conf/httpd.conf
```

```
# Source function library.
. /etc/rc.d/init.d/functions

apachectl=/opt/IBMIHS/bin/apachectl
httpd=/opt/IBMIHS/bin/httpd
RETVAL=0

case "$1" in
start)
echo "Starting IBM HTTP Web Server..."
$apachectl -k start
RETVAL=$?
    ;;
stop)
echo "Stopping IBM HTTP Web Server..."
$apachectl -k stop
RETVAL=$?
    ;;
restart)
echo "Restarting IBM HTTP Web Server..."
$apachectl -k restart
RETVAL=$?
    ;;
status)
status $httpd
    ;;
  *)
echo "Usage: $0 (start |stop|restart|status)"
    ;;
esac
exit $RETVAL
```

Next run `chkconfig--add ibmhttpd` in a terminal session to create links to all the appropriate run levels. Then go to Server Settings ➪ Services, refresh the list, check ibmhttp, click Start, and click Save.

Do the following to verify the installation was correct:

1. Make sure the IBM HTTP Server is running.

2. Start the portal server by going to a terminal session, changing the directory to `/opt/WebSphere/AppServer/bin` and entering **./startServer.sh WebSphere_Portal**.

3. Enter in the address bar in your browser the URL `http://<hostname.yourco.com>:,port>/wps/portal`, where hostname.yourco.com is the WebSphere Portal fully qualified host name and port is the port number in the confirmation panel (usually 9081). Click Go and you should see the WebSphere Portal Welcome page similar to Figure 2-12.

Nongraphic Linux Installation

Very often in Linux environments, installations are done on servers through telnet or the console. WebSphere Portal provides support for these environments using a text-based interactive installation.

To perform a text-based WebSphere Portal installation, copy the Setup CD-ROM to a location on your hard drive. Change into the directory and enter **./install.sh –console** (**install.bat –console** for Windows). An output similar to Figure 3-14 should appear.

You can also use a response file. A response file contains the values that you use during an install and is also used to create a standard WebSphere Portal installation for multiple machines. The values can also be passed as parameters. To run an installation program with a response file enter `./install.sh--options response_file` where response-file is the name of the response file. For Windows it is `\install.bat--iptions response_file`.

A response file can be manually created or automatically during an install. The information entered during an installation is automatically saved in `<was_root>/PortalServer/Log/responselog.txt`. The

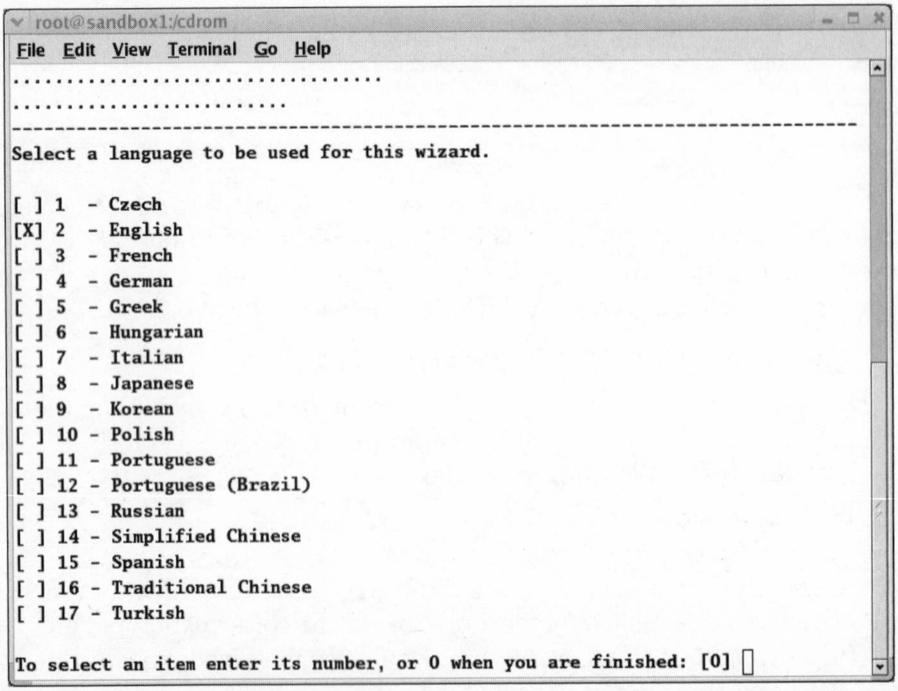

```
  root@sandbox1:/cdrom                                          _ □ ×
 File  Edit  View  Terminal  Go  Help
 ..................................
 .........................
 ---------------------------------------------------------------------------
 Select a language to be used for this wizard.

 [ ]  1  - Czech
 [X]  2  - English
 [ ]  3  - French
 [ ]  4  - German
 [ ]  5  - Greek
 [ ]  6  - Hungarian
 [ ]  7  - Italian
 [ ]  8  - Japanese
 [ ]  9  - Korean
 [ ] 10  - Polish
 [ ] 11  - Portuguese
 [ ] 12  - Portuguese (Brazil)
 [ ] 13  - Russian
 [ ] 14  - Simplified Chinese
 [ ] 15  - Spanish
 [ ] 16  - Traditional Chinese
 [ ] 17  - Turkish

 To select an item enter its number, or 0 when you are finished: [0] []
```

Figure 3-14   Console installation screen.

following is an edited version of the response log created by the Linux Install. Even though this abridged file is quite lengthy, we are showing it because the comments describe the syntax and semantics of the installation commands that are used within a response file. For space reasons, many of the comments have been edited from this example.

```
# Response File for WebSphere Portal Version 5.0 Silent Installation
#
# IMPORTANT: ALL VALUES MUST BE ENCLOSED IN DOUBLE QUOTES ("").
#
#
# INSTALL WEBSPHERE APPLICATION SERVER
#
# Description: Indicate whether you want to install a new instance of
WebSphere
# Application Server or use an existing instance.
# Values:
#
#   install - Install a new instance of WebSphere Application Server.
#   use     - Use an existing instance of WebSphere Application Server.
#   migrate - Upgrade an existing WebSphere Application Server to the
supported
#             level.

    -W installWas.choice="install"


#
# WEBSPHERE APPLICATION SERVER INSTALLATION LOCATION
#
# Description: Specify the directory where you want to install WebSphere
# Application Server.
    -W was.location="/opt/WebSphere/AppServer"

# INSTALL WEB SERVER (IBM HTTP SERVER)
#
# Description: Indicate whether you want to install a new Web server or
use an
# existing Web server.
#
# Values:
#   install - Install IBM HTTP Server
#   use     - Use an existing Web server

    -W installIhs.choice="use"

# IBM HTTP SERVER INSTALLATION LOCATION
#
# Description: Specify the directory where you want to install IBM HTTP
Server.
# Application Server.
```

```
            -W ihs.location="/opt/IBMHttpServer"

# HTTP SERVER TYPE
#
# Description: Specify the type of Web server that you want to use with
# WebSphere Portal.
#
# Values:
#    ihs     - IBM HTTP Server
#    apache  - Apache(TM) Web Server
#    iis     - Microsoft(TM) Internet Information Services
#    iplanet - iPlanet(TM) Web Server
#    domino  - Lotus Domino(TM) Web Server


        -W httpServerType.choice="ihs"

#=============================================#
# IBM HTTP Server Configuration File Location #
#=============================================#

        -W ihsPlugin.file="/opt/IBMIHS/conf/httpd.conf"

# WEBSPHERE APPLICATION SERVER NODE NAME
#
# Description: Specify the node within the WebSphere Application Server
cell to
# which the WebSphere Portal application server will belong.
        -W node.name="sandbox1"


#
# WEBSPHERE APPLICATION SERVER HOST NAME
#
# Description: Specify the fully qualified host name or IP address of
# the computer running WebSphere Application Server. For example,
# "hostname.yourco.com".
#

        -W node.hostName="sandbox1.rigorconsultants.com"


#
# Begin Installing Services
#


# WEBSPHERE PORTAL INSTALLATION LOCATION
#
# Description: Specify the directory where you want to install WebSphere
Portal.
#
```

```
      -W portal.location="/opt/WebSphere/PortalServer"

# WEBSPHERE PORTAL ADMINISTRATIVE USER AND PASSWORD
#
# Enter the user ID and password for the Portal
# administrator

      -W portalAdmin.user="wpsadmin"
      -W portalAdmin.password="PASSWORD-REMOVED"
# SETUP CD LOCATION
#
# Description: Specify the directory path to the Setup CD.

      -W cdSetup.cdPath="/mnt/cdrom"


#
# WEBSPHERE APPLICATION SERVER CD LOCATION
#
# Description: Specify the directory path to the WebSphere Application
Server
# installation images.
      -W userInputCDLoc2.cdPath="/mnt/cdrom"

# WEBSPHERE APPLICATION SERVER FIXPACK AND EFIXES CD LOCATION
#
# Description: Specify the directory path to the WebSphere Application
Server
# Fixpack and eFixes installation images.
      W wasfix1MediaLocation.cdPath="/mnt/cdrom"


#
# WEBSPHERE PORTAL CD LOCATION
#

      -W WPSCDLoc.cdPath="/mnt/cdrom"



#
# PORTAL BASIC CONFIGURATION OPTION
#
# Description: Specify whether you want to perform basic
configuration of
# WebSphere Portal automatically when WebSphere Portal is installed.
# Values:
#
#   yes - Basic configuration is performed automatically as part of the
#         WebSphere Portal installation. This is the default value and
is
#         assumed if the basicConfig.choice parameter is not specified.
#
```

```
#    no  - Basic configuration is not performed during installation and
must be
#         performed manually after installation.

# -W basicConfig.choice="no"

# The options above make this a custom install

    -W setupTypePanel.selectedSetupTypeId="custom"
```

If you have problems creating the response file then before you install, copy the setup CD to a local drive and CHMOD 777, the `installre-sponse.txt` file. The file `installresponse.txt` is a template of the response file.

Uninstalling WebSphere Portal on Linux

To uninstall WebSphere Portal on Linux, go to `<was_root>/PortalServer/uninstall` and execute `./uninstall.sh`. To uninstall the IBM HTTP Server, go to `<ihs_root>/_uninst` and enter **java -jar uninstall.jar.**

> **NOTE** Even though the IBM Http installed the IBM Global Security Kit, it will not uninstall it. To uninstall the Global Security Kit, find the name by entering `rpm -qa | grep gsk`; then `rpm -e the package`.

But what happens if the uninstall does not work, is corrupt, or is accidentally deleted? Then, a manual uninstall is necessary; however, this only works if you uninstall both WebSphere Portal and WebSphere Application Server. We are also assuming that you do not have any data that you want to save. To perform a manual uninstall perform the following steps:

1. Create a backup.
2. Kill all Java processes by typing the command **killall -9 java.**
3. Edit in the root home directory the `vpd.properties` file and remove any entries starting with WS.

Directory Structure

To understand the WebSphere Portal installation in more detail, let's see exactly what it creates. In Windows, installation places the information in the directories as an extension of `<was_root>\PortalServer` while in

Linux/Unix, they are an extension of <was_root>/PortalServer. The following describes the WebSphere Portal directory structure:

```
wp_root                    Root directory for WebSphere Portal
|
•    uninstall             Files used to uninstall WebSphere Portal
|
+-- app Transcoding tag library definition in the /wps.ear/wps.war/WEB-
INF/tld subfolder
|
+-- bin                    WebSphere Portal tools
|
+-- cloudscape             Cloudscape database files
|
+-- config Portal          configuration files
|
+-- deployed               Copies of the .ear and .war files for
installed portlet applications.
|
+-- dev                    Resources for portlet developers, including
Struts
|
+-- doc WebSphere          Portal InfoCenter and Javadoc
|
+-- IBMTrans               Transcoding component
|
+-- installableApps        WAR files prior to deployment
|
+-- installedApps          Active portlet applications extracted to the
WAR file directory structure
|
+-- launchPad              Images used by the WebSphere Portal First
Steps
|
+-- license                WebSphere Portal license agreement
|
+-- log                    WebSphere Portal log files
|
+-- migration              Scripts used to assist in migrating from
previous releases of WebSphere Portal
|
+-- odc                    On-Demand Client files
|
+-- package                Response files and utilities for install
|
+-- pb                     Property broker files for cooperative portlets
|                          XML files for installing portlets individually
+-- portletscripts
|
+-- shared
```

```
| |
| +-- app WebSphere Portal runtime JARs, TLDs, and other resources
| |
+-- config Portal configuration files
| | |
| |
+- services Portal services configuration files (*.properties)
| |
| +-- nls WebSphere Portal NLS files
|
| +-- WEB-INF Resources for the WebSphere Portal
| |
| +- tld Portal JSP taglibs
|
+-- uninstall Resources for uninstalling WebSphere Portal and components
|
+-- version Version information for various components
|
+-- wmm Member Manager configuration, including attributes of portal
users
|
+-- wpcp WebSphere Portal Content Publisher runtime and resources
|
+-- wts Resources for Transcoding Technology
```

The WebSphere Portal applications are stored in the WAR directory under `<was_root>/AppServer/installedApps/<hostname>/wps.ear/wps.war`:

```
wps.war
|
+-- c2a Cooperative portlet resources
|
+-- dtd Document Type Definitions (DTDs) for Portal Server
|
+-- html HTML files for the portal
|
+-- images Graphics for the portal
|
+-- menu Files for MenuService
|
+-- META-INF Metadata for the portal Web application
|
+-- peopleawareness Files for PeopleService
|
+-- screens Screen JSPs for the portal
| |
| +--  markup_name Subdirectory for each markup type
|
|-- skins Skin JSPs for the portal
```

```
| |
| +--  markup_name Subdirectory for each markup type
|_
|-- themes Theme JSPs for the portal
|
| +--  markup_name Subdirectory for each markup type
|
+-- WEB-INF Resources for the Portal Server Web application
```

Installing When WebSphere Security Is Enabled

In most production environments, WebSphere security will be enabled. Installing WebSphere Portal with WebSphere security can be unnecessarily challenging, so disabling security temporarily is highly recommended.

Using the WebSphere administrative console, disable security, install WebSphere Portal, configure WebSphere Portal to use WebSphere Application Server security (discussed in great detail in Chapter 19), and then re-enable WebSphere Application Server Security.

Summary

In this chapter you learned the tricks to installing WebSphere Portal in a Linux environment for both graphic and console desktops. However, all of our installations have dealt with "simplistic" installations. In the next few installation chapters, we are going to discuss how to configure WebSphere Portal with more robust databases and to integrate the various supporting products.

Customizing WebSphere Portal

You have now installed WebSphere Portal on both your Windows and Linux platforms. You are amazed how much easier the installation was compared to WebSphere Portal 4.X. A few questions to answer, pop in four CDs, and—voilà!—WebSphere Portal is installed. Now you might be looking at the other 58 CDs and wondering, "what are these for?" Like a person who has put together a bicycle and finds a few parts left over, you wonder if you missed something.

Well you haven't! To simplify the installation process, WebSphere Portal mandates that the basic configuration is installed and then the user modifies it using the tool WPSconfig. You use WPSconfig when you want to do the following:

- Change the database from Cloudscape
- Use a Directory server
- Use a remote Web server

The reason for this design decision is to enable the user to modify the configuration without having to reinstall the program. This capability clearly makes sense. Initially, when you install the program, you are testing out the features, writing some small portlets, and maybe doing a couple of pilots. For these requirements, you really don't need security and Cloudscape is suitable as a database. However, when you want to roll out a real application with scalability requirements you will need to add a security model and a database that satisfies your load, change, and operation requirements. With this new installation model, you will just need to run WPSconfig to change the database and/or directory server configuration and migrate the data. You will not need to reinstall the product.

WPSconfig

WPSconfig is a script file that invokes configuration tasks. The configuration tasks are implemented using the Apache Ant Tool, which is included as part of WebSphere Application Server.

Apache Ant (http://ant.apache.org/index.html) is a Java-based build tool whose functionality is extended using Java classes instead of scripts, as for most other build tools. Ant's build files are written in XML. They define the project and the tasks that need to be performed during the configuration. Configuration values are passed as parameters during invocation or through property files.

Each build file contains one or more projects. The project tag defines the name of the project, the default target to use when no target is supplied, and optionally the base directory where all path calculations are done. Each project has one or more target(s). A target is a set of tasks that need to be executed. On the target you can specify the order in which a target gets executed or a property that must be set (or not) for it to be executed.

A project can have a set of properties that are either set in the build file by the property task or can be set externally to Ant.

WPSConfig is invoked by typing the following:

```
* Unix: <wp_root>/config/WPSconfig.sh task_name [task_name...]
{-Dproperty =value]
* Windows: <wp_root>\config/WPSconfig.bat task_name
[task_name...] {-Dproperty =value]
```

task_name is the configuration task and -Dproperty is the property flag that enables you to pass the property value to be used by the task. Normally you would set the property values in WPSconfig.properties rather than pass them as parameters. When a value is invoked from property parameter, it temporarily supersedes the value set in WPSconfig .properties but does not overwrite it. The precedence order (highest to lowest) for setting properties is as follows:

1. Properties set on the command line

2. Properties set in parent properties file

3. wpconfig.properties

4. WPSconfig.xml

WPSconfig script invokes the Ant build tool, which receives its project and configuration task definitions from WPSconfig.xml. WPSconfig defines the configuration tasks you can invoke; see Table 4-1 for a description of the tasks.

Table 4-1 WebSphere Portal Configuration Tasks

TASK NAME	DESCRIPTION
enable-security-ldap	Configures the WPS50 and WMM databases for use with an LDAP directory. Sets WebSphere Application Server security to use the LDAP directory
database-transfer-export	Exports existing data from Cloudscape
database-transfer-export-linux	Exports existing data from Cloudscape on Linux
create-local-database-db2	Creates all the databases needed by WebSphere Portal and WebSphere Portal content publishing for a locally installed DB2 instance
database-transfer-import	Imports data collected by the database-transfer-export task
httpserver-config	Configures WebSphere Portal for use with HTTP server. The WpsHostPort value must be set first in the `wpconfig.properties` file

Configuration Templates

WebSphere Portal derives the values for the configuration tasks from the `wpconfig.properties` file. This file contains a centralized reference for all the configuration settings. However, this file contains a large number of properties, many of which the user does not need to change. To make the property file more workable, WebSphere Portal introduces the concept of configuration templates, which are special-purpose property files that contain the properties for a specific task.

Configuration templates is a parent property file. A parent property file has values that when invoked supersede the same property value in the `wpconfig.properties` file. A parent property file can also be a copy of `wpsconfig.properties` with set values. This can be used to define a common configuration over multiple machines.

In the `<wp_root>/config/helpers` directory, WebSphere Portal provides configuration templates. See Table 4-2 for a description of these templates.

To use the configuration templates, copy the template from `<wp_root>\config\helpers` to `<wp_root>\config`. Edit the file and change the property values to those that are appropriate to your environment (later on we will expand this much further). In the template, above the value are comments that go into great detail on what the value should be and what the default value is. More often than not, the default value does not need to be changed.

Table 4-2 WebSphere Portal Configuration Templates

CONFIGURATION TEMPLATE	DESCRIPTION
transfer_db2.properties	Configures WebSphere Portal to use a DB2 database, including transferring your data from Cloudscape to DB2
transfer_informix.properties	Configures WebSphere Portal to use an Informix database, including transferring your data from Cloudscape to Informix
transfer_oracle.properties	Configures WebSphere Portal to use an Oracle database, including transferring your data from Cloudscape to Oracle
transfer_sqlserver.properties	Configures WebSphere Portal to use an SQL Server database, including transferring your data from Cloudscape to SQL Server
config_http.properties	Configures WebSphere Portal to use an external Web server, instead of the internal HTTP transport provided by WebSphere Application Server
security_active_directory.properties	Configures WebSphere Portal to use WebSphere Application Server security with Active Directory as its Lightweight Directory Access Protocol (LDAP) directory
security_disable.properties	Disables security for WebSphere Application Server if you have previously configured WebSphere Portal to use security
security_domino.properties	Configures WebSphere Portal to use WebSphere Application Server security with Domino as its LDAP directory
security_ibm_dir_server.properties	Configures WebSphere Portal to use WebSphere Application Server security with IBM Directory Server as its LDAP directory
security_sun_one.properties	Configures WebSphere Portal to use WebSphere Application Server security with Sun ONE as its LDAP directory

After you have modified the configuration template, execute WPSConfig passing the configuration template as a parent properties file using the following syntax:

```
* UNIX: ./WPSconfig.sh -
DparentProperties=<wp_root>/config/<configuration_template> -
DSaveParentProperties=true
*Windows: WPSconfig.bat -
DparentProperties=<wp_root>\config\<configuration_template> -
DSaveParentProperties=true
```

Note that when you call WPSconfig, you are not specifying a task. When you do not specify a task, the configuration program updates the wpconfig.properties file with values from the configuration template. Of course, this happens if and only if the configuration tasks execute successfully.

Of course, you do not have to use the configuration templates provided by IBM. You can create your own. Just copy a configuration template that matches as close as possible to the configuration you want to make and modify the file adhering to the conventions specified in the file.

Using DB2 with WebSphere Portal

Now that you understand how WPSconfig works, you need to know how to modify the WebSphere Portal for a real-life scenario. In Figure 4-1, in the DMZ, the WebSphere Portal is on Windows 2000 Advance Server on sandbox1.rigorconsultants.com. In the secured zone, data is stored on DB2 UDB 8.1 Enterprise database server. In this configuration, the data is stored in a more robust database with features to support enterprise operation management, backup and recovery, performance turning, and change

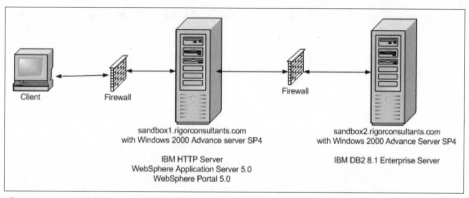

Figure 4-1 WebSphere Portal using DB2 database on a separate server.

management. Also by placing the database on its server, you can prevent the application server from impacting the database server and vice versa.

Configuring the DB2 Server

The first step is to configure the remote DB2 Server, which for the example is `sandbox2.rigoroconsultants.com`. Assume the following:

- You have installed DB2 UDB 8.1.
- The database user wpsdbusr has been set up and has administrative rights.
- You are logged in as wpsdbusr.
- Port 50000 and 50001 can access the client. This implies that the firewalls are configured to allow these ports.
- A db2 instance is available with enough storage allocated for the defined databases.

Three databases need to be created: wps50, wpcp50, and fdbk50. The database wps50 stores information about user customization and member management. Size is dependent on the number of portal objects and users. Database wpcp50 is used by the content publishing and the document management and the storage requirements are based on the number and size of documents being published or stored. The last database fdbk50 is the WPCP feedback database whose size is based on the site traffic.

Now you are ready to configure your remote server. This is somewhat complicated. Many of these commands are in the installation manual so a good trick is to find the installation manual (wpf-install-ent) in pdf format and copy and paste the commands from the manual to a command prompt.

The following are the steps to configure the remote database:

1. Log in to the DB2 server as wpsdbusr.

2. Enter the following commands in a DB2 Command Window to set up the WebSphere Portal database:

```
db2 create database wps50 using codeset UTF-8 territory us
db2 update database configuration for wps50 using applheapsz 16384
app_ctl_heap_sz 8192
db2 update database configuration for wps50 using stmtheap 60000
db2 update database configuration for wps50 using locklist 400
db2 update database configuration for wps50 using indexrec RESTART
db2 update database configuration for wps50 using logfilsiz 1000
db2 update database configuration for wps50 using logprimary 12
db2 update database configuration for wps50 using logsecond 10
db2set DB2_RR_TO_RS=yes
```

3. Enter the following commands in a DB2 Command Window to set up WebSphere Portal content publishing database:

```
db2 create database wpcp50 using codeset UTF-8 territory us collate
using identity
db2 create database fdbk50 using codeset UTF-8 territory us collate
using identity
db2 update database configuration for wpcp50 using applheapsz 4096
db2 update database configuration for fdbk50 using applheapsz 4096
db2 update database configuration for wpcp50 using logfilsiz 4096
db2 update database configuration for fdbk50 using logfilsiz 4096
db2 update database configuration for wpcp50 using logprimary 4
db2 update database configuration for fdbk50 using logprimary 4
db2 update database configuration for wpcp50 using logsecond 25
db2 update database configuration for fdbk50 using logsecond 25
```

4. Edit `C:\WINNT\system32\drivers\etc\services` and ensure the following entries for the DB2 connection and interrupt service ports:

```
db2c_db2       50000/tcp   # DB2 connection service port
db2c_db2CTLSV 50001/tcp   # DB2 interrupt service port
```

5. In a DB2 Command Window, set DB2COMM to TCP/IP and then set up the service name:

```
db2set DB2COMM=TCPIP
db2 UPDATE DBM CFG USING db2c_db2
```

6. Restart the database server.

Installing DB2 Client on WebSphere Portal Server

Next, you need to install the DB2 client on the WebSphere Portal Server so that it can access the remote DB2 server. This means you have to install the DB2 client and then configure it. Assume the following:

- WebSphere Portal, IBM HTTP Server, and WebSphere Administrator Server are on one machine and that it is a Windows 2000 Advance server.

- The user wpsdbusr has been set up and has administrative rights, is defined locally, can act as part of the operating system, and is able to create a token object, increase quotas, and replace a process level token.

- You are logged in as wpsdbusr.

- Port 50000 and 50001 can access the client. This implies that the firewalls are configured to allow these ports.

The following are the steps to do this:

1. Place the DB2 Enterprise Edition for windows CD into the drive. If autorun is enabled, you will see the Welcome screen. If not enter <D> :**Setup,** where <D> is your CD drive.

2. Click Install Products.

3. On Select the Product You Like to Install, click Next.

4. The Welcome to DB2 Setup screen appears. Click Next.

5. Accept the license agreement and click Next.

6. Choose Custom as the installation type and click Next.

7. Keep the default installation action and click Next.

8. The next screen will list the features you want to install. Unclick all features except Client Support. Also choose the installation directory. Click Next. See Figure 4-2.

9. A warning screen will appear if you have a firewall enabled. Click OK; however, it is strongly recommended to install the product with the firewall disabled.

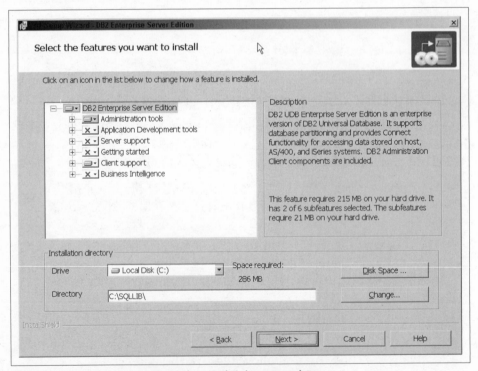

Figure 4-2   DB2 features required on WebSphere Portal Server.

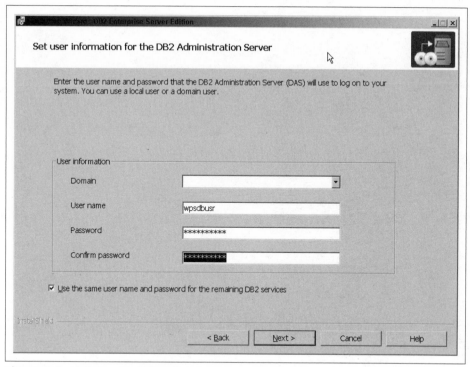

Figure 4-3   Defining the DB2 administrator.

10. Select installation language and confirm folder. Click Next.

11. Input user information for DB2 administrator and click Next. We have defined the DB2 administrator to be wpsdbusr. See Figure 4-3.

12. Set up your administrator contact list as per your company policies and click Next.

13. Keep the default Create a DB2 Instance and click Next.

14. Under Configure DB2 Instances, keep the default values and click Next. The name of the DB2 Instance on the client must be the same as the name of the DB2 Instance on the server.

15. Under Prepare the DB2 Tools catalog, keep the default value and click Next.

16. Specify your health contact as per your company policies and click Next.

17. Under Request Satellite Information, specify a satellite ID. This field is optional. If not specified, your login ID or wpsdbusr will be used.

18. Next will appear a screen listing the components you will be installing (for example, Figure 4-4). Click Install.

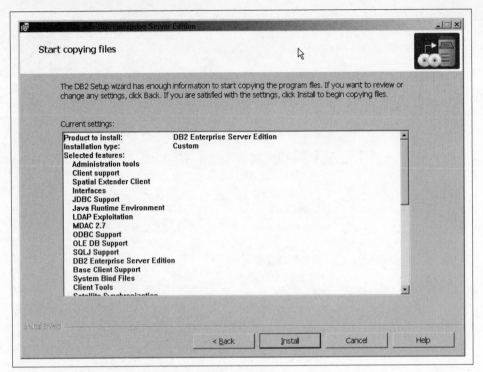

Figure 4-4   DB2 Client installation component list.

19. After you have successfully installed the client and restarted the server, log in as wpsdbusr.

20. In a DB2 Command Window, set DB2COMM to TCP/IP;

```
db2set DB2COMM=tcpip
```

21. In a DB2 Command Window, catalog the TCP/IP node with the IP address of the remote database;

```
db2 catalog tcpip node was1 remote sandbox2.rigoroconsultants.com
server db2c_db2
```

Here was1 is the node name we are assigning to the WebSphere Application Server node, sandbox2.rigorconsultants.com is our remote database server host name, and dbc_db2 is the name of the DB2 connection service port.

22. In a DB2 Command Window, catalog WebSphere Portal Server databases as aliases on the client.

```
db2 catalog db wps50 as wps50 at node was1
db2 catalog db wpcp50 as wpcp50 at node was1
db2 catalog db fdbk50 as fdbk50 at node was1
```

In this particular example, the name of the database on the server is the same as the alias on the client.

Using Oracle and SQL Server with WebSphere Portal

After you have installed DB2 on the client and server and created the appropriate tables, the next step is to modify WebSphere Portal configuration to support the database. But first let us go on a bit of a tangent to examine the support of other databases, since the last step is pretty independent of the database.

Although DB2 is an excellent database and comes with WebSphere Portal Extend and WebSphere Portal Experience, many sites have standardized on other databases. Two most popular databases are Microsoft's SQL Server and Oracle's database. In this section, you will find out what you need to do if you want to use SQL Server 2000 or Oracle 9i as the database instead of DB2 for the configuration in Figure 4-1. For the purpose of conciseness, let's assume that the databases have already been installed on the remote server and configured and tested to communicate with the WebSphere Portal Server. For Oracle, this implies that you are using the Oracle JDBC/OCI Type 2 drivers and that you copied the `classes12.zip` file from the remote Oracle server to the WebSphere Portal Server.

Step 1: Create the Databases

On `sandbox2.rigorconsultants.com`, create the databases wps50, wpcp50, and fdbk50. For SQL Server 2000, insure that your Collation Name is a case-sensitive collation. For English, set the collation name to SQL_latin1_General_CP1_CS_AS. For Oracle 8i, insure that the databases are created as UTF-8 character set databases.

Step 2: Create the Database Users

To use Oracle 9i or SQL Server 2000 with WebSphere Portal, we recommend six users be created in uppercase format: WPSDBUSR and WMMDBUSR that are associated with the database wps50, PZNADMIN, EJB, and WCMD-BADM that are associated with wpcp50, and FEEDBACK that is associated with fdbk50. WPSDBUSR will own approximately 76 tables, which will consist of WebSphere Portal core objects. WMMDBUSR will own approximately 17 pages consisting of Member Manager objects. PZNADMIN will own approximately 11 tables and EJB will own approximately 2 tables and they will both jointly own the tables for personalization information. WCMDBADM will own approximately 61 tables consisting of content publishing information. Lastly FEEDBACK will own 48 tables for the purpose of logging site and personalization usage. Note again this table size might fluctuate greatly depending on site usage, so configure it carefully.

Step 2a: Create SQL Server 2000 Database Users

To create database users for SQL Server, use SQL Server Enterprise Manager as follows:

1. Right-click SQL Server Group ⇨ Local ⇨ Security ⇨ Login and left-click on New Login.
2. Enter the database username (**WPSDBUSR, WMMDBUSR, PZNADMIN, EJB, WCMDBADM, or FEEDBACK**).
3. Select SQL Server Authentication.
4. Set a password for the selected user.
5. Select the default database for each user using the mappings discussed in the beginning of this section. For instance, WPSDBUSR default database is wps50.
6. Click on the Server Role tab and make sure that no Server Role is selected.
7. Click on the Database Access tab. Enable permissions based on what's shown in Table 4-3.
8. Click OK to save the user changes.

Table 4-3 Recommended Database Access Roles

USERNAME	DATABASE	DATABASE ROLE
WPSDBUSR	wps50	public, db_owner
WMMDBUSR	wps50	public, db_owner
PZNADMIN	wpcp50	public, db_owner
EJB	wpcp50	public, db_owner
WCMDBADM	wpcp50	public, db_owner
FEEDBACK	fdbk50	public, db_owner

Step 2b: Create Oracle Database Users

To create the database users for Oracle, use SQL*Plus:

1. Enter username: **system/manager@wps50.** This will log the administrative user system with a password of manager into the wps50 database. Replace manager with the System Administrator's password.

2. Create the WebSphere Portal users and grant them appropriate privileges.

```
create user WPSDBUSR identified by PASSWORD default tablespace USERS
temporary tablespace TEMP;
create user WMMDBUSR identified by PASSWORD default tablespace USERS
temporary tablespace TEMP;
grant connect, resource to WPSDBUSR;
grant connect, resource to WMMDBUSR;
```

3. Connect to the content publishing database by entering **connect** and then username: **system/manager@wpcp50.** This will log the administrative user system with a password of manager into the wpcp50 database. Replace manager with the System Administrator's password.

4. Create the content publishing users and grant them appropriate privileges.

```
create user PZNADMIN identified by PASSWORD default tablespace USERS
temporary tablespace TEMP;
create user EJB identified by PASSWORD default tablespace USERS
temporary tablespace TEMP;
create user WCMDBADM identified by PASSWORD default tablespace USERS
temporary tablespace TEMP;
grant connect, resource to PZNADMIN;
grant connect, resource to EJB;
grant connect, resource to WCMDBADM;
grant insert any table to WCMDBADM;
```

5. Connect to the Feedback database by entering **connect** and then username: **system/manager@fdbk50.** This will log the administrative user system with a password of manager into the fdbk50 database and again replace manager with the System Administrator's password.

6. Create the content publishing feedback user and grant it appropriate privileges.

```
create user FEEDBACK identified by PASSWORD default tablespace USERS
temporary tablespace TEMP;
grant connect, resource to FEEDBACK;
```

7. Type **exit.**

Configuring WebSphere Portal to Access a Remote Database

Now that the database is installed and configured, you need to configure WebSphere Portal to access and populate the database with WebSphere Portal system and user data. The method used, as stated previously, will be the same for any remote database, except that the property values will be different. The configuration for a local database is simpler, because configuration templates exist for Oracle, SQL server, Informix, and DB2 that configure and transfer the data all in one step.

However for a remote database, such as the one shown in Figure 4-1, the process is more difficult. Perform the following steps to configure a remote database for WebSphere Portal on a Windows 2000 Advanced Server:

1. Open a command prompt and change the directory to `<wp_root>\config`.

2. Export the current database data by entering **WPSconfig.bat database-transfer-export**. Execution of this command can take some time; if execution is successful, a message will be displayed indicating success. You can also see if it has executed successfully by looking at the logs at `<wps_root>\log\configmessages`. Executing the command is similar under Unix except for the OS syntax differences. However in Linux the task name is database-transfer-export-linux. After the command has executed, all the data will be stored in the directory `<wps_root>\config\DBTRansfer`.

3. Copy `<wp_root>\config\wpconfig.properties` to `<wp_root>\config\wpconfig.bkp`.

4. Using a test editor, edit `<wp_root>\config\wpconfig.properties` and for the properties described in Tables 4-4–4-6, enter the appropriate values. The values entered in the table support the example defined in Figure 4-1. Note that this is a Java properties file, so a backward slash (\) is represented as a forward slash (/).

5. Save the file.

6. Test that the properties are valid by entering the following commands in a command prompt:

```
WPSconfig.bat validate-database-connection-wps
WPSconfig.bat validate-database-connection-wmm
WPSconfig.bat validate-database-connection-wpcp
```

These commands will test the database connection. If the response is positive go to the next step, otherwise check your properties to see if they are valid. Very often it is an invalid port or a port/IP address that is inaccessible due to a firewall configuration.

Table 4-4 Configuration Database Properties

PROPERTY	DESCRIPTION	PROPERTY VALUE		
		DB2	ORACLE	SQL SERVER
DbSafeMode	If this property is set to true, no database-specific updates are performed	False	False	False
DbType	Database used to store information for WebSphere Portal	db2	oracle	sqlserver
WpsDbName	Database name or alias name if remote where WebSphere Portal objects are stored	wps50	wps50	wps50
DbDriver	Name of the JDBC provider used to import SQL files	COM.ibm.db2. jdbc.app.DB2 Driver	oracle.jdbc.driver. OracleDriver	com.microsoft. jdbc.sqlserver. SQLServerDriver
DbDriverDs	The data source for the JDBC provider that WebSphere Portal used to import SQL files	Not applicable	oracle.jdbc.pool. OracleConnection-PoolDataSource	com.microsoft. jdbcx.sqlserver. SQLServerData Source
DbUrl	The database URL used to access the WebSphere Portal database	jdbc:db2:wps 50	jdbc:oracle:thin:@ sandbox2 .rigorconsulta nts.com:1521: wps50	jdbc:microsoft: sqlserver:// sandbox2 .rigorconsultants .com:1433:Database Name = wps50
DbUser	The database administrative username	wpsdbuser	WPSDBUSER	WPSDBUSER
DbPassword	The 1database administrative username password	—	—	—

(continued)

Table 4-4 *(continued)*

PROPERTY	DESCRIPTION	PROPERTY VALUE		
		DB2	ORACLE	SQL SERVER
DbLibrary	Location `db2java.zip` for DB2	`C:/Program Files/SQLLIB/ java/db2/ java.zip`	`C:/Program Files/oracle/ jdbc/lib/ classes12 .zip`	`C:/Program Files/mssql/lib/ mssqlserver.jar;` `C:/Program Files/ mssql/lib/msbase .jar;` `C:/Program Files/mssql/lib/ msutil.jar`
WpsDsName	The name of the datasource used for the WebSphere Portal database	`wps50DS`	`wps50DS`	`wps50DS`
WpsXDbName	The TCP/IP alias for the database to be used as dsname. Only needs to be set for Unix or Linux servers	`wps5TCP`	Not applicable	Not applicable
WpsDbNode	The node name of the WebSphere Portal database. Only needs to be set for Unix or Linux servers	`wpsNode`	Not applicable	Not applicable

Table 4-5 Configuration Content Publishing Database Properties

PROPERTY	DESCRIPTION	PROPERTY VALUE		
		DB2	ORACLE	SQL SERVER
WpcpDbHost Name	Host name of the machine running SQL Server	Not applicable	Not applicable	sandbox2.rigor-consultants.com
WpcpDbNode	The node name of the WebSphere Portal content publishing database. Only needs to be set for Unix or Linux server	wpcpNode	Not applicable	Not applicable
WpcpXDbName	The TCP/IP alias for the WebSphere Portal content publishing database. Only needs to be set for Unix or Linux server	wpcp5TCP	Not applicable	Not applicable
FeedbackXDb Name	The TCP/IP alias for the feedback database. Only needs to be set for Unix or Linux server	fdbk5TCP	Not applicable	Not applicable
WpcpDbName	The database name or alias name where the WebSphere Portal content publishing objects are created	wpcp50	wpcp50	wpcp50
WpcpDbUser	The database administrative username	wpsdbusr	WCMDBADM	WCMDBADM
WpcpDb Password	The password for the database user associated with WpcpDbUser			
WpcpDbUrl	The database URL used to access the WebSphere Portal content publishing database	jdbc:db2:wpcp50	jdbc:oracle:thin:@sandbox2.rigorconsultants.com:1521:wpcp50	jdbc:microsoft:sql-server://sandbox2.rigorconsultants.com:1433;Database Name = wpcp50

(continued)

Table 4-5 *(continued)*

PROPERTY	DESCRIPTION	PROPERTY VALUE		
		DB2	ORACLE	SQL SERVER
WpcpDbEjb Password	The password for the Enterprise Java Bean (EJB) user	Not applicable		
WpcpDbPznad-min Password	The password for the PZNADMIN user	Not applicable		
FeedbackDb HostName	host name of the machine	Not applicable	Not applicable	`sandbox2.rigor-consultants.com`
FeedbackDb Name	The database name where the feedback objects are created	fdbk50	fdbk50	fdbk50
FeedbackDb User	The database administrative username	wpsdbusr	FEEDBACK	FEEDBACK
FeedbackDb Password	The password for the database user associated with FeedbackDbUser			
FeedbackDbUrl	The database URL used to access the feedback database	`jdbc:db2:fdbk50`	`jdbc:oracle:thin:@sandbox2.rigor-consultants.com:1521:fdbk50`	`jdbc:microsoft:sql-server://sandbox2.rigorconsultants.com:1433;Database Name = fdbk50`

Table 4-6 Configuration Member Manager Properties

PROPERTY	DESCRIPTION	PROPERTY VALUE		
		DB2	ORACLE	SQL SERVER
WmmDsName	Name of the datasource to be used for the Member Manager database	wmmDS	wmmDS	wmmDS
WmmDbName	The database name or alias name where the Member Manager objects are created	wps50	wps50	wps50
WmmDbUser	The database administrative username	wpsdbusr	WMMDBUSR	WMMDBUSR
WmmDb Password	The password for the database user associated with WmmDbUser			
WmmDbUrl	The database URL used to access the Member Manager database	jdbc:db2:wps50	jdbc:oracle:thin:@ sandbox2 .rigorconsultants .com:1521:wps50	jdbc:microsoft:sql-server://sandbox2 .rigorconsultants .com:1433;Database Name=wps50

Figure 4-5 Successful database configuration.

7. Enter the following command to import your old database data into your new database:

   ```
   WPSConfig.bat database-transfer-import
   ```

   After some time, the length being dependent on the volume of data imported, you should see a success message as indicated in Figure 4-5.

8. Restart WebSphere Portal and verify the installation by accessing your portal.

For DB2, you should perform a reorg check on all the database tables and if you installed WebSphere Portal on a pre-existing instance of WebSphere Application Server, make sure that the path to the required DB2 JDBC provider files was added to the WebSphere Application Server. You can verify that the classpath has been set up correctly by doing the following steps:

1. Go to administration console.

2. Click Servers Application Servers.

3. Then click WebSphere Portal from the list of application servers.

4. Click Process Definition from the list of additional properties.

5. Finally, click Java Virtual Machine from the list of additional properties.

Summary

In this chapter you saw how to configure WebSphere Portal after a basic installation. We focused on enabling WebSphere Portal to store its objects in

DB2 8.1, Oracle 9i, or SQL Server 2000. Configuration of WebSphere Portal for LDAP will be covered in Chapter 19. You saw that with WSConfig utility, you could easily change your configuration without reinstalling the product and the configuration utility also handled data migration.

In the next chapter we will discuss how to install some specialized tools that come with WebSphere Portal and also introduce you to some tools and features that help you analyze installation and runtime problems.

## CHAPTER 5

Installing WebSphere Portal Tools and Problem Analysis

WebSphere Portal comes with a couple of tools that are critical to the development and usage of portals: Portal Toolkit 5.0.2 and IBM Lotus Workplace Web Content Management version 1.1. In this chapter we will show you how to install them, since the installation methods are not that straightforward.

Lastly, we will discuss what you should do if you encounter a problem and show the tools that are available for identifying your problems and correcting them. This will include a discussion on Tivoli Web Site Analyzer that comes with WebSphere Portal Enable. The Tivoli Web Site Analyzer allows you to analyze your portal usage.

We will look at the 10 most common problems customers have encountered and propose some best practices.

Portal Toolkit 5.0.2

Portal Toolkit 5.0.2 is a plug-in for WebSphere Studio that enables you to easily develop and debug portlets and then test them either using an integrated local WebSphere Portal Test Environment or on a remote WebSphere Portal server. The local WebSphere Test Environment can be WP V4.2, WP 5.0, or WP 5.0.2. The usage of the Portal Toolkit is discussed in Chapter 15. Here we are going to discuss how to install Portal Toolkit 5.0.2 with a local WebSphere Portal 5.0.2 Test environment.

First we are assuming that you have installed WebSphere Studio Application Developer V5.1.0 or WebSphere Studio Site Developer V5.1.0. Do not install WebSphere Studio 5.1.0. Interim Fix 001 if you need to use the Web Service Client Portlet Project Wizard. Also when you install WebSphere Studio, insure that the installation directory has a short path. The toolkit installation tends to have problems with long path names.

The Portal Toolkit has the following system and software requirements:

1. Processor: 800 MHz Pentium III minimum.

2. Memory: 1 GB of memory minimum.

3. Disk space: 2.5GB +.

4. Operating system: Windows 2000 SP2+ or Windows XP SP1. Include all security patches.

5. Browser: IE5.5 SP2 +.

6. Tools: Adobe Acrobat, Zip Utility.

7. WebSphere Studio Application Developer 5.1.0 or WebSphere Studio Site Developer 5.1.0.

8. WebSphere Portal Toolkit V5.0.2 MP from WebSphere Portal Zone for developers; `http://www-106.ibm.com/developerworks/websphere/zones/portal/`.

9. Download WebSphere Application Server 5.0.2 Fix Pack and the WebSphere Portal 5.0 Fix Pack 2, which can be found at `http://www-1.ibm.com/support/docview.wss?rs=0&q1=portal+5.0.2&uid=swg24006309&loc=en_US&cs=utf-8&cc=us&lang=en`.

Updating WebSphere Studio's WAS Runtime Environment

The first step is to update the WAS V5.0.2 runtime environment used by WebSphere Studio to enable local debugging for WP V5.0.2. You do this by taking the following steps:

1. Unzip WebSphere Application Server 5.0.2 Fix Pack into `c:\fixes`.

2. Open a command prompt, change directory to `C:\fixes\win` and set `JAVA_HOME=<WSAD>\runtimes\base_v5\java` and hit Enter.

3. Type **updateWizard.bat.** and hit Enter.

4. Using the drop-down box, select a language for the wizard to use.

5. Read the Welcome screen and click Next.

6. Verify that Specify Product Information is checked and then browse to `<WSAD>\runtimes\base_v5` and click Next.

7. Select Install Fixes and click Next.

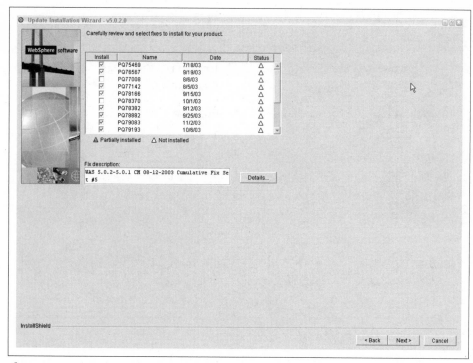

Figure 5-1   Fixes for WebSphere Studio runtime environment.

8. Verify/update the Fix directory to C:\fixes\win\efixes and click Next.

9. As shown in Figure 5-1, select all the fixes in the list except for PQ77008, PQ78370, and WAS_Plugin_09-03-2003_5.0.X_cumulative and then click Next. If you choose PQ77008, PQ78370, and/or WAS_Plugin_09-03-2003_5.0.X_cumulative, the installation will fail.

10. Review the fixes to be installed or refreshed and then click Next.

11. Check that the Update Wizard reports that the fixes have been installed successfully and then click Finish.

Installing WebSphere Portal Toolkit V5.0.2 MP

The next step is to install the actual Portal Toolkit with the WebSphere Test Environment V5.0. Perform the following steps to do this:

1. Shut down your HTTP servers.

2. Double-click PortalToolkit502MP.exe.

3. Enter a temporary directory and click Next.

4. Select a language for the wizard to use from the drop down box and click OK.

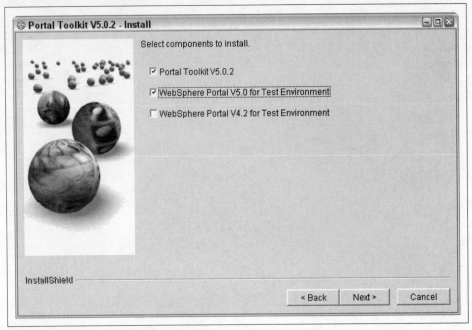

Figure 5-2   Portal Toolkit components.

5. Read the Welcome screen and click Next.

6. Read the License Agreement, select I Accept the Terms in the License Agreement, and click Next.

7. In the list of components to install (as seen in Figure 5-2), select Portal Toolkit V5.0.2 and WebSphere Portal V5.0 for Test environment. Click Next.

8. In the WebSphere Portal V5.0 installer field, place CD 2 of WebSphere Portal Enable or Extend. Browse to the location of `wpsinstaller.jar`, which is the wps directory (see Figure 5-3). Click Next.

9. Review the install location of the WebSphere Portal V5.0 for Test Environment and click Next.

10. Once the installation is completed successfully, click Finish. It will take 20–30 minutes.

11. Double-click the WebSphere Studio shortcut on the desktop.

12. In the WebSphere Studio dialog box, verify your workspace directory and click OK.

13. As seen in Figure 5-4, a Configuration Changes dialog should appear. Expand the detected changes and verify whether the Server

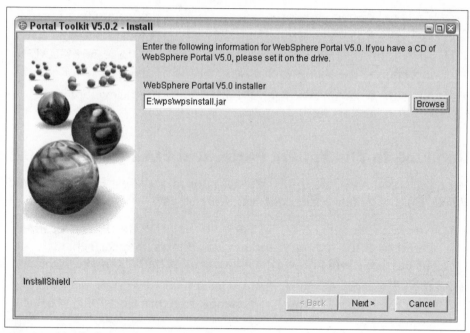

Figure 5-3   WebSphere Portal V5.0 location.

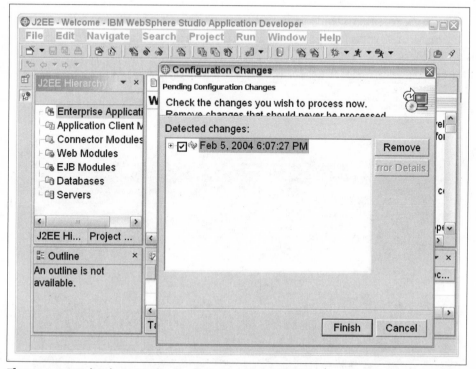

Figure 5-4   WebSphere Studio Configuration Changes dialog.

Tools for WebSphere Portal version 5.0 Test Environment 5.1.0 and WebSphere Portal Toolkit have been detected. Click Finish.

14. An Install/Update dialog appears and asks you to restart WSAD to incorporate the changes, click Yes.

15. After the restart, WSAD should display the basic development environment again.

Updating to WebSphere Portal Test Environment V5.0.2

Next you have to update the WebSphere Portal V5.0 Test Environment to V5.0.2. Do this by performing the following steps:

1. Extract WebSphere Portal Fix Pack 2 to c:\fixpack2. The location should be at the root path and have no blanks or special characters. The batch file will not work with a complex path. So make your life easier and use c:\fixpack2.

2. Open a command prompt and change directory to <WSAD>\Portal Toolkit.

3. Run updatePortalTestEnv502 C:\fixpack2. It should take approximately 20 minutes for the update to complete.

4. Check results in the command prompt (as seen in Figure 5-5) for updatePortalTestEnv502.bat to make sure it ended successfully.

5. Verify the WebSphere Portal V5.0.2 Test Environment upgrade by doing the following.

Figure 5-5   A successful update of the Portal Test Environment.

a. Double-click the WebSphere Studio shortcut on the desktop.

b. In the WebSphere Studio dialog box, verify your workspace and then click OK.

c. Click File ⇨ New ⇨ Project ⇨ Portlet Development Portlet Application Project.

d. To define the Portlet Project, enter **Portlet1** for the Project Name and click Finish.

e. After the wizard finishes creating the project, right-click on Portlet1 in the Project Navigator and select Debug on Server.

f. In the Server Selection dialog, select WebSphere Portal V5.0 Test Environment under the Create a New Server Area. Check the Set Server as Project Default (do not prompt) and click Finish.

g. The project will be published to the WebSphere Portal V5.0 Test Environment server and the server will be started. Server startup information will be displayed in the Console view in the bottom center area.

h. After sometime, a browser should display a Debug page with Portlet1 portlet on it (as seen in Figure 5-6). This verifies that the Test Environment is running properly.

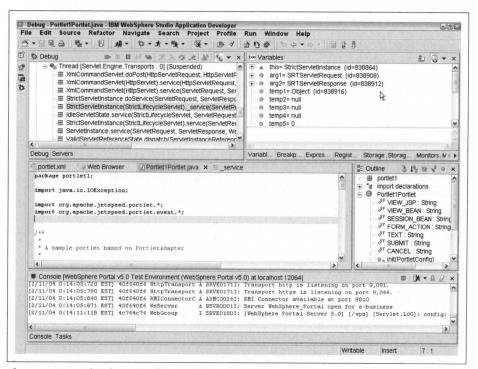

Figure 5-6   WebSphere Studio running Server in Debug mode.

IBM Lotus Workplace Web Content Management Version 1.1

Included with WebSphere Portal V5.0.2 is IBM Lotus Workplace Web Content Management (ILWWCM) version 1.1, which eventually replaces WPCP. However, this component must be installed after you have installed WebSphere Portal.

On a separate CD you will find a file called C53YLML.exe. You will also need to download JRE 1.3.1_09 and install it. To install ILWWCM, perform the following steps.

Updating the Initialization Parameters

1. Log in to Windows as an Administrative user.

2. Double-click C53YLML.exe and unzip the files to c:\wcm.

3. Open the WebSphere Application Assembly Tool by clicking Start ⇨ Programs ⇨ IBM WebSphere ⇨ Application Server V5.0 ⇨ Application Assembly Tool.

4. In Welcome to the Application Assembly Tool, select the Existing tab.

5. Browse to C:\wcm\app\config\websphere\ilwwcm.war. Click Select and then click OK.

6. Navigate to and select Initialization Parameters by clicking ILWWCM ⇨ Web Components ⇨ ILWWCM Framework ⇨ Initialization Parameters.

7. As seen in Figure 5-7, replace parameter [ILWWCM_HOME] with C:/wcm/app and click Apply. Click Save and exit the Application Assembly Tool.

Installing the ILWWCM Web Application

1. Start WebSphere Application Server.

2. Open the WebSphere Administration Console.

3. Select Applications ⇨ Install New Applications.

4. Select Local Path, browse to C:\wcm\app\config\websphere\ ilwwcm.war, and click Open.

5. As seen in Figure 5-8, enter **wcm** in the Context Root field and then click Next.

6. On all the next four screens, accept the defaults and click Next until you see the last screen. Then hit Finish.

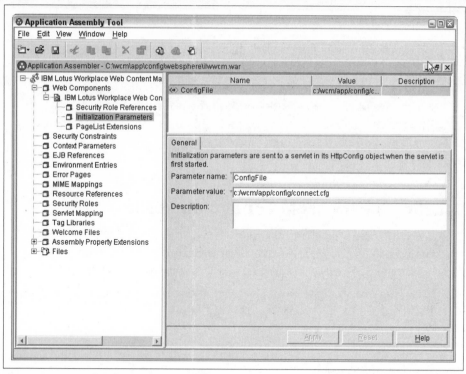

Figure 5-7 Configuring ILWWCM in WebSphere Application Assembly Tool.

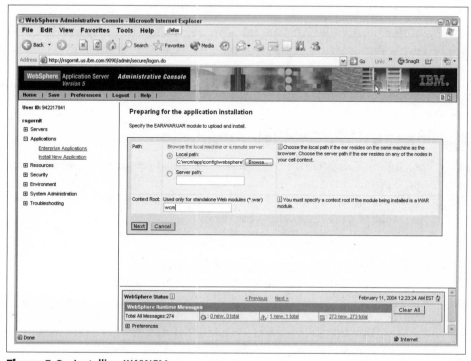

Figure 5-8 Installing ILWWCM.

7. If the installation is successful, click Save to Master Configuration and then in the Save to Master Configuration window click Save.

8. Copy the contents of C:\wcm\web-app, which consists of three directories (ac_admin, WEB-INF, and webinterface) to paste the directories into the <WAS>\installedApps\<short_server_name>\ilwwcm_war.ear\ilwwcm.war directory.

Updating the ILWWCM Configuration Files

1. Copy the configuration files aptrixjpe.properties, aptrixsearch.properties, and connect.cfg from C:\wcm\app\config\samples to C:\wcm\app\config.

2. Now this process is tedious. Replace the following variables with the given values in all the configuration files.

```
[HOST]         = Your host name.
[PORT]         = 9080
[CONTEXT_ROOT] = wcm
[ILWWCM_HOME]  = C:/wcm/app
[WEB_APP_HOME] = <WAS>/installedApps/<short_server_name>/
ilwwcm_war.ear/ilwwcm.war
```

Note that since these files are Java property files, the backward slash used for Windows directory is represented as a forward slash. This is not a typo in the book.

3. Save each file.

Starting the ILWWCM Web Application

In the WebSphere Administration Console, find and select the ilwwcm_war Enterprise Application and click Start. Verify ilwwcm_war has started by checking for the green arrow in Enterprise Applications. You can also just restart the WebSphere Application Server.

ILWWCM Administrative Client Setup

1. Make sure that JRE 1.3.1_09 is installed.

2. Initialize the ILWWCM Web application by entering **http://localhost:9080/ilwwcm/connect/?MOD=AJPEGUI** in an Internet Explorer browser. Figure 5-9 indicates a successful initialization.

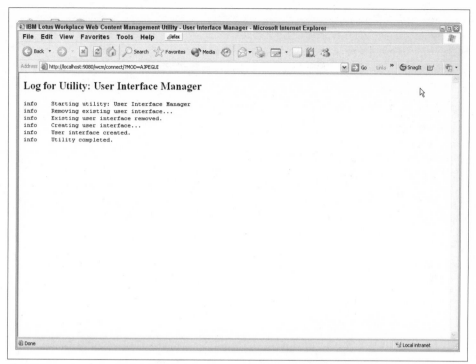

Figure 5-9   A successful initialization of the ILWWCM Administrative Client.

3. In Enter Network Password, enter **Administrator** for the User Name and password for Password. Verify that the Utility to update the User Interface Manager is completed without errors.

4. Enter **http://localhost:9080/ilwwcm/connect/aptrix** in a browser. In 'Java Plug-in Security Warning' click Grant Always to allow the Verisign authenticated ILWWCM applet to install and run. Expand the components of the Home area and verify that Aptrix exists as a Site Framework. If you see Figure 5-10, your ILWWCM administrator client is now running.

Installing the WebSphere Portal Content Management Portlet

To install the portlet, which will enable you to view your content managed by ILWWCM, log on WP as an administrator:

1. Go to the Portal Administration screen.
2. Go to the Install Portlets view and Click Browse.

Figure 5-10   The ILWWCM Administrator Client.

3. Select the `wpsV5-j-ilwwcm-cportlet.war` file to install and click Next. It is located at `c:\wcm\contentportlet\wpsV5`.

4. The Web Content Management Portlet is displayed (as seen in Figure 5-11). Click Install to install. The portlet will be labeled as Content Viewer, Java Edition when you look for it under Manage Portlets.

Problem Analysis

The one law that most professionals in the computer field believe in religiously is Murphy's law: whatever can go wrong will go wrong. This is why problem analysis is so important. You know something will go wrong. The question is how fast you can diagnose it, correct the situation, and prevent it from recurring.

WebSphere Portal is not a simple product. It is a framework that interacts with numerous other disparate products. Many problems occur with these interactions.

The first step to determine a problem is to isolate and simplify the environment. Try to duplicate problems in self-contained networks free of

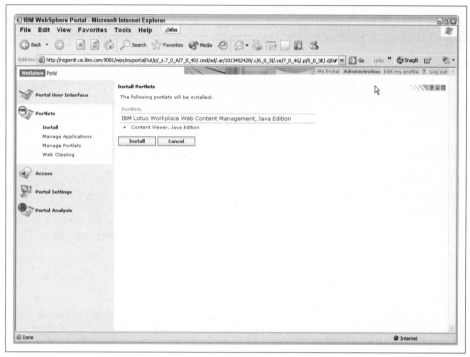

Figure 5-11   The ILWWCM Content Viewer Portlet.

firewalls and external HTTP servers. In other words, try to duplicate the error using WAS internal HTTP server on a single machine. When trying to isolate a problem, change only one parameter at a time. Check the infocenter and the WebSphere Portal developer Community Zone. The probability is that you are not the first to encounter the problem.

Try to find the errors before production by doing extensive load and stress testing. The time you spend on load testing will be one-fifth the time you will spend if you find the error during production (and a lot less stressful on yourself).

Remember, there is nothing magical about WebSphere Portal. It is a collection of applications that run under WebSphere Application Server and as such suffer the same problems as many other WebSphere Applications such as misconfigured HTTP plug-ins, memory, native, and application heap leaks. You can also suffer because of problems from misconfigured secured, classloaders, JVMs, and Session Managers. Problems can also be caused (most probably) by poorly written portlets.

WebSphere Portal helps you find your problems by logging everything. During the installation, log files are created in `<wp-root>\log`. However, before the Portal Server directory is created, the install logs are in the

Table 5-1   WebSphere Portal Installation Logs

LOG FILE NAME	DESCRIPTION
`wpinstalllog.txt`	Installation trace information
`installmessages.txt`	Installation messages that are generated during installation
`wpcpInstallLog.txt`	Trace information generated by WPCP
`wpsinstalllog.txt`	Trace information generated by WP
`portletinstall.txt`	Portlet installation messages
`wpwasfp1.txt`	WebSphere Application Server Fix Pack 1 trace information
`wppmefp1.txt`	WebSphere Application Server Enterprise Edition Fix Pack 1 trace information
`log.txt`	WebSphere Application Server trace information. Located in `<was_root>/logs` directory
`WAS.PME.install.log`	WebSphere Application Server Enterprise Edition trace information. Located in `<was_root>/logs` directory

system temporary directory. The logs created during installation are shown in Table 5-1.

Finding problems during WebSphere Portal provides extensive trace capability (see Chapter 10 for grammar and trace string configuration). Trace logging is set by enabling properties in the `<wp_root>/shared/app/config/log.properties` file. When the trace is set, it creates a file `<wp-root>/log/wps_<date_time>.log`. In the WebSphere Portal Administration guide under Using Logs, IBM lists in detail the trace settings needed to analyze if a component is having a problem.

Tivoli Web Site Analyzer

A useful tool to help you understand your WebSphere Portal site characteristics is Tivoli Web Site Analyzer. This tool comes with WebSphere Portal Enables and also comes with features preconfigured to help analyze WebSphere Portal.

Tivoli Web Site Analyzer analyses WebSphere Portal data that is stored in site analysis logs. You have to enable these logs by doing the following:

1. Open `<wp-root>/shared/app/config/services/SiteAnalyzerLogService.properties` with a text editor.

2. Accept the default values. Data will be stored in `log/sa.log` and the backup log will be `log/sa_$CREATE_TIME.log` where $CREATE_TIME is the time and date when the file was created.

3. Accept the default date and time format used as part of the log file name. The default value is yyyy.MM.dd-HH-mm.ss

4. Uncomment one of the following parameters to control the interval at which the log file is being backed up.

   - `SiteAnalyzerFileHandler.minutesPerLogFile` if you want to log in intervals of minutes, and set the value to an integer in the range 1–60.

   - `SiteAnalyzerFileHandler.hoursPerLogFile` if you want to log in intervals of hours, and set the value to an integer in the range 1–24.

   - `SiteAnalyzerFileHandler.daysPerLogFile` If you want to log in intervals of days, and set the value to an integer that indicates the number of days.

5. Enable the logger you want activated by removing the comment indicator (#). If you disable the logger, you re-add the comment indicator in front of it. Table 5-2 shows which WebSphere Portal URLs the loggers track.

6. Restart WebSphere Portal.

For purpose of demonstration, we enabled all the loggers, logged in as **wpsadmin**, and clicked on various pages and portlets. Remember, this is for demonstration. Normally you would not enable all the loggers (unless you are doing a major stress test on the box) and you would monitor more than one user.

Once enabled, WebSphere Portal started tracking the URL usuage as `sa.txt`. If you look in sa.txt, you would see entries like the following:

```
rsgornit.us.ibm.com - wpsadmin [10/Feb/2004:17:34:32 +0000] "GET
/Portlet/5_0_6B/YourCo_Financial_Latest_News_Portlet?PortletPID=5_0_6B&P
ortletMode=View&PortletState=Normal HTTP/1.1" 200 -1
"http://rsgornit.us.ibm.com/Page/6_0_6A/Home" "Mozilla/4.0 (compatible;
MSIE 6.0; Windows NT 5.1; .NET CLR 1.1.4322)" "JSES-SIONID=QUXWVc
_MeJHUly4BYAPd07u"
```

These entries show the following:

- The IP address or the domain name: `rsgornit rsgornit.us.ibm.com`

- The identifier used to identify the client. If it is not known then a dash (-) is used.

Table 5-2   Tivoli Web Site Analysis WebSphere Portal Loggers

PORTAL SERVER ANALYSIS LOGGER DESCRIPTION	URL ACTIVITY LOGGED
`SiteAnalyzerSessionLogger .isLogging`	/Command/Login /Command/Logout
`SiteAnalyzerUserManagement Logger.isLogging`	/Command/UserManagement/CreateUser /Command/UserManagement/DeleteUser /Command/UserManagement/CreateGroup /Command/UserManagement/DeleteGroup
`SiteAnalyzerPageLogger .isLogging`	/Page/* /Command/Customizer/CreatePage /Command/Customizer/EditPage /Command/Customizer/DeletePage
`SiteAnalyzerPortletLogger .isLogging`	/Portlet/*
`SiteAnalyzerPortletAction Logger.isLogging`	/PortletAction/*
`SiteAnalyzerErrorLogger .isLogging`	/Error/Portlet /Error/Page

- The WebSphere Portal user ID: `wpsadmin`.

- The date and time of the HTTP request: `[10/Feb/2004:17:34:32 +0000]`

- The HTTP request:

```
"GET
/Portlet/5_0_6B/YourCo_Financial_Latest_News_Portlet?PortletPID=5_0_6
B&PortletMode=View&PortletState=Normal HTTP/1.1"
```

- The HTTP status code: `200`.

- The number of bytes transferred from the client due to the request. -1 means unknown: `-1`.

- The URL that linked the client to the Web site:

```
"http://rsgornit.us.ibm.com/Page/6_0_6A/Home"
```

- The type of Web browser:

```
"Mozilla/4.0 (compatible; MSIE 6.0; Windows NT 5.1; .NET CLR
1.1.4322)"
```

- The name and value of the cookie sent:

```
"JSESSIONID=QUXWVc_MeJHU1y4BYAPd07u"
```

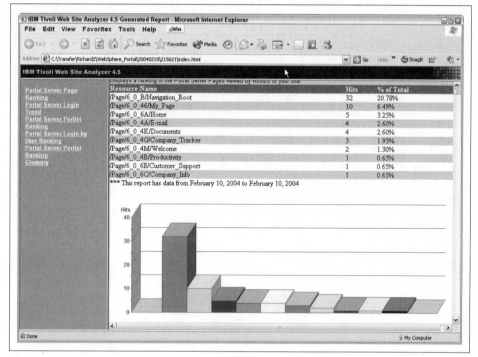

Figure 5-12   Tivoli Web Site analysis of the log.

You can then import your logs into Tivoli Web Site Analyzer or have it sample the logs automatically at scheduled intervals. Tivoli Web Site has special report elements defined for portal server. You can view pages, portlets, and logins rank by visitors. You can summarize statistics by commands or view hoe many times a page has been edited. Figure 5-12 shows how many times each page has been hit based on the logs generated.

Summary

In this chapter we reviewed how to install two very important tools: Portal Toolkit and ILWWCM. We also discussed problem analyses and using Tivoli Web Site Analyzer helped you understand the performance and user characteristics of your Web site. We slightly touched on the Tivoli Web Site Analyzer with the objective that you just understand the power and wealth of information that it can provide.

Now that we have dealt with installation issues in detail, the next logical step is to discuss migration, which is the topic of Chapter 6.

Migrating to WebSphere Portal Version 5.0

It would be great if you didn't have to worry about migration. However, you have dealt with a previous version so you have to deal with it even though it can be a tedious and difficult process. In this chapter, we will discuss the supported migration paths for WebSphere Version 5.0 and show you how to migrate the security attributes, portlets, skins, and themes. Due to the nature of this topic, this coverage is straightforward. For the purpose of being succinct, we will mention our examples using Windows format; however, you can easily determine the Unix/Linux format for 95 percent of the examples by using the appropriate directory format and replacing `WPMigrate` with `WPMigrate.sh`. In this chapter, `<wp4_root>` refers to the WebSphere Portal 4.x root directory, `<wp5_root>` refers to the WebSphere Portal 5.x root directory, `<was4_root>` refers to the WebSphere Administration Server 4.x root directory, and `<was5_root>` refers to the WebSphere Administration 5.x root directory.

Preparing for a Migration

In order to prepare for a migration, you must identify the supported migration path, any constraints, and your environment. There are numerous constraints on the migration paths supported by WebSphere 5.x. Table 6-1 lists the various versions of WebSphere Portal Server that can be migrated to WebSphere Portal 5.x. Basically, you can only migrate from WebSphere Portal Version 4.1.2 and higher. The left column lists the version that can be migrated to the WebSphere Portal version in the right column.

Table 6-1 Supported Migration Paths

WEBSPHERE PORTAL 4.X	VERSION 5.X VERSION
WebSphere Portal Enable Version 4.1.2, 4.1.3a, 4.1.4, 4.1.5, 4.2, or 4.2.1	WebSphere Portal Enable Version 5.x
WebSphere Portal Extend Version 4.1.2, 4.1.3a, 4.1.4, 4.1.5, 4.2, or 4.2.1	WebSphere Portal Extend Version 5.x
WebSphere Portal Experience Version 4.1.2, 4.1.3a, 4.1.4, 4.1.5, 4.2, or 4.2.1	WebSphere Portal Extend Version 5.x
WebSphere Portal Express Version 4.1, 4.1.5, or 4.2.1	WebSphere Portal Express Version 5.x
WebSphere Portal Express Plus Version 4.1, 4.1.5, or 4.2.1	WebSphere Portal Express Plus Version 5.x

The following are some other constraints:

1. Migration between WebSphere Portal environments across operating system (for example, Linux to Windows) is not supported.

2. Migration across database servers (for example, DB2 to SQL server) is not supported.

3. Migration of bookmarks or internal URLs is not supported.

4. Migration of WebSphere V5.x in a cluster is done by migrating data from the WebSphere Portal V4.x cluster main node to a standalone WebSphere Portal V5.x, making the V5.x server a main node, and then creating new clone nodes from it.

5. Content organizer in WebSphere Portal V4.x has been replaced with Document Manager and WPCP has been replaced with WCM. Presently there is no migration path for either new component.

6. The WebSphere Member service must be cataloged locally.

Recommended Migration Environment

To migrate WebSphere Portal V4.x to WebSphere Portal V5.x, both systems should be on separate machines. While it is possible to run both systems on one machine, the amount of resources required and the complexity of the configuration make it an exercise for a masochist.

The migration should be isolated to WebSphere Portal. Any changes in LDAP or database version should be made beforehand and verified with WebSphere Portal V5.x. If you are changing LDAP servers, you should export the LDAP database information as an LDIF file and re-import it into your new LDAP databases.

Before you perform your migration, you need to do the following:

1. Apply the `42_421_Multiplatform_Cumulative_Fixes.jar` (found on CD 2) to WebSphere Portal server V4.2.1.

2. Add the following line to the `XmlAccessService.properties` file in `<was5_root>\lib\app\config\services\`

   ```
   :com.ibm.wps.command.xml.groupexport.GroupExportEngine=-//IBM//DTD
   GroupExport//EN,
   /com/ibm/wps/command/xml/groupexport/GroupExport.dtd.
   ```

3. If WPS 4.x uses an external security manager, copy the `<wp5_root>\migration\efixes\ESMMigration.jar` file to `<was4_root>\lib\app` directory.

4. Apply fixes `PQ77682_WP50_Migration_iFix` and `PQ77683_WP50_iFix` to the WP V5.x server.

5. Go to your WebSphere Portal 5.x machine and in the directory `<was5_root>\migration\efixes` and copy `WP42X_MP_EXPRESS_Patch.jar` file to `<was4_root>\lib\app` directory on your WPS 4.2.1 machine. If you have a WPS 4.1 machine, copy `WP41X_MP_EXPRESS_Patch.jar` file. Extract the update by typing **jar-xvf WP42X_MP_Express_Patch.jar**, which will result in the file `42X_fix.jar`. Then extract `42X_fix.jar` by typing **jar-xvf 42X_file.jar**.

Remember that before applying fixes, you should stop the servers (Server1 and WebSphere Portal) and restart them after the fixes have been applied. Also verify that both portals are working by accessing them and clicking on various pages and portlets.

Performing the Migration

You will now find out how to do a migration using an example migration environment like the one shown in Figure 6-1. The goal is to migrate Web-Sphere Portal 4.2.1 using LDAP authentication and store data remotely on DB2 to a WebSphere Portal 5.0 portal with configuration similar to version 4.2.1 except that the database and LDAP versions have been upgraded. The custom place (Place), the custom pages (Page1 to Page3), and the portlets (Portlets1, Portlets2, and Portlets3) will be migrated. Assume that, before the migration, all the servers (`sandbox1.rigorconsultants.com` to `sandbox6.rigorconsultants.com`) have been configured and the

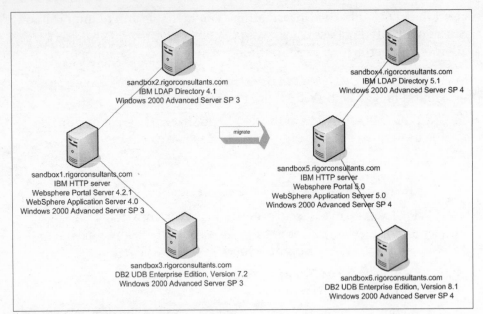

Figure 6-1　Migration example infrastructure.

WebSphere, Web, database, and LDAP software have been tested. Also assume that the appropriate tables and user permissions have been created and set in the remote databases and the user schema and data has exported from `sandbox2.rigorconsultants.com` and imported into the LDAP server on `sandbox4.rigorconsultants.com` using the LDIF utility. All servers and software are running during the migration process. Lastly, assume that both WebSphere Portal versions are configured and get requests through IBM HTTP Server using port 80.

Setting up the Migration Property Values

Much of the migration process is automated using defined automated tasks. To run these tasks, you have to set the values in the migration property files. You will find the migration property files on the WebSphere Portal 5 server (`sandbox5.rigorconsultants.com`) in the directory `<wp5_root>\migration`. But before you modify the files, copy the WebSphere Portal Server `wpsconfig.properties` files on `sandbox1.rigorconsultants.com` to `<wp5_root>\migration` on `sandbox5.rigorconsultants.com`. If you are migrating WebSphere Portal version 4.1.2, then you must add the `WPFamilyNameKey` to the `wps.properties` file. `WPFamilyName` key identifies the WebSphere Portal packaging. For instance, if you installed WebSphere Portal Enable then you would set `WPFamilyName=enable`.

Table 6-2   Core Migration Properties

PROPERTY	VALUE	DESCRIPTION
WpsHostName4x	`sandbox1.` `rigorconsultants.com`	Fully qualified host name of the WebSphere Portal V4.2.1 machine; `sandbox1` `.rigorconsultants` `.com`
WpsPort4x	80	Port number to which WebSphere Portal V4.2.1 receives requests
WpsContextRoot4x	wps	Base URI for WebSphere Portal V4.2.1
WpsDefaultHome4x	portal	Default home for WebSphere Portal V4.2.1
PortalAdminId4x	wpsadmin	WebSphere Portal V4.2.1 administrator ID
PortalAdminPwd4x	wpsadmin	WebSphere Portal V4.2.1 administrator password
wpsinstallLocation4x	`C:/WebSphere/` `PortalServer`	Root directory of WebSphere Portal V4.x
includePlaces	Place1	Comma-separated names of the custom places you want to migrate
includePages	Page1, Page2, Page3	Comma-separated names of the custom pages you want to migrate
includeApps	Portlet1, Portlet2, Portlet3	Comma-separated names of the portlet applications you want to migrate

The first migration property file to modify is `mig_core.properties`, which specifies the core migration properties. Table 6-2 lists the properties we set for our example.

Migrating Access Controls

Now that your migration environment is all set up, the first step is to convert the access control. This is significant migration since access controls have changed from permission base in WebSphere Portal Version 4 to role-based

Table 6-3 Mapping of Permissions to Roles

V4.X PERMISSIONS	V5.0 ROLES
View	User
Edit Privileged	User
Manage	Manager
Delegate	Security Administrator
View + Edit	Privileged User
View + Manage	Manager
View + Delegate	Security Administrator + User
Edit + Manage	Manager
Edit + Delegate	Security Administrator + Privileged User or Security Administrator + Editor
Manage + Delegate	Administrator
View + Edit + Manage	Manager
View + Edit + Delegate	Security Administrator + Privileged User or Security Administrator + Editor
View + Manage + Delegate	Administrator
View + Edit + Manage + Delegate	Administrator
Create	Not Applicable in WP 5.0

access control (more on this in Chapter 10). Table 6-3 shows the migration process mapping of permissions to roles.

Inheritance blocks will be created by the migration process for all roles except the Administrator and Security Administrator.

To migrate the access controls, do the following tasks:

1. Open a command prompt on your WebSphere Portal V5.0 machine (sandbox5.rigorconsultants.com) and go to <wp5_root> \migrate directory.

2. Enter **WPmigrate migrate-user-groups-ac**.

3. Wait for the Build Successful message and then check the MigrationReport.xml file for any errors.

4. Enter **WPmigrate optimize-roles**. This will eliminate obsolete roles and role blocks.

5. Wait for the Build Successful message and then check the
   `MigrationReport.xml` file for any errors.

6. On WebSphere Portal V5.0 portal, go to Administration ➪ Access ➪
   Users and Group Permission and review carefully that all the roles
   assigned to the Users and Group are correct and set the inheritance
   blocks as per your company policies.

Migrating Extended User Attributes

In WebSphere Portal 4.x, user attributes are stored in the WebSphere Member Services database while in WebSphere Portal 5.x, user attributes are stored in WebSphere Member Manager. If you just use the seven default user attributes (uid, userPassword, cn, sn, mail, preferredLanguage, and givenName) and do not use a look-aside database (as in 95 percent of the cases), then you can skip this section. If you have extended user attributes, then you must take the following steps:

1. Copy the files `attributeMap.xml` and `attributeMap.dtd` from
   `<wp4_root>\wms\xml` directory to the `<wp5_root>\template\`
   `wmm\xml\migration` directory.

2. In the `<wp5_root>\template\wmm\xml\migration` directory,
   you will find three files: `wmmDBAttributes.xml`,
   `wmmLAAttributes`, and `wmmMigrationAttributesInfo.xml`.
   The file `wmmDBAttributes.xml` is edited only if you have a
   database-only WMS configuration while the file
   `wmmDBAttributes.xml` is used if your WMS configuration uses
   both a database and an LDAP. The `wmmDBAttributes.xml` file
   specifies the WMM attributes that will be inserted into the
   WMMDBATR table while the `wmmLAAttributes.xml` file specifies
   the WMM attributes that will be inserted into the WMMLAATR
   table. The wmmMigrationAttributesInfo.xml is read by the migration
   utility to determine where the attribute value data is coming from for
   each attribute in the `wmmXXAttributes.xml` file. The file
   `wmmXXAttributes` refers to either the `wmmDBAttributes.xml` or
   the `wmmLAAttributes` file. In WMS, most attributes are stored in
   the MBRATTR table and their corresponding values are stored in the
   MBRATTRVAL table. The exception is that a column name for certain
   WMS tables can become a WMM attribute and the values associated
   with the attribute are the WMS column data (now that is confusing!).

3. For each attribute that you are migrating, add the following XML
   code to the appropriate `wmmXXAttributes` file and save it:

```
<attributeMap wmmAttributeName=subdepartment
              pluginAttributeName=subdepartment
```

```
                          applicableMemberTypes=Organization
                          dataType=String
                          valueLength=256
                          multiValued=true />
```

where `wmmAttributeName` is the attribute name in WMM and
`pluginAttributeName` is the plug-in attribute name in LDAP,
`applicableMemberTypes` is the member type which the attribute
is associated with, `dataType` is the attribute data type, and
`multiValued` is a flag specifying whether the element is
multivalued. `ValueLength` is an optional field that applies only to
string data type and specifies the maximum length of the attribute
value.

4. Now edit the `wmmMigrationAttributesInfo.xml` file and for
   each attribute (that does not come from a WMS column name) add
   the following XML code:

```
<AttributeInfo tableName=MBRATTR
                          wmsAttributeName=subdepartment
                          attributeType=String
                          wmmAttributeName=subdepartment />
```

where `tableName` is the table where the attribute is coming from
(usually MBATTR), `wmsAttributeName` is the WMS attribute
name, `attributeType` is the attribute data type, and
`wmmAttributeName` is WMM attribute name. If the attribute comes
from a WMS column name then use the following XML code instead:

```
<AttributeInfo tableName=wms_table
                wmsColumnName=wms_column
                attributeType=String
                wmmAttributeName=registration />
```

where `tableName` is the table where the attribute is coming from
(usually MBATTR), `wmsColumnName` is the column name of
`wms_table`, which contains the attribute value data,
`attributeType` is the attribute data type, and
`wmmAttributeName` is WMM attribute name. If the attribute comes
from a WMS column name then use the following XML code instead;

5. Next you have to edit the `mig_wmm.properties` file found in
   `<wp5_root>\migration`. This file only needs to be modified if you
   are using a look-aside database. Table 6-4 shows the values you
   would need if you were using a look-aside database for our example
   infrastructure.

6. Open a command prompt on your WebSphere Portal V5.0 machine
   (`sandbox5.rigorconsultants.com`) and go to `<wps_root>\`
   `migrate` directory.

7. Enter **WPmigrate migrate-wmm**.

Table 6-4 Properties to Migrate Look Aside Database

PROPERTY	VALUE	DESCRIPTION
WmsDbName	wps42db	Alias name of WebSphere Portal V4.x database
WmsDbUrl	jdbc:dbc:wps42db	WebSphere Portal V4.x database JDBC URL
WmsDbUser	db2admin	db2 administrator user ID
WMSDbPassword		db2 administrator password
WmmConfigType	2	LDAP + look-aside database configuration
WmmUid	DB1	The value of the UUID element. The UUID is an ID that uniquely identifies the member from all other members. You can find the value in `<wp5_root>\shared\app\wmm\wmm.xml` file under the node databaseRepository
Db2Home	C:/SQLLIB	DB2 root installation directory on `sandbox6.rigorconsultants.com`
LDAPHasUid	true	States if your LDAP already has a UUID attribute defined
LdapUuidName	ibm-appUUID	LDAP UUID Name

8. Wait for the Build Successful message and then check the `MigrationReport.xml` file for any errors.

9. On WebSphere Portal V5.0, check the `trace.log` file under `<wp5_root>\templates\wmm` directory for errors and check the `loader.log` file in the directory `<wp5_root>\template\wmm\db2\database` or `<wp5_root>\template\wmm\db2\lookaside` to see if all the rows are loaded correctly.

Migrating Themes, Skins, and Style Sheets

The migration of themes, skins, and style sheets that you may have customized is a manual process. The steps to do it using our example infrastructure are as follows:

1. Copy the WPS 4.2.1 customized themes and skins directories to `<was5_root>\installedApps\sandbox5\wps.ear\wps.war` on the WP V5.0 server.

2. Scan the JSPs used by the themes and skins and change the following:

   a. Remove the following tags: `<wps:pageGroupLoop/>`, `<wps:pageGroup/>`, `<wps:pageLoopInit/>`, `<wps:page/>`, and `<wps:frameURL/>`. They are no longer supported.

   b. Replace `<wps:pageLoop/>` by `<wps:navigationLoop/>`, `<wps:pageLoopShift>` by `<wps:navigationShift/>`, `<wps:pageRender/>` by `<wps:compositionRender/>`, and `<wps:URLSelect>` by the `<URLGeneration/>` tags.

   c. The behavior of `<wps:text/>` and `<wps:textParam/>` has changed. If the content is provided in the body of the `<wps:text/>` tag, then it will always be written to the page.

   d. The attributes `computeSelectionPath` and `useModelFromRequestAttributeNamed` of the `<wps:navigation/>` tag are no longer supported.

   e. For `<wps:if/>` and `<wps:unless/>` tags, the attributes `error`, `pageGroupSelected pageSelected`, and `frameMode` are no longer supported. The attribute `pageGroupAvailable` has been replaced by `nodeInSelectionPath` and `pageAvailable` has been replaced by `navigationAvailable`.

3. Update the style sheets used by the themes by looking at the Science theme in WP V5.0, find the classes that have a comment associated with them, New in V5, and copy them to your theme. Then modify the classes to match the look of your theme.

4. Log in to `http://sandbox5.rigorconsultants.com/wps/portal` and go to Administration ⇨ Manage Themes and Skins.

5. Add your customized skins.

6. Test the themes and skins by creating a root page using the Page Customizer, assign the customized theme to the new page, and assign some portlets.

7. Go to the new page and test to see if the new page is similar to the customized skin and themes in your WPS 4.2.1 portal.

Migrating Portlet Applications

The next step is to migrate your portlet applications. Copy your custom portlets from `<wp4_root>\deployed` on WPS 4.2.1 (`sandbox1.rigorconsultants.com`) to a temp directory on your WP 5.0 machine (`sandbox5.rigorconsultants.com`). Expand the WAR file. If your portlets worked on WP 4.2.1 then minimal modifications are required of the source code. The only changes you might need are the following:

1. Methods `getAttribute()`, `getAttributeNames()`, and `getLastLoginTime()` are no longer supported.

2. The portlet helper classes JSP, File server, and RSS (XSLT) portlet have been deprecated.

3. `PortletURI.addAction(java.lang.String simpleaction)` should be used instead of `PortletURI.addAction(PortletAction action)`.

4. `ActionEvent.getActionString ()` should be used instead of `ActionEvent.getAction`.

5. `PortletRequest.getUser()` must be used instead of `PortletSession.getUser()` especially since `PortletSession.getUser()` returns a null value.

6. Make sure there is no `portlet.tld` file in the WAR file. If there is, remove it.

7. If you used Java Authentication and Authorization Service to access the user credentials, you must rewrite the code using the credential vault service.

8. Click-to-action portlets behave differently in WP 5.0. Output parameters will not automatically propagate unless they are explicitly wired to input parameters. You may have to rewrite them as a cooperative portlet, which is just an enhance click-to-action portlet.

9. You need to copy the `pbportlet.jar` file found in `<wp4-root>\pb\lib` directory on you WPS 4.2.1 server (`sandbox1.rigor consultants.com`) to each of your migrating click-to-action portlets `WEB-INF\lib` directories. If within the click-to-action portlet WAR file there is another copy of the `pbportlet.jar` file in another location, then you must remove it to avoid classloading conflicts.

10. Ensure you are not referencing any deprecated tags mentioned in the previous sections.

11. Make sure that multiple portlets within a portlet application do not point to the same servlets definition in `web.xml`.

After you have modified the files, archive the files back into a WAR file and copy them to `<wp5_root>\installableApps` on your WP 5.0 server. Next perform the following tasks:

1. Ensure that in the `mig_core.properties` file, you have set the includeApps property with the names of all your custom portlets.

2. Open a command prompt on your WebSphere Portal V5.0 machine (`sandbox5.rigorconsultants.com`) and go to `<wp5_root>\migrate` directory.

3. Enter **WPmigrate export-apps**.

4. Wait for the Build Successful message and then check the `MigrationReport.xml` file for any errors.

5. On WebSphere Portal V5.0 portal, verify that all your portlet applications that you migrated are present under Portlets ⇨ Manage Applications ⇨ Web Modules. Click Modify Parameters and see that they are correct. Next go to Administration ⇨ Access Resource Permissions and under Resource Permissions click Portlet Applications and then verify that the access control settings are correct. Lastly, add them to a test page and perform a function test.

Migrating Places

In WebSphere Portal V5.0, the concept of a Place was eliminated. The migration tool converts them to a top-level page. Do the following tasks to migrate them:

1. Ensure that in the `mig_core.properties` file, you have set the includePlaces property with the names of all your custom Places.

2. Open a command prompt on your WebSphere Portal V5.0 machine (`sandbox5.rigorconsultants.com`) and go to `<wp5_root>\migrate` directory.

3. Enter **WPmigrate migrate-places -DdeployPages=false-DdeployApps=false -DconfigThemesSkins=false**.

4. Wait for the Build Successful message and then check the `MigrationReport.xml` file for any errors.

5. On WebSphere Portal V5.0 portal, click on Administration ⇨ Portal User Interface ⇨ Manage Pages. Then under Content Root, click on My Portal and verify that your Places were migrated. Check the page properties, including the properties under Advance Options to see if they are correct.

Migrating Pages

1. Ensure that in the `mig_core.properties` file, you have set the includePages property with the names of all your custom Pages.

2. Open a command prompt on your WebSphere Portal V5.0 machine (`sandbox5.rigorconsultants.com`) and go to `<wp5_root>\migrate` directory.

3. Enter **WPmigrate migrate-pages -DconfigThemesSkins=false**.

4. Wait for the Build Successful message and then check the `MigrationReport.xml` file for any errors.

5. On WebSphere Portal V5.0 portal, click on Administration ⇨ Portal User Interface ⇨ Manage Pages. Then under Content Root, click on My Portal and verify that your pages were migrated. Check the page properties, including the properties under Advance options to see if they are correct.

Migrating All User Customizations

This task migrates all skins referenced by themes.

1. Ensure that in the `mig_core.properties` file, you have set the includePages property with the names of all your custom Pages.

2. Open a command prompt on your WebSphere Portal V5.0 machine (`sandbox5.rigorconsultants.com`) and go to <wp5_root>\ `migrate` directory.

3. Enter **WPmigrate migrate-user-customization**.

4. Wait for the Build Successful message and then check the `MigrationReport.xml` file for any errors.

5. On WebSphere Portal V5.0 portal, click on Administration ⇨ Portal User Interface ⇨ Manage Pages. Then under Content Root, click on My Portal and verify that all your customization were migrated.

Migrating Credential Vault Slots and Segments

1. Open a command prompt on your WebSphere Portal V5.0 machine (`sandbox5.rigorconsultants.com`) and go to <wps_root>\ `migrate` directory.

2. Enter **WPmigrate migratecredential-slots-segments**.

3. Wait for the Build Successful message and then check the `MigrationReport.xml` file for any errors.

4. On WebSphere Portal V5.0 portal, click on Administration ⇨ Credential Vault ⇨ Manage Vault Segments and verify that the segments have been migrated. Then click Administration ⇨ Credential Vault ⇨ Manage Vault Slots and verify that your vault slots were migrated.

Migrating Credential Vault data

After you have migrated the credential vault slots and segments, you have to migrate the actual data. You do this by exporting the data from the tables

VAULT_DATA and VAULT_RESOURCES found on your WPS V4.0 database (sandbox3.rigorconsultants.com) and importing them to your WP V5.0 database on sandbox6.rigorconsultants.com. The tables on the VP V5.0 database gave the same names: VAULT_DATA and VAULT_ RESOURCES.

Verify the migration by clicking Access ⇨ Credential Vault ⇨ Manage System Vault Slots and reviewing the data for accuracy and completeness.

Migrating Everything at One Time

If you are feeling very confident (and lucky), you can do a complete migration with one command by following the steps given below:

1. Open a command prompt on your WebSphere Portal V5.0 machine (sandbox5.rigorconsultants.com) and go to <wp5_root>\migrate directory.

2. Enter **WPmigrate migrate-all**.

3. Wait for the Build Successful message and then check the MigrationReport.xml file for any errors.

4. On WebSphere Portal V5.0 portal, verify the migration by reviewing all your pages, portlets, credential vault slots/segments, and all the access controls for your users, groups, and resources.

XML Configuration Interface

Another tool you can use for migration and batch changes is the XML Configuration Interface. This tool enables you to export a part of or entire configuration and then re-create it on another portal. You can also use XML Configuration tool to help back up or restore complete portal configuration, copy parts of a configurations, install additional resources, or perform reproducible administration tasks.

The XML Configuration can be used to perform a complete re-creation of a portal. It cannot deal with War files, cannot be used for WPCP, and is not suitable for large volumes of data. Backup and restoration should be performed by regular database and file backup tools.

XML Config is invoked by typing **xmlaccess** on the command line. It can be invoked on the actual portal server or on any client. To invoke it on a remote client you need to have a Java engine and the tool.jar file that is found in <wp_root>/bin directory.

As can be seen in Figure 6-2, the XML Config tool takes an input file consisting of XML tags (1), sends it by HTTP from the client (2) to the WP

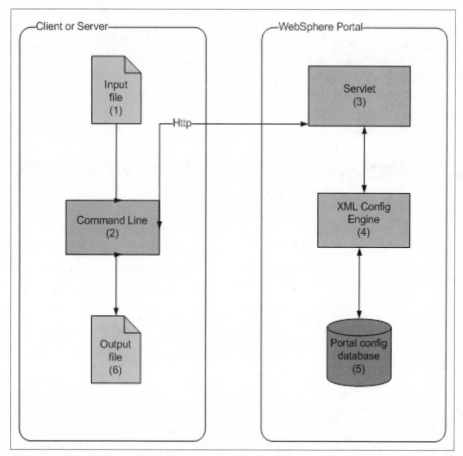

Figure 6-2 How the XML Configuration Interface utility works.

servlet (3), which passes the data to the XML Config engine (4). The XML Config engine stores and retrieves data specific to the configuration actions from the Portal config database (5). The output is sent back to the client via HTTP as XML tags (6), which can then be used as input.

The XML Configuration Interface handles two types of requests: Export and Update. Export results in complete or partial portal configuration into XML. Update causes the portal configuration to be modified based on the XML script values.

The syntax for the command is as follows:

```
xmlaccess-in inputfile-user user-pwd password-url URL-out
output_file
```

where `-in` is the input file, `-user` is the authorized portal user id, `-password` is the password, `-url` is the portal URL for processing the command (such as `http://www.rigorconsultants.com/wps/config`), and `-out` is the output file.

The user must be a super user with manager role on XML_ACCESS and administrator role on portal. The usernames and passwords are sent unencrypted, so send them over the intranet or use VPN.

The XML Configuration interface models your portal as XML tags with the defined hierarchical structure shown in Table 6-5. (This table can also be found in the Portal infocenter.)

Table 6-5 Description of XML Access Tags

XML	DESCRIPTION
portal	Main element of every XML request
global-settings	Global portal settings
services-settings	Global portal settings for portal services
virtual-resource	Virtual resources that have associated access control settings
user	Users defined in the portal user management system
group	Groups defined in the portal user management system
markup	Markups that can be supported by portal pages
client	Client devices (browsers) that the portal knows about
event-handler	Definitions of event handlers that can react to events in the portal
skin	Visual appearance settings that can be applied to user interface elements
theme	General visual settings that can be applied to the user interface
web-app	Web modules containing portlets
servlet	Servlets that are defined in the Web module
portlet-app	Portlet applications that are defined in the Web module
portlet	Portlets that are defined in the portlet application
content-node	Elements of the portal content tree (pages or labels)
component	Layout components of pages
portletinstance	Occurrences of a portlet on a page with customized settings
credential-segment	Segments for storing credentials in the credential vault
credential-slot	Slots in a credential segment that hold a credential
url-mapping-context	User defined URLs that map to pages in the portal

Obviously, the XML files generated can be quite complex and cryptic, especially with a detailed portal.

XML Input File

The XML Configuration Interface requests are defined in an input file with the following structure:

```
<?xml version="1.0" encoding="UTF-8"?>
    <request
    xmlns:xsi="http://www.w3.org/2001/XMLSchema-instance"
    xsi:noNamespaceSchemaLocation="PortalConfig_1.2.xsd"
    type="export | update">
        <portal . . . >
        definition of configuration parts to be exported or updated
        </portal>
        <status . . . >
        success or failure indication for the processing
        </status>
    </request>
```

You must always use the schema reference with no namespace to the schema "`PortalConfig_1.2.xsd.`"

Actions are carried based on the value of the request type parameter. You have two types of requests: update or export. Update performs a modification to the portal while export is used for extracting information.

Each request has actions associated with it. For update, only locate, create, update, and delete are permitted while export is limited to locate and export.

The locate action finds the portal resource associated with a specific XML element. Create action creates a portal resource with attributes you specify. Update action modifies the corresponding portal resource with a given configuration data. Delete action removes the portal resource based on the specified XML element. Finally, export action generates an XML representation of the portal resource.

To understand how to set up a configuration request, let's walkthrough a sample request file provided by IBM. You can find this code at `<WebSphere >\PortalServer\doc\xml-samples`. Normally you would look for a sample that performs a function similar to what you want to do and perform any necessary modifications. This XML request file will create the user Homer Simpson and add it to the group Springfielders. Note that in the update request, we set create-oids to "true." This enables object IDs to be symbolically created and valid only within the XML script which prevents the portal from choosing an already existing object-id and overwriting it.

```
<?xml version="1.0" encoding="UTF-8"?>
<request
    xmlns:xsi="http://www.w3.org/2001/XMLSchema-instance"
```

```
        xsi:noNamespaceSchemaLocation="PortalConfig_1.2.xsd"
    type="update" create-oids="true">
        <portal action="locate">
        <user action="update" name="hsimpson" firstname="Homer"
        lastname="Simpson" password="secret">
            <description>My favorite TV star</description>
            <parameter name="preferredLanguage" type="string"
                update="set">en</parameter>
                </user>
        <group action="update" name="springfielders">
            <description>Inhabitants of Spring
            field</description>
            <member-user update="set" id="hsimpson"/>
        </group>
        </portal>
    </request>
```

XML Configuration Interface Special Properties

The XML Configuration Interface has some special properties of which you should be aware. Since the portal is represented in XML, the XML Configuration utility must have some way of representing the order of elements on a GUI screen or the sorting order. This is done using three methods. If the resource is identified as an integer, it will be sorted into position relative to the ordinals of existing siblings. If a position indicator is specified (hash (#) mark followed by an integer), it will appear in that position in its content parent. Lastly, you can specify the special values with first and last, which indicates that the resource is sorted either in the first or last position.

You should also be careful with unique names in XML scripts especially if these scripts run on many portal installations. If a unique name is assigned by the XML script and that unique name is already used on the system, the script will fail.

XML Configuration Interface Transactional Support

The XML Configuration Interface provides limited transactional support. Changes in the portal database are grouped into transactions when you create, update, or delete resources. All changes that are part of the transaction are either executed completely or not executed at all.

The main request element has a transaction attribute, which defines the grouping value. The value can be Resource (default value), which means that every top-level resource is processed in one separate transaction or Request, which means the entire XML script is executed in one transaction.

The transactional support is limited because it only applies to changes to the portal database. This means changes to portlets, users, and groups stored in LDAP, or role assignments in external access control systems cannot be rolled back if a transaction fails. Similarly, if the latter changes failed, changes to the database will not be rolled back.

Changes in XML Configuration Interface for Version 5.0

The XML Configuration Interface utility is not compatible between different versions of WP. Version 5.0 of the utility has been enhanced using the following steps:

- Use of XML Schema instead of DTD file.
- Support for mandatory type attribute.
- Support for event handlers, URL Mappings, and property broker wires. A wire connects a source and a target portlet instance enabling changes to the source to be propagated to the target.
- Ability to manage users and groups.
- Support of object IDs, unique names, and the ordinal attribute
- Support of role administration.

In version 4.2 the portal navigation structure was expressed as a tree of components of type layered inside Root.Composition while in WebSphere Portal version 5.0, labels and pages are organized in a tree that is expressed by their content-parentref attributes. The navigation structure in the portal is the same as the structure of the content tree. There is no root composition defined in the XML scripts anymore.

Do the following to migrate your XML Configuration scripts to WP V5.0,

1. Open a command prompt on your WebSphere Portal V5.0 machine (`sandbox5.rigorconsultants.com`) and go to `<wps_root>\migrate` directory.

2. Enter

```
WPmigrate migrate-xmlaccess-script -DScriptPath=<path>
-DScriptSrc=<scriptname> -DScriptDest=<convertedscriptname>
```

where `<path>` is the complete path to your script file, `<scriptname>` is the script file name to be converted, and `<convertedscriptname>` is the name of the converted script file.

3. Wait for the Build Successful message and then check the `MigrationReport.xml` file for any errors.

Summary

In this chapter we reviewed the tasks and tools that are provided to assist you in migration. We clearly did not cover all the situations such as migration of collaboration portlets, portlets based on struts, portlet toolkit, and portlets using transcoding technology. We also did not bother with migration of WPCP and Personalization since they are both being replaced by WCM.

The purpose of this chapter was to help you in the migration of the most common components. For more detail information, we refer you to the WebSphere Portal Migration manual.

At the end of the chapter, you are probably saying to yourself, "boy this is complicated." Well it is, and partly this is due to the rapid infusion of functionality with each version of WebSphere Portal. With version 5.x, you are seeing the product mature and the product becoming simpler to use. We believe that migrations in the future will become easier as more effort is put into delivering configuration and migration wizards.

Well, now that you have got WebSphere Portal up and running, it is now time to actually use the product. In the next chapter, you will learn how to easily define the look-and-feel components of your portal.

Building and Administering Portals with WPS

Defining Portals and Pages

Portals and pages provide the framework for content delivery within Web-Sphere Portal. Everything the user sees upon entering your portal is part of a page. In this chapter you will learn the basic skills required to define and customize the content delivered by your portal.

Pages are essentially scaffold around which your portal is built, and in this chapter we focus on defining portal structure. The concepts involved are quite simple, and we will guide you through the most common tasks associated with the construction and customization of your portal.

Portals and Pages

Complex data is usually stored in hierarchical structures, a common example being files and folders in an operating system. WebSphere Portal follows this approach and uses a hierarchical structure to maintain the set of resources and components used to generate the user experience.

In order to view the structure of the portal, you click the Administration tab in the portal toolbar. To do this, you must be logged in as an administrator. As we saw in Chapter 2, to log in as administrator, you need to access the URL `http://<hostname>:<port>/wps/portal`, where *hostname* is the server on which WebSphere Portal Server is installed and port is 9081 (unless you modified the default settings), and click Log in. Once you are in the Administration tab, click Manage Pages under Portal User Interface. WebSphere Portal Server will configure your Portal Settings.

Logical Structure of a Portal

The Manage Pages window allows you to add, delete, edit, and reorder pages in your portal. The portal uses a treelike hierarchical structure, where the root of the tree is called Content Root. Nodes in this hierarchy belong to one of the following types:

- Pages
- Labels
- URLs

Pages are the basic building block used for displaying content in the form of portlets. Page nodes may contain other nodes, including other pages. A label is a placeholder for pages. Labels may contain other nodes, but display no content, and are used to provide logical grouping of nodes. This logical grouping is used to define common attributes such as access permissions. URLs are used to access any resource that can be addressed with a URL. URLs obviously do not contain any other nodes. URLs are useful for addressing external Web sites or another part of the portal.

Note that there is no built-in notion of a "portal." You may define multiple portals inside WebSphere Portal by using the abstractions of pages or labels. For example, you can create different subhierarchies for different sets of users and consider each such subhierarchy as a portal.

Figure 7-1 shows the composition of the Content Root as per the default configuration, immediately following product installation. We have five different nodes under Content Root of which three are labels and two are pages.

My Portal is a label containing the default portal configuration shipped with the product. By default, users who do not have administrative privileges can only access this node. The Administration label is accessible by users with administrative privileges, and incidentally is the label through which you have reached the current page. The last label is Page Customizer, which contains several portlets used for configuring page layout and content. This label is not accessible directly, but is invoked through the button in the portal toolbar. The two pages under Content Root are Page Properties and Organize Favorites. As the names imply, the former shows a portlet used to edit some properties of pages, and the latter allows users to organize favorites through the My Favorites drop-down menu in the portal banner. Note that Page Properties is hidden from navigation, which means you cannot see a corresponding entry in the portal toolbar.

This is in fact the default behavior for entries that are directly under Content Root. Typically, one would add new content at lower levels, for example, under My Portal (in the next chapter you will see how to customize the portal toolbar allowing you to access from there entries that are directly

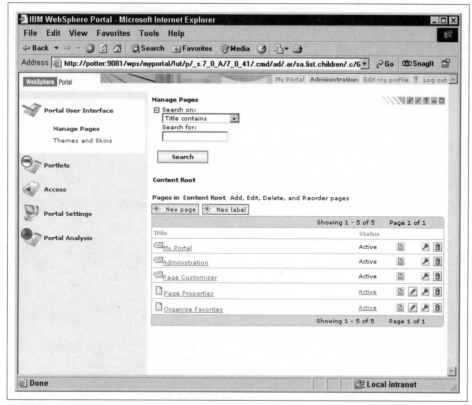

Figure 7-1   Default Content Root composition.

under Content Root). The page properties are accessed when you click the context-sensitive Properties icon on a window or under Manage Pages.

Browsing through the Content Hierarchy

The Manage Pages window allows you to browse through the content hierarchy. For example, clicking on My Portal would go to the next level down this hierarchy and show the nodes under My Portal, as shown in Figure 7-2. Note that the options at the top of the page allow you to search for a page by various criteria, and below that you see the current node you are viewing, as well as the path in the hierarchy leading up to it, starting with Content Root. Each of the parent node names is a clickable link, bringing you to that page. On the right-hand side of the current node name are some buttons (Figure 7-3 summarizes the buttons available under Manage Pages):

- Editing page properties
- Editing page layout (only for page nodes)

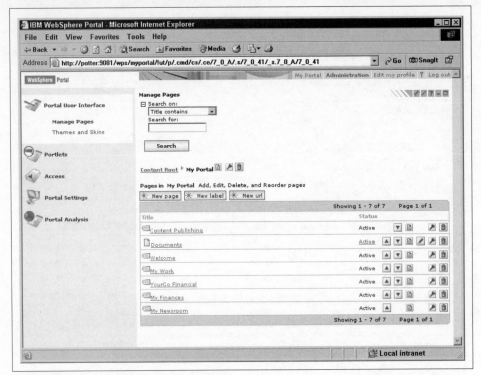

Figure 7-2   Default My Portal composition.

- Controlling access permissions
- Deleting the node

A table below the current node summarizes the children nodes for this node. In the case of My Portal in Figure 7-2, we have six groups and one page. Clicking on any of the child node names brings you to that node, allowing you to drill lower in the portal structure. Each one of the children pages has three or four buttons similar to the ones beside the current node name. In addition, each such children page has an up arrow, or down arrow, or both. These arrows allow you to change the ordering of children nodes. The ordering of children nodes controls their order in toolbars.

Button	Meaning
✏	Edit Page Layout
🗑	Remove Page
▼	Move down in current node
▲	Move up in current node
📄	Edit Properties
🔑	Set Page Permissions

Figure 7-3   Buttons available under Manage Pages.

Customizing the Portal Structure

WebSphere Portal provides several levels of customization. Here we will look at customizing the structure—that is, adding new pages and editing their attributes. In the next chapter we will look into customizing the Web design of the portal. It is important to remember that the most powerful way of customizing the portal is by adding new portlets, but we will get to this only in Part 3 of the book.

Adding New Nodes

To add a new node under My Portal, go to Manage Pages and navigate to the My Portal page (as shown in Figure 7-2).

1. Click the New Label button.
2. Enter **My Stuff** in the Title field.
3. Select OK.
4. Select OK in the confirmation window shown next.

The new group will be added under My Portal as shown in Figure 7-4. Now add a new page in this group.

1. Click My Stuff in the table of children nodes shown in Figure 7-4.
2. Click the New Page button.
3. Enter **Sample Page** in the Title field.
4. Click the Advanced Options button.
5. Click the two-column under A Content Page with These Properties (second option).
6. Select OK.
7. Select OK in the confirmation window shown next.

Finally, add a new URL under the same group. As mentioned above, we can use a URL node to point to any URL-addressable resource.

1. Click the New URL button.
2. Enter **Thinkpad** in the Title field.
3. Enter **http://www.ibm.com/thinkpad** in the HTML field.
4. Select OK.
5. Select OK in the confirmation window shown next.

Now you should see both new nodes under My Stuff, as shown in Figure 7-5.

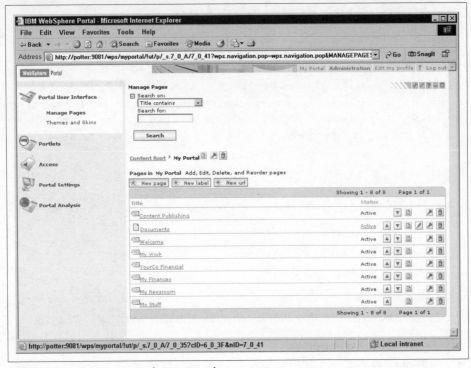

Figure 7-4 New group under My Portal.

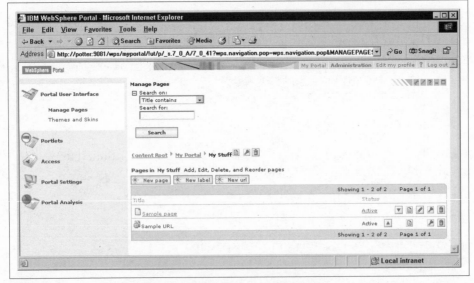

Figure 7-5 User view of new group My Stuff under My Portal.

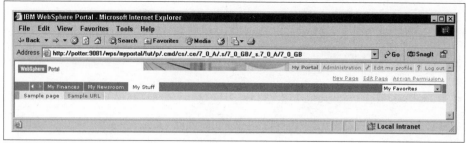

Figure 7-6   Viewing My Stuff through My Portal.

To see the new group from the user perspective, click My Portal on the portal toolbar, and then click My Stuff on the second layer toolbar. You should see the window shown in Figure 7-6. As you can see, the page Sample Page is empty, and clicking on Sample URL gets you to the IBM ThinkPad site.

The interesting thing to note at this point is how smoothly the new components were integrated into the portal as perceived by the user. If you have any experience with WebSphere Application Server (or any other application server), you will appreciate this seamless update of the configuration without the need to restart the server or any container.

Defining Page Content

In the previous section we added a new page but it remained empty. To place some content in the page, we can edit the page layout. To edit a page layout you need to go to the page and click the Edit Page link just below the portal toolbar. Another way is to go to Manage Pages, navigate to Sample page and click the Edit Page Layout button (denoted by a pencil icon).

The Edit Layout page (shown in Figure 7-7) allows you to choose between six layout types:

- One column
- Two column
- Three column
- T layout
- Reverse T layout
- I layout

Our page was defined as a two-column page, so it includes two adjacent containers. Each of these containers is a column container, which means elements within it will stack vertically.

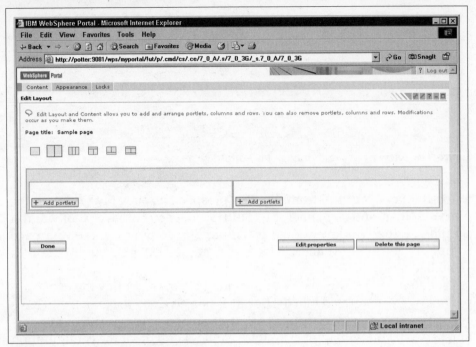

Figure 7-7   Page Customizer Content tab.

Below the layout type you can insert portlets into each of the containers. In our case we have two containers, and each can have several portlets. To add a portlet in the left column, simply click the Add Portlet button below that column.

A new window opens, and here you may select which portlet to add. The set of portlets available depends on whatever portlets were installed. Later in the book we will see how to develop our own portlets, but for now we will stick to the ones packaged into the default installation. For example, add the World Clock portlet (in version 5.0, it is the 41st entry shown on the 5th page). Once we add the portlet, it is visible inside the column container, with the following two buttons:

- Left arrow. Move to the container on the right
- Trashcan. Delete portlet

You may add a portlet on the right column as well, for example the Currency Calculator portlet. Note that this portlet will have a button for moving it to the container on the left. In general, a portlet will have a button for moving it in each of the four possible directions (left, right, up, and down) where there is a container (see Figure 7-8).

Button	Meaning
🖉	Edit Page Layout
🗑	Remove portlet
▼	Move portlet down
▲	Move portlet up
🗈	Move portlet left
🔑	Move portlet right

Figure 7-8 Page Customizer Portlet buttons.

Note that at this point you may also edit the page properties via the Edit Properties button and delete the page using Delete this Page button.

Once you click the Done button, the page is instantaneously updated, and you may view it going back to My Portal.

Editing Node Properties

Node properties are edited as part of addition of a new node, as we have seen earlier for both page and label nodes. When editing the properties of a label node we may modify the following properties (see Figure 7-9):

- Title. Text field controlling the title of the label
- Theme. Theme used for Web design (more on themes will be discussed in the next chapter)
- Advanced options.

  - This page supports: WML, cHTML, HTML. Markup language support. The default markup language for all pages is HTML, and a markup is only available for selection if supported for the parent node of the label.
  - I want to set titles and descriptions. Allows you to set the title and description for this label in each of the locales defined (24 of them by default).

When editing a page node, you may modify the following properties:

- Title. Text field controlling the page title
- Advanced options.

  - This page can be added to a user's My favorites list. A check box determining whether a user may bookmark (using the portal's My favorites drop menu) the page. This check box is checked by default.

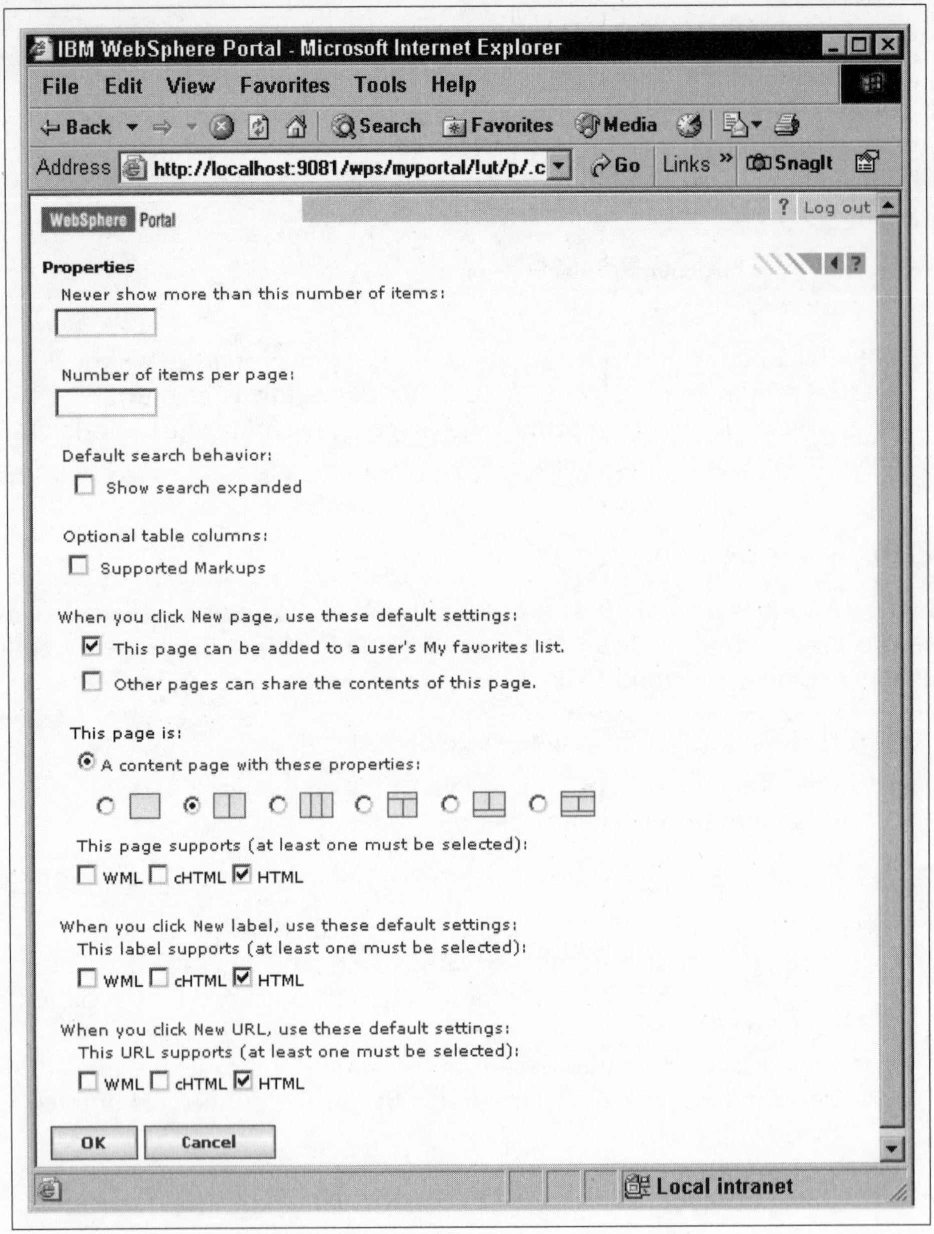

Figure 7-9   Editing node properties.

- Other pages can share the content of this page. Check box indicating whether the page can be shared (see discussion below). This check box is unchecked by default.
- This page supports: WML, cHTML, HTML. Markup language support. The default markup language for all pages is HTML, and

a markup is only available for selection if supported for the parent node of the page.

- This page has a list of allowed portlets. If this check box is clicked, the set of portals allowed within the page is limited. To set the list of allowed portlets, click the text beside the check box. This check box is unchecked by default.
- I want to set titles and descriptions. Allows you to set the title and description for this page in each of the locales defined (24 of them by default).

Page Inheritance with Shared Pages

When adding a new page, Advanced Options (shown in Figure 7-10) allows choosing the page content based on one of the six default layouts or based on another page. In the latter case, the other page must be one that was defined as a page that can be shared. When content of a new page is based on another page, the new page is essentially the aggregation of the existing page with a new specialized layer on top of the latter. This implies that a prerequisite for accessing a page using a shared page is that both the page and the shared page must be accessible by the user.

Shared pages essentially implement a form of inheritance. A page based on a shared page inherits the layout and content of the latter. An important characteristic of shared pages is that any changes made to the shared page are reflected on all the pages referencing it. For example, the addition or removal of a portlet from a shared page is immediately reflected in all referencing pages. This makes shared pages useful for implementing cascading portals.

Cascading portals are used in environments where the portal needs to meet the requirement of a central organization as well as those of units within the organization. For example, a portal for a certain department might share the structure of the basic portal of the whole company but add on department-specific content. In this case, one would like to share the page layout as well as visual elements reflecting the company identity.

WebSphere Portal provides a powerful paradigm for building cascading portals through the shared page mechanism. A shared page can reference another shared page, thus creating a chain of page references. From a practical standpoint, this means that top-level administrators may define a certain set of pages, and allow lower-level administrator to further refine and enhance the layout and content of pages as required to implement the needs of users within their respective subunit in the organization. This customization process can continue for a number of levels until end users are reached. End users may also customize pages, based on the permissions assigned to them by administrators.

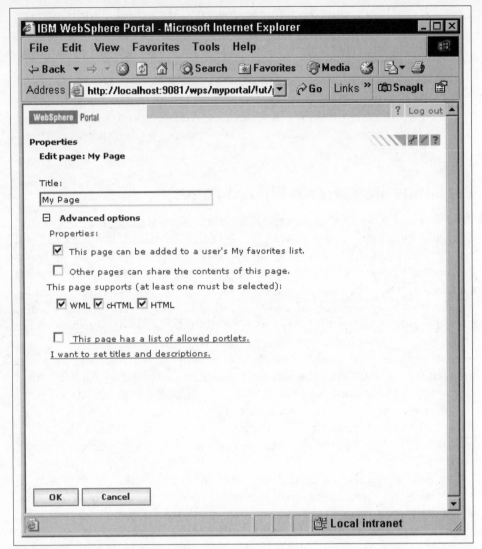

Figure 7-10   Editing Advanced Page properties.

Advanced Layout Editing

WebSphere Portal allows six different page basic layouts. While these might cover most simple cases, a real portal usually aggregates a variety of information sources, and fine-tuned control of layout is needed. To this end, WebSphere Portal provides *layout tools*. Layout tools are invisible by default. To enable them (for example, in our new page created earlier) follow these steps:

1. Go to Manage Pages under Administration.
2. Navigate to the Sample Page under My Stuff.

3. Click Edit Page Layout (second icon from the left following the page name).

4. Click the Configure button in the top-right corner of the window (that is, the leftmost button in the title bar).

5. Check the box reading Show Toggle Link for Show Layout Tools/Hide Layout Tools.

6. Click Done.

In the same configuration window you may also select whether users may modify the page layout, and if so what layouts (out of the six default ones) are allowed.

Once you have the Show Layout Tools link available in the layout editing window, you can click it. Once you do this, the six layout patterns are no longer visible and you may customize your layout by adding as many containers as you want. For each column container you may set its width, as well as add row containers within it. You may add column containers within a column container, and of course you may add portlets in both. This allows you to create a complex nested structure, which would provide the exact layout you are interested in.

Locks

In the page customization mode, where we edit the layout, there are two tabs in addition to the Content tab that opens by default. The Appearance tab can be used to customize appearance and will be discussed in the next chapter, and the Locks tab allows the administrator to limit the flexibility of a user in editing the page layout and content. For each container (row or column) you may lock or unlock the container and the content of the container. Locking the container prevents users from removing this container from a page, whereas locking the container content prevents users from adding or removing portlets and subcontainers from the container. You may also lock specific portlets, preventing the user from removing them.

Locks are applicable to shared pages, and allow top-level administrators in cascading portals to define content that is mandatory in a page, as lower-level administrators and end users cannot override the decisions of top-level administrators.

Removing Nodes

Removing nodes is a straightforward process. You just navigate in Manage Pages to a location you can see the node (to do this you navigate to the node or to its parent), and click the Delete button.

Note that removing a node implies removing all children nodes of that node, so a delete operation can have far-reaching consequences (just like deleting a folder in a file system). Furthermore, removing a shared page removes all reference pages.

Creating a New Portal

As previously mentioned, there is no built-in notion of portal within WebSphere Portal. Usually you can think of a portal within WebSphere Portal as a high-level label, available from the topmost navigation bar. In this section we will guide you through the process of addition of a new such label. This process is essentially identical to the process we went through earlier in this chapter, but it will allow us to define a structure we will use in the following chapters.

In order to define a new label, follow these steps:

1. Enter the Administration section.
2. Select Manage Pages.
3. Make sure you are viewing Content Root.
4. Click the New Label button.
5. Enter **New Portal** in the Title field.
6. Select OK.
7. Select OK in the confirmation window shown next.

To add a new label under this portal, follow these steps:

1. Select the New Portal entry.
2. Click the New Label button.
3. Enter **Company** in the Title field.
4. Select OK.

Now, follow the same steps to add two other labels named "Work" and "Personal." The following sequence of steps places some pages within these labels. We start with the Company page:

1. Select the New Portal entry.
2. Select the Company entry.
3. Click the New Page button.
4. Enter **Welcome** in the Title field.
5. Select OK.

Similarly, you add **Transactions** under Company; **Mail, Calendar,** and **Contacts** under Work, and **My Page** under Personal. Next we proceed to putting some content into these pages:

1. Select the new Welcome page.
2. Click the Edit Layout button.
3. Click the One Column button.
4. Click the Add Portlet button.
5. Select Interesting Links.
6. Select Breaking News.
7. Select Welcome to Your Co.
8. Select OK.
9. Click twice the Move Portlet Down button on Interesting Links.
10. Click the Move Portlet Up button on Welcome to Your Co.
11. Select OK.

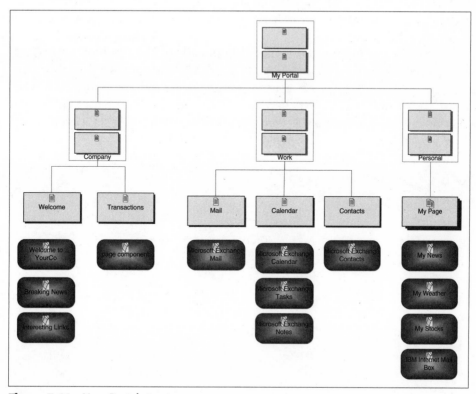

Figure 7-11 New Portal structure.

Note that after choosing the portlets to be placed within the page, they were ordered according to their ordering within the list of available portlets. In steps 9 and 10 we customize the ordering.

To complete the construction of our portal, we need to place content in all pages. To do this you need to follow the same sequence of steps choosing different portlets for each page. Figure 7-11 summarizes the structure and content of this portal.

Once you have finished the other five pages finished, you might want to see how this new portal looks like. Unfortunately, the default behavior of WebSphere Portal prevents users from accessing new label New Portal, as the set of top-level labels is fixed. In the next chapter we will see how to make this portal accessible, and we will continue the process of customizing it.

Summary

In this chapter we saw how the structure of a portal is defined and modified. We went through the process of modifying the default preinstalled portal, as well as defining our own new portal. This chapter provided a glimpse into the ease with which WebSphere Portal is configured and customized. At this point you should be able to define new portals and pages, and to place portlets within pages.

It goes without saying that controlling portal structure is merely the first step in customizing your portal. An important aspect of your portal design that has a strong impact on usability and user adoption is the look and feel of the portal. In the next chapter we will expand on the topic of portal customization, going into the visual (or Web design) aspects. Later in the book you will learn how to develop your own portlets.

## CHAPTER 8

Tailoring the Portal Web Design

In the previous chapter we described the process of customizing the structure and content of WebSphere Portal. In this chapter we focus on visual aspects of the portal. The visual aspects of your portal have a significant impact on the quality of user experience, and thus indirectly on the success of your portal. You would like the look and feel of your portal to be appealing, and usually you would like it to be unique. In this chapter you will learn how to customize the visual appearance of your portal. For the most part, such customization requires at least basic JSP programming skills.

Themes and Skins

A WebSphere Portal theme is an abstraction that captures the look and feel of a Web site. The theme is used to determine the global visual appearance of a page. Thus the choice of theme affects the navigational structure, logos, banners, fonts, and colors. For example, the theme determines whether navigation is performed using a toolbar on top of the page or a menu on the side of the page. It also determines the colors and fonts used.

Skins control the look and feel of borders around components. Skins can be either independent or associated with themes. For example, you may have a skin for which portlets have no borders, or another skin where borders are rectangular with rounded corners.

It is important to realize that both themes and skins are not necessarily fixed throughout the portal. It is possible to have a page of a set of pages with one theme and other pages with another theme. Similarly, portlets even within a single page can have different skins.

Similar to other aspects of WebSphere Portal customization, theme and skin customization can take place at three different levels:

- Portal Administrator. Controls user access permissions, and defines the extent to which a user may customize pages in the portal

- Web Designer. Controls visual aspects usually going into the level of HTML

- End user. Controls content and appearance as much as is permitted by the administrator

Default Themes and Skins

One of the easiest ways of understanding how something is built is to look at some existing examples. The themes and skins available to WebSphere Portal are stored in the directory `<WAS ROOT>/installedApps/<HOSTNAME>/wps.ear/wps.war`. In this location you can find two directories named `themes` and `skins`. On a Windows machine called Potter and using the default installation location for WebSphere, you have these directories under `C:\Program Files\WebSphere\AppServer\installedApps\potter\wps.ear\wps.war`. Each of the two directories contains subdirectories for the different markup types supported. By default HTML, cHTML, and WML are supported, and each has a separate directory. However, in the default configuration WebSphere Portal supports themes only for HTML. This makes perfect sense, as cHTML and WML are used to deliver text-based content to cell phones. In the HTML directory, the JSP page `Default.jsp` is used as the entry point for the default theme. Additional themes have their own subdirectories under the directory HTML:

- Corporate
- Engineering
- Finance
- Science

Each of these directories has its own `Default.jsp` page, and in addition it contains CSS style sheets and images. The default style sheet in each theme is called `Styles.css`, and the default version of this file is directly under the HTML directory. Images are used as much as they would in the context of ordinary HTML content, and for example the file `Banner.jpg` holds the banner shown on top of each page. Figure 8-1 shows the default theme as well as the other four preinstalled themes. Note that the file `preview.gif` in the directory corresponding to each theme shows a downsized version of a page rendered with the theme.

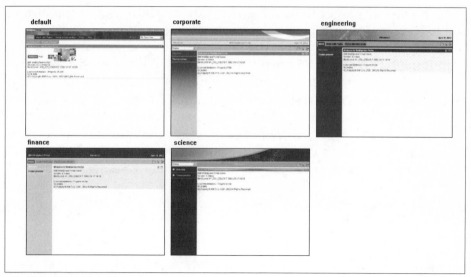

Figure 8-1 Preinstalled themes.

At this point you might wonder why WebSphere Portal organizes the portal resources in such a complicated way, where the default theme is defined in one directory and all other themes are defined in subdirectories. This organization stems from the fact that the portal provides fully dynamic aggregation of information, depending on locale, client, theme, and markup. In order words, whenever a certain resource is needed (be it a JSP, image, or CSS style sheet), the portal looks for it based on the directory structure. For example, when looking for the `Banner.jpg` file, the directory of the current theme is searched, and if nothing is found, the same file in the `HTML` directory is used. More generally, each research is sought for by traversing a set of directories, starting from the most specific location and moving higher in the hierarchy. The location is based not only on theme, but also on locale, client, and markup. For example, consider the file `Styles.css` when you are in the `Engineering` theme, using an Internet Explorer client using an `en` (English) locale. The search sequence would be as follows:

- `/themes/html/Engineering/ie/en/Styles.css`
- `/themes/html/Engineering/ie/Styles.css`
- `/themes/html/Engineering/en/Styles.css`
- `/themes/html/ie/en/Styles.css`
- `/themes/html/ie/Styles.css`
- `/themes/html/Styles.css`
- `/themes/Styles.css`

While this method of organizing resources might be confusing at first due to its complexity, it is quite powerful in allowing you to adapt style and content to different users. The search sequence starts with the most specific definition to the most general and stops when the needed resource is found. The way resources are sought allows you to minimize duplication of resources. By placing a resource at a high level of the hierarchy, you make it available for all locales and clients, and you can make customized copies of it when needed. It goes without saying that if a resource is nowhere to be found, the resulting HTML content might be erroneous. To this end, it is important to keep a default copy of important resources in the root directory.

Similar to themes, there is a directory `skins` under the `wps.war` directory. The default skins are:

- Album
- Clear
- Corner
- Diamonds
- Fade
- Hint
- Noborder
- Noskin
- Outline
- Pinstripe
- Shadow
- Wave

The visual effects of the various skins are shown in Figure 8-2. The differentiation between skins is through the look and feel of the title bar and window borders.

Choosing Themes and Skins

In the previous chapter, we saw how the Manage Pages window allows you to browse through the content hierarchy, and edit various properties of pages and labels. One such property is the theme, which may be edited through the Edit Page Properties button. An example of this is shown in Figure 8-3 where the theme for the My Portal label is set. The drop-down menu lists the available themes, as well as Portal Default Theme. For lower-level

Figure 8-2   Preinstalled skins.

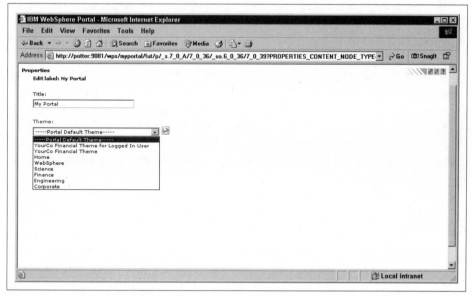

Figure 8-3   Choosing a theme.

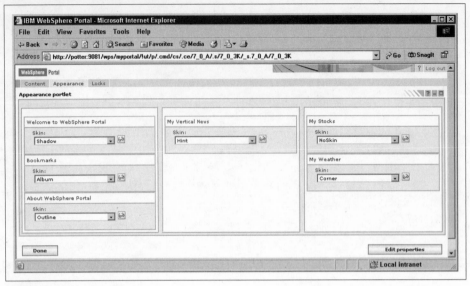

Figure 8-4   Choosing a skin.

nodes in the content hierarchy, the first entry (and the default one) is In-herit Parent Theme. This implements the simplest policy, which implies a uniform look and feel for the whole portal.

Clicking the Appearance bar brings the appearance portlet, which enables the selection of skins. Figure 8-4 shows this window for the default welcome window used when WebSphere Portal is first installed. Note that there are six different portlets, and each one may have its own skin.

End users can customize themes according to their own preference, as long as they have permission to do this. End-user editing is made through the page itself using the Edit Page link when available.

The easiest way to see the effects of different skins would be to choose six different skins for each of the portlets here, and going back to My Portal to see the visual effect. Figure 8-5 shows the Welcome portlet with a Hint skin.

Screens

In addition to themes and skins, WebSphere Portal defines a notion of screens. A screen is defined as a template for a page of portal content. Don't confuse this definition of a screen with that of a portal page, which is the end result of a process involving the screen. A portal page that is visible to the user is the product of the aggregation of several information sources, which include the portal page (which is part of the portal hierarchy as discussed in the previous chapter), page theme, skins, and the screen.

Figure 8-5 Welcome portlet with Hint skin.

The default screen is the Home screen, located in the file Home.jsp. This file is located in the directory screens\html under the aforementioned wps.war directory.

A portal page is only loaded when the tag <wps:screenRender/> is found in the page. This tag is a WebSphere Portal Server JSP tag, as implied by the wps: prefix. The Portal Server defines dozens of tags to support the customization of your portal, and we will cover most of them in the remainder of this chapter. Literally, the screenRender tag indicates the location where the current screen is to be rendered. This specific tag can only be used once within a portal JSP. We will see an example of its use in a short while.

Switching to a different screen is usually done through toolbar links. This is done using a special tag wps:url. This tag generates a URL pointing into a page in the portal. This tag can use the attributes screen, home, or command. These attributes specify respectively a screen name, the home page (using the value public for non-logged-in, and protected for logged-in users), or a specific command (using one of the attribute values LoginUser, LogoutUser, and ShowTools).

Defining Your Own Themes

Unless you are only exploring WebSphere Portal server or using it to build very small implementations, it is almost certain that you will want to create your own themes and possibly your own skins. While IBM made an effort to include a variety of themes and skins, to allow you to use the portal out of the box, in reality you would need to conduct some further customization. As with any Web site or Web application, you need to fine-tune the visual appearance to make it appealing to users and to ensure that it follows the standards used throughout your organization.

Creating a New Theme

To create a new theme, you need to go back to the directory `<WAS ROOT>/installedApps/<HOSTNAME>/wps.ear/wps.war` where themes and skins are located. Here, you create a new directory with a new name corresponding to the theme name. For example, to add a theme called `NewTheme` you need to create a directory with this name.

Once the directory is created, you need to populate it with the various resources needed, for example, JSP, images, and CSS style sheets. One way to go about this is to just copy an existing theme, for example, the `Corporate` theme.

Inside the theme directory, the most important JSP is the previously mentioned `Default.jsp`, which is the entry point for the theme. We have also discussed the CSS style sheet `Styles.css`. A lot of small image files are used for the various buttons (for example, `go.gif`, `help.gif`) and you may customize each one. The banner is stored in `Banner.jpg`, and the file `navfade.jpg` provides the background for the navigation bar on the left side of a page. As starters, we will change the banner. To do this, you need to replace the file `Banner.jpg` with your own file. For example, we will use the banner shown in Figure 8-6.

At this point you have your `New Theme` ready to be used, and we need to make WebSphere Portal aware of it. To do this, you need to perform the following sequence of operations:

1. Click the Administration button on the main toolbar.

2. Click Portal User Interface.

3. Click Themes and Skins.

4. You will now see the window as shown in Figure 8-7; click Add New Theme.

Figure 8-6   New `Banner.jpg`.

Figure 8-7   Themes and skins management.

A new window will be shown (see Figure 8-8). Here you need to follow these steps:

1. Enter the theme name, for example, **New Theme**.
2. Enter the theme directory name, in our case New Theme (note this is a relative path).
3. Choose which themes may be used in this theme.
4. You may click Set locale-specific titles to choose local-specific names for this theme.
5. Select OK.

Finally, you can see the new theme (and specifically the new banner) just by returning to My Portal.

In the window shown in Figure 8-7 you may also remove a theme or edit a theme. Removing the theme is important whenever you accidentally create an erroneous theme, as leaving it in the portal might allow users to apply it. Theme editing is quite limited, and allows you to control its local-specific naming and allowed skins.

It is usually a good idea to prepare a preview of your theme, and store it in the preview.gif file in the theme directory. This will allow users (or other administrators) to associate the name with the theme.

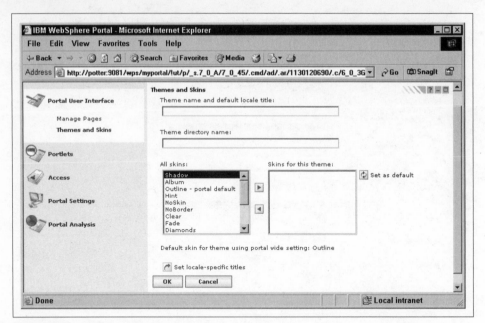

Figure 8-8   Adding a new theme.

Figure 8-9 shows the portal main page following the banner change. Notice that the Portal Server automatically concatenated several copies of the image provided to fill the full width of the page.

The Anatomy of a Theme

A theme in WebSphere Portal Server is implemented via a set of JSPs. We have mentioned the `Default.jsp` page, which serves as the entry point for the generation of content. This page includes other JSPs, which are part

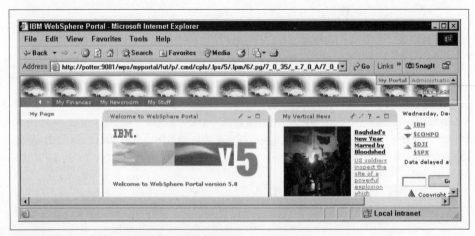

Figure 8-9   New banner within portal page.

of the theme definition. If a theme does not include any of these files, the default version of the JSP is used.

The other JSPs are as follows:

- `AdminToolBarInclude.jsp`. Displays links used by the Administrator for customizing pages and creating new pages:
  - Edit Page
  - Assign Permissions
  - New Page

- `ToolBarInclude.jsp`. Displays the toolbar available on the top of the page, offering options such as Sign Up or Log in when the user is not logged in, and options such as My Portal or Administration when the user is logged in

- `Head.jsp`. Displays the text in the <HEAD> element of the generated HTML page

- `PlaceBarInclude.jsp`. Displays a second level navigation toolbar

- `PageBarInclude.jsp`. Displays a third level navigation toolbar

In addition to JSP file, a theme directory contains other files used as building blocks for JSPs, such as GIF image files, and CSS style sheets.

Customizing Themes

In the previous section we added a new theme, but in fact we did not change much in terms of layout or functionality.

One of the first things you would like to change is the company name and company logo used in the portal. There are two ways to go about doing this. One way is to go to a file called `engine.properties` located in `<WPS Root>/shared/app/nls`, and edit the resource called title. Alternatively, you can modify this in the file `Default.jsp` of your theme. In order to do this, you must have some basic acquaintance with JSPs, which we will assume you have (if not, you can skip to the next section).

Given below is the default content of the file `Default.jsp`. This is a relatively short, albeit not very readable JSP. This JSP determines the general layout of pages in the portal, using an HTML table construct. The most notable feature in this page is that it uses tags, which are specific to WebSphere Portal. As mentioned above, these tags are identified by the `wps:` prefix.

The file `Default.jsp` starts with some standard headers.

```
<%@ page session="false" buffer="none" %>
<%-- Must be Transitional DTD or Mozilla/Netscape 6 will not correctly
display tables used for visual layout. --%>
<!DOCTYPE HTML PUBLIC "-//W3C//DTD HTML 4.0 Transitional//EN">
<%-- @copyright jsp --%>
```

We then include the `engine.tld` taglib, with the prefix `wps`, as well as some additional tag libraries.

```
<%@ taglib uri="/WEB-INF/tld/engine.tld" prefix="wps" %>
<%@ include file="./extension/TagLibInclude.jsp" %>
<%-- This includes Extend/Express specific tag libraries. --%>
```

Next comes a `<wps:constants/>` tag. This tag makes the two constants `wpsBaseURL` and `wpsDocURL` available in the remainder of the page. Later this page uses the former, which indicates the base URL for WebSphere Portal, e.g. `http://localhost:9081/wps/`.

```
<wps:constants/>
```

The HTML page starts here, including the file `Head.jsp`. This file defines the HTML page header using a `<head>` tag. The `Head.jsp` page is of course customizable, and in fact it is taken from the theme (that is, you may define a different implementation for different user groups). By default, the header reads "IBM WebSphere Portal."

```
<html>
<%@ include file="./Head.jsp" %>
```

Next starts the page body, with some browser-specific directives.

```
<%-- Set margins to 0 here in addition to stylesheet to support old
versions of Netscape --%>
<body marginwidth="0" marginheight="0" <%=bidiDirAttr%>
onLoad="if ( document.forms['wpsPageGroupSelectionForm'] != null )
  document.forms['wpsPageGroupSelectionForm'].reset();" >
```

At this point, immediately after the `<body>` tag, the file `PageBeginInclude.jsp` is included. The content of this file is dependent on the version of WebSphere Portal Server used, but it is typically empty.

```
<%@ include file="./extension/PageBeginInclude.jsp" %>
 <%-- This includes Extend/Express specific page logic. --%>
```

Finally we get to add the table, which is used to ensure a uniform width for the components of the page. You can notice the use of the tag `wps:text`, for example `<wps:text key="title" bundle="nls.engine">`. This returns the text for the key `title` in the locale of the user. Replacing this with a hard-coded title will be equivalent to changing the `engine` file residing in the directory `shared\apps\nls` under the Portal Server root, or one of the locale-specific variants of it. Obviously, to have a locale-specific title it might be easier to stick to the latter solution.

```
<%-- This table is here so the banner is the same width as the portlets
--%>
<table border="0" cellpadding="0" cellspacing="0" width="100%"
 height="100%">
```

```
<tr> <!-- logo -->
<td valign="top" align="<%=bidiAlignLeft%>" nowrap>
<img align="absmiddle" alt='<wps:text key="title"
 bundle="nls.engine">Portal Title</wps:text>'
 title='<wps:text key="title" bundle="nls.engine"/>'
 src='<wps:urlFindInTheme file="logo.gif"/>'>
<a href="#wpsMainContent"><img width="1" height="1" border="0"
 src='<%= wpsBaseURL %>/images/dot.gif'
 alt='<wps:text key="link.skiptocontent" bundle="nls.engine"/>'
 title='<wps:text key="link.skiptocontent" bundle="nls.engine"/>'>
</a>
</td>
<td width="100%" height="1" valign="top" align="<%=bidiAlignRight%>">
```

We include the file `ToolbarInclude.jsp` that controls the top-level navigation, allowing you to switch between `My Portal` and `Adminis-tration`. This would be the page to modify if you want to include another visible node directly under the `ContentRoot`. Following it, another tool-bar `AdminLinkBarInclude.jsp` is loaded based on the tag `<wps:if portletSolo="no">`. This is a standard condition statement and several conditions can be checked with its attributes. WebSphere Portal provides a multitude of attributes, which can be checked, such as the locale, whether a user is logged in or not, or client capabilities. Here only one condition is checked and that is `portletSolo` is set to no, i.e. the portlet is not running solo state. Portlets are running in one of the following four states: `normal`, `maximized`, `minimized`, and `solo`. There is another possible condition attribute for testing the portlet state, called `portletState`. Thus the con-dition `portletSolo="no"` is equivalent to `portletMode="solo"`. The `wps:if` below is used to enclose an include statement for adding the nav-igation JSP, which we will discussed later.

```
<%@ include file="./ToolBarInclude.jsp" %>
   <%-- Don't show navigation in solo mode --%>
        <wps:if portletSolo="no">
                <%@ include file="./AdminLinkBarInclude.jsp"%>
        </wps:if>

</td>
<tr>
    <td colspan="2">
```

If navigation is to be used, include `PlaceBarInclude.jsp`, providing the next level of navigation below the top-level one (for example, within `My Portal`, between Welcome and the other options), and `PageBarInclude.jsp` provides the next level of navigation. Obviously, by removing the JSP include statements for either of these files, you can remove this level of navigation altogether from a specific theme.

These pages provide specific implementation of a general concept in Web-Sphere Portal, which is navigation. Using the <wps:navigation> tag you can define your own navigation menus, which are not necessarily limited to two or three levels down.

```
                <%-- Don't show navigation in solo mode --%>
                    <wps:if portletSolo="no">
                    <%@ include file="./PlaceBarInclude.jsp" %>
                    <%@ include file="./PageBarInclude.jsp" %>
                </wps:if>
        </td>
    </tr>
    <tr>
    <td width="100%" height="100%" valign="top" colspan="2">
        <a name="wpsMainContent"></a>
        <wps:screenRender/>
    </td>
    </tr>
    </table>
```

We conclude with a product-specific PageEndInclude.jsp.

```
<%@ include file="./extension/PageEndInclude.jsp" %>   <%-- This
includes Extend/Express specific page logic. --%>
</body>
</html>
```

An important caveat to note about included files is that if you change them, you need to make the Portal Server aware of this by modifying the Default.jsp command (for example, using the UNIX touch command).

Using the WPS tags, you may create intricate logic to customize your portal. WebSphere Portal provided dozens of other tags, which are available. These tags are described in the next section.

Portal JSP Tags

In the previous section you saw how the tags wps:constants, wps:text, wps:screenRender, wps:navigation, and wps:if are used.

The Portal Server provides many more JSP tags. The taglib file for these tags is called engine.tld and is located in the <WPS ROOT>/shared\app \WEB-INF\tld directory. The main purpose of these JSP tags is to allow the JSP designer to leverage some of the information and capabilities available inside the Portal Server engine.

The remainder of this section describes some of the more commonly used JSP tags provided by the Portal Server. A full list can be found in the IBM product documentation.

The most commonly used portal JSP tag is wps:if. In the Default.jsp listing above you saw how to use it with the portletSolo attribute, which checks whether the portlet is in solo state. There are a multitude of other conditions that can be checked:

- capableof="*capability*". Tests whether the client has a specific capability (for example, HTML_4_0, HTML_FRAME).

- locale="*locale*". Tests for a specific locale (for example, in_US). The notLocale="*locale*" attribute checks if the locale is different than the one specified. The notLocale form is required as the syntax of the wps:if tag does not allow for fully blown logical expressions.

- loggedIn="yes|no". Tests whether the user is logged in. This condition is used extensively in Toolbarinclude.jsp, discussed in the next section.

- navigationAvailable="yes|no". Tests the availability of navigation.

- newWindow="yes|no". Tests whether portlet is running in a separate browser window.

- screen="*screen*". Checks if the current screen is the one specified. There is also a notScreen version available.

- pageAvailableNext="yes|no". Checks if there is a following page available. A similar tag pageAvailablePrevious checks for the availability of a previous page. Both of these are used in Banner.jsp to add a scroll icon allowing the user to access additional tabs if all of them are not visible concurrently.

- pageCompletelyActive="yes|no". Tests if the current page and its parents are all active.

- pageBookmarkable="true|false". Tests if a page can be bookmarked (as per the definitions in the administrator's Manage Pages). This condition can be used to enclose a bookmark link.

- portletMaximed="yes|no". Tests if the portlet state is maximized.

- portletMode="edit|view|configure|help". Tests what modes the portlet supports. This is important for the title bar display in customized skins.

- showTools="yes|no". Tests whether additional controls should be placed in the portlet title bar (usually, clicking the wrench icon in the top-level toolbar sets this to **yes**).

- resumeLevel="0|1|2". Tests for the setting of the level of session preservation as set by the administrator (0 means no persistent session state, 1 means portlet states and modes are stored, and 2 means all portlet settings are stored).

- resumeOption="0|1". Tests whether users are being offered to restore their most recent session upon login. 0 means no, 1 means yes.

In addition to the wps:if tag, there is a negative wps:unless tag. With this tag, if any of the conditions is true, the following text is not written to the output page.

In order that you are able to access files and resources, the Portal Server provides the tags wps:urlFind, wps:urlFindInSkin, and wps:url FindInTheme. All three have a file="*filename*" attribute. The urlFind also has path and root attributes to specify where to look for a file, and the other two just have an id attribute, which allows you to place the URL into a scripting variable instead of to the output stream. All forms of urlFind use the hierarchical search sequence described earlier, and thus depend on the locale and markup of the client.

While urlFind is sufficient for accessing static resources, you need to use wps:urlGeneration to generate URLs for portal pages. This tag places the generated URL into a variable wpsURL and has attributes called root, navigationNode, contentNode, and compositionNode used to iden-tify the node where the page or portlet is located. Other attributes available with this tag are as follows:

- portletWindowState="maximized|solo|normal". Indicates the state of the portlet window when it is displayed. This is only applicable to portlets.

- pacCheck="CreatePage|EditLayout|DeletePage|Assign Roles|NoCheck". Indicates what kinds of permissions are required from the users and should be checked. If NoCheck is specified, no checks are made.

- useReqID="true|false". This attribute determines whether a request ID is appended to the URL. By default this is true, thus allowing users access to a new browser window without the links getting invalid.

- newWindow="true|false". Opens a new window or new iFrame.

If you need to pass parameters to a generated URL, <wps:urlGeneration /> together with <wps:urlParam/> can be used. The latter tag has two attributes: name specifying the parameter name and value specifying the parameter value.

Some other tags are as follows:

- `wps:date`, d `wps:time`. These can be used to insert the date and time in various formats.
- `<wps:user attribute="userID|fullName|familyName">`. Returns an identification of the user based on the attribute, if the user is logged in.
- `<wps:captureContext contextKey="context">`. Captures the content of the tag (that is, whatever is placed between the tag beginning and ending markers) and places as a string attribute in `PageContext`. This is useful when you need to use data, which can only be generated by JSP tags from within JSP Java code.

Adding Top-Level Links

Recall that during our review of the `Default.jsp` page, the file `ToolbarInclude.jsp` was included to control the top-level navigation. In order to enable the "New Portal" entry defined at the end of the previous chapter, you need to understand how navigation works. To this end, let's take a look at `TooBarInclude.jsp`. For brevity, some of the comments were removed, and we only show the code for the first two navigation buttons. The code for each is denoted by a comment.

```
<table border="0" cellspacing="0" cellpadding="0" >
<tr>
<%@ page import="com.ibm.portal.*"%>
<%-- My Portal button --%>
<wps:if loggedIn="yes" portletSolo="no">
     <td class="wpsToolBar" nowrap><b>
     <wps:text key="link.my.portal" bundle="nls.engine"/></b></td>
</wps:if>
<%-- Administration button --%>
<wps:if loggedIn="yes" portletSolo="no">
   <wps:urlGeneration contentNode="wps.Administration"
   portletWindowState="Normal">
   <td class="wpsToolBar" valign="middle" align="<%=bidiAlignRight%>"
    nowrap>
   <a href="<% wpsURL.write(out); %>"
    class="wpsToolBarLink"><wps:text key="link.administration"
    bundle="nls.engine"/></a>
   </td>
   </wps:urlGeneration>
</wps:if>
```

What you can see is that if the user is logged in, and the portlet mode is not `solo`, the JSP provides button linking to My Portal. Notice this link has no `href` tag, since it is only used within the portal and not from the administration pages.

The Administration button does sport an actual link using an `href` tag obtained by using the `generateURL` tag.

In order to provide buttons for top-level New Portal label, we may add the following and replace the code after the My Portal button with the following:

```
<%-- New Portal button --%>
<wps:if loggedIn="yes" portletSolo="no">
<wps:urlGeneration contentNode="wps.New Portal"
 portletWindowState="Normal">
<td class="wpsToolBar" nowrap>
<a href="<% wpsURL.write(out); %>" class="wpsToolBarLink">
New Portal</a>
</td>
</wps:urlGeneration>
```

Once you implement this change, you have a new button allowing you to navigate to the new top-level page. However, once users go there, they have no way to return. To tackle this difficulty, you must create a different theme for the New Portal label, and implement there `ToolBarInclude.jsp`. The implementation should be such that the New Portal button is boldfaced instead of the My Portal button, but the latter would have a link. Incidentally, this is exactly the reason for having an `Admin` theme preinstalled with the Portal Server. You can notice that when entering the `Admin` mode the Administration button becomes bold and the My Portal button becomes active. To have the New Portal button available from the administration mode, this theme needs to be modified as well.

In some cases, it is desired to use different screens, especially for top-level links. For example, in the preinstalled themes, a different screen is used for logging in or for users who have forgotten their password. The following excerpt from `ToolBarInclude.jsp` shows the code for the "forgot password" button. This code uses the `wps:url` tag with the `screen` attribute.

```
<%-- forgot password button --%>
<wps:if loggedIn="no" notScreen="ForgotPassword">
<td class="wpsToolBar" valign="middle" align="<%=bidiAlignRight%>"
nowrap>
<a class="wpsToolBarLink"
href='<wps:url screen="ForgotPassword" home="public"/>'><wps:text
key="link.password" bundle="nls.engine"/></a>
</td>
</wps:if>
```

Defining Your Own Skins

Skins are less powerful constructs than themes. For this reason they are much easier to generate, but on the flip side it might not be as important to you to change the skins available in WebSphere Portal.

Creating a New Skin

To create a new theme, we have to go back to the directory <WAS ROOT>/ installedApps/<HOSTNAME>/wps.ear/wps.war where skins are located. As was the case with themes, you need to create a directory under the directory skins. In the new directory you need to place the JSP and image resources for your skin. The only mandatory file is Control.jsp, a JSP file defining the behavior of the skin. Essentially, this JSP uses several WPS tags to determine the portlet status (for example, minimized, maximized), and to generate the needed HTML appearance, using several images. Each of the preinstalled skins includes several images as needed, for the title bar buttons, the title bar background, and for window borders.

Once you have a new directory, say New Skin, ready with your Control.jsp file and any images needed, you may follow these steps to install it into WebSphere Portal:

1. Click the Administration button on the main toolbar.
2. Click Portal User Interface.
3. Click Themes and Skins.
4. You will now see the window as shown in Figure 8-6. Click Add New Skin.

A new window will be shown. Here you need to follow these steps:

1. Enter the skin name, for example, **New Skin**.
2. Enter the skin directory name, in our case New Skin (note this is a relative path).
3. You may click Set Locale-Specific Titles to choose local-specific names for this theme.
4. Select OK.

To use the skin, you need to add it to your portal default theme as discussed above.

Just like themes, you may edit skins (but only to change their names), and remove them. Also, you can provide a preview of skins in a file preview.gif in the skin directory.

Modifying Styles

CSS style sheets are an essential tool in designing Web pages. For this reason, the Styles.css file is part of each theme. This file defines a set of styles used in HTML files generated by the portal. You may change some of the font, color, and layout definitions given in the file to control the look and feel of portlets including the IBM administration portlets.

For example, the color in which active links and visited links are shown can be modified by changing the color definitions in the following snippet out of the Styles.css file:

```
a, .wpsLink, a:active, .wpsLink:active {
    font-family: Verdana, Arial, Helvetica, sans-serif;
    font-size: x-small;
    color: #3366CC;
}
a:visited, .wpsLink:visited {
    font-family: Verdana, Arial, Helvetica, sans-serif;
    font-size: x-small;
    color: #666699;
}
```

Summary

In this chapter we learned how to customize the portal Web design. The portal Web design can be customized with themes, skins, and styles. You learned how to create new themes and skins, and how to modify them. In the next chapter we will discuss personalization in WebSphere. Some level of personalization is provided in the Portal Server by allowing users to customize pages with themes and skins. IBM takes personalization to the next level with WebSphere personalization as described in the next chapter.

WebSphere Portal Personalization

The evolution of Web applications in general and Portals in particular places a lot of emphasis on the issue of personalization. Personalization is the process of producing and delivering individually tailored content based on previous information associated with a specific user.

Personalizing your portal in an appropriate way you can have the distinct advantage of making information and tools more accessible to users. As the quantity of Web-based content grows, the importance of filtering information and providing each user with the most relevant content becomes crucial. User loyalty and satisfaction tend to grow as content gets more personalized.

WebSphere Personalization

The need for customizing Web page content is a common thread in many applications. For example, in the e-commerce realm, it is important to provide customers with personalized recommendations and advice.

Generating personalized content from within a Web application is not very difficult. You can plug in a couple of "if" statements into your JSP to achieve some crude form of personalization. Personalization becomes a bit more difficult to tackle when you need to apply complex considerations in the customization of content. Alternatively, you might want to apply certain personalization processes across several applications, and to allow nonprogrammers to manage the personalization process.

WebSphere Portal Server provides some form of personalization through its out-of-the-box functionality as described in the previous chapter. The portal may allow users to customize the layout and themes for portlets and pages, and different content can be delivered to different users by using access control.

Personalization is essentially a process of matching content to users, based on well-defined attributes of users and of content. IBM WebSphere Personalization provides a framework that facilitates content personalization based on previous user interactions with the system. To this end, it provides a way to track users and analyze their activities, as well as store content in a manner that facilitates matching it against user attributes.

The personalization support in WebSphere allows you to use two different technologies: *rules-based personalization* and *recommendation-based personalization*.

Rules-based personalization relies on having a person define a set of business rules that determine which content is displayed for a given user. Rules-based personalization is tightly integrated into the WebSphere Portal Server.

Recommendation-based personalization uses a technology called collaborative filtering, implemented in a recommendation engine. The recommendation engine uses complex statistical models and other techniques to learn the usage patterns of a Web application or Web site in order to provide personalization without the need to provide explicit rules.

Rules-Based Personalization

As the name suggests, rules-based personalization involved using rules to determine what content to present to a given user. To this end, rules-based personalization requires three kinds of resources: users, contents, and rules to map users to content.

The basis for personalization is collecting and maintaining information regarding users. The collection of all the pieces of information relating to one user is referred to as a user profile. User information can be collected either directly from the user (via a user-profile form) or from other sources, such as tracking the user's online activities. Users can be grouped into categories to facilitate personalization.

Web content consists of the full array of data delivered through the portal, such as JSP, and static HTML or XML pages. It is important to note that on a typical portal page only a portion of the page need be personalized. In other words, some parts of the page are static, and the remainder of the page consists of "spots" where personalized content is to be placed.

Personalization rules allow nonprogrammers to specify what content to show in a "content spot" based on a user profile. For example, consider the following simplistic illustration of rules in a credit-card company customer portal:

```
When UserType is Platinum_member, Show Platinum News
When UserType is Gold_member, Show Gold News
```

In order for these rules to work, there must be a way to identify whether a member is a platinum card holder or a gold card holder. Furthermore, content should have an indication of whether it belongs to platinum news or gold news.

Resources

In WebSphere personalization, both users and content are considered personalization resources. Each resource has one or more fixed attributes defined by the schema for the resource. For instance, the user data schema may include the name, address, and phone number of a customer visiting your Web site. A schema for Web content includes attributes about the content, indicating to which Web visitors it is relevant. Typically the content itself is accessible via a URL, which will be part of the schema.

There are two ways to go about creating and managing resource in WebSphere personalization. One way is to use the WebSphere Portal user and content wizards in WebSphere Studio Application Developer. The other option is to provide Java classes implementing the resource class APIs.

Clearly, personalization requires having permanent storage of both user and content resources. Resources are stored in a content repository, and are loaded into the Portal Server by the Resource Engine. In WebSphere Portal Server 5.0, the Resource Engine is shared with WebSphere Portal Content Publishing (WPCP). Going forward, WPCP is taken out of the WebSphere Portal Server distribution, and it would be replaced with Aptrix/Lotus Workplace Web Content Management. In addition, it seems likely that at some point IBM will adopt the JSR 170 standard for content management, thus removing the need for the Resource Engine. Content Management in WebSphere Portal is discussed in detail in Chapter 11.

Content Spots

The result of personalization is the delivery of personalized content. This content is concentrated in content spots. Content spots usually do not take up the full space on a page, as some content need not be personalized (for example, a company logo would appear on every page regardless of the individual user). Technically speaking, a content spot is a Java wrapper bean that is placed inside your Web page. This bean is essentially a placeholder for a rule, and can invoke the rule to display personalized content or perform data updates.

The following JSP code snippet illustrates the use of such beans within a JSP. In this example we assume a bean called HelloContentSpot provides a message, which is based on user classification. To retrieve the content derived from the rule, the method getRuleContent() is invoked.

```
<!DOCTYPE HTML PUBLIC "-//W3C//DTD HTML 4.0 Transitional//EN">
<HTML><HEAD>
<TITLE> Sample Personalized Page </TITLE>
</HEAD>
<BODY BGCOLOR="#FFFFFF">
<jsp:useBean class="HelloContentSpot"
    id="helloContentSpot">
<% helloContentSpot.setRequest(request); %>
</jsp:useBean>
<%= helloContentSpot.getRuleContent()%>
</BODY>
</HTML>
```

Defining Rules

Rules define interactions between your Web site and users. Rules are structured as easy-to-read statements, in order to make rules accessible to non-programmers. WebSphere personalization introduces the concept of campaign to group together a set of rules, which are used to achieve a certain goal over a defined period.

To define new rules, you need to perform the following actions:

1. Go to the Personalization entry under the Content Publishing tab.
2. Select Rules on the left-hand panel.
3. Click the New Folder icon to create a new folder.
4. Name the new folder Rule.
5. In the new folder, click the New Rule button to create a new rule.

At this point, you reach the rule definition screen, as shown in Figure 9-1.

Editing Rules

The screen shown in Figure 9-1 allows you to specify the rule name and description, as well as choose the rule type and edit the rule itself. Rule editing is performed in the bottom part of the window. The rule editor provides HTML links to help you identify a variable, and items are color coded to help you recognize your options. For each such link, once you

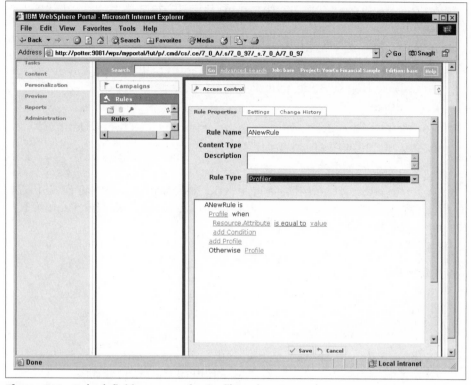

Figure 9-1   Rule definition screen for Profiler rule.

click it a new window opens. In this window you may choose a value out of a list of options. Once a selection is made, it is reflected in the rule text.

The color of links is as follows:

- Blue indicates an item that is completed. It may still be clicked for editing.
- Red indicates an item that must be edited to finish the rule.
- Magenta indicates an item that is optional. It is not required to complete the rule.

WebSphere personalization provides several types of rules, which are as follows:

- Profilers—allow you to define types of visitors based on current user properties and other object properties.
- Select Content—allows you to choose content to be displayed, and also allows to sort the order of returned results.

- Update—allows you to perform updates to data (for example, user profiles).

- E-mail—allows you to send an e-mail.

- Bindings—combine profilers with an action (select, update, or e-mail), so that specific actions can take place under defined conditions.

- Recommend Content—allows you to define rules for content recommendation. This type of rule will be discussed in the next section.

In order to complete editing a rule, you need to click all the blue links. In the example of a profiler rule, you need click the links for Profile, Resource.Attribute, and value.

To enter a new profiling rule, perform the following sequence of actions:

1. Click the Profile link.

2. In the window that opens, enter the desired profile name (see Figure 9-2).

3. Click the Resource.Attribute link.

4. In the window that opens, choose the resource and attribute. For example, Figure 9-3 shows the selection of the current date.

5. Click the value link.

6. In the value window, select the date, as shown in Figure 9-4.

7. Click Save.

Note that prior to saving you could add additional conditions or additional classifications of users (for example, using the else clause).

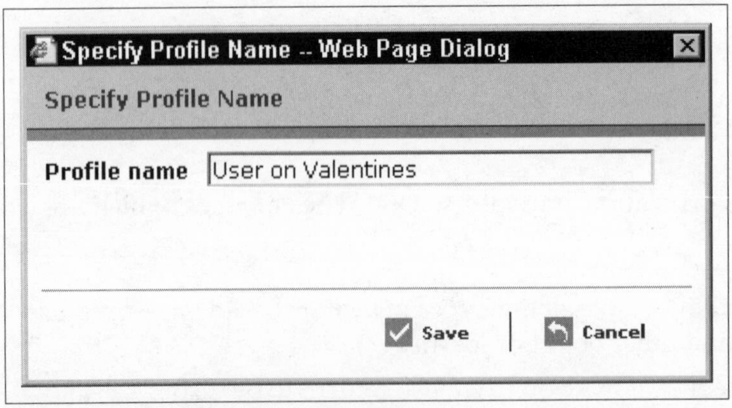

Figure 9-2 Specifying the profile name.

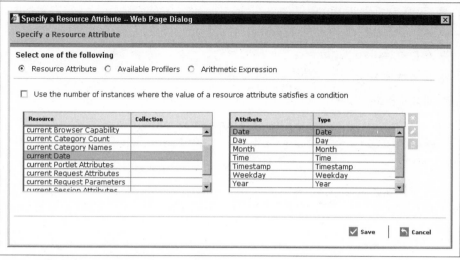

Figure 9-3   Specifying the resource attribute.

Furthermore, the Resource.Attribute link allows you to use other profilers (via the Available Profilers radio button) or an arithmetic expression combining several attributes (via the respective radio button). The `is equal to` link can be clicked to choose another type of comparison, out of the following options:

- includes
- includes any of
- is between
- is between but not equal to
- is equal to
- is greater than

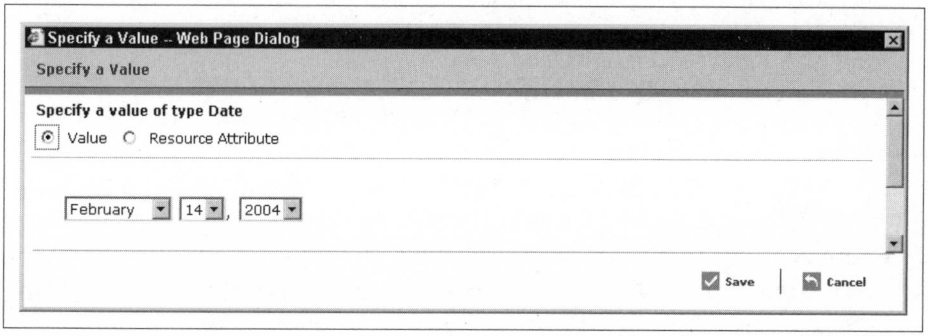

Figure 9-4   Specifying a date.

- is greater than or equal to
- is included in
- is less than or equal to
- is less than
- is not equal to

Other types of rules are edited in a similar fashion, only that the building blocks for these rules are different. Select content rules have the following structure:

```
Select content
Whose Resource.Attribute is equal to value
add Condition
order as is
show all items
```

The whose clause is similar to the one used in profiler rules. The two bottom links in this rule allow ordering of the results, and limiting their number. The ordering options are either "as is" (the default), in random ordering, or sorted by some attributes. Show all items may be replaced by putting a limit on the number of content elements to show. The limit may either be a fixed numeric value or extracted from a resource attribute.

Update rules follow a similar structure:

```
Update
Resource.Attribute set to value
```

Binder rules have a more complicated structure:

```
When Profiler is
     Profile do Action
    Otherwise do Action
    Always do Action
    Exclude do Action
order as is
show all items
```

The binder rule defines an action to take place for a certain profile. The action to perform can be defined to be any previously defined select content or update rule. The Otherwise clause allows you to define actions to run in case the profile is different, and the Always clause allows defining actions that are to run regardless of the profile. None of these actions are compulsory. The Exclude clause allows you to define an action whose result shall be removed from the result set of the rule. In other words, it allows you to remove items from the output of this rule. The ordering and item limit clauses are identical to those used in the select content rule.

The e-mail rule allows you to define an action by which e-mail is automatically sent. The e-mail rule has the following fields:

- Recipient
- Sender
- ccRecipient
- bccRecipient
- Subject
- bodyURI

These fields are extracted from select content actions.

Campaigns

Campaign Management is a component of Personalization that allows you to make rules to work. The portal personalization has a "default" set of rules, referred to as the *Normal View*. The Normal View defines the personalization of your Web site when there are no active campaigns. Normal View displays all of the content spots on your Web site, what content type they use, and their assigned rules.

Campaigns provide a platform for setting business goals and specifying a path for a Web site to achieve these goals. Campaigns are defined by three components: a set of rules, a specific period of time when the campaign is active, and content spots to be filled. Through the rules, campaigns may deliver personalized information via the Web or e-mail. They may also display forms to users where they can provide information to the site.

Campaigns are accessible via the Personalization tab in the portal, above the rules.

The Campaigns view shown in Figure 9-5 summarized all currently available campaigns. A campaign includes a collection of rules assigned to content spots on Web pages. These rules override the Normal View rules during the specified period. It is possible to prioritize campaigns to determine which one takes precedence in case there is an overlap in dates. It is possible to have two campaigns with the same priority. In that case, both are used based on the split percentage defined.

For example, Figure 9-6 shows a 30-70 split between two campaigns, which means the first will be shown for 30 percent of the time and the other in the remaining instances.

Within a campaign or within the Normal View, you may assign rules to each of the content spots, as shown in Figure 9-7.

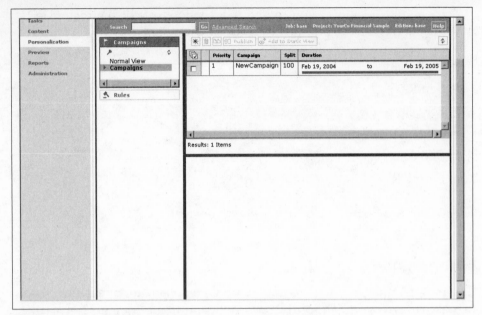

Figure 9-5   The Campaigns view.

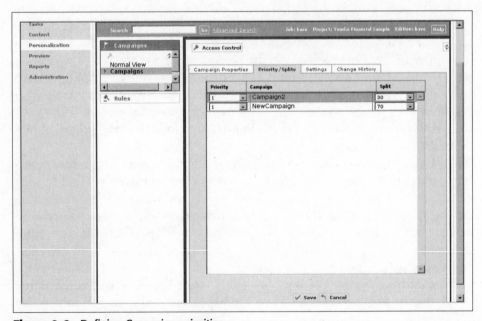

Figure 9-6   Defining Campaign priorities.

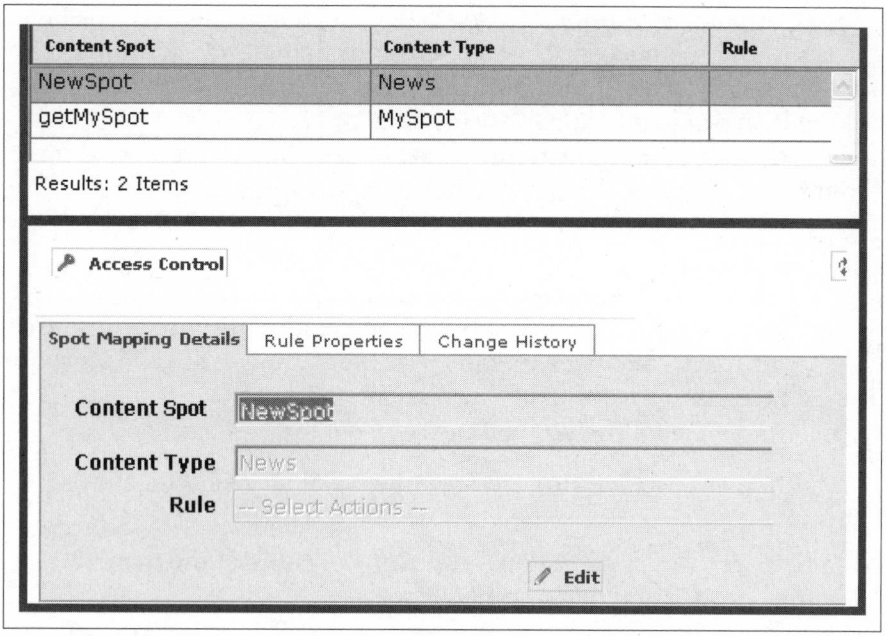

Content Spot	Content Type	Rule
NewSpot	News	
getMySpot	MySpot	

Results: 2 Items

🔑 **Access Control**

| Spot Mapping Details | Rule Properties | Change History |

Content Spot   NewSpot

Content Type   News

Rule   -- Select Actions --

✎ **Edit**

Figure 9-7   Assigning rules to content spots.

The Personalization APIs

The WebSphere Portal Personalization provides open APIs that allow the portal and WebSphere Studio Advanced Edition to access your own user and content data in customer data stores.

The WebSphere application server provides user-profile functionality via the packages:

```
com.ibm.websphere.userprofile.UserProfile
com.ibm.websphere.userprofile.UserProfileManager
com.ibm.websphere.userprofile.UserProfileExtender
```

WebSphere Personalization provides a more powerful mechanism with better support and larger flexibility in implementing resources (both user and content) for personalization. Flexibility is achieved via the support for data modeling. You can define user models and content models suitable for your own requirements. The APIs supplied by IBM to access resources in your own data store are as follows:

```
com.ibm.websphere.personalization.resources.Resource
com.ibm.websphere.personalization.resources.ResourceDomain3
com.ibm.websphere.personalization.resources.ResourceManager3
```

To provide your own implementations of the Personalization APIs for accessing resources in the customer data store, you can use wizards included with Studio Advanced Edition or use an IDE, such as VisualAge for Java. Regardless of the method used, you need to be acquainted with the API. The following sections provide a brief summary of the API. For full details refer to the IBM product JavaDoc documentation.

The class files for your implementations of the resource access APIs must be placed in the Web module of your Enterprise Application.

Resource Interface

The interface com.ibm.websphere.personalization.resources.Resource allows you to map your user model or content model to data in your database. The resource essentially implements a property container. This interface requires the following methods:

- String getId()—returns an identifier (primary key) for the resource
- Object get(String prop)—returns the value of the named dynamic property in this resource
- Enumeration keys()—returns all property keys associates with the resource
- void put(String name, Object value)—sets the named dynamic property to a value
- void remove(String name)—removes the named dynamic property from the resource

In addition to these methods, you need to implement methods for setting and getting each fixed property defined in the data model for the resource. For example, for a fixed property surname defined for your user resource, the methods getsurname() and setSurname() must be implemented.

ResourceDomain3 Interface

The com.ibm.websphere.personalization.resources.ResourceDomain3 interface allows you to query and select resources based on fixed properties. The access is read-only mode. The methods ResourceDomain3 use the class ResourceContext. The latter is an object that can be instantiated in your JSPs to pass data to your resource classes. This interface requires the following methods:

- Resource findById(String name, ResourceContext context)—returns the named resource
- Enumeration findResourcesByQuery(Query query, ResourceContext context)—returns all resources meeting the

query specification (query specification is similar to the WHERE clause in an SQL SELECT statement)

- Enumeration findResourcesByPropertyQuery(`String name`, `String value`, `ResourceContext context`)—returns all resources having the named property with the specified value

ResourceManager3 Interface

The com.ibm.websphere.personalization.resources.ResourceManager3 interface supports the process of dynamically updating, adding, and deleting resources (of type Resource) in the customer data store. This interface requires the following methods:

- void add(`Resource resource`, `ResourceContext context`)—adds a new resource

- void delete(`Resource resource`, `ResourceContext context`)—deletes the specified resource

- Resource getForUpdate(`String id`, `ResourceContext context`)—returns a resource having the named id (recall the ID is unique, thus there is only one)

- void syncdelete(`Resource resource`, `ResourceContext context`)—synchronizes any changes made (that is, making the changes permanent by storing them in the datastore)

Recommendation-Based Personalization

Rules-based personalization, as discussed above, requires a lot of work for defining the various criteria for delivering content.

Recommendation-based personalization relies on products external to the WebSphere application server to recommend content or to recommend content to visitors of your Web site. Recommendation-based personalization is powered by LikeMinds, which is not part of the WebSphere Portal Server Distribution.

Recommendation-based personalization complements and does not replace rules-based personalization. It uses collaborative filtering to capture subtle behavior patterns not captured in rules, and thus it adapts to changes without the need to create new rules. However, it can be used in the same page as rules-based personalization.

When defining new rules in the rule editor, the last option available under the rule type is Recommend Content. The rule structure for this rule type is shown in Figure 9-8. The content to be recommended is defined

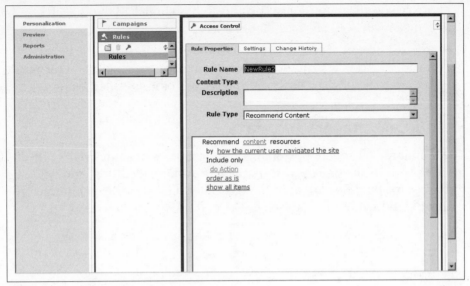

Figure 9-8 Defining a recommendation rule.

by a resource collection. The recommendation can be made by one of the following three options shown in Figure 9-9:

- **how the current user navigated the site**—this recommendation method is used to generate recommendation based on the user navigation sequence through the site. This method uses the LikeMinds ClickStream engine and is the default method. The

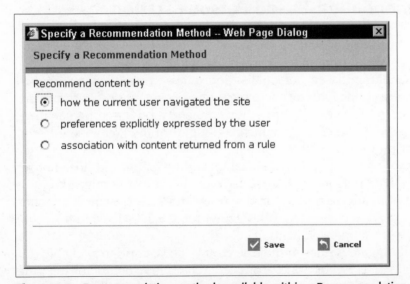

Figure 9-9 Recommendation methods available within a Recommendation rule.

ClickStream engine captures each navigation even within a bean called the Action bean.

- `preferences explicitly expressed by the user`—this recommendation method is used to generate recommendations based on the ratings users give to items. This method uses the LikeMinds Preference engine. Resources are rated using a Rating bean, and data is stored by LikeMinds for later use.

- `association with content returned from a rule`—this method generates recommendations based on market-based analysis. It associates resources that the user has interest in with items that other users have previously been interested in or have purchased. This method uses the LikeMinds Item Affinity engine. This engine makes use of transaction data being collected.

The action, sort, and limit output clauses of the rule are similar to other rules discussed above.

Summary

In this chapter we have reviewed the WebSphere Personalization solution. This solution relies heavily on content management solutions to store the actual content to be displayed based on personalization rules and recommendations. To implement personalization in your portal, you would need to get acquainted with the content management concept described in Chapter 11. In addition, content spots are deployed in the portal through portlets. You will learn to develop your own portlets in Part 3 of the book.

The next chapter describes the various facets of portal administration.

Portal Administration

The administration component of WebSphere Portal is the "ship's bridge," the area that allows you to control the layout, portlets, server, users, groups, and resources. The Portal Administration consists of five sections: portal user interface, portlets, access, portal settings, and portal analysis. Portal User Interface was covered in Chapter 7 Defining Portals and Pages Installing portlets will be covered in Chapter 17 Portlet Interactive Debug and JSR 168 Example. In this chapter you will learn how to customize and configure your portal, use Web Clippings, administer your search engine, and perform simple portal analysis.

Your Portal Settings

To configure your portal, you first need to access the administration page. After logging in using a user ID with administrative rights (for example, wpsadmin), click Administration in the right-hand corner. This will bring you to the main administration page.

One of the first tasks you want to do after you have installed WebSphere Portal (WP) is to configure your Portal Settings. Within Portal Settings, your first stop is to click Global Settings.

Global Settings

The first setting you need to review is the default portal language. Each user can change the selected language during the enrollment process or by selecting Edit My Profile. WP comes with support for numerous languages including Arabic, Czech, Danish, Dutch, English, Finnish, French, German, Greek, Hebrew, Hungarian, Italian, Japanese, Korean, Norwegian, Polish, Portuguese, Russian, Spanish, Chinese, and Turkish. But just in case you speak a dialect not covered (such as Swahili), WP provides the flexibility to add a new language.

You add a new language by adding it to the file and then copying and translating a resource bundle and JSP pages. Texts displayed in JSPs or stored in Java code are maintained in resource bundles. To add a resource bundle, copy and translate it, name it using the resource bundle naming convention, and then with the JDK Native-to-ASCII converter native2ascii, convert to Unicode. For any JSPs that have text directly imbedded in them, you have to translate them and store them in the appropriate location.

The next global setting you have to set is how the first page will be displayed. You have three options. Set it to the default page, the most recently visited page, or let the user make the choice at log-on. However, the latter two imply that you set the session preservation levels to 1 or 2.

The user's session state is defined by the session preservation level variable that is found in ConfigServices.properties. There are three values. If persistent.session.level = 0 then no persistent session information is stored in the database and no settings can be restored after login. If persistent.session level = 1, then the portlet states and portlet modes are stored but information regarding the last page is not. If persistent.session level = 2, then all session state information is stored.

The last two settings define portal-wide Find URL and enable transcoding of portlet content. Enter the search engine URL you want used when the user clicks Find and click Enable Transcoding of Portlet Content if you want this function to be operative.

URL Mappings

Another useful feature of WebSphere Portal is URL mapping. URL mapping allows you to create user-friendly URLs and map them to portal pages. For instance, using the default portal that is installed with WP, you want to directly reference My Finance page. The URL is `sandbox1.rigorconsultants.com/wps/myportal/!ut/p/.cmd/cs/.ce/7_0_A/.s/7_0_6S/_s.7_0_A/7_0_6S`, which you must admit is somewhat difficult to remember. With URL mapping, you can replace that URL with a URL little easier to remember such as `sandbox1.rigorconsultants.com/wps/myportal/finance`. URL mapping can also be used to map several different contexts to the same internal URL. You can externalize and provide different access rights for each new context.

URL mapping is quite simple. Under Portal Settings, click URL Mappings. In Figure 10-1, you can see that we have already added three new

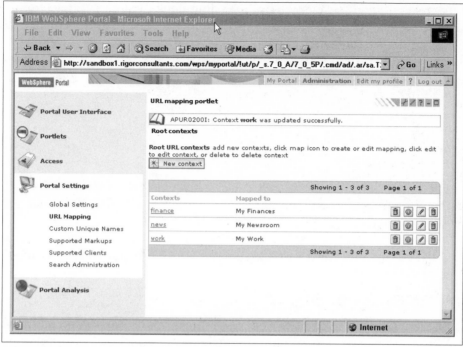

Figure 10-1 URL mapping administration.

contexts. To add a new context, click New Context and provide a label such as finance. If you wanted to add some more child contexts, you could then click Finance and create another context. However for simplicity, we are leaving it at one level. The label is appended to the portal prefix, which in this example is http://sandbox1.rigorconsultants.com/wps/myportal/. After you create the context, click the icon Edit Mapping and select the portal page that you want to be associated with the label and click OK. If there are too many pages, use the search capabilities. Choose the field you want to search (such as title) and then enter a value that will find the page you want to choose. If you need to change the label, click the icon Edit Label.

Custom Unique Names

Custom Unique Names allows you to associate a human readable name with the object IDs created by the portal. These object IDs are cryptic so that portal resources can be identified uniquely between different portals. Portal object IDs require human readable names since they are referenced when exporting or importing a portal configuration, linking to another portal resource, accessed by third-party vendor products, and so on.

To create or modify a custom unique name, click Custom Unique Names under Portal Settings. Select the resource type that you want to associate a custom unique name with. You can choose from the following:

- Pages
- Portlet Applications
- Portlets
- URL Mapping Contexts
- User Groups

Upon choosing the resource, a page will display the resource title, its unique identifier, and custom name. A search bar will also be displayed that will allow you to find the resource by title, description, keyword, last modified, unique name, or all available. If you click the Edit icon, you can enter a custom name for the unique identifier associated with the resource.

Supported Markups

Supported Markups is used to administer the markups associated with the portal. Upon clicking the Supported Markup portlet, you will be provided the options to add, edit, activate, show info, or delete a markup. When you add a markup, you need to give it a name, a MIME type (the Internet standard on how messages must be formatted), and default character set. More information on markups is provided in Chapter 24.

Supported Clients

This section is important if your portal supports unique devices. Supported Clients is where you define the types of devices that your portal supports. By default, most browsers and popular wireless devices are already supported. However, sometimes you want to add a unique device. To do so, you need to add support for the Sony Ericsson T310 device, which is done by performing the following steps:

1. Click Supported Clicks, which will display the Manage Clients page.

2. Click Add, and the Manage Clients page is displayed, with the Clients field.

3. In the User Agent field enter the name of the client surrounded with a period plus asterisk combination. This must match as close as possible to the user agent string the client sends in its request header. For T310, it is .*SonyEricssonT30/R201.*

4. Choose the markup from the drop-down box. These markups were defined in Supported Markups. For T310, it is wml.

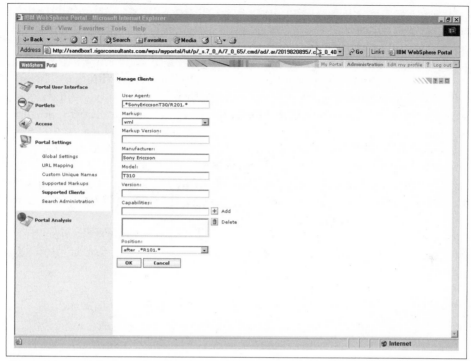

Figure 10-2   Adding a Sony Ericsson T30/R201 client.

5. Enter the markup version (optional). For this situation, leave this blank.

6. Enter the model or name of the client (optional). For T310 it is Sony Ericsson.

7. Enter the version associated with the model (optional).

8. Enter the capabilities of the client such as Frames or JavaScript. Click Add or Delete. Don't add anything since this is a dumb mobile device.

9. Choose the order from the drop-down box where the client will be entered in the client registry. The most specific user agent patterns should be placed close to the top. Add it before R201. Your screen should now look like the one shown in Figure 10-2.

Search Administration

WebSphere Portal provides a very sophisticated search and document collection capability. Basically you can create collections of various types of documents for other portal users to access. You create the collection using a very sophisticated search engine that supports a wide range of Internet search operators. Each collection is a set of documents that can be summarized and/or categorized. Collections can be automatically categorized using a predefined static taxonomy or can be user defined. Documents can be anything from HTML to Excel spreadsheets and then can be stored on local or remote sites. The collections can be scheduled and filters can be applied to exclude or include any documents. In this section, we will discuss how WebSphere Portal search and document collection, including administration, at a high level. Chapter 12 will discuss this in greater detail.

Under Manage Documents Collection, you can define Web sites or documents, which will be prefetched by WebSphere Portal Web crawler. WebSphere Portal will create indexes that will map key words and terms to the documents. These indexes are referenced by setting the `IndexName` parameter in the Document Search portlet.

In learning how to use this feature, create a document collection from information stored at `http://www.rigorconsultants.com`. Refer to Figure 10-3.

1. Click Administration ➪ Portal Settings ➪ Search Administration.

2. Under Document Collections, click Create Collection.

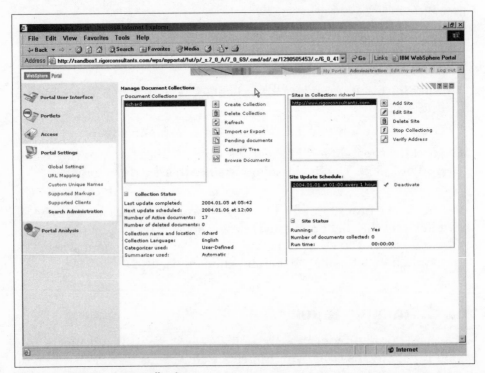

Figure 10-3 Creating a collection.

3. Specify directory path where you want the collection to be created. If you give it a name WP saves it as an appropriate directory under `<was_root>`. Call this collection Richard.

4. Specify Collection language; select English.

5. Select Categorizor. You have a choice of none, predefined, or user-defined. If you choose predefined, WP will automatically categorize your documents in over 2,300 subjects. Normally you will choose predefined; however, to show all the features you will choose user-defined. Note that when you choose user-defined, the Category Tree icon will appear on the Manage Documents Collection screen. It will not be there if you choose predefined.

6. Select Summarization. It can be either none or automatic. If you select automatic, WP will create a coherent narrative summary for each document, independent of language.

7. Check the Remove Common Words from queries box and then click OK.

Now, you have to create a custom categorization. Usually you set these up if you want to see all the documents associated with your product. In this case, you are going to create a category (surprise!) called WebSphere, which will find all Web pages that contain the word WebSphere. Refer to Figure 10-4 and perform the following steps:

1. Under Manage Document Collections, click Category Tree.

2. Under the root category, input **WebSphere Portal** as the sub-category name and click Create.

3. Expand the root tree on your left and highlight WebSphere Portal.

4. Under the Manage Category Rules Box in WebSphere Portal, click Create.

5. A new page will appear. In the Create Category Rule box, perform the following tasks:

   a. Input **WebSphere** as your rule name.

   b. Click Apply Rule to Content.

   c. Input **WebSphere** as the key word that you want to select documents with.

   d. Click Create.

6. Click the WebSphere Rule now appearing in the Manage Category Rules box.

7. Click Manage Rules.

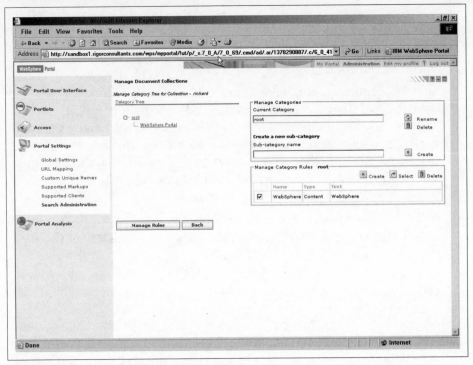

Figure 10-4   Creating a category tree.

Next, as seen in Figure 10-5, you need to specify from where documents are to be collected by following the steps given below:

1. Under Manage Documents Collection, highlight the collection.

2. Under Sites in Collection, click Create Site.

3. Enter the URL of the site. For this example, it is 5. Specify the level of linked documents to collect. This is the maximum number of levels the crawler will follow.

4. Choose number of linked documents to collect. This is the maximum number of documents that will be indexed.

5. Select the time to stop collection. The value of this field determines the maximum time the crawler will run in a single session.

6. Choose Stop Fetching a Document After (sec). This field defines the maximum time limit in seconds for completing the initial phase of the HTTP connection so that the crawler does not get stuck infinitely in a bad connection.

7. Select Link Expire After (days). Each document is time stamped. This field determines when documents will be removed from the collection.

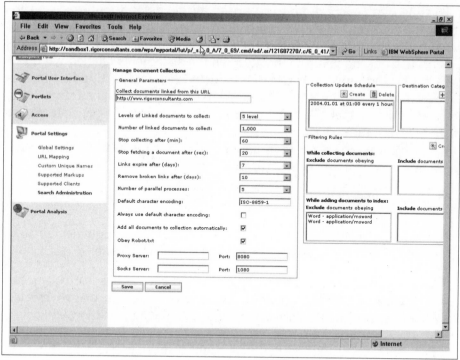

Figure 10-5   Manage Document collections.

8. Choose Remove Broken Links After (days). This field tells the crawler how many days to wait before removing documents that it found before but can no longer find because of invalid links.

9. Choose the Number of parallel processes. This is the number of threads that the crawler uses during a session.

10. Enter the default character encoding. If the crawler cannot determine the character set of a document, it uses this character set.

11. Click Always Use Default Character Encoding if you want the default character set at all times.

12. Click Add All Documents to Collection Automatically if you want the documents put in their destination folders and indexed, otherwise they are put in the pending documents folder until an administrator approves them.

13. Click off `Robot.txt` if you do not want the crawler to observe the restrictions specified in the `robot.txt` file.

14. Enter the proxy server and socks server if the crawlers uses on.

15. Click the Create button.

For this particular example, you used all the default values except Increase the Stop Fetching a Document to 20 seconds and you clicked Add all Documents to Collection Automatically. If you did not click Add all Documents to Collection Automatically, then the documents fetched would be held until an administrator released them by clicking Pending Documents (under Manage Document Collection). We also told it to obey `Robot.txt`, which is a file on Web sites that informs Web crawlers if a page should be excluded from the collection.

Next you need to create an update schedule, that is basically telling the robot how frequently to collect documents:

- Under Collection Update Schedule (as seen in Figure 10-5), click Create.
- Under Define Schedule choose the date, time, and frequency by clicking on the drop-down boxes and then click Create.

The schedule update will then appear in the right-hand side box. You can create multiple schedulers. In the schedule box you can see that we created a schedule to run the robot every hour starting at 1:00 P.M. on January 1, 2004.

After creating your scheduler, you might want to create some filters to include or exclude certain documents, Web sites, or files. In the example shown in Figure 10-6, we created a filter rule to exclude Word documents. To do this, perform the following steps:

1. Enter the rule name. Choose Word.

2. Choose your rule. Click Exclude.

3. Choose your file types. Choose Word files.

4. Click Create and click OK.

You may also want to add a destination category. If you do this all documents will be chosen based on your criteria and filters for this site will be associated with this category. To add a destination category do the following:

1. Under Destination Categories (as seen in Figure 10-5), click Add.

2. Expand the Category Tree, and click the sub-category.

3. Click Add to the List and click OK.

After you finish creating your site, click Save.

Now to verify whether it is working, under Manage Document Collections, click Start Collection, wait a few seconds, and click Browse Documents. You should see results similar to Figure 10-7.

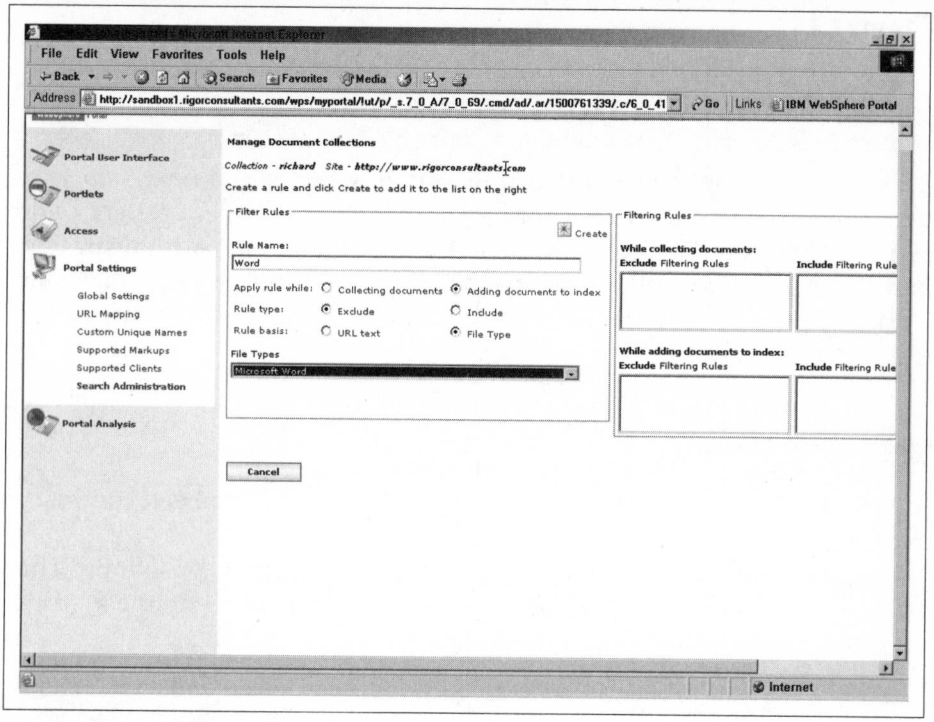

Figure 10-6   Creating a filter.

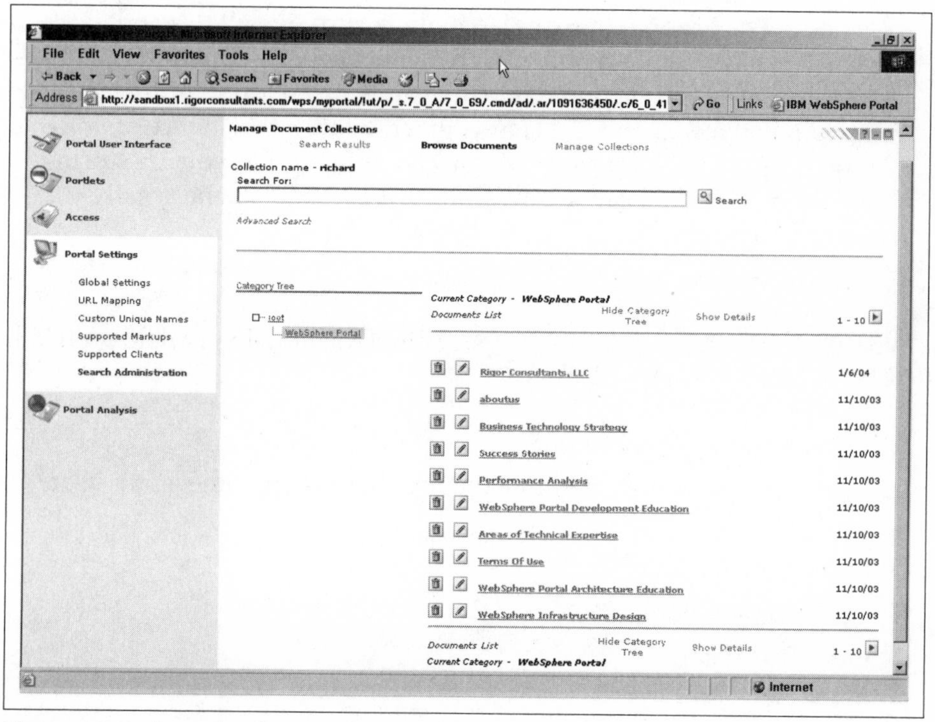

Figure 10-7   Browsing the Document Collection.

Portal Access Control

Once you have defined your default portal settings, the next step is to add some groups and users. Account information can be registered and managed by users themselves or an administrator. Under Administration, click User and Group Permissions. You first add the groups you want. Normally, you will have at least three groups: a group for administrators, managers, and users.

User and Groups

In WP V5, Manage User Groups and Manage Users have been combined into one portlet.

You have already defined the group for administrators, wpsadmin. This group was defined when you installed the program. Now define a group for general users called general as follows:

1. Click Users and Group.
2. Click the New Group button.
3. In the Name text field, enter a group name. We will call our group general. The group name can have blanks but like all IDs and password may contain only the characters a–z, A–Z, period (.), and underscore (_). The group name, like all IDs and passwords, can contain between 5 and 256 characters; however, the chance of your forgetting a 256-character password is quite high. If you are storing your names and passwords in an LDAP, the size will be greatly reduced because the schema fields are included.
4. Click the OK button.

Now click General and add a new user called Richard. Every field prefixed with an asterisk is mandatory.

1. Click the New User button.
2. Using the same rules mentioned above for group name, enter user ID.
3. Enter password.
4. Confirm password.
5. Enter first name.
6. Enter last name.
7. Enter the user's email (optional).

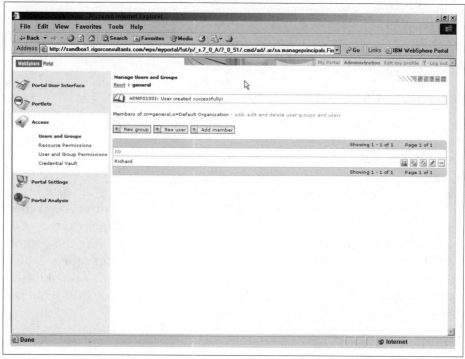

Figure 10-8   Creating and modifying users.

8. Enter his or her preferred language. This is the language that will appear on the portal pages after the user signs in.

9. Select OK.

In Figure 10-8, you will now see the user Richard with five icons associated with it. These will enable you to view the groups of which the user is a member, duplicate group or role assignments, edit a user, or remove a user. It is easy to understand the function of the icons for viewing and editing. The icons for duplicate group or role assignments allow you to choose another user or group and inherit its permissions. These are new for this version. Please note to remove the user from the group and do not delete it from the portal. To delete a user from the portal, find the user under all the authenticated user group, and click Delete.

Permissions

In WebSphere Portal, you can select, view, and modify only those resources for which you have access rights. Access rights are administered using the Resource Permission and the User and Group permission portlet found on the Administration page. They are usually defined by groups but can be defined by users. The access rights are stored in the default database; however, a third-party external security manager can be used. This will be discussed in greater detail in Chapter 20.

Resource, User, and Group Permissions

To assign permissions to a resource, click Resource Permissions on the Administration page. To assign permissions to a user or group, click User and Group Permissions on the Administration page.

If you clicked User and Group Permissions, you will see a page with Users and Groups (depending on the permissions set for your user id). If you click on users, you will see a user called anonymous portal user. When you click Edit, you can define what resources an unsigned user can access.

If you click User Groups, you get a list of groups including the default administration group. You will also see two virtual resources called all portal user groups that define all nonvirtual user groups and all authenticated portals, which are all known user groups. When you click Edit, you can define what resources a group can access.

If you clicked Resource Permissions, you will see the resource types listed in Table 10-1 on the page.

Click on the resource that you want to assign permissions. When you get to the resource, click Assign Access. You will see a page with a list of roles.

Roles

In WebSphere 5.0, access control changed with the introduction of roles. A role is a defined set of permissions associated with a resource (such as a page or a portlet). They enable access to specific operations within the WP such as viewing a page or modifying a layout. Roles use the convention Role@Resources since roles are tied to a specific resource. For example Manager + My Portal Page is defined as Manager@My Portal, see Figure 10-9.

There are seven different Websphere role types as shown in Table 10-2. They are hierarchical in the sense that each role from the top down has less permissions. For instance the top role is the administrator, which changes, reads, updates, and deletes any resource. The bottom role (excluding no role) is the user that can only view the resource it is associated with.

Roles can be explicit or implicit. You can explicitly associate a resource, such as a user, with a role. Alternatively, you can associate a group with a role and any members of the group will implicitly inherit the role. Practically, you would only associate roles with groups since the administrative overhead of associating a role with each resource will be huge.

Descriptions of these roles are shown in Table 10-2.

Table 10-1   Resource Permissions

RESOURCE	DESCRIPTION
Pages	Set permissions for pages within the portal. If you set the permissions for a parent page, the child pages will inherit them unless you specifically block a page
Web Modules	Set permissions for Web modules within the portal
Portlet Applications	Set permissions for portlet applications within the portal
Portlets	Set permissions for portlets within the portal
User Groups	Set permissions for user groups within the portal
URL Mapping Contexts	Set permissions for URL mapping contexts within the portal
Virtual resources	Virtual resources are resources that have access control definitions but are not actually represented in the portal. Here you can set permissions for the various virtual resources such as markups, portal settings, event handlers, and so on
WPCP Projects, WPCP Editions, WPCP resource Collections, WPCP Directories, WPCP Resources	Set permissions for WPCP resources within the portal

Table 10-2   Role Definitions

ROLE	DESCRIPTION
Administrator	Super-user. Can do everything including creating, configuring, and deleting resources. Administrator can also change the access control configuration
Security Administrator	Can create and delete role assignments for roles tied to specific resources
Delegator	Can assign users or user groups to roles
Manager	Creates, configures, and deletes new or existing resources for use by one or more users
Editor	Creates, and configures new or existing resources for use by one or more users
Privileged User	Can create new private pages, view portal content, and personalize portlets/pages
User	Can view portal content
No Access	Can do nothing

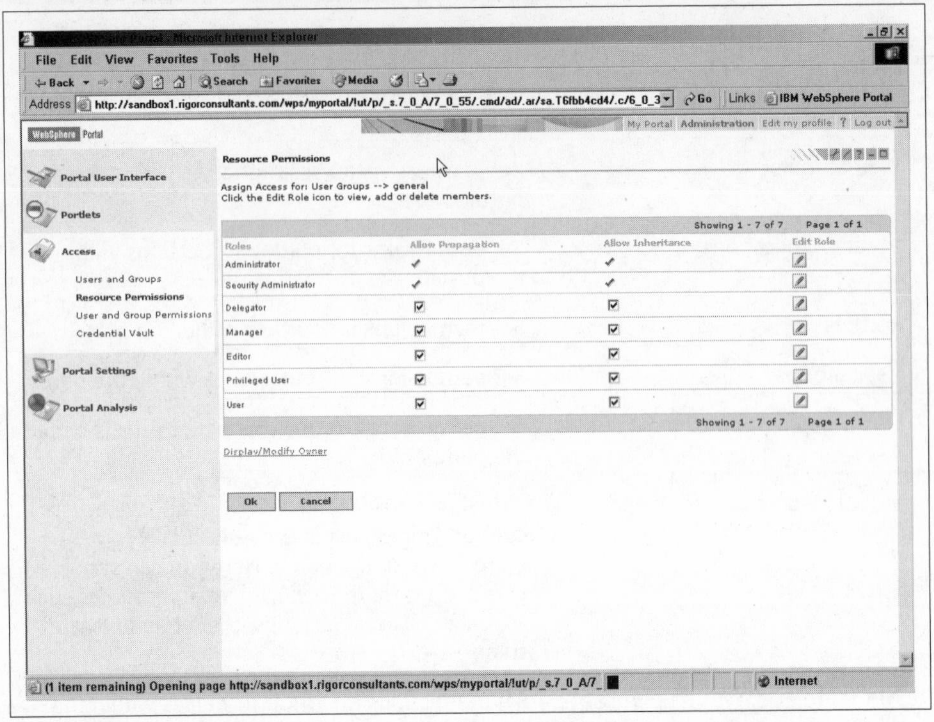

Figure 10-9 Assigning permissions and roles.

For a resource, you can determine which roles will allow propagation or inheritance with the exception of the administration and security administration roles, which always support both.

Inheritance and propagation are functions supported to reduce the overhead of administrating a large number of resources. Inheritance enables the role to inherit any permission from its parent while propagation allows the role to pass permissions to its children. If you uncheck the box, you are basically blocking the role from inheriting or propagating (based on which box you unchecked). However, the portal also provides traversal support. For Pages and URL Mappings resources, you can navigate to the resource even if you are blocked from the parent resources. You can view the navigation entities but you cannot see the contents.

When you click Edit Role when assigning a role to a resource, you can explicitly add or remove a user or user group from the role associated with the resource.

You can also change the ownership of a page by clicking Display/Modify Owner. When you create a resource, you automatically become the initial owner of that resource. As the owner you have permissions equivalent to the Manager role.

Another unique resource available to you is private page. Private page is created by Privileged User by personating a nonprivate page and optionally creating new private pages underneath it. Only the owner can access the private page.

Under User and Groups Permission, you can indicate whether a role is explicitly assigned or inherited. You click User if you want to define permissions for an anonymous user, since all other users are part of the group; authenticated user. To get a sense of how this can be done, do something controversial: allow any user to have a Manager role with the Web Clipping Portlet. To do so, perform the following steps:

1. Click User and Group Permissions under Administration page.
2. Click User.
3. Click Select Resource Type associated with anonymous portal user.
4. Click a resource type such as Portlets.
5. Click Assign Access associated with the resource such as the Web Clipping Editor Portlet.
6. Check the box associated with Manager.

Here is a more practical example. You are going to explicitly assign permission to everybody in the staff group to create, modify, or delete pages under My Portal.

1. Click User and Group Permission.
2. Click User Groups.
3. Besides staff, click Select Resource Type.
4. Click Pages.
5. Click Content Root.
6. Besides My Portal, click Assign Access.
7. Check the Manager Role box.

Credential Vault

If you are using a single-sign on package, sharing credentials amongst your portlets, or passing credentials to your back end, you will need to set up your Credential Vault. A Credential Vault is a repository that stores credentials such as private keys, user IDs, passwords, and certificates. Vaults are then segmented into two partitions: administrator managed and user managed. Vault slots are part of a vault segment and are used to store and retrieve credentials. For administrator managed, you access the Credential

Vault portlet on the Administrator page. With this portlet, you can do the following:

1. Add a vault segment.

2. Manage a vault segment.

3. Add a vault slot.

4. Manage system vault slots.

Chapter 20 will go into further detail on Credential Vaults.

Web Clipping

Under the portlets administration section, you will find a very useful feature called Web Clipping. Web Clipping allows you to quickly create a portlet that is composed of specific portions of Web site content. Of course, it can also be the content of a browser-based application so long as it can be accessed by a URL. The design concept of Web Clipping is to allow you to extract content/documents from sites that were designed to be displayed on desktops and allow the information to be displayed on other devices (such as PDAs) that have more display restrictions.

Web Clipping has certain limitations. Clipping decisions are based on the hierarchical format of the HTML tag structure so pages with JavaScript will cause irregular results. Also pages with Frames and double-byte character set support will not display correctly. Lastly old browsers such as Netscape Communicator and Navigator 4.7 or Internet Explorer 5.0 will also generate display irregularities. Even with these limitations, Web Clipping is very useful.

You also need to be aware of how the clipping portlets handle cookies. Normally clipping portlets preserve cookies set on the server side. If you need to preserve them on the client side, then go to Administration ⇨ Portlets ⇨ Manage Portlets ⇨ Modify Parameters and specify the cookie on the configuration parameter. For instance, if you wanted to capture the cookie name and password on the client side then you would set the configuration parameter to:

```
ClientCookies = name, password
```

You should be aware of a few other items regarding Web Clippings, which the WebSphere Portal InfoCenter goes into greater detail. Refer to this document if you need to change the restart settings, override preconfigure settings, or specify a clipping portlet caching timeout.

Now it's time to learn how to create a Web Clipping, see Figure 10-10. For example, extract a portion of the Service page of the Rigor Consultants, LLC Web site into a portlet (a little bit of self-promotion never hurts):

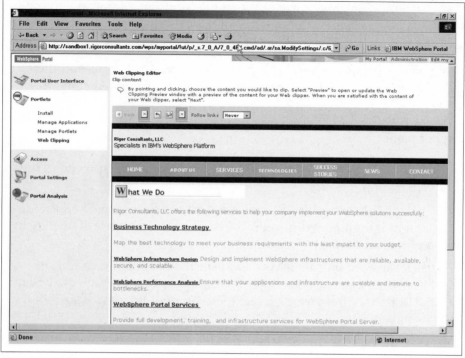

Figure 10-10 Web Clipping.

1. Click Portlets under Administration.

2. Click Web Clipping. You will see a page with a list of your Web Clippings where you can edit them or delete them.

3. Click New Portlet.

This brings you to the Add a Web Clipper function of Web Clipping Editor. Three fields need to be completed: the name of the portlet (rigor_clip), the fully qualified URL to clip (`http://www.rigorconsultants.com/services.htm`), and the description of the clip (Rigor Consultants, LLC Services). By selecting `I want to set titles and descriptions for other languages`, you can have the title displayed for different languages but this implies that you have enabled multilanguages.

If you want to select the entire page, then just select Next. However, if you need further control or security, click Advance Options. Advance Options allows you to do the following:

- Modify the clipping type. You can manually select the content type, keep all the content, or clip between specified texts. For this example, click HTML clipping and manually select the text.

- Configure for proxy server by clicking Modifying Firewall Options
- Modify authentication options or rules for URL rewriting. See Chapter 23 for further discussion.
- Remove JavaScript by clicking Modify Security Options and then clicking the check box Remove JavaScript from clipped content.

After you click OK in Advance Options, you will return to Add a Web Clipper page:

1. Click the Next button and the Clip content will be displayed in the Web Clipping Editor.
2. Click on the content for Rigor Consultant Services page and the content is highlighted in yellow. Click Preview and it will display in a separate window.
3. Click the Next button. If you don't see the Next, Back, or Cancel button, the content you clipped was too big and the page bled over the buttons. After you click Next, the Content Preview page is displayed.
4. Click the Finish button. A new portlet, clip_rigor, has been created, active, and ready to be added to a page layout.

Portal Analysis

WebSphere Portal provides a couple of portlets to help analyze and debug your portal. Clicking Portal Analysis ⇨ Frequent Users enables you to determine how many users are currently logged on. The other portlet, Enable Tracing, allows you to enable or disable trace logging for individual classes and entire packages.

To trace a class or package, you enter a trace string in the Append these Trace Settings field and click Add. This trace string is added to the shared/app/config/log.properties file. The trace values are written to the log file, which is usually stored in a file with a name similar to log/wps_2003.05.23-15.11.23.log (name changes based on the time stamp).

The trace string must conform to the grammar:

```
TraceString := <ClassString>(:<ClassString>)*
ClassString := <ClassName>=<type>=<state>(,<type>=<state>)*
ClassName := a java String
state := [enabled| disabled]
type := [all| low| medium| high]
```

This is used to identify the class (or set of classes) to apply the specified change. Either this ClassName may be an exact name or it may identify a point in the class hierarchy class by using the "*" wild card character. State indicates whether you want trace enabled or disabled for this class. For instance if you want to trace the World Clock Portlet, you would enter **com.ibm.wps.portlets.worldclock.*=all=enabled**. Remember that any changes to the trace setting are only valid for the current running portal. The type is specified at the discretion of the programmer imbedding the trace as low, medium, or high. If you set type to all, the all trace types will be included.

Summary

This chapter reviewed all the stations of the WebSphere Portal "bridge" and discussed some of the powerful new features available in WebSphere Portal V5.0 from URL Mappings, custom names, role permission to Web Clippings. Also covered were the powerful new features available for searching and document collection.

In the next chapter we will explore some of the powerful information management features that are available in Websphere Portal. You will learn how to use Websphere Portal Web Content and Document Management components.

Document and Content Management within WebSphere Portal

When you are implementing a portal (or any Web site), one of the key criteria is that content must be fresh, accurate, complete, and legitimate. To ensure this, you need a content management tool. WebSphere Portal provides IBM Lotus Workplace Web Content Management (ILWWCM). ILWWCM comes as a separate limited licensed product with WebSphere Portal 5.0.2.

WebSphere Portal also comes with Document Manager, a tool that enables you to create, edit, and share documents with other portal users.

This chapter examines the features of Document Manager and ILWWCM and shows you how to use these powerful WebSphere Portal tools.

Document Manager

Document Manager is new to WebSphere V5.0. It allows you to create and edit documents, store them, track changes and comments, and transfer them to an authorized person. A document is not just a text document but it can be a PDF, a word document, or a spreadsheet. Actually Document Manager supports importing over 100 document types. This tool is designed for business uses and entry level administrative uses. It is not a replacement for Microsoft Office or Lotus SmartSuite!

The first step in creating a Document Manager project is to log on as an administrator, click on the Document Manager tab, click Configure, and then click Create.

Enter Project Name and click OK. As shown in Figure 11-1, you will then see a number of fields. Do the following to each field:

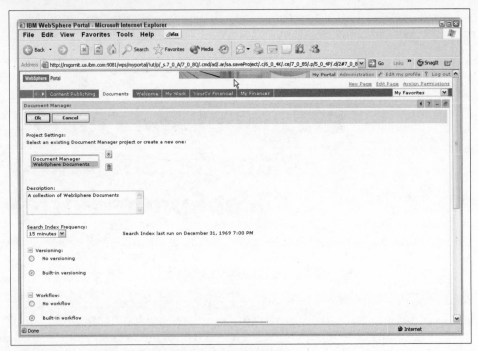

Figure 11-1   Defining a Document Manager project.

1. Highlight your Project Name.

2. Enter a description.

3. Indicate the search index frequency (the time to rebuild the search index).

4. Expand Versioning and select Built-in Versioning (if you want versioning).

5. Expand Workflow and select Built-in Workflow (if you want workflow) and select a default approver.

6. Expand Updates and select Enable Updates.

7. Expand Conversions and select Enable Document Conversions. This stores both the original document and the document converted to HTML. This is an important point, which will be discussed in more detail later.

8. Expand Editors and select Enable Portal Editors.

9. Select OK.

You, no doubt, now have some questions such as what workflow, versioning, and updates are.

Document Manager provides an optional simple workflow support. In the configuration, you assigned a group of reviewers. When an author creates or changes a document it appears in the task list of the assigned reviewer. Multiple users can have review authority but only one reviewer can approve it. If the document is approved then it becomes visible in the Document folder. If it is rejected then it goes back to the author task folder for modifications.

Document Manager also provides versioning. If versioning is activated, you are asked if you want to create a new version of the document you are saving. If you click OK, then a new version is created using automatic versioning numbering. If you want versioning, you must also check the versioning box when you create a document.

The Receive Updates option enables authorized users to see a document when it is created or updated. When a document is added or changed it shows up in your Updates folder.

After you create the Document Manager project, you need to assign access rights. In Administration ⇨ Access ⇨ Users and Groups, create two groups: wpsDocAuthor and wpsDocReviewer, and assign a user to wpsDocAuthor, and another user to wpsDocReviewer. You then click Access Control assigned to the Document Manager project (for you, it is WebSphere Documents) and associate wpsDocAuthor with editor role, wpsDocReviewer with manager role, and all authenticated portal users with the user role. Then you click Assign Access associated with Document Manager and add groups to the roles that they will be associated with. If you want some users to have read-only access to documents, then assign them the user role. The editor role is assigned to users who you want to have the ability to view and add new folders/documents or modify the properties of existing Productivity components within the current resource. The manager's role is like an editor who scans the above for all documents, deletes folders or documents within the current resource, and moves folders. An administrator can perform any operation.

Next log off as an administrator and log on as an author. Click Document Manager and then click New Folder. Give it a unique name, click OK, click the new folder, and then click Create New Document or Upload New Document.

As seen in Figure 11-2, if you click Create New Document, then you have the choice of three formats: Rich Text Editor file, Presentation Editor file, and Spreadsheet Editor file. Then choose whether you want versioning. The three productivity portlets provide you bare-bones Word Editor, Spreadsheet Editor, and Presentation Editor. However, you can also use a native editor. If you decide that you want to upload a file, Document Manager will convert the file into HTML for editing and displaying.

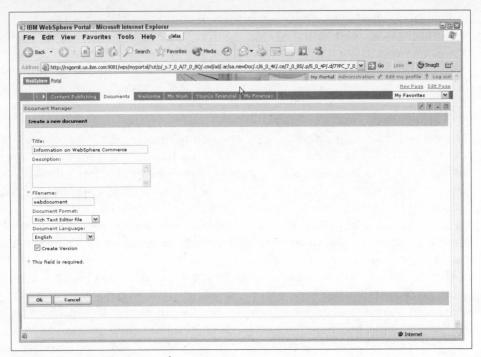

Figure 11-2 Creating a new document.

NOTE Because Document Manager converts the files into HTML, many of the original format features are not supported due to the limitations of HTML. Before using the productivity portlets, read the Document Manager InfoCenter section.

After you have modified your document, save and close it. Since Workflow is enabled, the document will be found under Tasks. All those who are authorized to see updates will also see it in their Update folder. Log off the portal as author and log back as a reviewer. When you click Documents, you will see under your Task folders documents to be approved. You can approve them by clicking Approve Change or reject them by clicking Reject Change.

Figure 11-3 shows the Documents information on WebSphere Commerce waiting to be approved under Tasks.

Now let's say you have documents in the Updates folder. Normally the document will be viewable for one day; however, if you click Edit on Document Manager you can choose how long to display the document (1 to 14 days) in the Update folder and which editors you can use.

If you want to edit and restore a specific version (obviously versioning is on), click Edit Document and click the Version tab. Click Activate Next for the version you want and it will be restored from archives.

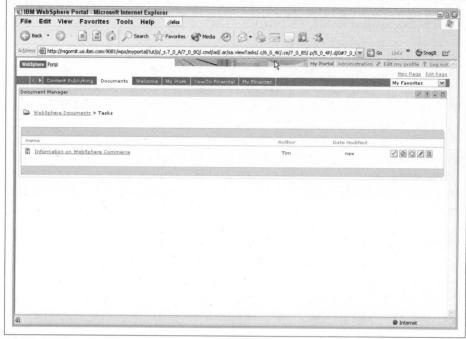

Figure 11-3 Document waiting to be approved.

WebSphere Content Management

ILWWCM provides full Web content management (WCM) services that facilitate integration of content that is accurate, authorized, easy to navigate, and complete. It is designed to replace WPCP. It provides a complete solution for creation, storage, management, and delivery of content. Services can be broken into three categories: Content Creation, Content Management, and Content Delivery. Don't get confused; ILWWCM is a Web content manager and not an enterprise content manager like DB2 Content Manager.

Content Creation enables you to develop and source content collaboratively using page design, distributed authoring, databases, and code. Content Management allows you to manage the integrity of the content and the process through staging, storage, workflow, versioning, and taxonomy. Lastly Content Delivery manages the delivery of content to the portal using features such as aggregation, syndication personalization, dynamic presentation, and caching.

The features of ILWWCM are best examined while performing a task, so, as an example, your task is to create and publish a sample site. You are encouraged to first review the material in Chapter 5, which discusses how to install ILWWCM, as you will be using the parameters defined in that chapter. (For instance, the context root used is wcm.)

Creating a Site

In your portal, you are going to have a page that consists of two portlets. The first portlet will list WebSphere Books, and the second will display the details of the book that you clicked in the first portlet.

You will now learn how to create a site using content templates and menu/navigator components and then integrate it into WebSphere Portal. A workflow will be created to ensure that the published content has been approved. In our example, four people are working on the project: Jim, Scott, Tim, and Ron. Ron is Content Approver, Tim is Content Editor, Scott is Page Designer, and Jim is Site Administrator.

Next, assume that you have started WebSphere that includes server1. Then go into the WCM administrative console as `http://localhost:9080/wcm/connect` aptrix. Make sure you using Sun JVM 1.3.1_09.

Setting Up Security

The first thing that you have to define for ILWWCM is the user's roles. At this time ILWWCM does not integrate into portals' access control; however, this limitation will be resolved very shortly.

First log in as an administrator. You will see in ILWWCM on your left side a tree that contains all the functions necessary to create, manage, and publish one or more sites.

To add a user, expand Home, expand Security and Workflow and then highlight Users and Group, as seen in Figure 11-4. For each user, do the following:

1. Click New.

2. Under Type, select User from the drop-down box. A window will appear like Figure 11-5 with a series of tabs that appear in almost every window for WCM.

3. Click the ID tab and enter the name and description. For this step, enter **Ron**.

4. Click the User tab and enter the password and e-mail address. Just enter the password: **password**.

5. Click the Profile tab if you want any objects associated with this use to be automatically categorized (which we don't for this site).

6. You click Security if you want to assign permissions to users directly. You can enable Live, Read, Write, or Edit, or Delete Access. Live permission enables the user or object to read an object rendered in

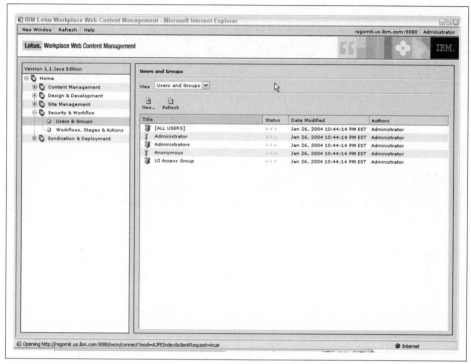

Figure 11-4 ILWWCM Security and Workflow Administration screen.

the Web browser. Selecting Delete Access automatically implies live, read, and write access. We don't recommend that you directly assign permissions to users; instead, define a group with the appropriate permissions and then assign the users to the group.

7. Lastly, you can click History, which tells you what was done to the object.

8. Click Close and then Save.

Repeat for user IDs Tim, Scott, and Jim. Next, create the groups to associate the user IDs with. Under Users and Groups, click New and choose Groups from the drop-down box and click OK. Then do the following:

1. Under ID, enter **Content Approvers**.

2. Under the Group tab, click Members and highlight Ron and click Move Right to add Ron to the group. Click OK.

3. Click Save, Close, and Refresh.

Repeat the above and create the groups Content Editors, Page Designers, and Site Administrators. Add Tim to Content Editors, Scott to Page Designers, and Jim to Site Administrators. Also add all the users and the groups to AprixUIAccessGroup so that they can log on to the Aptrix user interface.

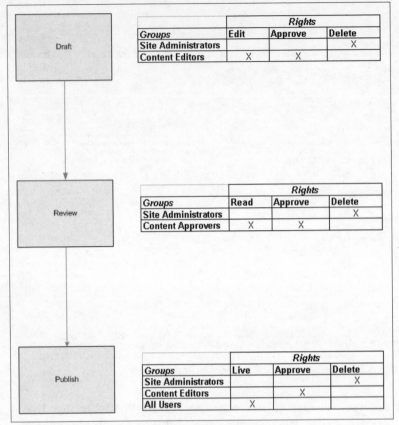

Figure 11-5   Workflow process with associated access rights.

Creating a Workflow

The next step is to create a workflow. A workflow is a defined process made up of stages for the purpose of determining if content should be published. Each stage has a list of users who can approve the content going to the next stage.

Figure 11-5 shows the stages of our workflow and the rights assigned to the stage. The Approve right enables a person to allow the document to proceed to the next stage.

Do the following to create the workflow:

1. Go to Home ⇨ Security and Workflow and highlight Workflows, Stages, and Actions.

2. Click New and click Stage from the drop-down box and then click OK.

3. Under Name, enter **Draft**.

4. Click Properties tab and then assign the rights, as shown in Figure 11-5.

5. Click Security tab and assign read access to AptrixUIAccessGroup and delete access to both Administrators and Site Administrators.

6. Click Close, Save, and Refresh.

Repeat for the Review and Publish stages. When defining the Publish stage, you must inform ILWWCM that it is the Publish stage by clicking on the Properties tab, clicking on Execute on Entering Stage, and selecting Publish (see Figure 11-6).

Next, you need to tell ILWWCM the order of the stages in the workflow. Under Security and Workflow, do the following:

1. Click Workflows, Stages, and Actions, and then click New.

2. Select Workflow from the drop-down box.

3. Name the Workflow **Workflow1**.

4. Click the Properties tab and then click Workflow stages and move them all to the right-hand window as seen in Figure 11-7. You define the order with the arrows on the right.

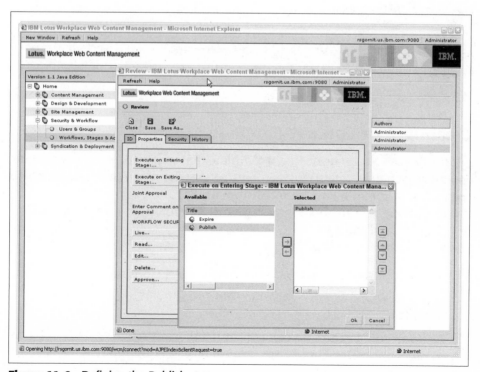

Figure 11-6 Defining the Publish stage.

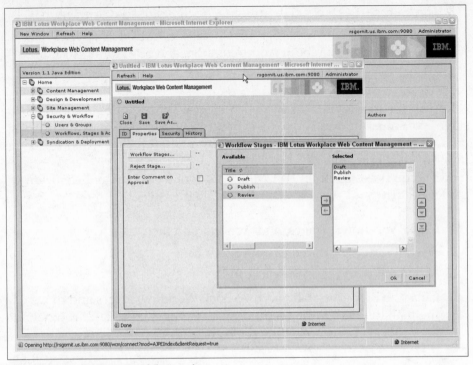

Figure 11-7   Defining Workflow order.

5. Click Security tab and assign read access to AptrixUIAccessGroup and delete access to both Administrators and Site Administrators.

6. Click Close, Save, and Refresh.

Creating Your Content Template

First, you need to create a content template that will be used by the content creators when they create new content. You can have as many as you want, each tailored for different types of content. For the particular Web site in this example, show the book title, a picture of the cover, some information on the book, and the book URL.

Do the following to create a content template WebSphere Books:

1. Expand Design and Development and Select Content Templates.

2. Click New and enter **WebSphere Books** as the name of content template.

3. Click Content Template tab.

4. In the Name field enter a description that will tell the author what information is needed such as [Enter Book Information].

5. Next click the Workflow button and select the workflow process associated with the template. For this particular workflow, it is **workflow1**.

6. Next click Component Manager and click Add. Enter BookTitle and select the type as text. Then go back and add BookCover, BookDescription, and BookLink as another component where picture is an image component, BookDescription is a Rich Text component, and BookLink is an HTML component.

7. Click Content Template and you will notice that fields for all the components have been added.

8. Click the Security tabs and give permissions to the appropriate people. Obviously, Page Designers will need delete access, Content Editors read access, and All Users will need live access.

At this point, you should be aware of the components that are used to build the template. You saw that ILWWCM supports not only text, but also various types of objects into a WCM object. Specifically, the following objects are supported:

- Text.
- Rich Text, which is Text with Web Content Management component tags. A Rich Text editor is included.
- HTML.
- File Resource—a file that is accessible from anywhere on the site or from syndication.
- Image file.
- Component-Reference—a reference to a library component.

Categorizing the Content

ILWWCM enables you to personalize content by defining content into categories. In ILWWCM you define a category tree that will enable you to display lists of content based on the category. For the example you have been using, you will define a very simplistic category tree with the taxonomy being WebSphere and the categories being Portal, Application Server, J2EE, and EJB. Do the following to create the category tree:

1. Expand Site Management, Click Category Management, and click New.

2. Select Taxonomy from the drop-down box and click OK.

3. Under the ID tab, give it a name and description. Call it **WebSphere**.

4. Under the Security tab, all security settings must be the same for the categories and the taxonomy. Give Site Administrators delete access, Page Designers and Content Editors read access, and All Users live access.

5. Click Close, Save, and Refresh.

Now under WebSphere, create the categories:

1. Expand Site Management, Click Category Management, and click New.

2. Select Categories from the drop-down box and click Next.

3. Highlight the Taxonomy with which the categories will be associated.

4. Under the ID tab, give it a name and description. Call it **Portal**.

5. Under the Security tab, all security settings must be the same for the categories and the taxonomy. Give Site Administrators delete access, Page Designers and Content Editors read access, and All Users live access.

6. Click Close, Save, and Refresh.

Repeat for the categories Application Server, J2EE, and EJB.

Creating Navigators and Menus

The next step in designing your site is to provide some sort of structure so that users can get around your site. ILWWCM provides navigators and menus. Navigators enable users to travel between areas of your site by showing the logical view of your site while menus are a list of related pages. A Navigator component consists of a start area, a child depth, a parent level, and a sibling value relative to the start area. ILWWCM is designed such that if you change your site using ILWWCM, your navigators and menus will reflect the changes. Navigators can also be used to create breadcrumbs or site maps. Breadcrumb shows a user where a page fits within his or her site while site map shows you the framework of your site.

Menus are usually just a list of hyperlinks on a page that, when clicked, will display the content. In ILWWCM, menus can search for content within matching site area, content templates, categories, key words, or any combination of the latter. Searches can also be based on category profiles. For the example in this chapter, you will create a menu that will list all the books that reference WebSphere in their title or description.

To get a sense of how WCM implements menu, create a menu that lists all the books on the site.

Do the following to create a Menu component:

1. Under Design and Development, go to Component Library

2. From the dropdown box, select Menu Component and click OK.

3. Enter ID Name. In this case, input **WebSphereList**.

4. Click the Menu Component tab.

5. Click Matching Content Templates and add select WebSphere Books.

6. Select Publish Date for the Results Primary Key and Name for the Results Secondary Sort Key.

You will then see a box for header, footer, and Component Design for Each Matching Content. The header and footer are for (surprise!) defining the header and footer. In these boxes, you place HTML for rendering the menus. The HTML consists of special ILWWCM tags used to display information about components.

In the header box, add `<h1>WebSphere Books</h1><br>`. This will provide a title to the menu page.

In Component Design for Each Matching Content, you enter your HTML code to display information about the Navigator component. In this case, enter:

```
<A HREF="<Placeholder tag="href"/>"><AptrixCmpnt context="autoFill"
key="BookTitle" type="content"/></A><br>
```

The placeholder tag can have multiple values. In this case, you instructed it to insert the URL of the matching content detail using Book Title as the link text.

Don't forget to set security; otherwise, nobody will be able to use these components. The Page Designer needs delete access, Content Editors need read access, and All Users need live access.

Page Design

The Page Design component accepts content and library components and enables them to be displayed in a formatted layout.

1. Under Design and Development, highlight Page Design and click New.

2. Under ID, assign a name. In this case, give it the name **WebSphere Page design**.

3. Click the Page Design tab and add the HTML code, as shown in Figure 11-8. Basically, all you need is to add straight HTML code with special ILWWCM that point to our content, site, or site area objects,

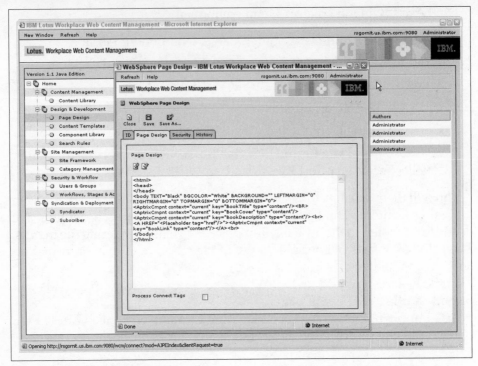

Figure 11-8 Page design HTML code.

as illustrated in Figure 11-8. The `<AprtrixCpmt>` tag is pointing to the components we defined from our content template. You can also click Import and bring in other saved HTML code. The contact parameter refers to whether the object is in the current site or whether it will be determined from the Name tag or the Menu, Navigator, or Taxonomy component.

4. Under Security, the Page Designer needs delete access, Content Editors need read access, and All Users need live access.

Building the Site

Now it's time to set up your site and define the content. Like categories, IL-WWCM enables you to define your site in a hierarchical manner by defining your site framework. The top node is your site, and the children are your site areas. For the example in this chapter, the WebSphere site will be very simple. It will consist of a WebSphere Area, your portlet. Do the following to define the site:

1. Expand Site and Framework and click New.
2. Select Site from the drop-down box and click OK.

3. Click ID tab and assign a name: WebSphereSite.

4. Select the Properties tab.

5. Click Content Template and highlight WebSphere Books. Click OK.

6. Choose Page Design and highlight WebSphere Page Design.

7. Under the Security tab, give Site Administrators delete access, Page Designers and Content Editors read access, and All Users live access.

8. Click Save, Close, and Refresh.

9. Click New and select Site Area from the drop-down box. Click Next.

10. Highlight the site area or site framework that is the parent and choose the link order, which specifies where the site area is below the parent.

11. Click the ID tab and assign a name. In this case, use the name **WebSphereArea.**

12. Select the Properties tab.

13. Choose Content Template and highlight WebSphere Books. Click OK.

14. Click Page Design and highlight WebSphere Page Design.

15. Under the Security tab, give Site Administrators delete access, Page Designers and Content Editors read access, and All Users live access.

16. Click Save, Close, and Refresh.

Adding Content

Up to this point, you have spent a significant amount of time defining the site, and the menus, security, workflow, and the content templates. Now, it's actually time to add content. Do this by performing the following steps:

1. Expand Content Management group and highlight Content Library.

2. Click New and select a content template. For this example, it is WebSphere Books.

3. Choose your site area and associate it with the content template. Expand WebSphereSite and move it to the selected area. Click OK.

4. Under the ID tab, enter a name. Call it **Portal Book 1.**

5. Click the Contents tab and enter the information in each of the fields. We added information on the WebSphere Portal book with a link back to Wiley's Web site. For our example, we added content about three WebSphere Books (including our own).

6. After you enter each document, click Save, Close, and Refresh.

You now need to view Content Library with Content by Workflow. You can now preview each document and edit it for correctness. If it is correct,

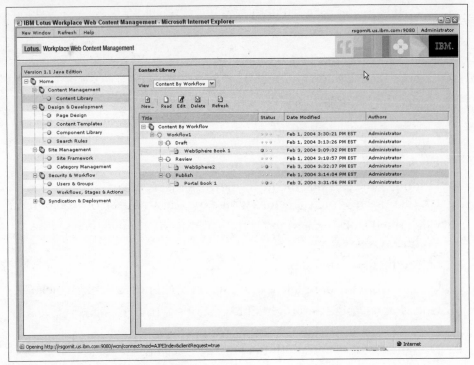

Figure 11-9   Content in various approval stages.

you click Read and then Next Stage. Content Editor will then review it and if he or she likes it will then authorize it to the next stage.

In Figure 11-9, you see that you have one document in the draft stage and one in the review stage and one ready for publishing.

Next, move all the documents into the Publish stage so that they can be accessible by WebSphere Portal.

Configuring WebSphere Portal

The next big question is, "How you see your content on WebSphere Portal?" Chapter 5 discussed installing ILWWCM; the Content Viewer portlet was installed. If you go to Administration ⇨ Portlets ⇨ Manage Portlets, you will see a portlet called Content Viewer, Java Edition. This portlet will enable you to see the content you are managing with ILWWCM.

Making a Copy of the Content Viewer, Java portlet

You will want to view content using two portlets. Since you are really using the same portlet twice on the same page, you need to make a copy; otherwise, the settings on one portlet will be the same as those on the other.

So to make a copy, under Administration ➪ Portlets ➪ Manage Portlets, highlight Content Viewer, Java Edition, click Copy, and highlight the copy version (it should stay inactive). Click Modify Parameters and then click the English button. Click Set Title for Selected Locale and change to something unique such as WebSphere Book Detail. Click Save, Close, and Activate. We repeated this for our other portlet WebSphere Book List.

Creating a Credential Vault

In order for the portlet to access the data in ILWWCM, it needs to authenticate against the ILWWCM server. This means that you need to set up a Credential Vault slot with the user ID and password that you use to log in to ILWWCM. You do not need to use the Credential Vault if you pass the portal user and it is defined in the ILWWCM or if you are using LDAP authentication and the user is mapped to the ILWWCM group.

As shown in Figure 11-10, create a vault slot called ILWWCM, set the vault slot to Shared, and enter your user ID and password.

Setting Up Your Portlets on a Page

The next step is to create a page and place your portlet on the page. Do so by performing the following steps:

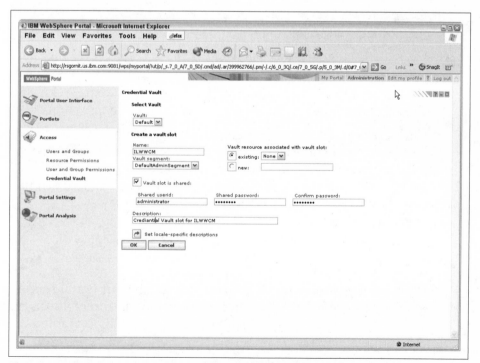

Figure 11-10 Setting up the Credential Vault for ILWWCM Viewer portlet.

1. Go to Administration ⇨ Portal User Interface ⇨ Manage Pages ⇨ My Portal and click New Label. Enter your Title. Call it **Books**.

2. Click the label Books and add a new page called WebSphere and click OK.

3. Click Edit Page Layout, add your portlets, and click Done. In this case, add WebSphere Book List to the left-hand column and WebSphere Book Detail to the right-hand column.

4. Navigate to the page, and you will see your two portlets with a message asking you to configure them.

5. To configure your portlets, click Configure.

   a. Enter the Portlet Display Title.

   b. Enter the ILWWCM server host name. For us it was http://192.212.131.100:9080. You need to use IP (Known issue). You need to use the IP address because if you use the same host name for both the portal and ILWWCM, then the session gets invalidated when you try to configure the WCM portlet. The workaround is to define multiple host names on client machines <etc>\host file.

   c. Enter the Web Content Management Server Path, which for us is /wcm/connect.

   d. Enter the Web Content Management Portlet Module, which is AJEPortletModule (see Figure 11-11).

   e. Click the Credential tab, click Override User Logon, and enter the Credential Vault Slot Name: **ILWWCM**

   f. Click the Links tab and choose Receive Links from Other Portlets and this Portlet so that the left portlet can send you an action.

   g. Click Content tab, select Content, and then click Edit under Content Component. The content site tree will appear. Choose the default content that you want to appear under the portlet. Choose Portal Book 1, as shown in Figure 11-12. If the Content tree 41is not displayed and you get an SHA1 error, then open the wpsV5-j-ilwwcm-Cportlet.war file using a Zip utility and extract AptrixClientApplet.jar to C:\Program Files\WebSphere\PortalServer\installedApps\wpsV5-j-ilwwcm-Cportlet_PA_1_0_69.ear\wpsV5-j-ilwwcm-Cportlet.war\ (or the equivalent location in your Portal Server) overwriting the correct AptrixClientApplet in the applet directory. The error was caused by the applet signature getting corrupted.

   h. Click the Edit button under Alternative Page Design and choose a path. A path must be given even if you are not using it.

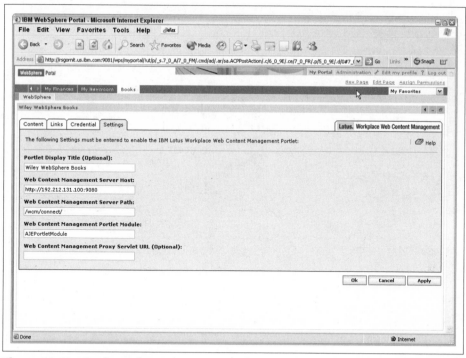

Figure 11-11   Portlet settings.

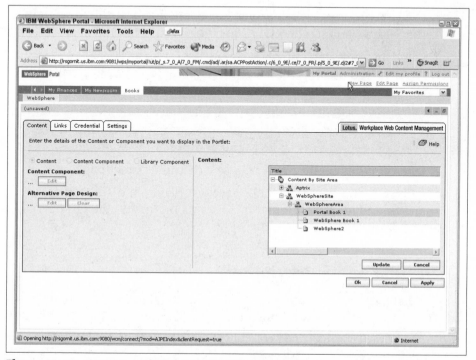

Figure 11-12   Content settings for ILWWCM Portlet Viewer.

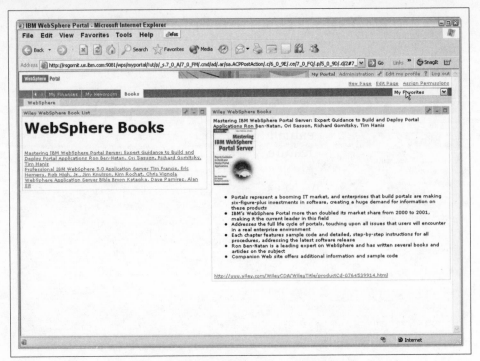

Figure 11-13 Content from ILWWCM displayed through WebSphere Portal.

i. Click Configure on the portlet on the left side. Use the same values for Settings and Credential as for the right portal.

j. Click the Links tab and click Broadcast Links to This Page, so a click the left portlet will cause a broadcast to the right portlet on the same page when an action is taken.

k. Click the Content tab and then click Library Component and Edit. When the Component Type tree appears, expand until you see WebSphereList. This is the Menu component we defined.

l. Click Default Context and choose a default context page.

m. Click OK and then you should see your content displayed as shown in Figure 11-13. If you click a menu link on the left portlet, the detail will appear on the right.

Syndication and Subscription

ILWWCM supports syndication and subscription. Syndication enables the WCM engine to replicate data from one engine to another so that distributed editing and separation of the development and production servers can be supported. Syndicator is the server making the objects available and

Subscriber is the server subscribing to the objects. WCM uses a syndication engine based on the Information and Content Exchange standard.

Summary

This chapter examined the WebSphere Portal Document Manager and ILWWCM, which will eventually replace WPCP. You saw that Document Manager provides some features for creating and managing documents; however, its productivity portlets have limited functionality for most users. With the advent of ILWWCM came a powerful, easy-to-use Web Content Manager that integrates into WebSphere Portal. Only a few of its features are examined in these paragraphs, which should give you a taste of its power. You are heartily encouraged to explore more.

In the next chapter, we will further explore how WebSphere Portal aids employee to employer facilitation by exploring WebSphere Portal's comprehensive collaboration and search components.

Adding Collaboration and Search Components to Your Portals

A portal is by definition a Web site that gives users a single point of access to a variety of resources and tools. In this chapter we focus on two specific types of tools that are of interest to users: collaborative features and search.

The need for collaborative features in a portal is obvious: Any portal, be it a B2B, B2C, or an intranet portal internal to an organization, can benefit from some sort of person-to-person interaction. Furthermore, collaboration is a key ingredient in promoting portal adoption within any organization, as it shifts existing stand-alone applications into the portal boundaries.

The explosive growth of the Internet has given rise to the notion of search engines. One of the main offerings of first generation portals such as Yahoo!® was (and still is) their search capability.

In this chapter you will learn how to make use of the collaborative features and the search capabilities that are provided with the WebSphere Portal Server.

Collaborative Features

The motivation for the collaborative features is to provide physically distributed teams with ways to work in a virtual office environment, through tools such as instant messaging, e-mail, calendar sharing, and information sharing in general. In a more general setting, such tools can be used to develop and support user communities, such as customers or business partners.

The WebSphere Portal Server collaborative components are shipped as part of the WebSphere Portal Extend offering. Namely these are Lotus Sametime 4.0, Lotus QuickPlace 3.0, and Lotus Collaborative Components.

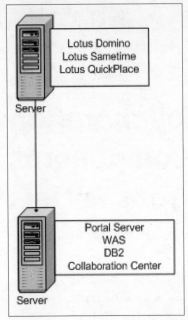

Figure 12-1   Minimal configuration for portal with collaboration.

Lotus Sametime provides a platform for instant messaging and application sharing. It is seamlessly integrated into the WebSphere Portal Server. Lotus QuickPlace facilitates shared virtual workspaces for sharing and organizing data, be it ideas, documents, or schedules. Lotus Collaborative Components provide a Java API to allow developers to implement customized portlets making use of features of Lotus Domino, Lotus QuickPlace, and Lotus Sametime.

The minimal configuration for the collaborative features is shown in Figure 12-1. It is advisable to place the Lotus Domino server and the Sametime and QuickPlace product on a separate machine, to avoid conflicts between the Lotus Domino server and the IBM HTTP server used with WAS.

In a production environment with large quantities of users, it would be more practical to place each product on a separate server (that is, use three different machines for the Lotus Domino, Sametime, and QuickPlace products).

Lotus Notes Integration

With Lotus Notes integration, WebSphere Portal Server provides access to mail, appointments, contacts, and tasks in Lotus. Since these are functions used extensively by nearly every user, placing them inside the portal increases the use and acceptance of the portal.

WebSphere Portal Server provides two different ways for Lotus Notes integration. On one hand you have the Domino Web Access (iNotes) portlet, and on the other hand the Notes and Domino portlet.

The former portlet uses Domino's own iNotes Web access, and consequently it has two distinct disadvantages: It requires browser support from iFrames, and it does not apply the portal's theme to the generated pages.

The Lotus and Domino portlet replaces five different portlets in earlier versions of the WebSphere Portal Server (for example, version 4.2). This single portlet can be configured to provide access to the following types of Notes databases:

- NotesMail—To access a Note Mail database
- NotesView—To access any view of any Notes database
- MyNotesMail—Access to a specific Notes Inbox, based on the login identity
- MyNotesCalendar—Access to a specific Notes Calendar, based on the login identity
- MyNotesToDo—Access to a specific task list, based on the login identity
- NotesTeamRoom—Access views of a Notes TeamRoom
- NotesDiscussion—Access to Notes Discussions

The Lotus and Domino portlet supports single sign-on (SSO) to the Domino server and the Notes database, with an LTPA token. This portlet has the following configuration parameters (accessible through the Manage Portlet entry in portlet administration), as shown in Figure 12-2.

- `NotesServer`—Host name of the Domino server where the Notes database resides
- `NotesDatabase`—Filename of the Notes database used as an information source for the portlet
- `VAULT_SLOT`—Name of the slot in the WebSphere Portal Credential Vault used for this portlet
- `NotesView`—Name of view to use, default is ($All)
- `PortletType`—One of the values NotesView, NotesMail, MyInbox, MyCalendar, MyTodo, NotesDiscussion, NotesTeamRoom.

Note that the default portlet type is NotesView, which is the most general one. While being the most flexible and powerful type, it also requires the most tweaking by users.

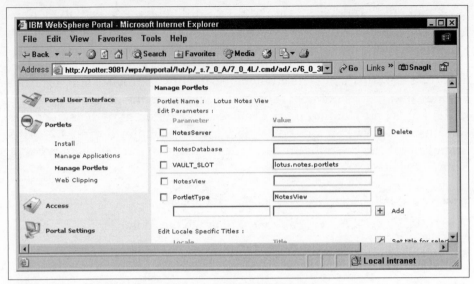

Figure 12-2 Configuration parameters for NotesView portlet.

Microsoft Exchange Integration

Understandably, WebSphere Portal Server has tight integration with Lotus products. Even so, it provides means for integration with Microsoft Exchange. Five different portlets are provided for Microsoft Exchange Integration:

- Microsoft Exchange Tasks
- Microsoft Exchange Notes
- Microsoft Exchange Contacts
- Microsoft Exchange Calendar
- Microsoft Exchange Mail

Each of these portlets provides a respective view into the Microsoft Exchange server.

Before using any of these portlets, users need to customize the portlet, by choosing a credential slot in which their user ID and password shall be stored, and by entering the details of the exchange server as shown in Figure 12-3.

Lotus Sametime Integration

Lotus Sametime allows teams to collaborate through instant messaging and online meetings. WebSphere Portal Server provides a Sametime portlet which allows users to launch the Sametime connect applet.

The Sametime portlet is shown in Figure 12-4. There are not a lot of configurable parameters for this portlet, just the host and port number. Once

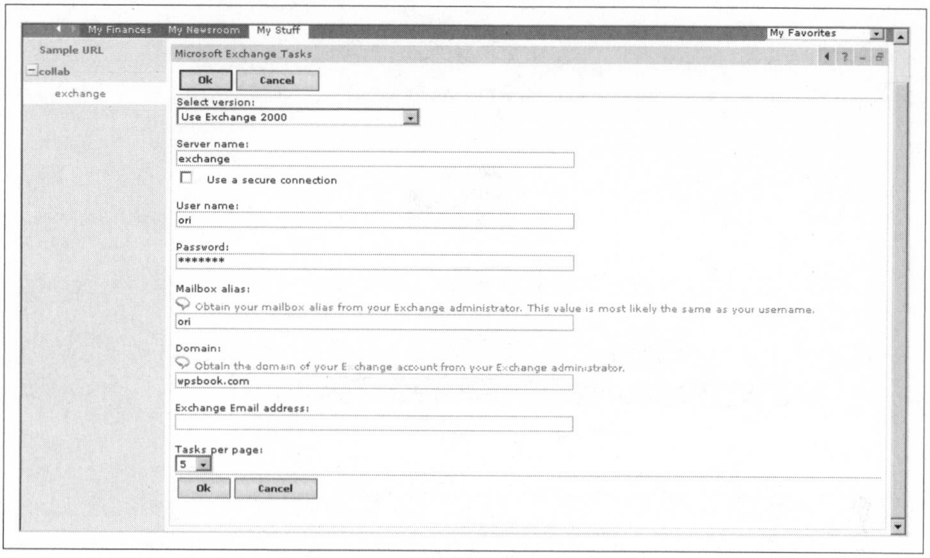

Figure 12-3   Editing Microsoft Exchange Tasks portlet.

you launch the Sametime connect applet, you need to log in to Sametime (as shown in Figure 12-5).

An important advantage of using Sametime through the portal is single sign-on. In other words, users need not log in to Sametime; instead their session with the portal is extended to Sametime, using the same username. In order for SSO to take place, you need to configure Sametime, by importing an LTPA token exported by the WebSphere Application Server.

Once logged into Sametime, users can send instant messages and start electronic meetings. The Sametime user interface is straightforward, and resembles most other instant messaging products. Each Sametime user has a contact list. The contact list typically contains individuals with whom the

Figure 12-4   Lotus Sametime portlet.

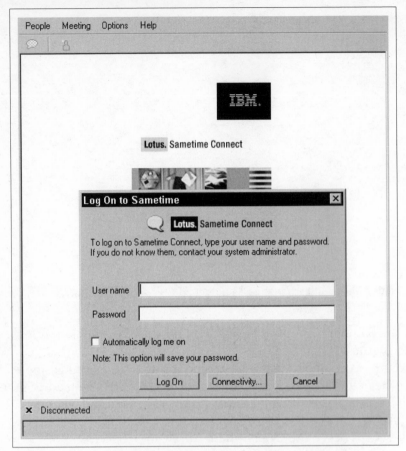

Figure 12-5 Lotus Sametime Connect, launched from portlet.

user intends to interact with frequently. Users are able to set their online status, to indicate whether they are available. Through the Meeting menu it is possible to initiate a variety of communication modes: text-based chat, audio, video, whiteboard, or application sharing. Once a meeting is initiated, other people (either from the contact list or outside of it) may be invited to join in.

Lotus QuickPlace Integration

Lotus QuickPlace (now known as IBM Lotus Team Workplace) allows teams to establish a team workplace to facilitate collaboration. Workplaces can store documents, discussions, plans, tasks, and resources.

QuickPlace provides tools for asynchronous collaboration, in contrast to the online and synchronous collaboration tools of Sametime.

Figure 12-6   Lotus QuickPlace portlet.

WebSphere Portal Server is shipped with two QuickPlace portlets. The QuickPlace portlet shown in Figure 12-6 is used to direct users to one or more QuickPlace places. Users may customize the portlet in the edit mode by specifying up to six different places. For each place the name and URI need to be specified. The inline QuickPlace portlet is associated with a specific place, which launches immediately within the same page.

When new places are created, users sharing the place are specified along with their respective access rights.

Microsoft NetMeeting Integration

WebSphere Portal Server includes a portlet for launching a Microsoft Net-Meeting client. The client is invoked through the NetMeeting Active-X component, which can be embedded into a portal page.

The NetMeeting portlet is not installed by default in the portal, and it is located in the netmeeting.war file. This portlet does not have any configuration parameters, as the user profile is entered through the NetMeeting interface.

People Finder

A prerequisite for any sort of collaboration is finding the people with whom you want to collaborate with. While that is a nonissue in a small to medium-sized organization, it is much more difficult within a larger organization.

WebSphere Portal Server is shipped with the People Finder portlet. It is not installed by default, but is available in the `PeopleFinder.war` Web module.

In order for the People Finder portlet to work, you need to have the Directory Connector Web application (LDAPConnector.ear) to be installed. This is automatically done by the Collaboration Center installation program. The Directory Connectors bridges between the portal server and your LDAP directory. The Directory Connector uses the data store of the underlying WAS (be it the default CloudScape, DB2, or Oracle) to store data.

The Directory Connector uses an XML configuration file to define the LDAP server to which the People Finder portlet connects to. The Collaboration Center installs a sample file `PFSampleConnection.xml` under the directory `CollabCenter` under the portal installation root. You may direct the Directory Connector to use another XML file by opening it at

```
http:// yourHostName/PFDirectoryConnector0
```

Here you can load new XML files, validate them (that is, make sure that they are well formed), and activate them. The XML file defines the connection settings, as well as configuration data relating to the data stored in the LDAP server.

The connection settings include the following elements, which must be set correctly for the People Finder portlet to work:

- hostURI—Fully qualified LDAP URI (that is, `ldap:://ldapServer:ldapPort`).
- baseDN—The starting point for any searches (that is, the topmost node from which a search will start).
- bindDN—Name of user used to access the LDAP server. If empty, anonymous bind is made.
- privateCredentials—Password, if applicable
- securityProtocol—`none` if anonymous binding, or `simple` if using a password.

The XML file indicates what LDAP attributes are exposed to the People Finder portlet. For each exposed attribute a meaningful name can be given. For example, the first attribute in the sample file is

```
<exposedAttribute label="DisplayName">
    <description/>
    <mappedAttrbiute>displayName</mappedAttribute>
    <type>String</type>
</exposedAttribute>
```

Figure 12-7 People Finder portlet.

The label controls the naming of the attribute in the People Finder portlet, and the `mappedAttribute` indicates the respective LDAP attribute.

The XML file can also specify exposed filters, custom queries, and recursive queries. Filters are used to limit the results given. For example, the default XML file includes a filter `objectclass=person` to ensure that only person records are retrieved. Custom queries are used to define queries that look at more than one attribute, for example searching in several name fields. Recursive queries allow traversing the directory recursively. In the sample XML file there is a query `ReportsTo` which recursively searches for the managers of a specific person.

Once the LDAP connection is configured, it is possible to use the People Finder portlet, by adding it to any page, as shown in Figure 12-7.

The People Finder portlet is customizable in several ways. To configure it click the wrench button on the portlet title bar. The configuration window is shown in Figure 12-8.

In `Configuration Basics` you can connect the People Finder portlet to connect the portlet to the LDAP directory by selecting one of the loaded XML configuration files, and to invoke the Directory Connector application. You can also choose what fields to display and for each such field its display format (for example, as a mailto link for mail addresses or as a Web page link for home pages).

In `Shared Elements` you can customize the business card display used by the People Finder portlet, as well as define sections where information shall be placed. Sections apply to both the Person Record and Advanced Search. Default sections are Contact Information, Current Job, and Background, and of course you can add, rename, or remove sections.

`Person Record` allows you to customize the Person Record display and the Organizational View. You can rearrange the fields, and place fields in the various sections defined.

The `Quick Search` and `Advanced Search` entries allow you to customize the search options, by choosing the fields available and the output fields.

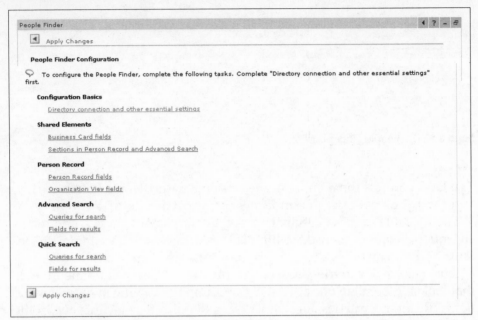

Figure 12-8 People Finder portlet configuration.

Collaborative Components

In addition to the out-of-the-box collaboration provided by the portlets described here, WebSphere Portal Server includes the Lotus Collaboration Components. These components are a set of Java APIs and taglibs for integrating the functionality of Lotus products into portlets. The Lotus products supported are Lotus Domino, Lotus Sametime, Lotus QuickPlace, and Lotus Discovery Server.

In contrast to the previous sections, the current one requires some basic understanding of JSP. In addition, to actually make use of the Collaborative Components, you need to develop and deploy portlets, which you will learn later in this book.

The Collaborative Components Java APIs are packaged in the file `cs.jar`, whereas the taglibs available are `people.tld` for people awareness and `menu.tld` for contextual menus.

The entry point to the Lotus Collaborative Components is the class `CSEnvironment`. To start using the Collaborative Components from within a JSP scriptlet, you need the following two lines of code.

```
CSEnvironment env = CSEnvironment.getEnvironment(request);
CSCredentials cred = env.getCredentials(request);
```

The first line initializes the Collaborative Components and sets the credentials for the currently logged-in user. The second line retrieves these credentials. The credentials are used to instantiate service objects. The following are the service objects available:

- Domino Service—Provides access to Domino databases
- DiscoverServer Service—Retrieves data from the Lotus Discovery Server
- PeopleService—Provides access to information about a person (aggregates information from Domino Service and DiscoveryServer service)
- Calendar Service
- QP Service—Provides access to QuickPlace places

Service objects are instantiated using the object `CSFactory`. For example, the following line of code instantiates a Domino Service.

```
DominoService ds = (DominoService)
              CSFactory.getService(cred, CSFactory.DOMINO_SERVICE);
```

In this case the Domino Directory server is specified in the `CSEnvironment.properties` file, located in the `Appserver\lib\config` directory under your Application Server installation root. It is also possible (though not advised) to use the `getService` method with a hard-coded server name and protocol.

Given a `DominoService` instance you can access Domino databases through views. For example, the following line of code retrieves a full view of a Lotus Domino address book called `names.nsf`.

```
ViewInfo vi = ds.getViewInfo("names.nsf", "($all)");
```

With the `ViewInfo` at hand, we can generate a list of names in the view. A typical use of names would be to provide people awareness. In other words, allow portal users to see whether other users are online and to interact with such users. To that end, the Collaborative Components provide the `people.tld` taglib. This taglib introduces the `peopleservice` tag. When you use this tag, a link menu is generated, allowing users to interact with the specific user.

The following piece of code combines the information extracted from the `ViewInfo` with the `peopleservice` tag to generate a list of names that can be clicked to initiate contact with the respective person. For simplicity, we retrieve only the first 10 names out of the address book.

```
<%
RowInfo[] ri = vi.getRowInfo("1", 10);
int i;
String values[];
String name;
for (i = 0; i < ri.length; i++) {
    values = ri[i].getValues();
```

```
        name = values[0];
%>
<br><peopleservice:person><%=name%></peopleservice:person>
<%
}
%>
```

Note that the `peopleservice` tag can be used directly without any use of the DominoService. For example, the following JSP shown within a portlet will provide a list of the authors of this book, with a menu for communicating with them. The actual entries shall be available only if the individuals can be located through the definitions of the `CSEnvironment` properties.

```
<%@ page language="java" import="com.lotus.cs.*"^>
<%@ taglib uri="/WEB-INF/tld/people.tld" prefix="peopleservice" %>
<%@ taglib uri="/WEB-INF/tld/menu.tld" prefix="menu" %>


<TABLE>
<TR><TD><peopleservice:person>Ron Ben-Natan</peopleservice:person>
</TD></TR><TR><TD>
<peopleservice:person>Richard Gornitsky</peopleservice:person>
</TD></TR><TR><TD>
<peopleservice:person>Tim Hanis>/peopleservice:person>
</TD></TR><TR><TD>
<peopleservice:person>Ori Sasson</peopleservice:person></TD></TR>
</TABLE>
```

If Lotus Sametime is enabled, each of these lines will show a status icon for the respective person, indicating his online status (for example, Active, Away, Offline). Clicking the person link will show a menu. The menu options depend on the system configuration. With Sametime enabled, it is possible to initiate instant messaging with the user, or add him to the Sametime contact list. If Lotus Discovery server is enabled, it is possible to send e-mail to the specified user, display the user profile, and find documents authored by him. If the People Finder portlet is available within the page, it is also possible to invoke it to show the person record or his location in the organizational view.

The `menu.tld` taglib is used by the `people.tld` taglib to implement pop-up menus. You may use it for any purpose other than collaboration, by using the `menu` tag and implementing JavaScript callback functions within your portlet.

Search Capabilities

With the huge amount of information stored both within the corporate intranet and the Internet, efficient searching is an important ingredient of the capabilities you expect to have in a portal.

IBM offers search capabilities in all versions of the WebSphere Portal Server. The Portal Server has a built-in search engine that supports full-text searching. The search engine allows users to specify the + and − query operators to indicate words that must be in the document or words that must not be in the sought document, respectively.

In order to keep down the search time, some preprocessing is required. To that end, the search engine building indexed document collections, which can then be searched.

To enable search in your portal, you need to prepare a document collection. The document collection is essentially the database of documents to be searched. The procedure for creating a document collection was covered in Chapter 10.

Searching a Collection

Once you have prepared a document collection, you are ready to provide search from within your portal. The Portal Server comes with a preinstalled search portlet called Document Search. This portlet is configured to use a specific document collection. Therefore, you need to create a copy of this portlet for each collection you want to use. You can avoid this only if you have a single collection, in which case you can configure the preinstalled instance of the portlet to use that collection.

To configure the portlet, follow these steps:

1. Log in to the portal as **Administrator**.
2. Enter the portal Administration section.
3. Go to Manage Portlets under Portlets.
4. In the Portlets list select the portlet Document Search.
5. Click Copy (on the right of the list).
6. Click Modify Parameters (on the right of the list).
7. In the IndexName field, type the path of the document collection, for example **C:\tmpindex**.
8. Click Save.
9. Click Activate (right of the portlet list).

Now you have a new instance of the Document Search portlet configured to use the index created in the previous section. To actually use it, insert this portlet into any page. Note that typically it would be at the end of the portlet list, since it was just created.

Once the portlet is placed within a container, it is ready to use. To search it, users need to specify text in the Search For field, and click the Search button. The portlet has an Advanced Search mode where users can limit the search

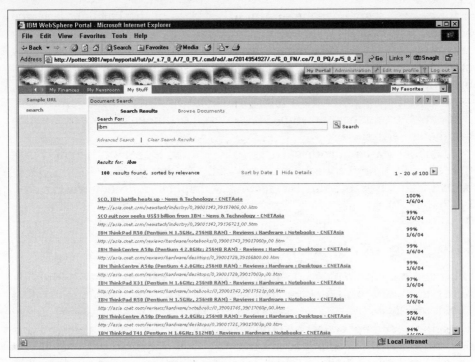

Figure 12-9 Sample Search Results.

to a specific part of the document (for example, Title, Keyword, Subject), and to limit document types. Figure 12-9 shows the result of searching for **ibm** within and index created from the URL http//asia.cnet.com.

Managing Taxonomy and Categorizing

In order to facilitate more efficient searching, the portal search supports categorization of documents. When documents are collected, they may be categorized. The basis for categorization is either a predefined static taxonomy or a dynamic user-defined taxonomy.

The predefined static taxonomy covers over 2,000 subjects in a variety of domains. You may customize this static taxonomy based on the needs of your organization. To that end, a Taxonomy Manager portlet is provided, which allows you to add synonyms to existing nodes, or to insert new nodes. New nodes may either be interior nodes, reflecting concepts and abstractions, or product nodes (reflecting specific products or terms relevant to your organization).

User-defined taxonomies have the advantage of being completely flexible, but the obvious downside is that you need to spend significant effort in defining the various categories. You will also need to define the associated rules.

For each document collection, you can define whether it uses a categorizer (see the document collection parameters as shown in Figure 12-9), and if it does whether it is predefined or user-defined.

When a categorizer is used, it eases the task of browsing through the documents, as well as the Advanced Search which allows focusing on specific categories.

Extended Search

The WebSphere Portal Extend ships with the IBM Lotus Extended Search product. It provides a search engine that is more powerful than the one integrated into the Portal Server. Extended Search supports a variety of data sources, ranging from text documents, and document repositories such as Lotus Notes, to fully blown RDBMS such as DB2 and Oracle.

Extended Search is installed separately from the WebSphere Portal, and once installed, you are able to define data sources. For each data source, Extended Search supports field mapping to allow common naming for fields that have different names in different subsystems.

IBM offers a portlet for using Extended Search from within the portal. This portlet allows the user to query using Web-style querying (using + and −), using GQL (Generalized Query Language, which is a language used by the Extend Search internally), or using native syntax when searching in databases (for example, SQL query syntax when searching an RDBMS).

Summary

In this chapter you learned how to use WebSphere collaboration and search capabilities within the Portal Server. These capabilities allow you to seamlessly integrate existing collaboration tools such as Lotus Notes or Microsoft Exchange into your portal. In addition, Lotus QuickPlace and Lotus Sametime, which are shipped with the Portal Extend offering, can be used to facilitate people awareness, instant messaging, and common workplaces. This chapter concludes this part of the book, and by now you should be familiar with the Portal Server basics. In the next part of the book you will learn how to develop new portlets. New portlets are required whenever you want to implement functionality that is not available within an existing portlet.

Portlet Development in WebSphere Portal

Extending Portal Functionality: Portlets

In this chapter you will learn about portlets, what they are, how they work, and how they are managed by WebSphere Portal. We will discuss the portal environment in which the portlets operate and some key portlet objects and services that portal provides. In addition, we will discuss the portlet life cycle, relevant aspects of the portal container, page aggregation and the differences between portlet applications and portlets, abstract and concrete portlets, and portlet instances. We will conclude the chapter with a discussion about the portlet event model and two-phase portlet processing.

What Is a Portlet?

Portlets are distinct, functional components of a portal. They are implemented in Java and are based on a well-defined portlet API. They are deployed through portal, packaged as a Web application, and are managed by portal through a portlet container. They process HTTP requests forwarded through the container and generate dynamic content in response.

From a user's perspective, portlets are functional entities represented on a portal page. A portal page typically contains several portlets that are arranged on the portal page in a grid of rectangles of varying size. Common examples of portlets are portal applications that show the local weather forecast, the stock ticker, or a user's email.

A portlet rendered on a page contains a title bar showing the title of the portlet, portlet navigation and behavior icons, and the dynamic content generated by the portlet. The content generated by the portlet is a portion (fragment) of the total markup that makes up the portal page. All portlets on the page contribute these markup fragments. The portlet navigation and behavior icons allow the user to minimize or maximize the portlet and to change portlet modes. We will discuss portlet modes and states in more detail later in this chapter. In addition to portlet content, the portal page consists of headers, banners, and a navigation area.

Portlets tend to implement very specific tasks with less page navigation and less complexity than a typical Web-based application may have. From a development perspective portlets are very similar to servlets. A servlet is an application within a Web application server. A portlet is an application within a portal.

From a deployment perspective portlets are packaged as J2EE WAR files and deployed into the portal environment using portal administrative utilities or administrative portlets.

Portlets benefit from functions and services of the portal, which provides a common user interface (UI) framework, a common user interaction model, single authentication, and common administration. Developers benefit by gaining access to supporting portal infrastructure for personalization, customization, and administrative functions such as security, access control, UI skins and themes support, and page layout.

Figure 13-1 shows the portal architecture. The portal receives the client HTTP request for a portlet page. Using the portal user and access control information the portlets on that page are determined. Each portlet is invoked to generate its content fragment in context of the requesting device type. Those fragments are aggregated in context of the device type and the

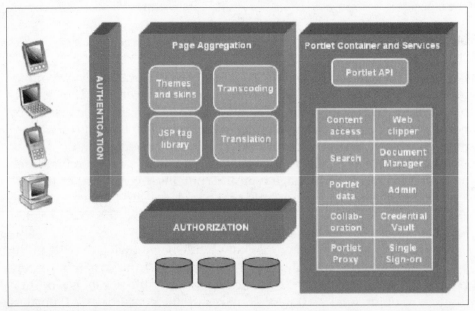

Figure 13-1 Portal architecture.

theme and skin definitions. The portlet container is the portion of the portal server that provides the runtime environment for the portlet.

The portal environment supports multiple device types and multiple markup languages. So, well written portlets that could be invoked from a variety of device types will respond with the appropriate markup and the portal will use markup specific aggregators to generate the correct markup response. These could be HTML, cHTML, or WML.

Portlet Container

Portlets run in the portlet container. The portlet container implements the portlet API and provides a runtime environment where portlets are instantiated, invoked, and destroyed. Through the API, portlets can access the logged-in users' profile, respond to events, communicate with other portlets, gain access to portal services such as the Credential Vault and content access service, persist application data, access portlet setting information, and access the portlet session object, the portlet request object, and the portlet response object.

WebSphere Portal provides two portlet containers that support two different portlet APIs. There is support for the javax.portlet API which is defined by JSR 168 and also support for the proprietary portlet API as it was defined by WebSphere Portal 4.1. All portlets written prior to Portal version 5 used only this API.

As shown in Figure 13-2, the portlet containers are components of the portlet environment. Portal itself runs as a Web application in WebSphere Application Server. The portal engine in that Web application talks to the portlet environment through the portlet invoker API and the information provider SPI. As portlets get invoked by the portal engine, they can communicate back to requesting portal information through the portlet API. The implementation of that API may need to gain access to the portal engine through the information provider SPI.

A portlet request will get directed to the correct portlet container depending on the implemented API of the portlet. The portlet then responds back with its markup fragment, which is passed back through the portlet container to the portal engine for aggregation.

Page Aggregation

One of the key differences between a portlet and a servlet is page aggregation. In a servlet the generated markup is solely the responsibility of the servlet to define and generate. In a portlet the portal aggregator is responsible for generating the resulting markup with assistance from the

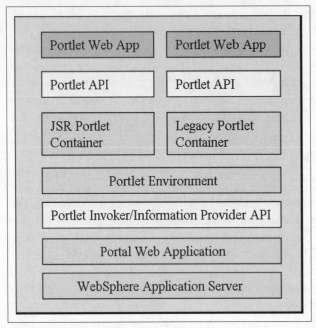

Figure 13-2 Portlet container.

portlets that are on the page to be rendered. Portlets have to be cautious that any generated markup is going to be in context of the markup generated by the aggregator and in context of the markup of other portlets on the page. For example, JavaScript that is generated by a portlet may conflict with JavaScript generated by other portlets contributing to the same portal page. Care should be taken to minimize the risk of name collisions.

Portlet Modes and States

Portlets inherit common UI behavior from the portal. One of these is the ability for users to select a portlet to be maximized or minimized. When maximized the portlet takes over the entire portal page. When minimized the portlet is reduced to just the title bar. This is known as the *state* of the portlet. The states that are allowed for a portlet are defined in the portlet deployment descriptor as a property of the abstract portlet.

The portal also provides infrastructure for common portlet behavior. Portlets often have requirements for runtime configuration and customization. Consider a portlet that shows the local weather. Typically we would expect that a portal administrator would deploy the portlet and provide portlet configuration. In this case, the portlet would probably be configured to specify the source of the weather information. The portal user would then need to customize the portlet to specify their location, probably in the form of a zip code or city and state. Then the deployed portlet can successfully execute for all portal users customized for each user but configured by an administrator for common settings such as the weather source provider. We will see later where to store this kind of information so that it is shared in one case but local to each user in another.

So, given this scenario and given that it is common behavior for many portlets, we would like the portlet container and portlet API to provide the common infrastructure to remove some of that work from the portlet developer and also to make sure that we have a consistent user interaction model.

The first commonality is the need for the portlet API to implement portlet modes. The defined modes are view, configure, edit, and help, as shown in the sample portlet control icons in Figure 13-3. All portlets support view

Figure 13-3 Sample portlet.

mode and this is the initial mode when the portlet is displayed. View mode is the main mode of the portlet. Configure mode is for shared portlet configurations as we discussed. Edit mode is for user-specific portlet customizations. Help mode is naturally for displaying portlet help.

The other common function requirement here is the need to make a distinction on the user's access rights not just at the portlet level but for the portlet and for modes within the portlet. We want to allow all users access to the portlet's view, edit, and help modes but give only portal administrators the ability to execute the configure mode of the portlet.

Keep in mind that it is up to the writer of the portlet to determine what, if any, configuration and customization processing needs to be accomplished, and implement it accordingly. Portal provides the infrastructure to associate access control permissions with portlet modes, to provide the Portlet API with mode support, and provides access to portlet settings, portlet application configuration parameters, and servlet initialization parameters. It provides access to a persistence store for user-specific application data. It is up to the portlet writer to determine which values should be shared and which should be user-specific.

Portlet Applications and Portlets

Portals are defined within the context of a portlet application. A portlet application may contain one or more portlets. Portlet applications are used for administrative management of a set of portlets.

Portlets are defined in the portlet deployment descriptor, an XML file that gets consumed by portal during the process of installing or updating a portal application. As we said before a portlet is deployed in a Web application so we also have a Web deployment descriptor for our portlet application. The Web application deployment descriptor defines one or more servlets and each of those servlet definitions is tied to a portlet definition in the portlet descriptor (via a mapping of the servlet id to the portlet href).

The portlet deployment descriptor defines portlet properties such as portlet display name, caching preferences, supported portlet states, modes, and markups, and portlet configuration parameters.

Portlet application properties are minimal and include the display name and an application unique identifier. A portlet application will have one or more concrete portlet applications defined in the portal deployment descriptor.

A concrete portlet application is differentiated by a set of Context Parameters that are shared across its concrete portlets. One or more concrete portlets are defined in the portlet deployment descriptor. They are mapped to the abstract (nonconcrete) portlets by the href attribute of the concrete portlet mapping to the id attribute of the abstract portlet. Concrete portlets are differentiated by a set of additional properties that include the defined language locales (and default), the portlet-language-specific portlet title, short title, description and keyword properties, and defined setting parameters.

Although the portlets and servlets have many similarities, there are some key differences. Portlets cannot issue a redirect or forward a request. Since portlets only contribute to the response markup output stream rather than write the entire response, they have some limitations in what markup they can generate. In general, portlets should generate only markup that could be contained within a table. A portal provides dynamic administration of portlets, and dynamic updates can be made to change the portlet settings, to copy portlets, and to delete portlets. Portlet applications are installed into a running portal.

Figure 13-4 shows the relationship of portlet application to Web application and the attributes associated with portlet applications, concrete portlet applications, abstract portlets, and concrete portlets.

While administrative tasks can target portlet application and concrete portlet applications, only concrete portlets are put on pages to be used by the portal user.

The portlet class that implements the required portlet API and provides the function of the portlet is defined as the servlet class in Web application deployment descriptor. Portlet application and portlet configuration information is linked from the Web descriptor and the implementation of the portlet is invoked from the Web descriptor servlet class.

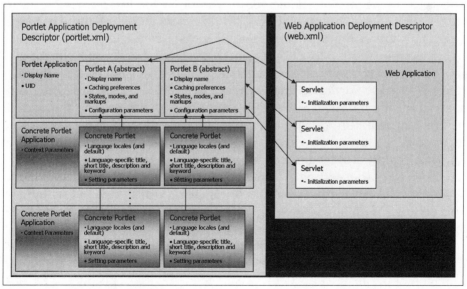

Figure 13-4   Portlet application.

To deploy a portlet to a portal there is a bit more work to do. We don't simply add a portlet to the portal. We define an abstract portlet in a portlet application and a concrete portlet in a concrete portlet application in the portlet deployment descriptor. We create a Web application and a servlet definition in a Web deployment descriptor and map the servlet to the abstract portlet. We package the deployment descriptors with the portlet class files and any associate resource files into a WAR file. Then we use the administrative tools in portal to deploy the WAR into portal. Under the covers, portal generates an Enterprise Application for the Web application and deploys the Enterprise Application to the Portal Application Server.

Portlet Life Cycle

Portlets have a life cycle similar to servlets. The portlet container is responsible to manage the portlet life cycle. As we would expect, portlets move through the life cycle by virtue of being deployed, being placed on a user's page, or having that page invoked by the user. They also progress as a result of configuration data that is associated with them.

As we see in Figure 13-5, an abstract portlet is loaded when the portal is initialized. Legacy portlets extend the Portlet API implementation class org.apache.jetspeed.portlets.AbstractPortlet, which in turn extends org.apache.jetspeed.portlets.PortletAdapter. PortletAdapter provides the default implementations for the methods referenced in Figure 13-5.

Prior to being first used the settings defined for the portlet are held in a PortletSettings object. With the association of the Portlet Settings object the portlet is referred to as a concrete portlet. We can use the administrative function of portal to create many copies of the abstract portlet, each with its own portlet settings and each referred to as a concrete portlet. Portlet settings are read and write properties. They can be dynamically modified either through portlet function using the portlet API or through administrative services. Modification of these settings is required to be performed while the portlet is in configure mode if using the portlet API. Portlet settings are persisted by portal. They are initialized with the concrete portlet setting parameters defined in the portal deployment descriptor. We can then have multiple concrete portlets defined with their own setting information allowing a single portlet deployment to provide tailored behavior.

Like many representations of the portlet in the life cycle described here, there is no ConcretePortlet object. Rather the concrete portlet is a representation of the abstract portlet when associated with a specific Portlet-Settings object.

Portlet Representation	Action	Portlet API invoked	Associated Portal Objects	Result
	During portal initialization	ExamplePortlet init() method		ExamplePortlet class loaded and represented as an abstract portlet
Abstract portlet	Prior to first portlet access	ExamplePortlet initConcrete() method	PortletSettings	PortletSettings object created and associated to form a new concrete portlet
Concrete portlet	User or Administrator places ExamplePortlet on a page.		PortletData	PortletData object created and associated to form a concrete portlet instance
Concrete portlet instance	User access a page with ExamplePortlet	ExamplePortlet service() method	PortletSession	PortletSession object is associated to form a user portlet instance
Concrete portlet	Administrator deletes portlet	ExamplePortlet destroyConcrete() method		
Concrete portlet	Portal is stopping	ExamplePortlet destroy() method		

Figure 13-5 Portlet life cycle.

When the portlet is placed on a portal page, a `PortletData` object is created for the concrete portlet. This `PortletData` object is associated with the concrete portlet to generate a reference to a concrete portlet instance. There can be multiple concrete portlet instances for each concrete portlet. The `PortletData` object is available for portlet writers to persist application data. `PortletData` must be written when the portlet is in Edit mode but can be read from all modes. `PortletData` can be scoped to either a user or a group of users depending on the scope of the page on which the portlet was added. If an administrator puts a portlet on a shared page then the users that have view access to that page will share the portlet data. Users that have edit access to the page will get user-specific portlet data. Likewise, if users put a portlet on their own page, they will have private access to the portlet data.

Finally, when a user accesses a portal page, user portlet instances for the portlets on that page are created. User portlet instances are the association of the user `PortetSession` object with the concrete portlet instance. Of course, there can be many user portlet instances for each concrete portlet instance. A `PortletSession` object is created for each user portlet when the user logs in to the portal. As we have discussed, for a new portlet deployment the deployment descriptors contain the information by which one or more abstract portlets and one or more concrete portlets are defined. When the portlet application is installed (deployed) to portal, the abstract portlet(s) are created, and when associated with their portlet settings their concrete portlet representations are also available. In this case, the portlet's `init()` and `initConcrete()` methods are invoked. Similarly, when the administrative function is used to copy a portlet a new `PortletSettings` object is created and associated with the new concrete portlet representation. This is performed by the `initConcrete()` method.

Portlet Configuration Objects

In the previous section on portlet life cycle we saw that changes in a portlet representation was marked by the association of a configuration object. They were `PortletSettings`, `PortletData`, and `PortletSession`. In addition, there was configuration defined in the portlet deployment descriptors that get encapsulated in other configuration objects including `Portlet ApplicationSettings` and `PortletConfig`. In this section we will take a closer look at these objects.

PortletConfig

In the Web deployment descriptor we can define a number of servlet context parameters. These configuration parameters provide the initial configuration for the abstract portlet and are available to all of its concrete portlets. This information is read-only and cannot be modified by the portlet. These parameters are encapsulated in a `PortletConfig` object and that object is passed to the abstract portlet on the `init()` method. Parameters are accessible using the `getInitParameters()` method on the `PortletConfig` object.

Figure 13-6 shows an example of a Web deployment descriptor with a configuration parameter named `persist_to_DB` defined.

PortletApplicationSettings

In the portlet deployment descriptor for each concrete portlet application we can define context parameters. Figure 13-7 shows an example portlet deployment descriptor with a portlet application setting parameter highlighted. There can be multiple parameters defined although only one is

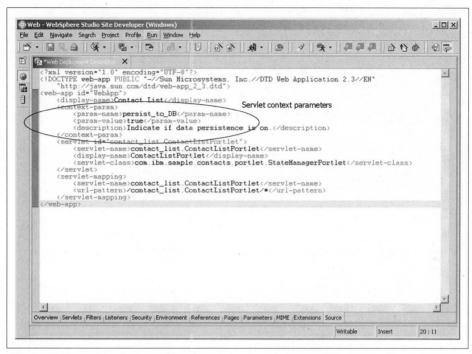

Figure 13-6   web.xml—context parameter.

shown here. When deployed these context parameters are encapsulated in a `PortletApplicationsSettings` object and are available to the portlet. This information is shared with all concrete portlets included in the portlet application. The `PortletApplicationsSettings` object can be read by the portlet in any mode but can only be updated in configure mode. It can be retrieved from the `PortletSettings` object using the `get ApplicationSettings()` method.

PortletSettings

Also in the portlet deployment descriptor, for each concrete portlet we can define a number of configuration parameters. Figure 13-8 shows the example portlet deployment descriptor with a portlet setting highlighted. There can be multiple parameters defined although only one is shown here. When deployed these configuration parameters are encapsulated in a `PortletSettings` object and are available to the portlet. This information is shared with all concrete portlet instances. The `PortletSettings` object can be read by the portlet in any mode but can only be updated in configure mode. It can be retrieved from the `PortletRequest` object using the `getPortletSettings()` method.

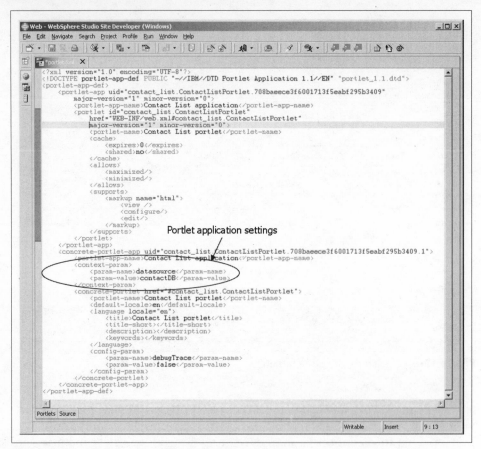

Figure 13-7   portlet.xml—portlet application settings.

The `PortletData` object manages persistent data for a concrete portlet instance. As we discussed in the section on portlet life cycle, when a portlet is placed on a portal page a `PortletData` object is created for the concrete portlet and then a concrete portlet instance is generated. The `PortletData` instance associated with the portlet can be retrieved using the `getData()` method of the `PortletRequest` object. Data is stored as name and value pairs, with the name represented as a string and the value as a serializable object. The `store()` method is used to persist the values set using the `setData()` method and as we discussed this can only be performed while the portlet is in edit mode.

`PortletData` can be scoped to either a user or a group of users, depending on the scope of the page on which the portlet was added. If an administrator puts a portlet on a shared page then the users that have view access to that page will share the portlet data. Users that have edit access to the page will get user-specific portlet data. Likewise, if users put a portlet on their own page, they will have private access to the portlet data.

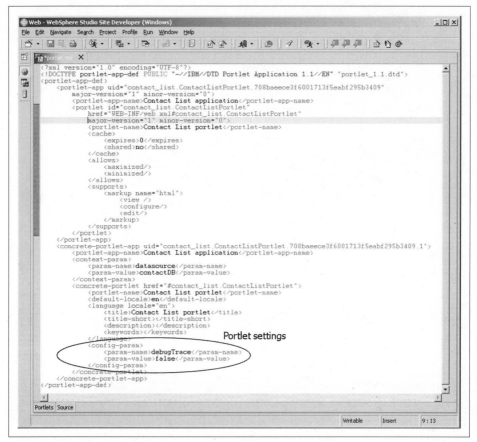

Figure 13-8   portlet.xml—portlet settings.PortletData.

PortletSession

A `PortletSession` is very similar to an `HttpSession`. Its function is to provide a facility to maintain transient user application data across multiple HTTP requests. A `PortletSession` object is created for all user portlets on authenticated pages when the user logs into the portal. Portlet user instances are differentiated from portlet instances (or other portlet user instances) by their `PortletSession` objects.

The `PortletSession` object is accessible from the request object using the `getPortletSession()` method.

A portlet placed on an unauthenticated page on the other hand will not have a `PortletSession` object assigned automatically. The portlet write can ask to have one created using the `getPortletSession()` or `get-PortletSession(true)` method. Portlets should verify that they have a valid session object by testing the results of the `getPortletSession (false)` method.

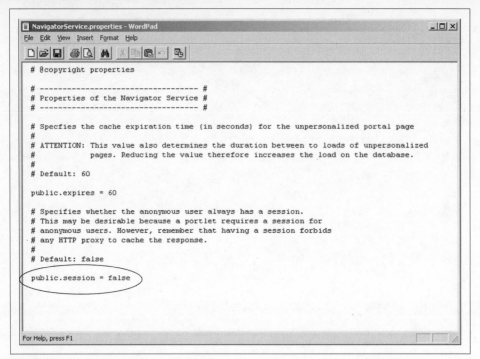

Figure 13-9 NavigatorService.properties.

A portal configuration change can be made to request a `Portlet Session` object also by default for portlets on unauthenticated pages. Keep in mind that the session object will be available when the portlet is executed but will be transient. That is, a new `PortletSession` object will be created by the portlet container for each request to that portlet. Change the `public.session` property to true in the `NavigatorService.properties` (see Figure 13-9) file to have the `PortletSession` object created for unauthenticated page portlets. The `NavigatorService.properties` file can be found in `<wp_root>/shared/app/config/services`.

As with `HttpSession` objects, good programming practice is to be careful and limit how much data is put on the session. Application memory requirements and database overhead if the session data is persisted can grow quickly and limit performance and scalability.

This is especially true in a portal environment as there are as many "application sessions" active as there are portlets on pages that the user is visiting during the current logged-on session.

Portlet Objects

There are a number of portlet objects that are defined by the portlet API. The following section describes the `PortletRequest`, `PortletResponse`, `PortletContext`, `PortletLog`, and `User` objects. These represent the key portlet objects in addition to the objects already defined in the section on portlet configuration (`PortletConfig`, `PortletSettings`, `Portlet ApplicationSettings`, `PortletData`, and `PortletSession`).

PortletRequest

The `PortletRequest` object provides the portlet access to HTTP request specific information and to portlet configuration information as well. The `PortletRequest` object is passed to the portlet as a parameter on the service method.

Through the `PortletRequest` the portlet can get and set attributes, can get parameters sent in the URI query string, and get the user agent information to determine client support information such as the markup name and the MIME types. As we have mentioned before, through the `Portlet Request` object, we can also retrieve the `PortletData`, `Portlet Session`, and `PortletSettings` objects. We can also get the current mode and state of the portlet.

PortletResponse

Like the `PortletRequest` object the `PortletResponse` object is passed to the portlet as a parameter on the service method call. Typically, the `PortletResponse` object is used to return output to the client using a `PrintWriter`. The `PortletResponse` is also used to generate encoded URI strings that can be used to reference the portlet, and associated portlet actions, in context of the portal.

PortletContext

The `PortletContext` provides the portlet access to some context information in the portlet container including providing access to portlet services. Application scoped resources, attributes, and initialization parameters are all available through the `PortletContext`. Portlet-to-portlet messaging is also possible through the `PortletContext` as well as access to portlet services and the portlet log.

PortletLog

The `PortletLog` object is available from the `PortletContext` using the `getPortletLog()` method. It provides common trace logging services for portlet writers. Messages can be informational, warning, or errors. Logging at various levels can be switched on/off by changing a properties file setting or, dynamically, through portal administrative function.

One of the important benefits to applications running in a portal is the availability of common services and function. Some of these we have already mentioned, such as the common user interaction model and common UI facades through portal managed themes and skins. Another common service is user authentication and authorization (access control). Both of these services are provided by the underlying portal services, and portlet developers can focus on the application requirements and use the portlet API to determine user information.

The `User` object represents the profile of the user logged in to portal. The `User` object can be retrieved from the `PortletRequest` object using the `getUser()` method. While the `PortletSession getUser()` method is available as well, it has been deprecated in the current version of Portal.

Portlet Event Model

Unlike a servlet, which does all request processing in the `service()` method, a portlet has two processing phases. The first phase is the event phase and the second is the rendering phase.

Various types of events can be handled in the event phase. These can be action events, message events, portlet settings attributes events, and portlet application settings attributes events.

The `Event` interface is the basis for all events that are managed within the legacy portlet container. Portlets that implement the appropriate listener interface for these events will get notified during the event processing phase.

The portlet container is responsible to signal all event listeners before any rendering phase processing begins. Events can be generated by other event listeners during their event phase processing. In this case the portlet container will deliver that, and any subsequent events, before event processing completes. In addition, no events will be delivered after the event phase completes.

The listener interface defines the methods that will get invoked during event processing. For example, action events will get handled by the `actionPerformed()` method and message events by the `messageReceived()` method.

The rendering phase is sometimes referred to as the content generation phase. The portlet `service()` method is invoked to handle this request. Portlets typically inherit from `PortletAdapter` and the `service()` method implemented in that class performs the following:

```
public class Sample extends PortletAdapter {

    public void service(PortletRequest request, PortletResponse response)
        throws PortletException, IOException {
      if(request.getMode() == Portlet.Mode.VIEW)
```

```
        doView(request, response);
    else
    if(request.getMode() == Portlet.Mode.EDIT)
        doEdit(request, response);
    else
    if(request.getMode() == Portlet.Mode.HELP)
        doHelp(request, response);
    else
    if(request.getMode() == Portlet.Mode.CONFIGURE)
        doConfigure(request, response);
  }


}
```

So, since our portlet typically would want to make a distinction in processing depending on the mode the portlet is currently in, typically the portlet writer will simply override `doView()`, `doEdit()`, `doConfigure()`, and `doHelp()` instead of `service()`.

All portlet state changes are handled during event processing. The `service()` method is called after the portlets event handling listener is invoked for portlets that are direct targets of the event. In addition, the `service()` method of a portlet is called when the portal page is refreshed. So, when a user is interacting with a portlet on a page, that portlet could have processing in both phases. Other portlets on the same page will have their `service()` method called for the rendering phase to generate response markup fragments for the entire page to be generated.

Typically, the portlet class is used as the event listener class as well. The event handling method has access to the `PortletRequest` object and can add attributes to the `PortletRequest` to be referenced during the rendering phase, as the `PortletRequest` object is the same between both processing phases.

Action Events

Action events are generated when an HTTP request is received by the portlet container for which an action has previously been associated with that clickable link on the page. So, when we create content for a portlet and want to generate HTML with a clickable link we will use the portlet API to associate with the URI for that link, an encoding that can later be interpreted as a specific action event. We will look at this API more closely in the following chapter.

Message Events

Message events are generated when a portlet using the portlet API to send a message to another portlet where both portlets are within the same portlet application and are on the same portal page. Also, a `Default-PortletMessage` can be sent to portlets not in the same portlet application to all portlets on the portal page. The portlet receiving the message event must implement the `MessageListener` interface. This API allows for portlet-to-portlet communication and the capability to create cooperative portlets. We will see in later chapters a more advanced framework for generating cooperative portlets.

Portlet Settings Attributes Events

Portlets that implement the `PortletSettingsAttributesListener` interface will be notified when changes to the attribute list on the portlet settings of a concrete portlet occur. Depending on the change that occurred, the method `attributeAdded()`, `attributeRemoved()`, or `attributeReplaced()` will get invoked.

Portlet Application Settings Attributes Events

Portlets that implement the `PortletApplicationSettingsAttributesListener` interface will be notified when changes to the attribute list on the settings of a concrete portlet application occur. Depending on the change that occurred, the method `attributeAdded()`, `attributeRemoved()`, or `attributeReplaced()` will get invoked.

Summary

In this chapter we discussed what a portlet is. We discussed portlets in context of a high-level view of the portal architecture and how portlets are managed by the portlet container. We started the discussion about portlet container and portlet interface differences between the legacy portlet API and the API provided that implements JSR 168.

We learned about portlet rendering and page aggregation and how portlets provide markup fragments that the portlet container uses to generate a complete markup page response. We looked at how portlets are defined within a J2EE servlet deployment and how a portlet deployment descriptor maps portlet-specific information to a servlet definition in a Web application deployment descriptor that is needed for portlet deployment. We looked that the portlet life cycle and saw how portlets take on different contexts as configuration objects are associated with the portlet.

Finally we reviewed the portlet event model and looked at how a two-phase processing design handles portal and user interaction events prior to the portlet rendering phase.

In the next chapter we will look at the portlet API in more detail.

Portlet Programming Model and API

In this chapter you will learn about the portlet Application Programming Interfaces (APIs) supported in WebSphere Portal. We will discuss in detail the API that exists for portlet development, starting with the existing API, which is based on Portal 5.0 and is referred to as the IBM Portlet API. We will discuss the Java Community Process portlet specification identified as Java Specification Request (JSR) 168.

JSR 168 is described as follows: "To enable interoperability between Portlets and Portals, this specification will define a set of APIs for Portal computing addressing the areas of aggregation, personalization, presentation and security."

We will review this specification in context of WebSphere Portal (version 5.02 or later) and compare this API to the IBM Portlet API.

The JSR 168 API

In the previous chapter we discussed portlets and the portal context under which they operate. Part of that discussion naturally relied on an understanding of the portlet API. The discussion in that chapter was based on the IBM Portlet API. In this chapter we will discuss the API based on JSR 168 and compare it with the IBM Portlet API.

Java Portlet Specification JSR 168 is a Java Community Process specification to provide a standard for interoperability between portlets and portals. The specification was approved in October 2003.

Portlet API in WebSphere Portal

As of version 5.0.2, WebSphere Portal provided support for the JSR 168 portlet API. However, at the time of this writing, there are functions and services provided in the IBM Portlet API that have not been defined in the JSR 168 specification. Therefore, the early implementation of JSR 168 API in WebSphere Portal does not contain all of the portlet functions available with the IBM Portlet.

As we mentioned in the previous chapter, WebSphere Portal provides two portlet containers to support the IBM Portlet API and the JSR 168 API. Portlets from both containers can reside on the same portal page. There is no difference to the portlet user as to which API is used as the administration and deployment of the portlets are the same. There are however functional differences in the API, which will be explored in this chapter.

Portlet API Comparison

In order to show an organized comparison between the two portlet APIs in total, we will review the API by functional area. The areas of the portlet API we will consider are:

- Portlet deployment descriptors
- Portlet processing model
- Portlet life cycle and configuration objects
- Portlet services and objects
- Portlet URI addressability
- Portlet window

Portlet Deployment Descriptors

In both portlet APIs, there is one portlet class instance for each portlet configuration in the Web deployment descriptor and one or more portlets are defined in a portlet application in a WAR file. And in both cases the portlet deployment descriptor (portlet.xml) defines the portlet application and portlets, while the Web deployment descriptor (web.xml) defines the associated Web application.

There are a few main differences with the JSR 168 portlet deployment descriptor. A change with the JSR 168 API is that a portlet is no longer a servlet. The portlet deployment descriptor is created in the format of an XML schema and it does not contain a reference to a corresponding servlet ID in the Web descriptor. As with the IBM Portlet API we can associate context parameters in the Web descriptor and retrieve them using the `PortletContext getInitParameter()` method.

In order to uniquely identify the portlet application, a unique identifier (UID) is added to the `<portlet-app/>` element. In the case of the IBM Portlet this was the UID attribute, for the JSR 168 descriptor this is the ID attribute. The default ID value, if not specified, is the WAR filename.

Within the portlet element definition the `<allows>` maximized and minimized do not need to be explicitly defined in the JSR 168 descriptor. The portlet must support the default window states. Custom state however will need to be defined here. Figure 14-1 shows this element set in the IBM Portlet descriptor.

```
<?xml version="1.0" encoding="UTF-8"?>
<!DOCTYPE portlet-app-def PUBLIC "-//IBM//DTD Portlet Application 1.1//EN"
    portlet_1.1.dtd">
<portlet-app-def>
    <portlet-app uid="com.ibm.sample.HelloWorldPortlet.30ef486bec"
            major-version="1" minor-version="0">
        <portlet-app-name>Hello World application</portlet-app-name>
        <portlet id="com.ibm.sample.HelloWorldPortlet"
            href="WEB-INF/web.xml#com.ibm.sample.HelloWorldPortlet"
            major-version="1" minor-version="0">
            <portlet-name>Mastering WP Sample portlet</portlet-name>
            <cache>
                <expires>0</expires>
                <shared>no</shared>
            </cache>
            <allows>
                <maximized/>
                <minimized/>
            </allows>
            <supports>
                <markup name="html">
                    <view />
                </markup>
            </supports>
        </portlet>
    </portlet-app>
    <concrete-portlet-app
        uid="com.ibm.sample.HelloWorldPortlet.30ef486bec.1">
        <portlet-app-name>Hello World application</portlet-app-name>
        <concrete-portlet href="#com.ibm.sample.HelloWorldPortlet">
            <portlet-name>Hello World portlet</portlet-name>
            <default-locale>en</default-locale>
            <language locale="en">
                <title>Hello World</title>
                <title-short>Hello World</title-short>
                <description>Say hello</description>
                <keywords>Portlet, World</keywords>
            </language>
            <language locale="de">
                <title>Hello Welt</title>
                <title-short>Hallo Welt</title-short>
                <description>Sagen Sie Hallo</description>
                <keywords>Portlet, Welt</keywords>
            </language>
        </concrete-portlet>
    </concrete-portlet-app>
</portlet-app-def>
```

Figure 14-1 IBM Portlet API descriptor.

```
<?xml version="1.0" encoding="UTF-8"?>
<portlet-app xmlns="http://java.sun.com/xml/ns/portlet/portlet-app_1_0.xsd"
    version="1.0" xmlns:xsi="http://www.w3.org/2001/XMLSchema-instance"
    xsi:schemaLocation="http://java.sun.com/xml/ns/portlet/portlet-app_1_0.xsd
                         http://java.sun.com/xml/ns/portlet/portlet-app_1_0.xsd"
    id="com.ibm.sample.jsr.api.HelloWorld.30ef486bec">
    <portlet id="Portlet_30ef486bec">
        <description xml:lang="EN">This is a Hello World portlet</description>
        <description xml:lang="DE">Dies ist ein Hallo Welt portlet</description>
        <portlet-name>Hello World portlet</portlet-name>
        <display-name xml:lang="EN">Hello World Portlet display name</display-name>
        <display-name xml:lang="DE">Hallo Welt Portlet Ausstellung Name</display-name>
        <portlet-class>com.ibm.sample.jsr.api.HelloWorld</portlet-class>
        <expiration-cache>0</expiration-cache>
        <supports>
            <mime-type>text/html</mime-type>
            <portlet-mode>VIEW</portlet-mode>
        </supports>
        <supported-locale>en</supported-locale>
        <resource-bundle>nls.HelloWorld</resource-bundle>
    </portlet>
</portlet-app>
```

Figure 14-2   JSR 168 Portlet descriptor.

Localization

The IBM Portlet API allows you to specify localized strings in the portlet deployment descriptor for the portlet title, the portlet short title, the portlet description, and the searchable keywords. You can see in Figure 14-2 in the example deployment descriptor that the concrete portlet is defined to default to English (en) but includes translated text to support English and German.

The JSR 168 API provides two mechanisms in the deployment descriptor to support localization. The first is the ability to specify localized strings in the descriptor for administrative value like the portlet display name and the portlet description. These elements allow you to specify an xml:lang attribute to allow you to specify multiple element definitions using different language strings.

You can see in Figure 14-2 the elements defining the description and display name in both English and German. Also you can see in the example that the portlet also defines the locales it supports using the <supported-locale> element.

The second mechanism allows for the localization of strings like the portlet title, the portlet short title, and the portlet search keywords in a resource bundle. The resource bundle is specified in the deployment descriptor using the <resource-bundle> tag. The resource bundle then defines the localized strings for these properties. The portlet has access through the PortletConfig object to the resource bundle at runtime.

The following shows the HelloWorld.properties file for this portlet.

```
#
# HelloWorld Resource Bundle
#
```

```
# English Resource Bundle
#
javax.portlet.title=Hello World Portlet
javax.portlet.short-title=Hello World
javax.portlet.keywords=Hello

#
# German Resourse Bundle
#
javax.portlet.title=Hallo Welt Portlet
javax.portlet.short-title=Hallo Welt
javax.portlet.keywords=Hallo
```

Portlet Content Types

The JSR 168 API allows the portlet container to define to the portlets the content types that the container supports. It also allows the portlet deployment descriptor to specify the content types that the portlet supports. Figure 14-2 shows a portlet descriptor where the supported content type is defined in the <supports> section.

Portlets must explicitly set the content type of their markup response. The RenderResponse setContentType() method is used. The content type specified must match one of the content types supported by the portlet, otherwise an IllegalArgumentException is thrown and the setContentType() method must be called before the response writer is committed. The getResponseContentTypes() method of the Render-Response object returns the list of supported content types. The method will only return content types that the portlet supports as defined in the deployment descriptor.

Portlet Class Definition

The Portlet interface defines the JSR 168 portlet class. Portlet can implement this interface directly or extend GenericPortlet, which implements Portlet and provides default method implementations.

By comparison, portlet classes using the IBM Portlet API typically extend AbstractPortlet and may also implement listener interfaces to participate in event model notifications.

Portlet Processing Model

Both APIs adhere to a two-phase processing model. A key difference in the JSR model is that the request and response objects are different between the two phases of processing. With the IBM Portlet API you could set attributes

Table 14-1   IBM Portlet API Events and Listeners

EVENT	LISTENER
`ActionEvent`	`ActionListener`
`MessageEvent`	`MessageListener`
`WindowEvent`	`WindowListener` **(depreciated in WebSphere Portal 5.0)**
`PortletSettings AttributeEvent`	`PortletSettingsAttributeListener`
`PortletApplication SettingsAttributeEvent`	`PortletApplicationSettingsAttribute Listener`
Render phase life cycle	`PortletPageListener`
Session life cycle	`PortletSessionListener`
Event phase life cycle	`EventPhaseListener`

on the `ActionRequest` object in the event processing phase and retrieve them from the `RenderRequest` object in the rendering phase. Using the JSR 168 API you cannot do this. Passing user instance objects from the first phase to the second needs to be done on the session object. However, you can set string parameters on the `ActionRequest` in the event phase and have them added to the `RenderRequest` object for the render phase.

Instead of the `service()` method being invoked as in the IBM Portlet API, the JSR 168 API defines a `render()` method. The `action Performed()` event listener method is replaced with the `process Action()` method. Also, during the action phase, the JSR 168 API allows portlets to redirect requests to other Web resources, a servlet for example.

The IBM Portlet API provided an event model to signal processing events such as a user action or a portlet message. As we mentioned previously, the action event listener method is replaced by a method on the portlet that gets invoked from the portlet container. The IBM Portlet API supports the events and associated listeners shown in Table 14-1. The JSR 168 API does not support events or listeners.

Portlet Modes

The view, edit, and help modes are the same between both APIs and can be invoked through the corresponding `doView()`, `doEdit()`, and `doHelp()` methods. The JSR 168 API provides the capability for portlets to define custom modes where configure mode can be implemented. Other suggested custom modes include about, preview, print, and edit defaults.

JSP Invocation and Tag Libraries

To invoke a JSP from the portlet render phase, the IBM Portlet API provided an `include()` method on the `PortletContext` object. The JSR 168 API provides a `PortletRequestDispatcher include()` method. We will define the `PortletRequestDispatcher` object later in this chapter. The following code example shows the invocation of a JSP using the JSR 168 API.

```
public void doView(RenderRequest request, RenderResponse response)
    throws PortletException, IOException {

  PortletContext context = getPortletConfig().getPortletContext();
  response.setContentType("text/html");
  String jspFileName = "/jsp/html/main_view.jsp";
  context.getRequestDispatcher(jspFileName).include(request,response);
}
```

In the JSP, the portlet tag library provides a `<portletAPI:init/>` tag that will initialize local variables to reference the `PortletRequest`, `PortletResponse`, and `PortletConfig` objects. Using the tag library with JSR 168 API the `<portlet:defineObjects/>` tag initializes variables for `RenderRequest`, `RenderResponse`, and `PortletConfig` objects.

Other taglib differences for creating portlet URI references and to encode namespace references are `<portletAPI:createURI/>` and `<portlet API:encodeNamespace/>` in IBM Portlet API and `<portlet:action URL/>` and `<portlet:renderURL/>` and `<portlet:namespace/>` in the JSR 168 API.

Render Parameters

Render parameters allow a portlet to store its navigational state. The `setRenderParameter()` and `setRenderParameters()` methods of the `ActionResponse` object allows portlets to set render parameters during an action request. The parameters will then be used for all render requests until the next action occurs.

The portlet should be written to store any information that is needed to successfully redisplay and use those parameters in the render phase. When the portlet encounters a new action, the render parameters are set again.

Portlet Life Cycle and Configuration Objects

In the IBM Portal API the `PortletSettings` object encapsulates the portlet configuration setting initially defined in the portlet deployment descriptor. It is through a `PortletSettings` object that the abstract portlet was

Table 14-2 JSR 168 Portlet

PORTLET REPRESENTATION	ACTION	PORTLET API INVOKED	ASSOCIATED PORTAL OBJECTS	RESULT
	Portlet container starts the portlet application			Portlet class loaded and instantiated
Portlet	Prior to first portlet access	`init()` method	`Portlet-Config`	Portlet is initialized
Portlet	User or Administrator places the portlet on a page		`Portlet-Preferences`	Portlet window

configured as a concrete portlet. There could be multiple concrete portlets for each abstract portlet. Similarly, an association of a `PortletData` object with a concrete portlet defines a concrete portlet instance.

When users edit the settings in a portlet according to their preferences, the settings are persisted using the `PortletData` object. There can be many `PortletData` objects associated with the same concrete portlet. Each `PortletData` object along with the concrete portlet comprises a concrete portlet instance.

The JSR 168 API does not define a concrete portlet or a concrete portlet application. Portlets are defined by a `PortletPreferences` object that encapsulates parameters in the portlet deployment descriptor. These parameters can be identified as read-only and in that case will be analogous to the IBM Portlet API `PortletSettings` object in that they can be modified only when the portlet is in configure mode.

Also since there are no concrete portlets, there are no life cycle methods such as `initConcrete()` or `destroyConcrete()` in the JSR 168 API. Table 14-2 shows this portion of the JSR 168 portlet life cycle.

The `PortletConfig` object in the IBM Portlet API provides access to the initialization parameters defined in the Web deployment descriptor. In the JSR 168 API, the `PortletConfig` object provides access to the initialization parameters in the portlet deployment descriptor.

Portlet Session

The JSR 168 API defines two session scopes, APPLICATION_SCOPE and PORTLET_SCOPE. Using APPLICATION_SCOPE allows the sharing of information between portlets. Any object that is set to the `Portlet Session` object using APPLICATION_SCOPE can be retrieved by any other portlet that is part of the same portlet application and that handles a request that is part of the same session. This sharing is among all components of the Web application so that you can share data between portlets or between a portlet and a servlet.

The code example below shows the JSR 168 API to set an attribute in the portlet session using APPLICATION_SCOPE.

```
PortletSession portletSession = portletRequest.getPortletSession(true);
MyAppBean myAppBean = new MyAppBean(portletRequest);
portletSession.setAttribute("app_bean", myAppBean,
  PortletSession.APPLICATION_SCOPE);
```

Portal Context

JSR 168 API supports a `PortalContext` that can be retrieved from the `PortletRequest` object. The `PortalContext` provides portal information to the portlet. This allows the portal vendor, portal version, and a set of portal properties to be defined by the portal and available to the portlet. The portlet can interrogate the portal information in the `PortalContext` and adapt accordingly.

Portlet Services and Objects

This section will discuss additional portlet services and portlet object differences between the two APIs.

Portal User Profile

In the IBM Portlet API the user profile information is accessed in the form of the `User` object, retrieved from the `PortletRequest` object. In an LDAP configuration the `User` object held attributes that mapped to an LDAP object, typically the `inetOrgPerson` LDAP object class.

In the JSR 168 API the user profile information (such as name, address, and userid) is stored in a map in the request and can be accessed through the Platform for Privacy Preferences (P3P) keys. In the JSR 168 API the deployment descriptor can define the user profile information that is to be made accessible. The recommendation from the JSR 168 specification is to use a list of standard P3P attributes but the portlet is not limited to that definition. The portal will map the requested user profile attributes to the supported profile attributes. The portlet can then determine which profile attributes are available by retrieving the map of attributes using the `getAttribute()` method of the request object for the attribute named `PortletRequest.USER_INFO`.

Portlet Caching

The two APIs use different mechanisms to implement portlet caching. The IBM Portlet API uses an invalidation-based caching mechanism where the portlet can explicitly invalidate the portlet cache using the `invalidate-Cache()` method on the `PortletRequest` object.

In addition, with the IBM Portlet API the portal queries a portlet to determine if the cache is still valid. The portlet deployment descriptor sets a cache time value for the portlet application. The value determines the length of time the cache is valid. The portal queries the portlet using the `getLastModified()` method to determine the time that the cache was last modified. By overriding this method the portlet can manage the portlet cache.

In Figure 14-1 you saw the cache value specifications in the portlet deployment descriptor for the portlet application. For this example, this entry looks like the following: The *expires* value of 0 indicates that the cache always expires. The *shared* value of "No" indicates that the portlet cache should not be shared between portlet instances. A value of −1 for *expires* indicates that the cache never expires and any other positive number indicate the number of seconds that the cache is to be valid.

The following xml is the cache definition from the portlet deployment descriptor:

```
<cache>
   <expires>0</expires>
   <shared>NO</shared>
</cache>
```

Caching is somewhat different in the JSR 168 as the portlet can attach an expiration time to the portlet definition. The JSR 168 API defines an expiration-based cache mechanism. As you saw in Figure 14-2 the `<expiration-cache>` timer value is set in the portlet deployment descriptor. It can be dynamically changed by the portlet using the `set Attribute()` method of the `RenderResponse` object referencing the `EXPIRATION_CACHE` attribute name.

The following xml shows the expiration cache timer value from the portlet deployment descriptor.

```
<expiration-cache>0</expiration-cache>
```

NOTE Sharing the cache entry across users is only possible in the IBM Portlet API. Dynamic fragment caching is not implemented for JSR 168 portlets in WebSphere Portal V5.0.2. Placing JSR 168 portlets on a page with other portlets that support caching results in incorrect page output. If you use dynamic fragment cache, make sure that there are no JSR 168 portlets on pages where portlets are cachable.

Property Broker

The property broker provided with WebSphere Portal and the IBM Portlet API is used to allow the dynamic integration of portlets. Portlets can be developed and deployed independently and then by using the property broker service, portlets can register for and receive notification of property changes.

Cooperative portlets declare, publish, and share data (properties) using the property broker, not with a specific portlet or portlets. Portlets that need to respond based on changed property values will associate actions with properties. This action processing in the portlet does not differentiate between a user initiated action event or an action that is the result of a property value change. In this way, portlets can behave in a coordinated fashion without depending on a close development–time association.

This service is not available with the initial implementation of the JSR 168 API.

Portlet Services

The IBM Portlet API provides a `PortletService` interface. This interface allows vendors and developers to make pluggable portlet services available to portlet developers. `PortletService` writers follow a few simple steps to create their service:

1. Define the service (class extends `PortletService`).
2. Implement the service (class implements `PortletServiceProvider`).
3. Optionally create a new service factory (if not using the predefined factories).
4. Register the service in the `PortletServiceRegistryService` `.properties` file in the `<wp_root>/shared/app/config/ services` directory.

Portlet developers can use the `PortletContext getService()` method to get the `PortletService` for the class of the given name. Two portlet services provided with this API are the `ContentAccessService` and the `CredentialVaultService`.

The `ContentAccessService` allows portlets to access remote systems or content from remote URLs, including URLs located on the other side of a proxy server.

The CredentialVaultService has two associated components. The credential service assists the portlet to handle basic authentication, LTPA Token authentication, and simple form-based userid/password login challenges from back-end systems being accessed on a user's behalf. The credential vault service is used to retrieve credentials from a secure, persisted store, a Credential Vault. This service can also pass Tivoli Access Manager or Netegrity SiteMinder single sign-on tokens to the back-end application in the appropriate HTTP headers.

Portlet services are not available with the initial implementation of the JSR 168 API.

Portlet Menus

The portlet menu service allows the portlet to add to the portal navigation menu, providing users easier navigation through the portal. This service is not available with the initial implementation of the JSR 168 API.

Portlet URI Addressability

References to a specific portlet, portal page, or portal resource must be encoded in the portal Web application URI. The IBM Portlet API creates a PortletURI object for this encoding, while the JSR 168 API creates a PortletURL object. In both cases you can set the portlet state or add parameters using these objects.

To encode the URI to reference portlet deployed resources, both APIs use the encodeURL() method on the PortletResponse object.

IBM Portlet API Addressability

The IBM Portlet API uses the createURI() or createReturnURI() method on the PortletResponse object to create a PortletURI object referencing the portlet. The createURI() method creates a PortletURI object pointing to the calling portlet with the current mode. The create ReturnURI() method creates a PortletURI object pointing to the calling portlet with the previous mode. The PortletURI toSring() method will return a URI string that can be used in the markup for a link (such as an action tag or href tag).

In order to associate a portlet action event with that URI, the Portlet URI can be modified to add an action event trigger. This is done by using the addAction(String actionName) method on the PortletURI object.

For example, you may want to have two buttons on a form input page on your portlet. One button is to "save" the form data and one to "cancel" to return back from the input page without saving. The following code segment shows the creation of the two URI strings.

```
// Create the URI with an action to save the form data
// Add the URI string to the request for use by the JSP
PortletURI saveURI = portletResponse.createURI();
saveURI.addAction("save");
portletRequest.setAttribute("saveURI", saveURI.toString());

// Create the URI to return to the previous (view) mode
// without saving. Add URI string for use by the JSP
PortletURI cancelURI = portletResponse.createReturnURI();
portletRequest.setAttribute("cancelURI", cancelURI.toString());
```

If the portlet class has implemented the `ActionListener` interface then that class's `actionPerformed(ActionEvent event)` method is invoked when the HTTP request associated with that URI is processed by the portal. The `ActionEvent` object that is passed when the `action Performed` method is invoked will contain the name of the action event, as is shown in the following code sample.

```
public void actionPerformed(ActionEvent event)
    throws PortletException {

  PortletRequest request = event.getRequest();
  String actionName = event.getActionString();

  if ("save".equals(actioName)) {
    // Retrieve the form data from the request
    // object and save it.
  }
}
```

This is the same name that was used in the `addAction(actionName)` method on the `PortletURI`. Using action names, you can distinguish the action event notifications that get processed by the portlet class and respond appropriately. The following `actionPerformed()` method shows how this is performed.

This same URI creation function is available through the portlet API JSP tag library. The following tags are available and behave as expected given the previous discussion. A required parameter "name" specifies the action name for the `URIAction` tag.

```
<portletAPI:createReturnURI />
<portletAPI:createURI />
<portletAPI:URIAction />
```

JSR 168 API Addressability

As we said, references to a specific portlet, portal page, or portal resource must be encoded in the portal Web application URI. The JSR 168 API creates a `PortletURL` to assist with this encoding. The `RenderResponse` object has two methods to create URLs, the `createActionURL()` method and the `createRenderURL()` method. The `createActionURL()` method will create an action URL while the `createRenderURL()` method creates a render URL.

There are two main differences to the portlet developer in the generation and handling of portlet URLs. The first is that with the JSR 168 API you do not have a single URL for the portlet to which you optionally add a named action event, which then triggers an event notification and listener. Instead, this API defines two different URLs, one for the action phase processing and one for the render phase.

The following code fragment shows the creation of two `PortletURLs` to handle our example to provide the links for a button to save the form data and a button to cancel without saving.

```
// Create the save URL for the page and add the
// URL string to the request for use by the JSP
PortletURL saveURL = renderResponse.createActionURL();
saveURL.setParameter("action", "save");
renderRequest.setAttribute("saveURL", saveURL.toString());

// Create the cancel URL for the page and add the
// URL string to the request for use by the JSP
PortletURL cancelURL = renderResponse.createActionURL();
renderRequest.setAttribute("cancelURL", cancelURL.toString());
```

The other difference between this approach and the IBM Portlet API is how the action is identified. Portlets can add parameters to the `Portlet URL`. Typically you would add a parameter (name–value pair) to an action URL to indicate the action to be performed. This name is analogous to the action name you added to the `PortletURI` in the IBM Portlet API. It is a name that you can later interrogate in the action phase's `process Action()` method.

The JSP tag library with the JSR 168 API defines custom tags that provide the creation of `PortletURLs` in the JSP. The tags are `<portlet:action URL/>` and `<portlet:renderURL/>`.

```
public void processAction(ActionRequest request,
    ActionResponse response) throws PortletException, IOException {

    String actionName = request.getParameter("action");
    if ("save".equals(actionName)) {
```

```
     // Retrieve the form data from the request
     // object and save it.
   }
 }
```

Portlet Window

Both APIs provide maximize, minimize, and normal window states. The JSR 168 API also allows portlets to define custom window states. Custom window states are defined by the portal. Portlets, in their deployment descriptors, declare the window states that they support using the custom-window-state element. These can be defined in the portlet deployment descriptor. The portlet can query these state definitions using the `get SupportedWindowStates()` method on the `PortletContext` object. The portlets can change their window state when processing an action request.

A portlet window is defined by the JSR 168 API as the occurrence of a portlet and a `PortletPreferences` object on a portal page. There can be more than one portlet window for a given portlet on a page. Each portlet window associated with its own portlet mode, render parameters, and `PortletPreferences`.

Developing JSR 168 Portlets for WebSphere Portal

The Portal Toolkit V5.0.2 includes JSR 168 API support. The toolkit provides the ability to generate a portlet application project that uses the JSR 168 Portlet API and also includes the JSR 168 portlet tag library declaration file (`std-portlet.tld`).

The toolkit provides a JSR 168 project wizard for creates new portlet application projects which extend the `GenericPortlet` class defined in the JSR 168 "Portlet Specification."

Enabling the Portlet Container for JSR 168

The JSR 168 support is provided in WebSphere Portal 5.0 with fix pack 2 (version 5.0.2) and subsequent releases. In version 5.0.2 you must apply interim fix PQ77263 to the WebSphere Application Server.

The portlet container for JSR 168 portlets is not enabled by default with WebSphere Portal 5.0.2. You can enable this support by setting the `portal.enable.jsr168` property to true in the `ConfigService` `.properties` file. That properties file is in the `<wp-root>/shared/app/`

`config/services/` directory. The portal server will need to be restarted for this change to take effect.

Which API Should You Use for Your Portlet?

While both portlet APIs are supported in the current version of WebSphere Portal and will be supported for announced future product enhancements, the focus of IBM's development effort and IBM's commitment to open standards should be on the JSR 168 API being the API of choice.

In the near term, the JSR 168 API implementation is not as functionally rich as the IBM Portlet API as we have seen in this chapter. However, that gap is expected to close quickly as the API and its implementation matures.

There is no immediate need to migrate existing portlets to the JSR 168 API. For development of new portlets you should consider using the JSR 168 API when the functional support meets the needs of the portlet, and also if the portlet is going to be published as a Web service since JSR 168 portlets can be published as a Web Service for Remote Portlets (WSRP).

Summary

In this chapter you learned about the portlet APIs supported in WebSphere Portal. We discussed the differences between both the IBM Portlet API and the JSR 168 API in the contest of key portlet topic areas.

In the following chapters we will develop an example portlet using both ofthese APIs to understand how these APIs are applied and to highlight the differences by using a common example.

WebSphere Portlet Development Environment

In this chapter you will learn about portlet development using WebSphere Studio and the IBM Portal Toolkit. Both of these components are part of the WebSphere Portal package. WebSphere Portal version 5.0 ships WebSphere Studio Site Developer (WSSD or WebSphere Studio) and the Portal Toolkit. We will introduce the WebSphere Studio development environment and the Portal Toolkit extension that assists in portlet development.

We will introduce a sample portlet application and then work through its design and development in the next chapter. We will focus on showing key aspects of the Portlet APIs and in the process show the Studio development environment. We will use WebSphere Studio version 5.1.0 and the Portal Toolkit version 5.0.2 throughout these examples.

This sample portlet will be implemented using both the IBM Portlet API and the JSR 168. We will then compare the results seeing the differences in the two implementations.

An Example Poll Portlet

In this example we will look at creating a portlet that handles an online poll. The portlet will present a question and a series of answer choices from which the user can make a selection and then register a vote.

Figure 15-1 shows a screen capture of a portal page that contains the Poll portlet. If the user who is logged in to the portal has not yet voted, the portlet displays the question and answer choices. When the user has voted, the view will change to display a graphical representation of the current voting totals for the answer options, as shown in Figure 15-2.

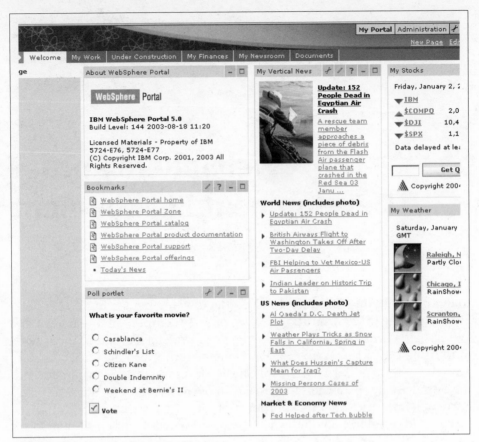

Figure 15-1   Portal page with poll portlet.

The portlet will also provide both an edit mode and a configure mode. In configure mode the administrator will (1) define the persistence store option for the portlet, (2) define the name of a new poll to be created or select an existing poll to be associated with this portlet instance, and (3) modify the poll question and answer selection choices. A portlet instance can be configured to display a poll that is in progress (votes have been recorded against the poll with that name), but in that case the poll question and answer choices cannot be modified.

Figures 15-3 to 15-5 show the configuration pages of the portlet. In the first page the persistence store is defined. The portlet will need to store the portlet question and answer choices as well as the number of votes cast. This poll information can be held in memory or in a database. If the data is held in memory then it is lost when the portal is restarted. This option is useful for demonstration and portlet testing purposes. The poll data is not actually persistent. If a database is used to store the poll information then the portlet

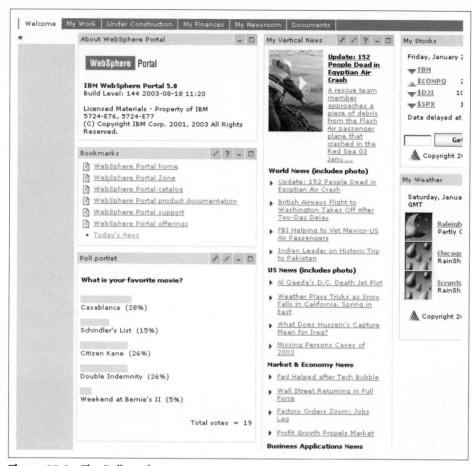

Figure 15-2   The Poll portlet.

Poll portlet

Provide the persistence type selection and if database is preferred then specifiy the datasource name, then select verify to validate that the database and tables are defined.

○ **Memory**

◉ **Database - specify datasource name**

pollDS

Verify

Next   **Cancel**

Figure 15-3   Portlet configuration page specifying persistence store.

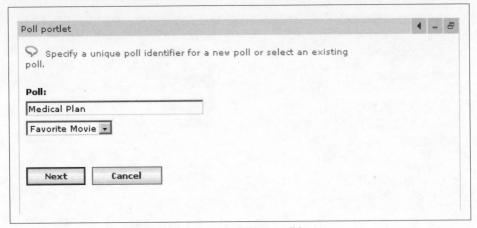

Figure 15-4 Portlet configuration page identifying poll by name.

must be configured to specify the database information. The database data source name must be specified here. The Verify button will test to ensure that the datasource name is defined correctly in the application server and that the tables have been correctly created to support the portlet.

In the next configuration page the portal administrator identifies the poll by a unique name (see Figure 15-4). A new poll can be created by specifying a unique name here or an existing poll can be chosen from the drop-down list.

In the last configuration page the portal administrator defines the poll question and the answer choices (see Figure 15-5). If the poll selected is an exiting poll that is in progress, then the question and answer choices cannot be modified.

These portlet configuration changes are applicable to the concrete portlet instance. You can copy the portlet multiple times and put the copied versions on portal pages each defining a different poll (also with potentially different persistent store options). These configuration parameters will be held in PortletSettings when implemented using the IBM Portlet API. When implemented using the JSR 168 API, these values will be managed through the PortletPreferences object.

Finally, there is an edit mode for the portlet. In edit mode the portlet user (as opposed to the portal administrator who configured the portlet) can customize the portlet (see Figure 15-6). For this simple portlet the level of user-specific customization is minimal. We allow the user to select the color that will be used on the bar graph, which displays the current voting totals for the poll. As with the configuration settings, the customization values can be specified uniquely for each poll portlet that the user has deployed on portal pages. Unlike the configuration portlet settings these options are

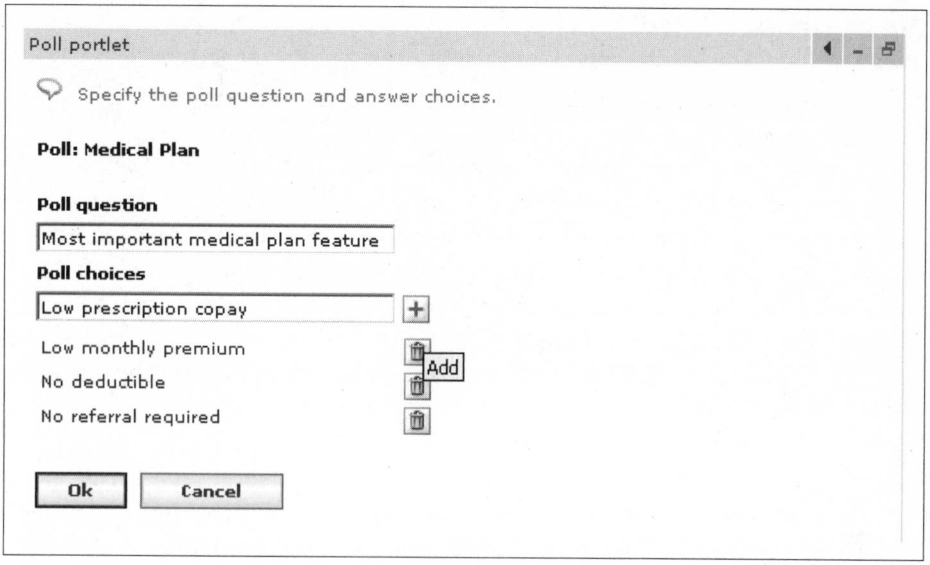

Figure 15-5   Portlet configuration page defining poll question and answer choices.

specific to a user. Using the IBM Portlet API these parameters are held in `PortletData`. When the portlet is implemented using the JSR 168 API these parameters are held in `PortletPreferences`.

In edit mode the user can select a specific color or select to have the color be the same as the color of the portlet toolbar as defined by the current portlet skin.

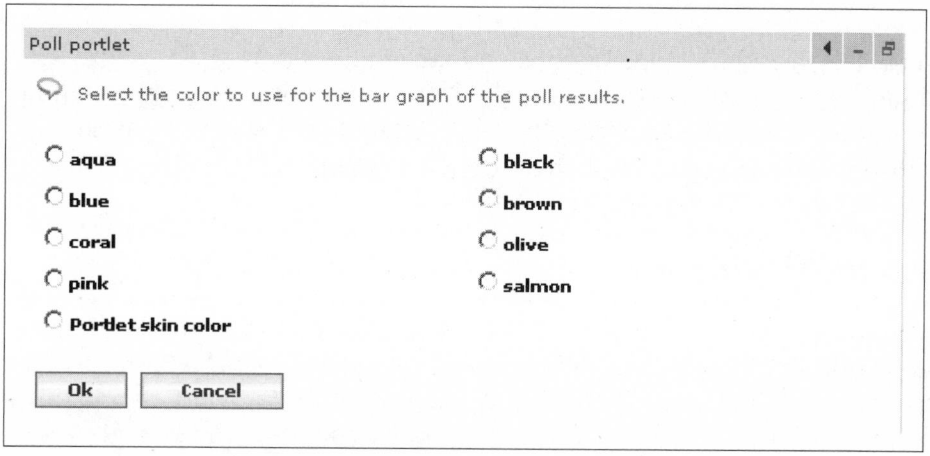

Figure 15-6   Edit mode: color selection.

WebSphere Studio

WebSphere Studio is the integrated development environment (IDE) platform of choice for building portlets for WebSphere Portal. It provides editors, builders, and wizards for Java application development. WebSphere Studio is built on Eclipse technology, an open platform for tool integration.

Eclipse provides common function on its open platform for tool vendors to provide advanced development environment functionality such as team programming, the user workbench and user interface, and interactive debugging. Eclipse is both an integrated development environment and a tool integration platform. WebSphere Studio provides functional enhancements to the Eclipse IDE.

WebSphere Studio version 5 supports JDK 1.3 and provides support for adding additional JRE definitions and switching between Java levels. The Java development environment provides automatic incremental compilation, local and remote interactive debugging, customizable and configurable workbench perspectives, views, and editors. The workbench also provides an extensive search capability and a scrapbook where Java code snippets can be evaluated easily and execution results inspected.

WebSphere Studio provides a rich set of tools to support Web application development. WebSphere Studio version 5 supports development of Web applications that meet the J2EE 1.3 specification, which includes the Sun Microsystems Java Servlet 2.3 specification and the Sun Microsystems JSP 1.2 specification. Web application support includes Web project creation. This creates an application project using the J2EE hierarchy and includes the creation of the Web application deployment descriptor file (web.xml).

The development environment supports Java Server Pages (JSP) creation, validation, editing, and debugging. JSP tooling also includes support for JavaScript editing and validation and custom JSP 1.2 tag development support. Web Archive (WAR) files can be imported, exported, and validated. There are a variety of additional tools for editing images and Cascading Style Sheets (CSS), a Web site designer, wizards for servlet creation, and integration with the WebSphere test environment.

Portal Toolkit

The IBM Portal Toolkit extends WebSphere Studio further by providing a complete set of tools for developing portlet applications. The Portal Toolkit provides support to create, debug, and deploy individual portlets and portlet applications. Wizards and templates assist in developing portlet project and portlets, while powerful interactive debugging capability dramatically reduces development and test time for portlet developers.

The mechanism for extending the Eclipse-based Studio environment is through plug-ins. The development environment is designed for extensibility. The Portal Toolkit is a plug-in for either WebSphere Studio Application Developer (WSAD) or WebSphere Studio Site Developer (WSSD). As mentioned before, WebSphere Portal ships with WSSD. We refer to either product generically as Studio.

NOTE The latest information, including documentation and downloads, about the Portal Toolkit is available on the WebSphere Portal Toolkit Web site at `www.ibm.com/websphere/portal/toolkit`.

The toolkit provides the following portlet development tools and IDE enhancements.

Portlet Project

A new project type is defined for portlet applications and a wizard tool is available to create portlet projects. A portlet project is similar to a J2EE Web application project and includes a Web deployment descriptor that defines the Web application. In addition, a portlet project contains a portlet deployment descriptor file (`portlet.xml`) that defines the portlet application and the portlets within that application.

The portlet application wizard assists in the creation of the project directory structure, the Web deployment and the portlet deployment descriptors, and a set of sample Java source files that make up the portlet application. The amount of generated code is dependent on the type of portlet application that was selected in the wizard: an empty portlet application or a basic portlet application.

Portlet Perspective

A new perspective is provided for portlet development. A perspective in Studio defines a set of views and the layout of those views along with a set of editors. Studio defines multiple perspectives each aimed at a specific task or a specific type of resource. For example, the Web perspective shows workbench views that are appropriate to Web application resources. The debug perspective shows views that apply to the interactive debug of Java applications.

The portlet perspective is similar to the Web perspective provided by Studio, showing views and editors for Web application resources. In addition, this perspective provides an editor specific for the portlet deployment descriptor file (`portlet.xml`). The `portlet.xml` editor also assists in keeping the portlet and Web deployment descriptors in sync. As discussed in a previous chapter there are links between the Web deployment descriptor and the portlet deployment descriptor. The servlet ID defined in the web.xml file must link to the portlet href attribute in the portlet application definition in the portlet.xml file. The portlet.xml editor manages this and other associative descriptor attributes. The editor also provides a validator to check the deployment descriptor definitions.

Portal Server Configuration

The Portal Server Configuration defines a WebSphere Studio server configuration that allows you to publish your portlet application to WebSphere Portal. Published portlets are deployed on a debug page of WebSphere Portal. Interactive debugging is supported.

A portlet application can be published and debugged in a local portal test environment or a remote (attached) portal server. Local debugging requires that you install the WebSphere Portal for a test environment. You can use the Portal Toolkit installer to set up the Portal test environment. Once installed and started you can interactively make changes to your portlet in Studio and immediately test the change on the local portal without an additional package, publish, or deploy step.

You can use remote debugging for portlets running on a portal server outside the Studio environment. To enable remote debugging you need to configure the JVM for the WebSphere Portal Application Server instance. Debug mode needs to be enabled, with the debug arguments set to

```
-Djava.compiler=NONE -Xdebug -Xnoagent -
-Xrunjdwp:transport=dt_socket,server=y,suspend=n,address=7777
```

We will look at portlet developing using Studio in more detail in Chapter 16 and explore interactive debugging using Studio in Chapter 17.

Portlet Preview

Portlet preview allows you to preview the portlet under development as deployed on a remote Portal system. This is different than executing the portlet in the test environment. The preview function works only with external Portal systems, not an installed WebSphere Portal for a test environment. It does not set up a debugging environment. Instead the portlet application is deployed on the remote Portal system using the XML configuration interface of Portal. The portlet is put on a preview page and Studio's internal Web browser opens that portal page.

Building the Portlet Application WAR File

A portlet application project is a J2EE-compliant Web application. You can easily build a deployable WAR file for your portlet application simply by using the Export utility in Studio. Similarly, you can import resources from a WAR file to your portlet application project using the Import function.

Creating the Poll Portlet Project

In this section you will create the portlet application project in Studio for our sample portlet application. This section assumes that you have already installed the Portlet Toolkit in Studio. If the Portal Toolkit is not already installed, follow the instructions that came with the toolkit (either downloaded from the Web site mentioned earlier or obtained from the Portal product CD) to run the toolkit.

The intention of this chapter is to introduce the Portlet development toolkit in the context of creating our example portlet application. This chapter is not intended as a tutorial on WebSphere Studio itself. The discussion here assumes you have a familiarity with Studio, its key concepts, and how to navigate the workbench. If you do not have experience using WebSphere Studio you may want to review the product help content, which has excellent information about the development environment and includes scenario-based tutorials.

The Portlet Perspective

First let's take a look at the portlet perspective in Studio (see Figure 15-7). Start WebSphere Studio and open the portlet perspective from the Window item on the menu bar.

The default perspective shows a number of views and an editor. The key views to consider are the Project Navigator view, the editor, and the tasks view. These will be used initially as you create the portlet project. The Palette view, Attributes view, and Quick Edit view are used primarily with the Page Designer editor when editing JSP or HTML files. Change to the Tasks view by selecting the Tasks tab on the bottom of the view with Quick Edit.

Create a portlet project for our Poll Portlet by selecting New ⇨ Portlet Application Project from the File menu item in the Studio toolbar. This opens the Portlet Project creation wizard (see Figure 15-8).

Enter the name of your portal project. Choose **Poll** for this example. The project location specifies the directory where the project files will be created. You may change the directory using the Browse button, but the selected

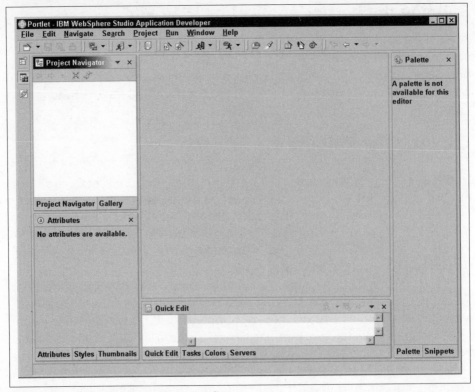

Figure 15-7   Portlet perspective in Studio.

directory must be empty. You can select to create either an empty portlet or a basic portlet.

An *Empty Portlet* creates a portlet project directory structure and the Web and portlet deployment descriptors. The wizard sets the Java build path for the project, including the required jar files for the portlet API. The portlet deployment descriptor that is created defines a portlet application and a single portlet in that application. You can add additional portlets to the portlet application by re-executing the wizard and specifying a *portlet* instead of a *portlet application*.

A *Basic Portlet* generation performs this function also but in addition generates source code for the portlet. The code generated will depend on the options selected in the wizard. At a minimum, a portlet class is created that extends `PortletAdapter` and implements a `doView()` method that invokes a sample JSP. Since the portlet class is created the deployment descriptors created can reference that class. This step is useful as both the Web descriptor references this as the servlet class for the Web application and the portlet class name is used in both descriptors. Create the Poll portlet using the *Basic Portlet* type.

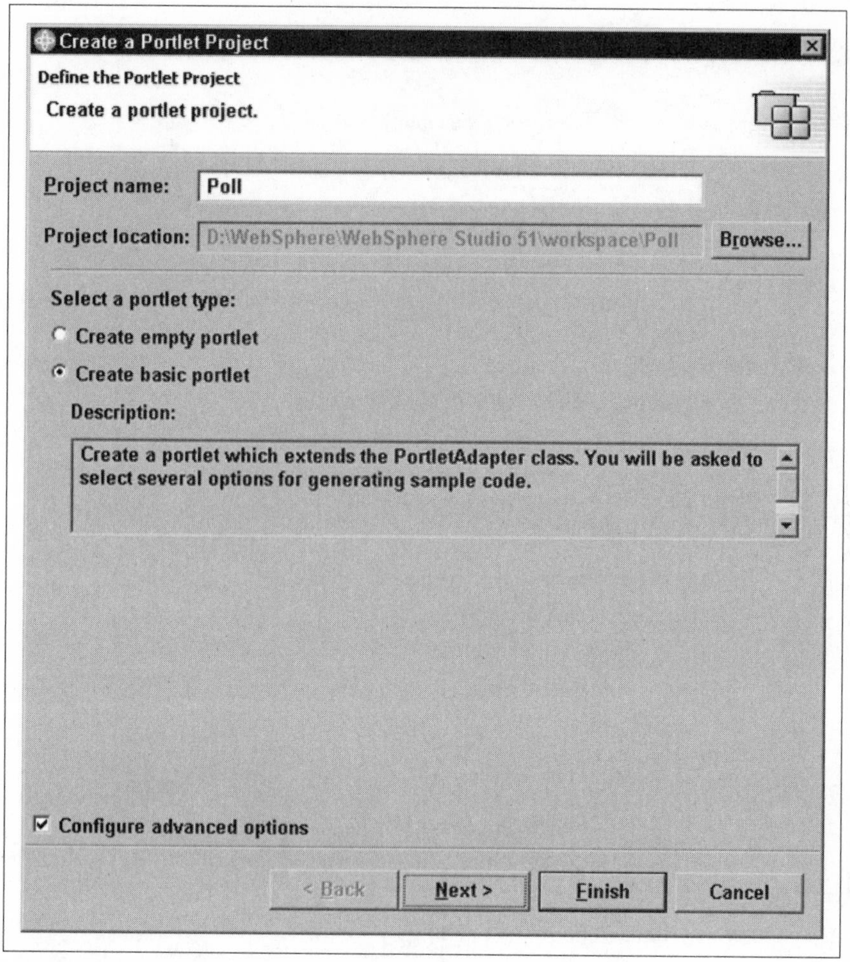

Figure 15-8 Portlet Project creation wizard.

After selecting Create Basic Portlet, select Configure Advanced Options and then Next. On the next page of the wizard you can specify the name of the Enterprise Application (EAR) project (see Figure 15-9). Since portlet applications are packaged and deployed to portal through a WAR file, the EAR file selected here will not affect that deployment. However, the EAR will be used for portlet deployment to the WebSphere Portal test environment. You may want to put portlet applications in separate EAR projects to be able to manage more easily the portlets that are executing in the test environment. This project being created is set, and can be modified later, in the EAR deployment descriptor. For this example portlet, leave the project set as the default EAR.

J2EE supports multiple Web applications running in the same server instance. The context root is a unique (within the server instance) identifier

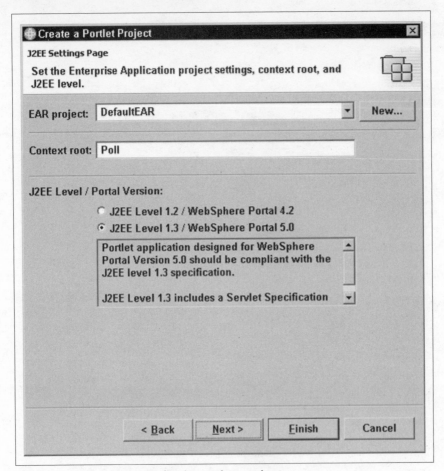

Figure 15-9   Enterprise Application project settings.

to ensure that an HTTP request reaches the correct Web application. The context root is a path identifier used in the URI immediately following the host name. The default value defined in the Studio wizard is the project name. This value is set, and can be modified later, in the EAR deployment descriptor with the Web module definition. For this example portlet use the provided default value.

Also on this page you can specify the J2EE level of the Portal into which you expect to deploy this portlet. WebSphere Portal 5.0 supports J2EE level 1.3. Select J2EE 1.3 for your example portlet and click Next.

The next page in the wizard gathers the final set of information needed for the portlet and Web deployment descriptors (see Figure 15-10). Here you specify the name of the portlet and the name of the portlet application. Also, you specify the default locale and the portlet title in the language of the default locale. Change these to values of your choice.

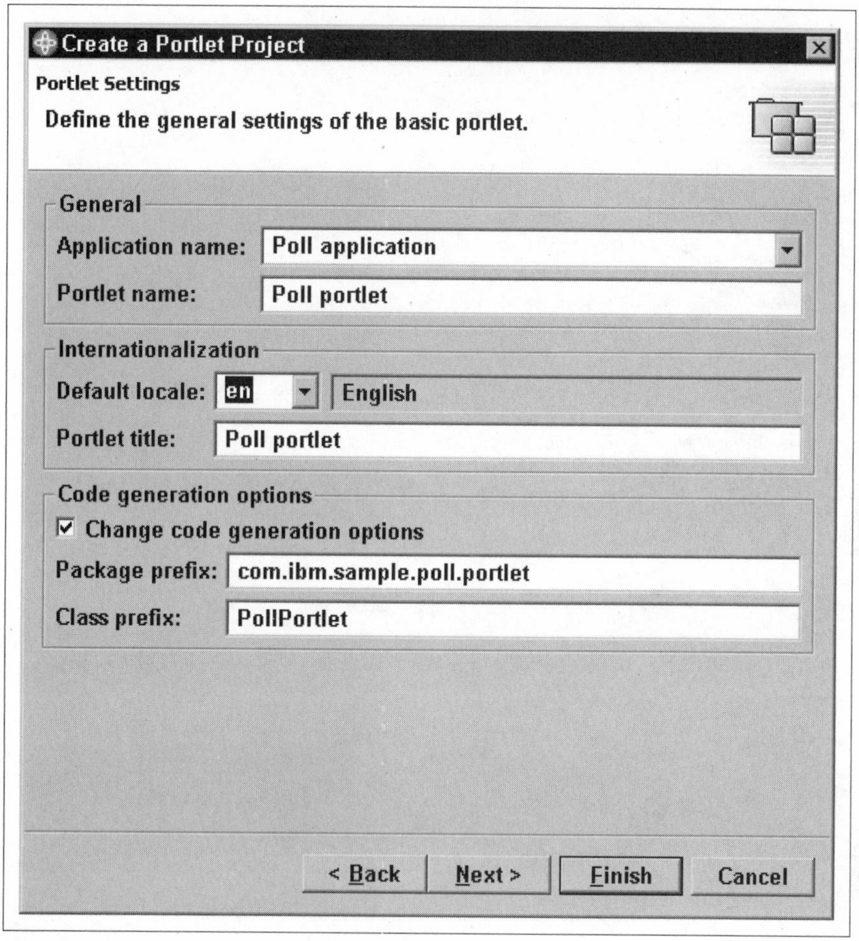

Figure 15-10   Specifying portlet settings.

Select Change Code Generation Options. The package prefix is the package name that will be created in this new project and it is the package that will be referenced in the Web deployment descriptor for the servlet class name. Change the package prefix to a package name of your choice. The class prefix will be used as the class name for the portlet class and also referenced in the Web deployment descriptor as the servlet class name (with the package prefix). A version of this package name will also be used to create a directory structure in the Poll Portlet project for other generated files such as JSP files. The default class prefix name is fine for our portlet, so click Next.

The final three pages in the wizard are used to determine what source code files to generate. This next page specifies portlet event handling options. Most portlets will have a requirement to implement an action event listener.

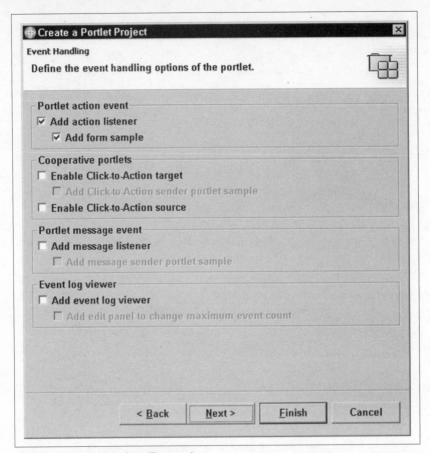

Figure 15-11 Event handling options.

This preselected choice will generate an `actionPerformed()` method in the portlet class and also modify that class definition to implement the `ActionListener` interface.

This selection will also generate a simple view bean and a simple session bean. The form bean has a getter and setter method for an instance variable to hold a portlet URI string. The session bean provides similar function for a text string. An example JSP using these beans will also be created.

Cooperative portlets are portlets that interact by sharing data elements through a broker mechanism that handles portlet requests to declare, publish, and share properties (see Figure 15-11). A portlet associates actions with properties that get invoked when the property change is received.

Selecting all three of these Cooperative Portlet options will generate a simple example of two cooperative portlets, their JSP files, and a control WSDL file. Selecting Enable Click-to-Action Target generates a control WSDL file so the target portlet can receive properties (select Add Form Sample to ensure a complete working example). Selecting Add Click-to-Action Sender Portlet Sample creates a simple property sender portlet. Selecting Enable Click-to-Action source updates the source portlet JSP to use the Click-to-Action tag library to publish properties. These options are available only for J2EE 1.3 applications.

Portlets that reside on the same portal page can communicate during the action processing phase using message events. Selecting these options updates the portlet class definition to implement the `MessageListener` interface and the `messageReceived()` method. You can choose to generate a sample portlet to send a broadcast message.

Finally, on this page you can select to generate code in the sample portlet to record action events in session so that they can be displayed later. Leave this page with the default values and select Next.

The next page allows you to generate sample code to handle user credentials that are managed through the Credential Vault (see Figure 15-12).

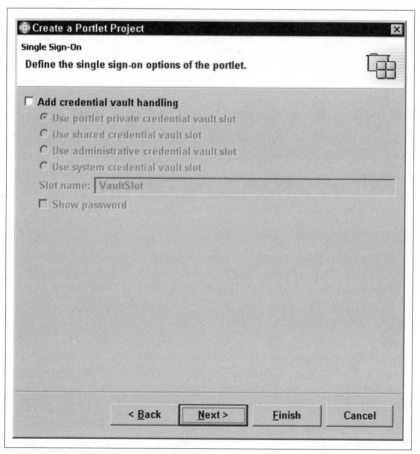

Figure 15-12   Credential Vault options.

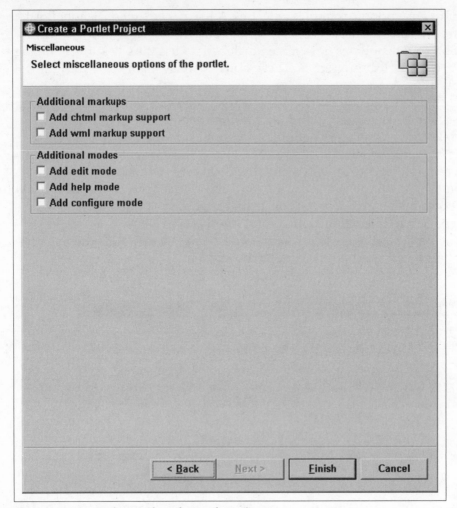

Figure 15-13 Markup and portlet mode options.

The Credential Vault is a secure store for user secrets and provides a portlet service to manage the vault and its contents and handle authentication to back-end applications.

Selecting options on this page will generate sample code to access credentials from the Credential Vault. There are several options to support credentials of various scopes. Leave this option unchecked and select Next.

The last page of the wizard allows you to modify the portlet deployment descriptor to support multiple markups and additional portlet modes (see Figure 15-13). In addition, when the markup options are selected, device-specific JSP files will be generated. The portlet will invoke the correct JSP depending on the client request type. Leave these options unchecked and select Finish.

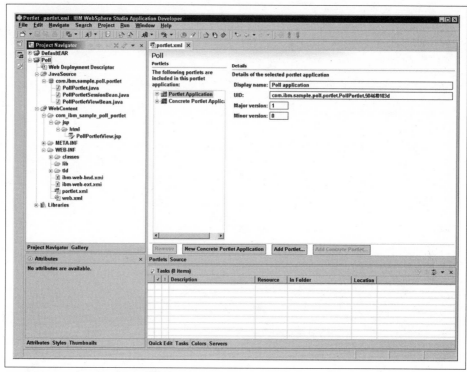

Figure 15-14 Poll project created.

As a result of completing the portlet application wizard the Poll project is created (see Figure 15-14). The project is shown in the Project Navigator view. It is created with the correct directory structure for a Web application, and so you can generate a deployable WAR file simply by selecting the Poll Portlet project and using the export function (File ➪ Export ➪ WAR File).

The appropriate portlet project build class path is also set when the project is created. The project properties view shows the Java build path along with other project metadata and preference settings. The properties view can be opened by selecting the project in the Project Navigator then selecting File ➪ Properties.

In addition the portlet deployment descriptor and Web deployment descriptor are created and the deployment descriptor editor is opened. We will take a closer look at this editor and the generated values next.

Deployment Descriptor Editor

Click on Portlet Application in the editor to see the portlet application details (see Figure 15-15). The display name for the portlet application is the name you provided to the wizard. The application unique identifier (UID)

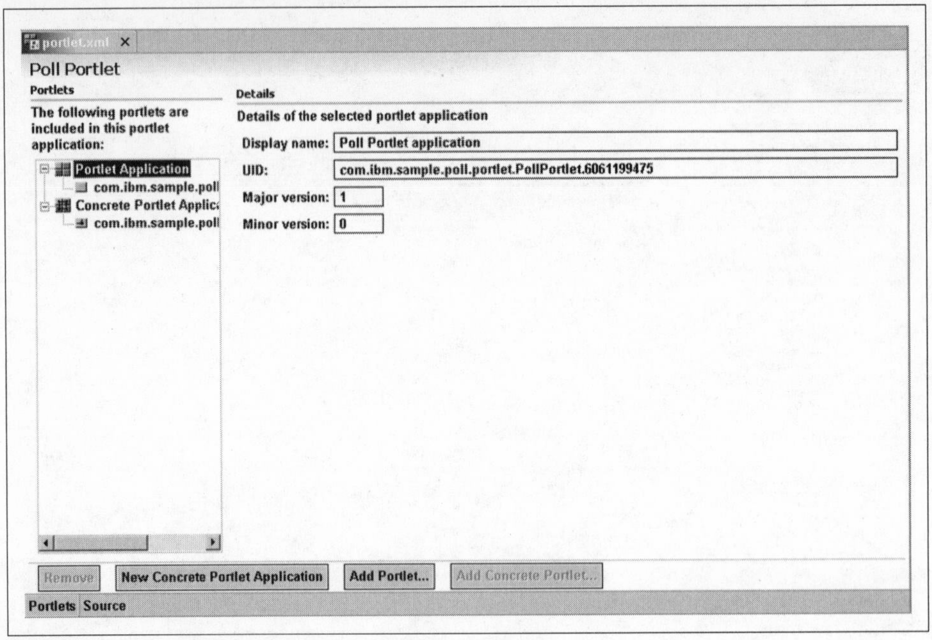

Figure 15-15   Portlet deployment descriptor editor.

is a generated value based on the portlet package and the portlet class name provided to the wizard. The major version and minor version default to 1 and 0 respectively. These values are used to track portlet application revisions.

Expand the Portlet Application and select the portlet. Its details are shown in Figure 15-16. Like the portlet application, the portlet name was provided to the wizard. The portlet ID is a generated value and the major and minor version values are the new portlet defaults.

The servlet name is set as the full class name of the portlet class. This value must map to the servlet name in the Web deployment descriptor. Using the wizard to create the deployment descriptors ensures that this mapping and the mapping between the abstract and concrete portlet definitions are set correctly.

The portlet cache defaults are to always expire and be nonshared. The portlet definition also includes the window states that are supported, the markup types supported, and the portlet modes supported. As we have seen, the Poll portlet will require configure and edit modes as well as its view mode. We could have specified this in the wizard but let's make the change here. Click None in the column labeled Configure on row labeled HTML, and from the drop-down list that appears select Fragment. Do the same for the column labeled Edit. This will enable our portlet to have icons for these three modes on the portlet menu bar.

Figure 15-16   Portlet application details.

There are no portlet configuration parameters set through the wizard but any of these values can be set here. Any configuration parameters set here are specified as init-param's in the Web deployment descriptor. This editor will modify both the portlet and web xml files.

Click on *Concrete Portlet Application* in the editor. The details view shows the concrete portlet application display name and its associated UID (see Figure 15-17). Both of these values are derived from input values to the wizard. The wizard does not capture portlet application context parameters but they can be set using this editor.

Expand the *Concrete Portlet Application* and select the concrete portlet definition (see Figure 15-18). Here the supported and default locales are defined. The portlet title, short title, description, and keywords (for search function) are specified by language. The concrete portlet settings are also defined here.

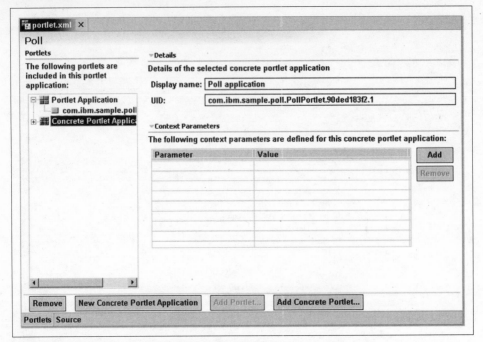

Figure 15-17   Concrete Portlet Application details.

The Poll portlet will require portlet settings but we will define them later. Close the deployment descriptor editor and save the changes.

Generated Source Code

Review the `PollPortletSessionBean` and the `PollPortletView-Bean` classes that were generated. The Poll portlet will not use these classes so they can be deleted.

The `PollPortlet` class will now have a number of errors that are displayed in the task view as a result of deleting those bean classes. Open the source editor on `PollPortlet.java`. Let's start our Poll project development with a fairly empty portlet. Delete the `getSessionBean` method. We will put our portlet constants in a separate class so delete the static instance variables. Change the `doView()` method to remove the references to `PollPortletSessionBean` and `PollPortletViewBean`. We will use the JSP tags to generate the PortletURIs so delete them as well. Similarly clean up the `actionPerformed` method and remove the `getJSPExtenstion` method. Also, delete the JSP file and its directory structure. So our very basic `PollPortlet` looks something like Figure 15-19.

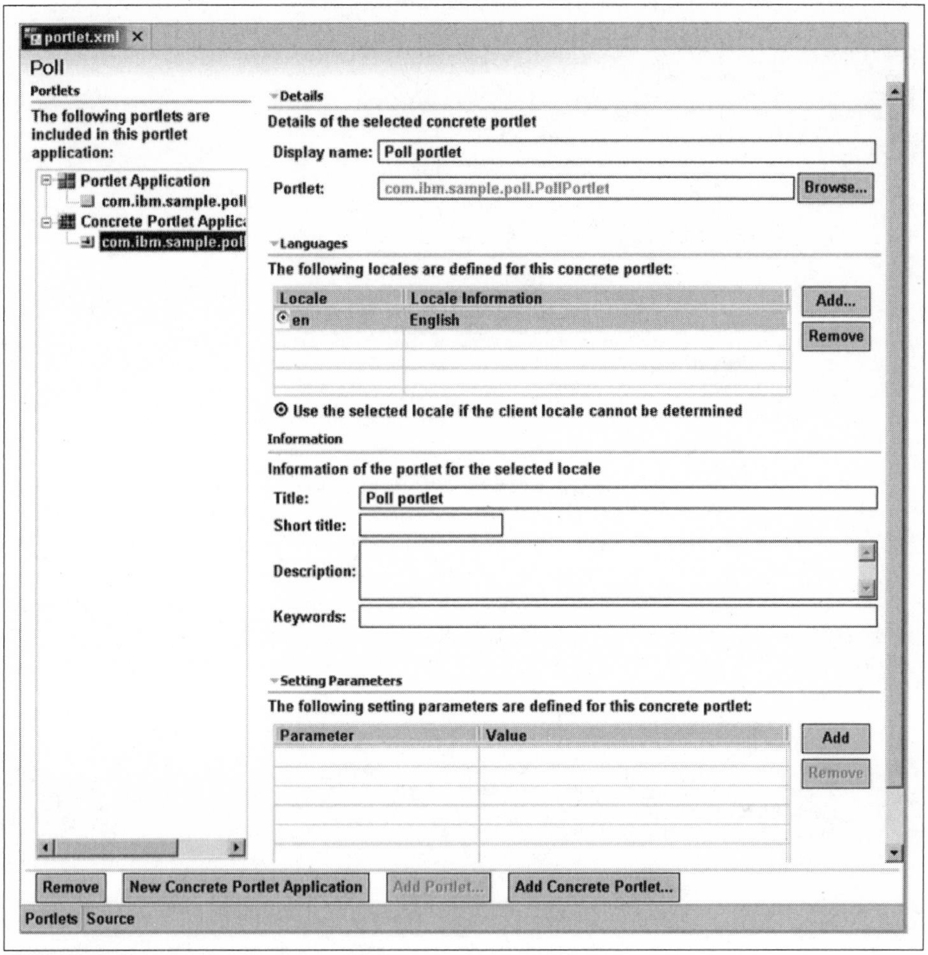

Figure 15-18 Concrete portlet definition.

Summary

In this chapter you reviewed the WebSphere Studio development environment. You learned about the capability of the Portal Toolkit and the value it brings to Studio for portlet development.

We introduced a sample application that we will develop using Studio. You used the portlet application generation wizard to help create our portlet project. You saw that the wizard was very helpful in creating the Portlet Project with the correct directory structure, setting the correct class path for the portlet project to build correctly, and creating the deployment descriptors needed for our portlet application. The wizard also generated portlet

```
package com.ibm.sample.poll.portlet;

import java.io.IOException;

import org.apache.jetspeed.portlet.*;
import org.apache.jetspeed.portlet.event.*;

/**
 * Poll Portlet
 */
public class PollPortlet extends PortletAdapter implements ActionListener {

    /**
     * Initialize the portlet
     */
    public void init(PortletConfig portletConfig) throws UnavailableException {
        super.init(portletConfig);
    }

    /**
     * Render the view mode
     */
    public void doView(PortletRequest request, PortletResponse response)
        throws PortletException, IOException {

        // Invoke the JSP to render
        getPortletConfig().getContext().include("jsp/view.jsp",request,response);
    }

    /**
     * Handle the action events
     */
    public void actionPerformed(ActionEvent event) throws PortletException {
        if (getPortletLog().isDebugEnabled())
            getPortletLog().debug("ActionListener - actionPerformed called");

        // ActionEvent handler
        String actionString = event.getActionString();
        // Add action string handler here
        PortletRequest request = event.getRequest();
    }
}
```

Figure 15-19   PollPortlet.

Java code as a starting point. Some of that we removed to leave a very minimal base on which to build.

In the next chapter we will develop our Poll portlet using this starting point.

Portlet Development

This chapter explores in detail the implementation of the example Poll portlet. In the previous chapter we introduced the WebSphere Studio development environment. Using the Portal Toolkit in Studio, you used the portlet application wizard to create a portlet project and create the portlet deployment descriptors.

The complete source code for this portlet is available for download. Most of the key sections of the portlet code are shown in listings here and from the discussion and code shown, you should be able to create the portlet implementation in your Studio project. However, not all of the project code is shown here. You may want to import the completed project in Studio to have the total reference available while you follow the discussion.

This implementation is based on the IBM Portlet API. In the following chapter we will use this base portlet implementation and modify it to use the JSR 168 API. While doing that we will compare the differences in implementation and functionality.

Poll Portlet

Recall the description of the Poll portlet from the previous chapter and the associated screenshots. This is a relatively simple portlet but still has enough complexity to demonstrate some key aspects of the Portlet API.

- Action event processing
- Page navigation within the portlet
- Multiple portlet modes—view, edit, and configure

- Portlet configuration parameters in `PortletSettings`
- User customization parameters in `PortletData`
- Database access
- Trace logging
- Internationalization

While this example portlet is simple, we will still employ good principles to its design. We will structure the application to ensure good separation of components based on areas of responsibility. The portal architecture itself provides a good foundation for portlet designs. Consider how a Model–View–Controller (MVC) pattern would apply to this portlet.

We would implement the View components as JSPs, one for each of the portlet pages shown in the previous chapter. The Model or domain components are minimal for our portlet. These components represent the business objects and logic of the application domain and for our portlet that is a small set of objects such as a `Poll` object or a `User` object. The Controller component of a portlet is the portlet class. It is responsible to respond to user requests from the View components and invoke behavior in the Model components. Our portlet requires access to a persistent store and therefore has components for infrastructure components as well.

Implementing the Controller

Open the Poll project in WebSphere Studio that we created in the last chapter (see Figure 16-1). Use the portlet perspective. In this project you should have a `PollPortlet.java` file in the `JavaSource` directory in the package called `com.ibm.sample.poll.portlet`. This is the portlet class. The name of the portlet class was specified when you ran the portlet application wizard and is now defined in the Web deployment descriptor. Open the source editor for this file.

First consider the implementation for the `doView` method. This method gets executed when our portlet is asked to render itself in view mode. The portlet should display either the view with the question and answer choices or the view with the voting results depending if the user has already voted. You have not yet created our business objects or broker classes, so you have to fill in those pieces next. But the `doView` method can look something like the following:

```
/**
 * Render the view mode
 */
public void doView(PortletRequest request, PortletResponse response)
```

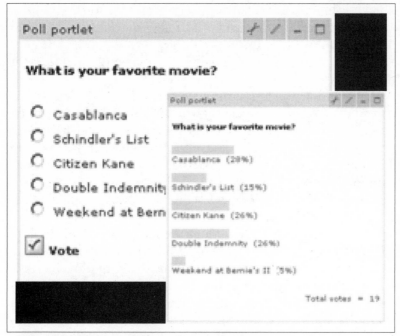

Figure 16-1   The Poll project in WebSphere Studio.

```
  throws PortletException, IOException {

  // Get the poll bean
  PortletSettings portletSettings = request.getPortletSettings();
  String persistType = portletSettings.getAttribute(PERSIST_TYPE);
  String datasource = portletSettings.getAttribute(DATASOURCE);
  String pollName = portletSettings.getAttribute(POLL_NAME);
  Broker broker = Broker.getInstance(persistType, datasource);
  PollBean pollBean = broker.getPoll(pollName);

  // If the user has not already voted show poll question
  // otherwise show poll results.
  String user = request.getUser().getUserID();
  boolean hasUserVoted = broker.hasUserVoted(user, pollName);

  if (hasUserVoted) {
    pollBean.initializeResults(broker);
    request.setAttribute("pollBean", pollBean);
      portletContext.include(VIEW_RESULTS_JSP, request, response);
  }
  else {
    request.setAttribute("pollBean", pollBean);
      portletContext.include(VIEW_QUESTION_JSP, request, response);
  }
}
```

You see from this code that the portlet configuration information that defines the name of the poll and the information that specifies the datastore are kept in the portlet settings. With that information, you can ask our datastore manager class (`Broker`) for an instantiated `Poll` object (`PollBean`) for the poll with the given name.

You can get the userid of the logged-in user from the `User` object. The `User` object is available from the `PortletRequest` object. Then determine if a vote for this poll for the current user has already been registered and if not invoke the JSP to show the poll question. If the user has voted, get the vote results from the `Broker` and invoke the JSP to show the results, as shown in Figure 16-2.

Next consider the configuration pages for this portlet. As you have just seen, the poll name and the persistent store information are retrieved from portlet settings. These can initially be configured in the portlet deployment descriptor but we want to allow the portal administrator to make modifications to these values after the portlet has been deployed. Also, the administrator will need to specify the poll question and answers, although that information will be kept in the persistent store, not the portlet settings. We want that information outside the scope of a single portlet instance since the information may be shared across multiple poll portlet instances. Also we don't want the data to be lost when the portlet gets reconfigured.

The implementation for configure mode will be very similar to what you just did for view mode, except now it gets a bit more complicated, as you have page navigation issues to consider and action event processing to handle.

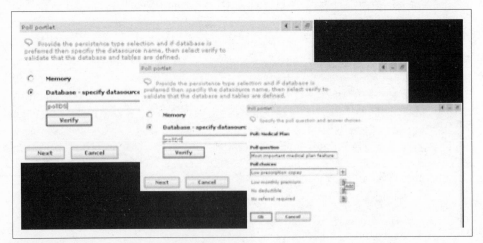

Figure 16-2 The results of the poll.

```
/**
 * Render the configure mode view
 */
public void doConfigure(PortletRequest request,
  PortletResponse response)
  throws PortletException, IOException {

    // Create a form data object and put it on session
    PortletSession session = request.getPortletSession();
    SessionData sessionData = new SessionData();
    session.setAttribute(SESSION_DATA, sessionData);
    ConfigureFormData formData = sessionData.getConfigureFormData();

    // Get the portlet settings
    PortletSettings portletSettings = request.getPortletSettings();
    String persistType = portletSettings.getAttribute(PERSIST_TYPE);
    String datasource = portletSettings.getAttribute(DATASOURCE);

    // Set the portlet settings in the form data bean on session
    formData.setDatasource(datasource);
    formData.setPersistType(persistType);

    // Invoke the JSP to render
    portletContext.include(CONFIGURE_JSP, request, response);

}
```

This implementation is still simple. We introduce a `ConfigureFormData` object that will hold the input data as the user steps through the configuration pages. This object will be held in session and so we also create a `SessionData` object to hold the portlet data that will go on the actual session object. Putting the portlet session data in a single object makes it easier to clean the session data and also reduces the number of attribute names that need to be managed.

Now the processing gets a little more complicated as we have three actions that can occur on the user interface for this first page. The user can *verify* the datasource definition. The user can advance to the next configuration page or cancel from configure mode completely. The specifications for these action events are in the JSP through encoding in the link URI. The JSP uses a custom tag from the portlet tag library to create a URI that can be specified on links defined by the `Action` attribute or an `href` attribute. Two examples of using the tag are

```
<portletAPI:createURI>
  <portletAPI:URIAction name="verify"/>
</portletAPI:createURI>
```

and

```
<portletAPI:createReturnURI/>
```

The first tag creates a URI that encodes both the portlet reference and a trigger for an action event. The portlet container will interpret this URI and call the portlet's `actionPerformed` method, that is, if the portlet class implements that `ActionListener` interface. The action event is named so the `actionPerformed` method can interrogate the `Event` object, retrieve the name, and execute the correct behavior for this action event. The same `actionPerformed` method will get called for all action events for this portlet so the event name is needed to distinguish events.

The second tag does not associate an action event with the URI and simply asks the portal container to return the portlet to its previous mode. For example, if the user had been in view mode prior to configure mode, then this URI will return the portlet to view mode.

The following listing shows a complete JSP for the first page of configure mode. This is slightly different than the version that is available via download. It has been changed somewhat to reduce the size. If you are implementing this in Studio, this file is named `configure.jsp` and is in a JSP directory under `WebContent`.

```
<%@ page contentType="text/html"%>
<%@ page import="com.ibm.sample.portlet.poll.beans.ConfigureFormData"%>
<%@ page import="com.ibm.sample.portlet.poll.portlet.PollConstants"%>
<%@ taglib uri="/WEB-INF/tld/portlet.tld" prefix="portletAPI"%>
<%@ taglib prefix="fmt" uri="http://java.sun.com/jstl/fmt"%>

<jsp:useBean id="sessionData"
class="com.ibm.sample.portlet.poll.beans.SessionData" scope="session"/>
<fmt:setBundle basename="nls.polling"/>
<portletAPI:init />

<%
  ConfigureFormData formData = sessionData.getConfigureFormData();
  String message = sessionData.getMessage();
  String dataSource = formData.getDatasource();
  String persistType = formData.getPersistType();
%>

<form method="post" name="<portletAPI:encodeNamespace value="form"/>">
<table align="left" width="400">

  <tr>
    <td class="wpsInlineHelpText" colspan="2">
      <img src='<%=response.encodeURL("/images/msg_inline_help.gif")%>'
```

```
      border="0"/> 
      <fmt:message key="configure.initinfo"/>
    </td>
  </tr>


  <tr>
    <td class="wpsPortletHead">
      <input type='radio' name='persist_type' value='memory'>
    </td>
    <td class="wpsPortletHead">
      Memory
    </td>
  </tr>


  <tr>
    <td class="wpsPortletHead">
      <input type='radio' name='persist_type' value='database'>
      >
    </td>
    <td class="wpsPortletHead">
      Database - specify datasource name
    </td>

  </tr>
    <td class="wpsPortletHead"></td>
    <td class="wpsPortletSmText">
      <input type='text' name='datasource' value='' size='40'>
    </td>
  </tr>


  </tr>
    <td class="wpsPortletHead"></td>
    <td align="left" valign="bottom" nowrap>
      <input class="wpsButtonText"
      type='submit' value='Verify' name='verify'
      onClick="document.<portletAPI:encodeNamespace
value='form'/>.action=
      '<portletAPI:createURI>
        <portletAPI:URIAction name="verify"/>
      </portletAPI:createURI>'">
    </td>
  </tr>


  <tr>
    <td class="wpsPortletSmText" colspan="2">
      <input class="wpsButtonText"
      type='submit' value='Next'
      onClick="document.<portletAPI:encodeNamespace
      value='form'/>.action=
      '<portletAPI:createURI>
```

```
        <portletAPI:URIAction name="config_pg2"/>
      </portletAPI:createURI>'">

      <input class="wpsButtonText"
      type='submit' value='Cancel'
      onClick="document.<portletAPI:encodeNamespace
      value="form"/>.action=
      '<portletAPI:createReturnURI>
        <portletAPI:URIAction name="Cancel"/>
      </portletAPI: createReturnURI>">
    </td>
  </tr>
 </table>
 </form>
```

Notice in the JSP that we namespace-encode the document object names. Instead of encoding each individually we encode the name of the form object. That way any references to objects within the form are namespace-protected as well. To do this we use the `<portletAPI:encodeName space/>` tag.

Also, as of Portal version 5 the preferred method to get text strings from resource bundles is through the Java Server Pages Standard Tag Libraries (JSTL) `fmt` tag library. You will need to get the open source libraries, `standard.jar` and `jstl.jar`, and add them to your portlet application libraries folder.

You will also notice a reference to an image file in the JSP. This file is packaged with the portlet in an images folder under `WebContent`. The URI reference to that resource must also be encoded to successfully resolve the reference. To do that we used the `encodeURL` method from the portlet response object:

```
<%=response.encodeURL("/images/msg_inline_help.gif")%>
```

The JSP also uses style definitions from the portal Cascading Style Sheet (CSS) file named `styles.css`. The JSP has access to this style sheet. The actual style sheet that is used for the portlet is dependent on the theme selected. Using these styles will allow the portlets to look and feel integrated well with other portlets and take on the selected theme's behavior. Look for the `styles.css` files in directories starting from

```
<was-root>/installedApps/<node>/wps.ear/eps.war/themes/...
```

Next, let's look at the `actionPerformed` method in the portlet class to handle the requests to verify the datasource and to move to the next page in configure mode. Don't add this code to your portlet just yet.

```java
/**
 * Handle all Action requests
 */
public void actionPerformed(ActionEvent event)
  throws PortletException {

  PortletRequest request = event.getRequest();
  PortletContext portletContext = getPortletConfig().getContext();
  PortletLog log = portletContext.getLog();

  // Get the action name
  String actionName = event.getActionString();
  if (log.isDebugEnabled())
    log.debug("actionPerformed() processing action "+actionName);

  if ("verify".equals(actionName)) {
    verifyAction(request, portletContext);
  }

  if ("config_pg2".equals(actionName)) {
    page2Action(request, portletContext);
  }

}

/**
 * Verify datasource action
 */
protected void verifyAction(PortletRequest request,
  PortletContext portletContext)
  throws PollException {

  try {
    // Get configuration form data bean from session
    SessionData sessionData = SessionData.getSessionData(request);
    ConfigureFormData formData = sessionData.getConfigureFormData();

    // Update the persistence type and the datasource from request
    // parameters, validate the input.
    formData.updateDbParms(request);

    // Check the datasource name and the database tables
    // If an exception occurs put the exception message out
    DbBroker dbBroker = new DbBroker(formData.getDatasource());
    dbBroker.verifyTables();

    // Success, put a message out
    ResourceBundle bundle = ResourceBundle.getBundle("nls.polling",
      request.getLocale());
    String msg = bundle.getString("configure.verify_success");
```

```
        sessionData.setMessage(msg);

    }
    catch (PollException e) {
      SessionData sessionData = SessionData.getSessionData(request);
      sessionData.setMessage(e.getLocalizedMessage());
     }

  }

  /**
   * Prepare for configure mode page 2
   */
  protected void page2Action(PortletRequest request,
    PortletContext portletContext)
    throws PollException {

      // Get configuration form data bean from session
      SessionData sessionData = SessionData.getSessionData(request);
      ConfigureFormData formData = sessionData.getConfigureFormData();

      // Update the persistence type and the datasource from request
      // parameters, validate the input.
      formData.updateDbParms(request);

      // Get the list of current polls (by name) from the data store
      // Get a broker instance using the form data parameters
      Broker broker = Broker.getInstance(formData.getPersistType(),
        formData.getDatasource());
      List pollNames = broker.getPollNames();

      // Put it in form data object
      formData.setPollNames(pollNames);

  }
```

You see in this example code that the actionPerformed method is passed an ActionEvent object. From the ActionEvent you can get the PortletRequest object and you can also get the name of the action event. So, this single method becomes the dispatcher for all action event processing for the portlet. In this example we show two action events, verify and config_pg2, and the code in separate methods that needs to execute for each of those events.

You can see that the actionPerformed method can become very cluttered with "if" statements while matching event name strings to invoke appropriate application behavior. You can solve this problem easily by changing the action event names from arbitrary strings to class names and then have the actionPerformed method in your portlet class get an instance of that class and invoke its actionPerformed method. This allows you to ensure better separation of responsibility in our code. You will see in the chapter titled *Struts Portlet Framework* that using the Struts framework to develop our portlets solves this problem.

Your JSPs will have to be changed to specify fully qualified class names in their `PortletURI` tags. We also introduce an abstract `Action` class as the superclass of our `Action` classes. The `ActionClassManager` is used to return `Action` subclass instances given a class name. Then our `actionPerformed` method is quite simple and looks like the following (this can be added to the `PollPortlet` in the Studio project):

```
/**
 * Handle all Action requests
 */
public void actionPerformed(ActionEvent event)
  throws PortletException {

  PortletRequest request = event.getRequest();
  PortletContext portletContext = getPortletConfig().getContext();
  PortletLog log = portletContext.getLog();

  // Get the action handler class and dispatch
  String actionClassName = event.getActionString();
  Action action = ActionClassManager.getAction(actionClassName);
  if (log.isDebugEnabled())
      log.debug("Dispatching to action class "+actionClassName);

  // Dispatch to that class event handler
  action.actionPerformed(request, portletContext);
  action.setView(request);
}
```

Now the code that was in the `verifyAction` method can be moved to the `actionPerformed` method of the new class `ConfigVerifyData-sourceAction`. Likewise, the code that was in the `page2Action` method can be moved to the `actionPerformed` method of the new class `ConfigPg2Action`.

The last structural change you will make will allow a similar separation of concerns in our implementation for the render phase processing as you just did for the action phase. You would have a similar problem with the `doConfigure` method, as it would need to handle all render requests for all configure pages in our portlet. You would need to determine which page in configure mode you should render, and then create any necessary beans and invoke the appropriate JSP. Again, you can segment this work out by introducing the idea of `View` classes and use the `Action` event processing to set the `View` class name to be dispatched to it during the render phase. You see that in the `setView` method in the `Action` classes.

Action Classes

The following is the `ConfigVerifyDatasourceAction` class:

```java
/**
 * Action - Handle the request to test the datasource
 */

public class ConfigVerifyDatasourceAction extends Action {
  public void actionPerformed(PortletRequest request,
  PortletContext portletContext) throws PollException {

    try {

      // Get configuration form data bean from session
      SessionData sessionData = SessionData.getSessionData(request);
      ConfigureFormData formData = sessionData.getConfigureFormData();

      // Update the persistence type and the datasource from request
      // parameters, validate the input.
      formData.updateDbParms(request);

      // Check the datasource name and the database tables
      // If an exception occurs put the exception message out
      DbBroker dbBroker = new DbBroker(formData.getDatasource());
      dbBroker.verifyTables();

      // Success, put a message out
      ResourceBundle bundle = ResourceBundle.getBundle("nls.polling",
        request.getLocale());
      String msg = bundle.getString("configure.verify_success");
      sessionData.setMessage(msg);

    }
    catch (PollException e) {
      SessionData sessionData = SessionData.getSessionData(request);
      sessionData.setMessage(e.getLocalizedMessage());
    }
  }

  /**
   * Set the next Portlet view... if this is a MODE change action
   * (createReturnURI) then set the next view to null to allow the
   * default view in the next mode
   */
  public void setView(PortletRequest request)
    throws PollException {
      setView(request, CONFIG_STATE);
  }
}
```

The setView method in the abstract Action class simply sets the View class name on the session object. During the render phase all you have to do is retrieve the View class name from the session object and dispatch to it. Realize that you can put the view class name on session using the portlet mode as the session attribute name. That is, you can have a view attribute on session, as well as configure, edit, and help attributes, each specifying a different View class name.

By implementing it this way, the user can leave configuration mode in page 2, for example, and when the user returns to configure mode he or she will return to that page instead of starting over from the initial page. Given this, you can dispatch not from the doView, doEdit, doConfigure methods in our PollPortlet class but from the Service method. So the Service method looks like the following:

```
/**
 * Service method
 */
public void service(PortletRequest request, PortletResponse response)
    throws PortletException, IOException {

  PortletContext portletContext = getPortletConfig().getContext();
  PortletLog log = portletContext.getLog();

  // Dispatch to the current View class for the current mode.
  // The View class name was set in the Action phase or is the
  // initial view.
  // View for the current portlet mode.
  View nextView = ViewClassManager.getView(request);
  if (log.isDebugEnabled())
    log.debug(Dispatching to view "+nextView.getClass().getName());
  nextView.performView(request, response,
    getPortletConfig().getContext());

}
```

The ViewClassManager simply retrieves the view class name from the session object using the current portlet mode as the attribute name and returns an instance of that class. If the attribute is not found on session then the initial view class for the current mode is returned.

Implementing the Action Classes

You have seen how the Action classes get invoked from the actionPerformed method in the Poll portlet class. You have also seen how a specific Action class is identified by name through the PortletURI tag in the

JSP and you have seen the implementation for the `ConfigVerifyData-sourceAction` class.

Configuration Mode

The configuration mode of this portlet has most of the action event processing. The view pages really have just one action and that is to register the user's vote. The edit mode we will see shortly also has only one action, to save the user's color preference for the results bar graph.

The configuration mode has the following actions to perform:

- Cancel the configuration (`CancelAction`)
- Add an answer choice (`ConfigAddChoiceAction`)
- Delete an answer choice (`ConfigDeleteChoiceAction`)
- Get user input and show next page (`ConfigPg2Action`)
- Get user input and show next page (`ConfigPg3Action`)
- Verify the datasource (`ConfigVerifyDatasourceAction`)
- Save the configuration updates (`ConfigSaveAction`)

The `ConfigAddChoiceAction` class and the `ConfigDeleteChoice-Action` class are very similar from a controller perspective. They simply get the current form data object from session, get the index of the select choice to be deleted or the choice string to be added, and call the appropriate method on the `PollBean` object. Here is the code for the action to add a choice.

```
/**
 * Action - Handle the request to add a poll choice
 */
public class ConfigAddChoiceAction extends Action {
  public void actionPerformed(PortletRequest request,
    PortletContext portletContext) throws PollException {

    // Get the form bean from session
    SessionData sessionData = SessionData.getSessionData(request);
    ConfigureFormData formData = sessionData.getConfigureFormData();

    // Get the updated choice and question values and
    // save them to the form data bean
    String pollQuestion = request.getParameter(POLL_QUESTION);
      formData.getPollBean().setQuestion(pollQuestion);
      String newChoice = request.getParameter(POLL_CHOICE);
      formData.getPollBean().addChoice(newChoice);
  }
```

```
      public void setView(PortletRequest request)
      throws PollException {
        setView(request,  CONFIG_P3_STATE);
    }
  }
```

The `ConfigPg2Action` class and the `ConfigPg3Action` class are also very similar. They get the current form data object from session, update the form data with the user settings from the request parameters, and update the form data object for the next page and invoke the JSP.

The following listing shows the `ConfigPg2Action` class. The datastore options from the first configuration page are retrieved and held in the form data and a list of existing polls (by name) is prepared for use by the JSP for the next configuration page. The `ConfigPg3Action` class is very similar to `ConfigPg2Action`, so we will not show it here.

```
/**
 * Action - Handle the request to move to the next
 * configuration page.
 */

public class ConfigPg2Action extends Action {

  public void actionPerformed(PortletRequest request,
    PortletContext portletContext) throws PollException {

    // Get configuration form data bean from session
    SessionData sessionData = SessionData.getSessionData(request);
    ConfigureFormData formData = sessionData.getConfigureFormData();

    // Update the persistence type and the datasource from request
    // parameters, validate the input.
    formData.updateDbParms(request);

    // Get the list of current polls (by name) from the data store
    // Get a broker instance using the form data parameters
    Broker broker = Broker.getInstance(formData.getPersistType(),
      formData.getDatasource());
    List pollNames = broker.getPollNames();

    // Put it in form data object
    formData.setPollNames(pollNames);

  }

  public void setView(PortletRequest request)
    throws PollException {
      setView(request, CONFIG_P2_STATE);
  }
}
```

The final action event is to save the configuration mode modifications. This is invoked from the last page and implemented in the `ConfigSaveAction` class. In the following listing you see that, like the other configuration action classes, the form data is retrieved from session and updated with the configuration values from the last page.

The poll name and the persistence options are saved to the portlet settings. Keeping those values there allows concrete portlet instances each to represent a different poll with potentially different persistent stores. The poll information itself is saved to the persistent store.

```
/**
 * Action - Handle the request to save the configuration
 * changes
 */
public class ConfigSaveAction extends Action {

   public void actionPerformed(PortletRequest request,
       PortletContext portletContext) throws PollException {

      try {

         // Get form data and poll bean from session
         SessionData sessionData = SessionData.getSessionData(request);
         ConfigureFormData formData = sessionData.getConfigureFormData();
         PollBean pollBean = formData.getPollBean();

         // Get the question and save it to the form data bean
         String pollQuestion = request.getParameter(POLL_QUESTION);
           pollBean.setQuestion(pollQuestion);

         // Update the portlet settings
         PortletSettings portletSettings = request.getPortletSettings();
           portletSettings.setAttribute(POLL_NAME, pollBean.getName());
         portletSettings.setAttribute(PERSIST_TYPE,
           formData.getPersistType());
         portletSettings.setAttribute(DATASOURCE,
           formData.getDatasource());

         // Save the portlet settings
         portletSettings.store();

         // Save the poll info
         Broker.getInstance(portletSettings).updatePoll(pollBean);

         // Clean up session data
         SessionData.removeFrom(request.getPortletSession());

      }
```

```
    catch (AccessDeniedException e) {
      ResourceBundle bundle = ResourceBundle.getBundle("nls.polling",
        request.getLocale());
      String msg = bundle.getString("exception.accessdenied");
      throw new PollWrapperException(msg, e);
    }
     catch (IOException e) {
      ResourceBundle bundle = ResourceBundle.getBundle("nls.polling",
        request.getLocale());
      String msg = bundle.getString("exception.io");
      throw new PollWrapperException(msg, e);
    }
  }

  public void setView(PortletRequest request)
    throws PollException {
      setView(request, null);
  }
}
```

View Mode

The view mode has only one action class and that is to register the user's vote. That class simply gets the userid from the User object for the logged-in user and retrieves the vote selection from the request parameter. It then calls the Broker class to register the vote. The following listing shows the VoteAction implementation.

```
/**
 * Action - Handle the request to cast a vote
 */
public class VoteAction extends Action {
  public void actionPerformed(PortletRequest request,
    PortletContext portletContext) throws PollException {

    // Get the userid and selected choice
    String userid = request.getUser().getUserID();
    String indexStr = request.getParameter(SELECTED_CHOICE);
    int index = new Integer(indexStr).intValue();
    // Register the vote
    PortletSettings portletSettings = request.getPortletSettings();
    String pollName = portletSettings.getAttribute(POLL_NAME);
    Broker.getInstance(portletSettings).vote(userid, pollName, index);
  }
  public void setView(PortletRequest request)
    throws PollException {
      setView(request, VIEW_STATE);
  }
}
```

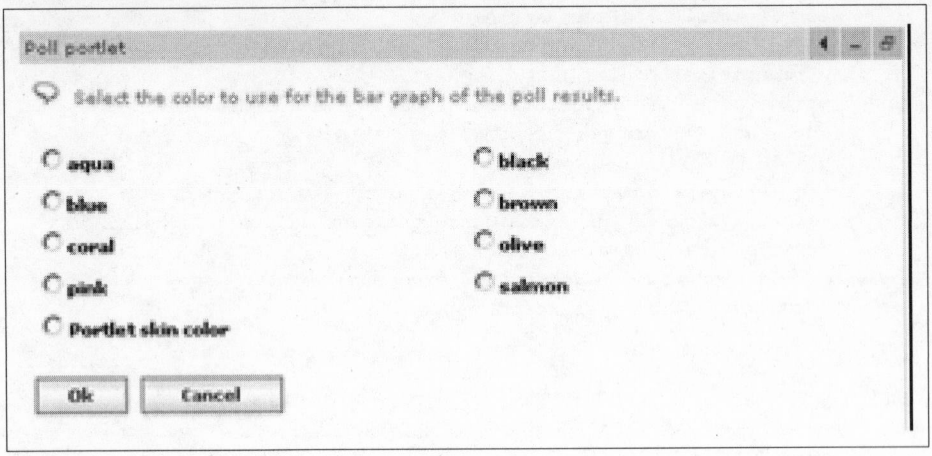

Figure 16-3 Edit mode.

Edit Mode

The final action class is for edit mode and it is the code to save the edit customization information (see Figure 16-3). The customization data is user-specific and so it is stored in portlet data. The following listing shows the implementation for the `EditSaveAction` class:

```
/**
 * Action - Handle the request to save the edit customizations
 */
public class EditSaveAction extends Action {

  public void actionPerformed(PortletRequest request,
    PortletContext portletContext) throws PollException {

  try {
    // Save the selected color to portlet data
    String color = request.getParameter(COLOR);
    if (color != null) {
      PortletData portletData = request.getData();
      portletData.setAttribute(COLOR, color);
      portletData.store();
    }
  }
  catch (AccessDeniedException e) {
    ResourceBundle bundle = ResourceBundle.getBundle("nls.polling",
      request.getLocale());
    String msg = bundle.getString("exception.accessdenied");
    throw new PollWrapperException(msg, e);
  }
  catch (IOException e) {
    ResourceBundle bundle = ResourceBundle.getBundle("nls.polling",
```

```
        request.getLocale());
      String msg = bundle.getString("exception.io");
      throw new PollWrapperException(msg, e);
    }
  }
  public void setView(PortletRequest request)
    throws PollException {
      setView(request, null);
  }
}
```

Implementing the View Classes

The `View` classes are invoked during the portlet rendering phase. Typically the view classes simply invoke the JSP. Beans needed to render the JSP are most often created during the action phase processing and put in session data for use by the JSP. You might be inclined to instead put these objects in the request object during action processing; however, they would then not be available on subsequent portal page refreshes when the portlet is asked to render itself without explicit user interaction with the portlet and so no action processing occurs.

The following view classes are used in this portlet:

- Initial configure view (`ConfigureView`)
- Configure view—page 2 (`ConfigurePg2View`)
- Configure view—page 3 (`ConfigurePg3View`)
- Initial edit view (`InitialEditView`)
- Initial view (`MainView`)

Only in the initial views do we need to execute processing logic. The `ConfigurePg2View` and `ConfigurePg3View` simply invoke their respective JSPs. Similarly, the initial edit view and the initial configure view do not require any processing prior to invoking their JSPs. The edit page simply shows a static set of color choices from which the user can make a selection. The initial configuration page shows static persistent store choices.

The main view is different however. This view requires that we get the portlet settings to determine the poll name and the persistent store information. Then we ask the `Broker` for the poll details and check if the user has already voted. If so, we need to call the `Broker` again for the current voting results. Since the voting totals are dynamic we want to refresh this information when the portlet is asked to render itself not just when the user is interacting with this portlet.

We have looked at the code to generate the main view earlier. Here it is again in complete form in the `MainView` class:

```
/**
 * View - Poll view
 */

public class MainView implements View {

public void performView(PortletRequest request,
    PortletResponse response, PortletContext portletContext)
    throws IOException, PortletException, PollException {

  // Is the portlet configured
  validateConfiguration(request);

  // Get the poll bean
  PortletSettings portletSettings = request.getPortletSettings();
  String pollName = portletSettings.getAttribute(POLL_NAME);
  Broker broker = Broker.getInstance(portletSettings);
  PollBean pollBean = broker.getPoll(pollName);

  // If the poll was not found generate an error message
  if (pollBean == null) {
    ResourceBundle bundle = ResourceBundle.getBundle("nls.polling",
      request.getLocale());
    String msg = bundle.getString("exception.notfound");
    throw new PollMessageException(msg);
  }

  // If the user has not already voted show poll question
  // otherwise show poll results.
  String user = request.getUser().getUserID();
  boolean hasUserVoted = broker.hasUserVoted(user, pollName);

  if (hasUserVoted) {

    // Get customization color value from portlet data
    PortletData portletData = request.getData();
    String color = (String)portletData.getAttribute(COLOR);
    request.setAttribute(COLOR, color);

    pollBean.initializeResults(broker);
    request.setAttribute("pollBean", pollBean);
      portletContext.include(VIEW_RESULTS_JSP, request, response);
  }
  else {
    request.setAttribute("pollBean", pollBean);
      portletContext.include(VIEW_QUESTION_JSP, request, response);
  }
 }
}
```

Implementing the Model Classes

Let's start with the implementation of the model classes for the polling portlet. There are two model objects that we should consider for this portlet. The most obvious is the object to represent a poll (PollBean). In addition, we need access to user information. For this, the User object is provided to the portlet developer through the portlet API. If we ensure that our portlet executes only on authenticated portal pages then we have access to the User object that represents the user that is logged in to portal.

The PollBean object needs to implement the behavior that we have seen so far. It needs to know its poll name, the poll question, and the collection of answer choices. The Poll object should also know the total number of votes cast, the number of votes cast for each answer choice, and the percentage value of votes for each choice. We will also implement an initializeResults method to explicitly initialize the votes cast information for the poll.

The PollBean implementation is pretty straightforward. Create a package in the Poll Project under the JavaSource directory. In the package create a new class called PollBean. The following listing shows most of the class implementation. Some of the accessor methods have been deleted in the interest of space.

```java
public class PollBean implements Serializable, PollConstants {

    // Poll attributes
    protected String name = "";
    protected String question = "";
    protected String choices = "";

    // Choice list
    protected int numberOfChoices = 0;
    protected List choiceList = null;

    // Votes cast on this poll
    protected int votesCast = 0;
    protected List voteCountList = new ArrayList();
    protected List votePercentageList = new ArrayList();

    /**
     * Set the current vote counts
     */
    public void initializeResults(Broker broker) throws PollException {

        votesCast = 0;
        for (int i = 0; i < numberOfChoices; i++) {
            int voteCount = broker.voteCount(name, i);
            voteCountList.add(i, new Integer(voteCount));
```

```java
        votesCast = votesCast + voteCount;
    }
    calcVotePercentages();
}


/**
 * Calculate the voting percentages for each choice
 */
protected void calcVotePercentages() throws PollException {

    int voteCount = 0;
    int voteLargestPercent = 0;
    int voteLargestIndex = 0;
    int votePercent = 0;
    int voteCumPercent = 0;

    for (int i = 0; i < numberOfChoices; i++) {
        voteCount = ((Integer) voteCountList.get(i)).intValue();
        votePercent = (voteCount * 100) / votesCast;
        votePercentageList.add(new Integer(votePercent));
        voteCumPercent = voteCumPercent + votePercent;
        if (votePercent > voteLargestPercent) {
            voteLargestIndex = i;
            voteLargestPercent = votePercent;
        }
    }

    voteLargestPercent = voteLargestPercent + (100 - voteCumPercent);
    votePercentageList.remove(voteLargestIndex);
    votePercentageList.add(
        voteLargestIndex,
        new Integer(voteLargestPercent));
}


/**
 * Sets the choices and parses the string
 *
 * @param choices The choices to set
 */
public void setChoices(String choices) {
    this.choices = choices;
    parseChoices();
}


/**
 * Parse the choices string
 */
public void parseChoices() {

    List choiceList = new ArrayList(3);
```

```
      int lastIndex = 0;
      int index = choices.indexOf(DELIMITER, lastIndex);
      while (index > 0) {
        choiceList.add(choices.substring(lastIndex, index));
        lastIndex = index + 1;
        index = choices.indexOf(DELIMITER, lastIndex);
      }

      // Set the number of poll choices
      this.numberOfChoices = choiceList.size();
      this.choiceList = choiceList;
   }

   /**
    * Add a poll choice
    * @param newChoice String
    */
   public void addChoice(String newChoice) {

     if (!newChoice.equals("")) {
       newChoice = stripDelimiter(newChoice) + DELIMITER;
       String newChoices = choices + newChoice;
       setChoices(newChoices);
     }
   }

   /**
    * Delete a poll choice
    * @param choiceIndex int
    */
   public void deleteChoice(int choiceIndex) {
     // Strip the choice from the choices string
     int index = -1;
     for (int i = 0; i < choiceIndex; i++) {
       index = choices.indexOf(DELIMITER, index + 1);
     }

     String prefix = choices.substring(0, index + 1);
     index = choices.indexOf(DELIMITER, index + 1);
     String suffix = choices.substring(index + 1);
     String newChoices = prefix + suffix;

     setChoices(newChoices);
   }

   /**
    * Strip the delimiter if it appears in the entered text.
    * No substitution or warning is provided.
    */
```

```
protected String stripDelimiter(String choice) {

  int index = choice.indexOf(DELIMITER);
  if (index == -1)
    return choice;
  return stripDelimiter(
    choice.substring(0, index) + choice.substring(index + 1));
}
}
```

A `Poll` instance will be created by a call to the persistent store access class. To simplify the persistence access for the answer choices they will be stored as a single string. When the choices field is updated, the setter method will also parse the string and update the list of choices that are held in the `choiceList` field as well as update the `numberOfChoices` field. This will be important when we define the persistence class definitions in the next section.

There will also be a method to initialize the poll results. This method will get the vote count for each answer choice from the persistent store and calculate the voting totals and the voting percentages.

Implementing Persistence Classes

There will be two implementations for persistence layers for this portlet. We will implement a database broker and a memory broker. Of course, the data "stored" in memory is lost when the server restarts. But, it is useful for demonstration purposes. Both broker types will extend the abstract broker that we will define.

The `Broker` class defines the following abstract methods:

- `getPoll(String pollName)`. Gets the poll information from the datastore for the poll of the given name. Creates and returns a Poll instance with that data.

- `getPollNames()`. Returns a list of the names of existing polls.

- `deletePoll(String pollName)`. Deletes the poll data with the given name.

- `updatePoll(PollBean poll)`. Updates the poll data.

- `vote(String userid, String pollName, int choiceIndex)`. Records a vote for the given user in the given poll for the choice index.

- `hasVotingStarted(String pollName)`. Returns true if a vote has been registered for a poll name; false otherwise.

- hasUserVoted(String userid, String pollName). Returns true if the userid has a recorded vote in the poll with the given name.

- voteCount(String pollName, int choiceIndex). Returns the number of votes for the given choice index for the poll with the given name.

The Broker class has static methods and static variables to return an instance of either a DbBroker or a MemoryBroker. The portlet configuration defines the persistent store type, memory, or database. If a type of database is selected, then a datasource name is specified as well. A call to the Broker getInstance() method will return either a DbBroker or MemoyBroker instance based on those values.

DatabaseBroker

The DatabaseBroker queries the poll and vote data from two tables in a database specified by the named datasource. The tables are POLL and VOTE and can be defined by the following SQL:

```
CREATE TABLE POLL (NAME VARCHAR(32) NOT NULL, QUESTION VARCHAR(256),
CHOICES VARCHAR(512), PRIMARY KEY(NAME))

CREATE TABLE VOTE (USERID VARCHAR(255) NOT NULL, POLL VARCHAR(32) NOT
NULL , VOTE INTEGER NOT NULL, PRIMARY KEY(USERID, POLL))
```

Implementing Utility Classes

Our portlet defines two exception classes. One is an exception to wrap another thrown exception and associate our own message with it. The other is a message exception that we can use to terminate processing and put a message out to the portlet page. These are PollWrapperException and PollMessageException. Both extend PollException.

Finally, the string constants needed for the portlet application are defined in the PollConstants interface. This completes the utility classes in use by the Poll portlet.

Summary

In this chapter you looked at the key elements of the code for the Poll Portlet implemented using the IBM Portlet API. We discussed the overall design of the portlet application and focused on a design that maintained good separation of concerns.

The portlet implementation should be in the use of `PortletSettings` and `PortletData` for configuration and customization data. We discussed issues of page navigation. The portlet demonstrated an implementation with multiple portlet modes. We accessed text strings from `ResourceBundles` in the java code as well as the JSP to enable the portlet for internationalization. We showed the use of the `PortletLog` to generate trace-logging messages. We implemented two `Broker` classes to manage a persistent store for our poll data.

In the next chapter you will fill in any missing pieces of this implementation from the download source code. We will execute the code using WebSphere Studio's test environment.

## CHAPTER 17

Portlet Interactive Debug and JSR 168 Example

This chapter will examine the interactive test environment of WebSphere Studio. You will execute the example Poll portlet discussed in the last chapter. You will learn about configuring the test server and how to use the debugging environment using a local Portal test environment.

You will also modify the example Poll portlet to use the JSR 168 API instead of the IBM Portlet API used in its initial development.

Poll Portlet Project

If you did not work through the complete portlet implementation in the last chapter you may want to download the source code and import it into an empty portlet project, allowing the import to overwrite any existing files. You can also use the import utility to create a new project. After the import is complete and the project is created, you will see a number of errors in the project. That is because required portlet jar files are not on the project build path. As we have discussed, one of the benefits of using the portlet toolkit to create portlet application projects is that it will set up the correct class path definition.

To add the needed IBM Portlet API jar files to the project build class path, open the properties on the newly created project by right-clicking on the project in the Navigator pane and selecting Properties from the pop-up menu. Select Java Build Path and then the Libraries tab. You can add the required jar files with the following steps:

- Select Add Variable, then select WPS_V5_PLUGINDIR in the New Variable Classpath Entry and click Extend. Select `portlet-api.jar` and click OK.

- Select Add Variable, then select WPS_V5_PLUGINDIR in the New Variable Classpath Entry and click Extend. Select `wps.jar` and click OK.

- Select Add Variable, then select WPS_V5_PLUGINDIR in the New Variable Classpath Entry and click Extend. Select `wpsportlets.jar` and click OK.

- Select Add Variable, then select WAS_50_PLUGINDIR in the New Variable Classpath Entry and click Extend. Expand the lib directory and then select `dynacache.jar` and click OK.

- Click OK to exit properties and save changes.

You may need to rebuild the project to resolve some JSP errors. Right-click onthe project in the Navigator pane and select Rebuild Project.

Portal Server Configuration

You can use Studio to debug portlet applications that are running on WebSphere Portal running locally within the Studio environment or on a remote machine. In this chapter we will discuss local environment debugging, which is referred to as *WebSphere Portal 5.0 Test Environment*. You will need to ensure that you have installed WebSphere Portal in WebSphere Studio using the Portal Toolkit installer.

In order to run the portlet in the local portal test environment, you must create a server and portal server configuration in Studio (see Figure 17-1). After the portal server configuration is defined, you can publish and debug your portlet application.

In Studio, select File ⇨ New ⇨ Other from the menu bar. In the dialog box that opens, select Server in the left pane and then Server and Server Configuration on the right. Select Next.

In the next dialog box, enter a name of your choice for the server and select Test Environment under *WebSphere Portal version 5.0* for the Server type. Click Next.

The next dialog box allows you to change the HTTP port number that will be used in the server configuration (see Figure 17-2). Make a change if needed and then click Finish. Change to the Server perspective. You will see the server you just created in the Server view. Open the server to edit the configuration.

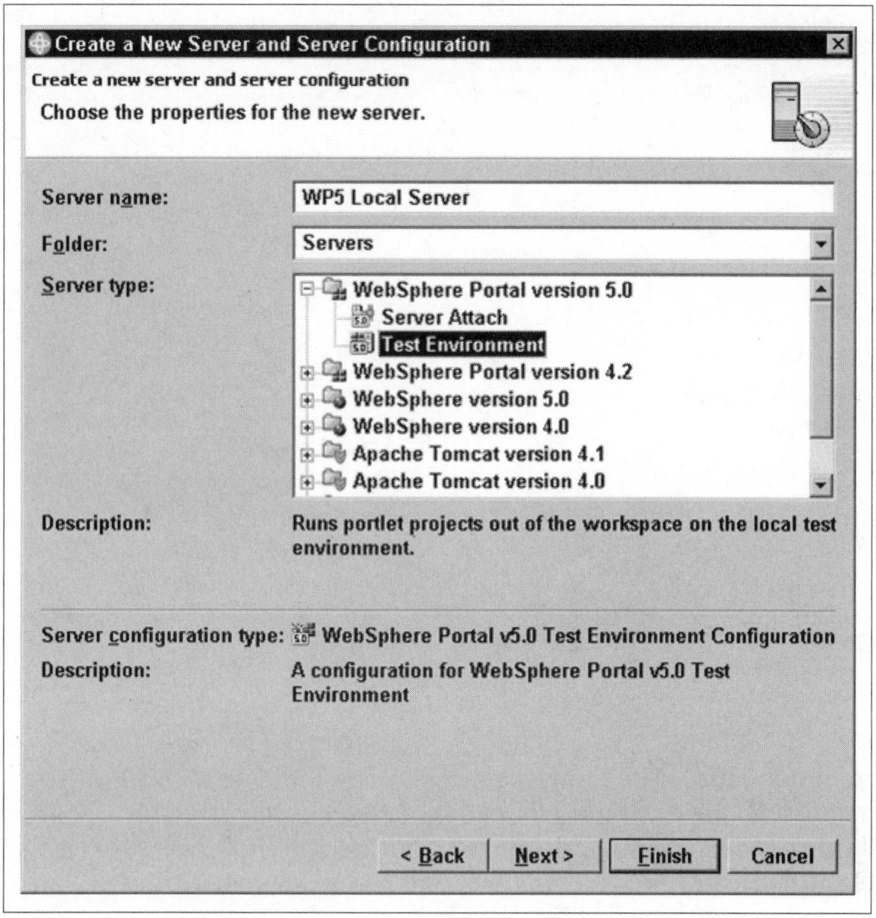

Figure 17-1   Creating a new server in Studio.

Here you can specify the data source for the poll application if you will use a database for storing the application data. First, select the Security tab to open the Security Options page. Create a JAAS Authentication Entry for the userid that will be used to authenticate to the database when a connection is requested. Then select the DataSource tab. From the Data Sources page create a JDBC Provider, if needed. For DB2, select IBM DB2 Database Type and DB2 Legacy CLI-Based Type 2 JDBC Driver for the JDBC provider type. On the second page make sure the class path is set to point to the correct JDBC driver library.

Select the JDBC Provider and click Add to add a data source. From the Create a Data Source dialog box, select the JDBC Provider and select Version 5.0 Data Source. Select Next. Provide a data source name of your choice. Enter a JNDI name of your choice, keeping the `jdbc/` prefix. The name you enter here (after `jdbc/`) is the data source name that you will use in the

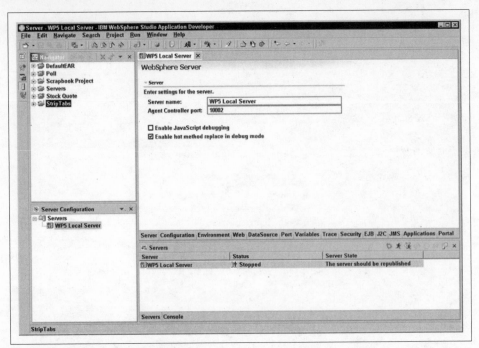

Figure 17-2   Server configuration.

portlet configuration. For Component-managed authentication alias select the JAAS Authentication Entry that you created. Uncheck the check box for Use this Data Source in Container Managed Persistence (CMP). This is the minimal set of changes you need to make. Make other changes as needed for your environment. Select Next.

Enter the database name on this page. This is the only required configuration on this page. Make other changes as needed for your environment. Select Finish. The data source has been defined. Close the server configuration edit and save the changes.

A portal server configuration is like a server configuration with the addition of portal-specific configuration information kept in the wps-info.xml file. You can view the configuration files through a filter change. Switch to the Web perspective and from the Project Navigator in the left pane click on the menu icon. From the drop-down list select Filters. From the Filters dialog box that appears, select Server in the project types list and select OK.

Back in the Server perspective, the server has been configured but we have not associated any portlet projects with it. Right-click on the server you just added from the Server view. Select Add and Remove Projects. You will add Enterprise Application (EAR) projects to the server configuration (see Figure 17-3). When you created the portlet project, it was associated

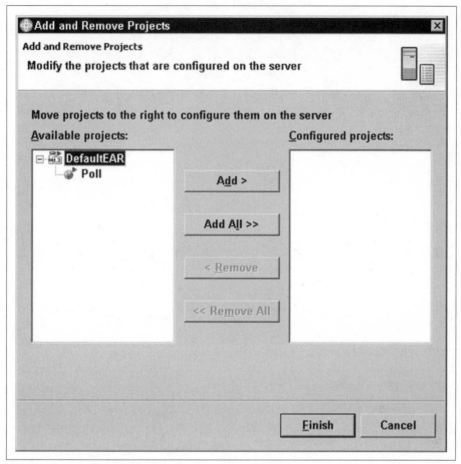

Figure 17-3   Adding and removing projects.

with an EAR, DefaultEAR, by default. If you did not change that then add the DefaultEAR project to the server configuration.

To change the EAR a portlet project is deployed into, open the EAR deployment descriptor (application.xml). Select the Module tab and use the Add and Remove buttons to change the Web applications associated with this EAR.

When the Portal test environment is started, the Poll portlet (and any other portlets in the DefaultEAR project) will be deployed on a debug portal page.

You can publish, start, and stop the server manually. Publishing copies the application project, resource, and configuration files to the correct server location. After the publishing is complete you can start the server. You can also start the server in debug mode. If not started in debug mode you will be

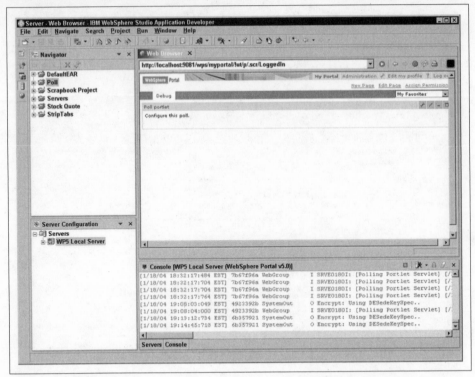

Figure 17-4 Portal page.

able to execute your portlets; in debug mode you can set breakpoints, interrogate code, and inspect variables. These actions can be performed from the Server view from the pop-up menu and the server. After the server starts you can open a browser to `http://hostname:9081/wps/myportal` where `hostname` is your server hostname and `9081` is the HTTP server port that was configurable when the server was created.

As an alternative you can start the server and launch your portlet in a Studio Web browser by right-clicking the portlet project and selecting either Debug on Server or Run on Server from the pop-up menu. After logging in with the default portal admin id (`wpsadmin`) the portlet is shown (see Figure 17-4).

Portal Debug Mode

When you start the server in debug mode you can set breakpoints in your Java source files or JSP files and then, using the Debug perspective, debug your code. You can step through the code, inspect variables, and evaluate expressions in context of the current thread's stack frame.

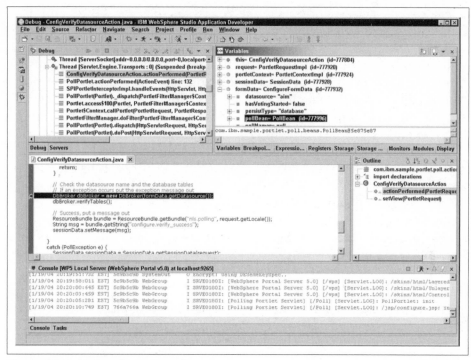

Figure 17-5   Debugging your code.

Breakpoints can be made conditional and they can be active based on a hit count. You can set exception breakpoints or breakpoints can be set on binary types where there is no source code available.

In our example application we added a breakpoint to the following line in the `ConfigVerifyDatasourceAction actionPerformed` method:

```
DbBroker dbBroker = new DbBroker(formData.getDatasource());
```

Then when we ran the portlet and clicked the Verify button in configure mode, the Debug perspective opened, with processing suspended at that breakpoint. Figure 17-5 shows the debugger opened, with execution suspended at that method. You see in the Variables view the current values of the method variables. The current stack is shown along with the current class outline. We can continue execution by stepping through the code to trace the application execution. We can also inspect code expressions in the current method or through the Expressions view.

We can make changes to our portlet code and have those changes immediately reflected in our executing test environment. There is generally no need to restart the server or republish the application in order to test code modifications. However, if changes are made to the deployment descriptors for example, those changes require a server restart. But, changes can be made to Java classes or JSPs in the Portlet perspective, saved, and then that code immediately executed.

Studio's ability to interactively debug portlet code in a test environment with dynamic changes provides an extremely powerful development environment. The portlet toolkit provides assistance for getting the portlet application development started by creating the portlet project and starting the base implementations. The portal test environment significantly enhances that by providing a highly productive execution environment that assists in application code debugging while allowing developers to more quickly understand the portlet API through its interactive nature.

The step-by-step debug mode of WebSphere Application Server lets you debug WebSphere Portal internal methods. This is enabled by default. To disable the step-by-step debug mode so that you stop only at the breakpoints that you set, do the following:

1. Select Window ➪ Preferences from the menu bar
2. Select WAS Debug mode to open the WAS Debug page.
3. Deselect the Use step-by-step Debug mode check box.
4. Click OK.

Portal Trace Logging

The IBM Portlet API provides a logging mechanism so that portlet developers can easily write trace messages to a common log. By default, the trace messages are written to a log file named wps_<date>.log in the <wp-root>/log directory, where <date> is the timestamp when the log was first created.

WebSphere Portal also supports the redirection of its trace logging to the WebSphere Application Server log. This function can be enabled in the <wp_root>\shared\app\config\log.properties file.

You can enable trace logging using an administrative portlet or through a properties file change. Using the Enable Tracing portlet will allow you to specify the trace settings temporarily. When the server is restarted, the trace settings return to the previous state. You can also update the same log.properties file and specify the trace setting there. In this case the change will get applied when the server is restarted.

In either case the trace specification is through a trace string. See the Portal Information Center in the section Using Logs for the definition of trace strings. For example, to enable tracing of portlets use the following trace string:

```
com.ibm.wps.portlets.*=all=enabled:org.apache.jetspeed.portlet
.PortletLog=all=enabled
```

Enable tracing in our Portal test environment. The portal root (`<wp-root>`) in Studio is `<studio-root>\runtimes\portal_v50`. So the log file is at `<studio-root>\runtimes\portal_v50\shared\app\log .properties`. Uncomment the `traceString` property and set it to the string shown above.

You will recall that we had two trace messages in our portlet code. In the `service` method and in the `actionPerformed` method we had the following. Note it is good practice to test if logging is enabled before attempting to write the trace message and also before constructing the trace message.

```
if (log.isDebugEnabled())
  log.debug(this.getClass().getName()+".service() dispatching to "+
  nextState.getClass().getName());

if (log.isDebugEnabled())
  log.debug(this.getClass().getName()+".actionPerformed() dispatching to
"+
  actionClassName);
```

So after executing our portlet with tracing turned on we should see portlet trace messages in the `<studio-root>\runtimes\portal_v50\log\ wps_2004.01.19-23.51.33.log` file (see Figure 17-6).

```
2004.01.19 23:56:59.405 1 org.apache.jetspeed.portlet.PortletLog debug Servlet.Engine.Transports : 1
  com.ibm.sample.portlet.poll.portlet.PollPortlet.service() dispatching to com.ibm.sample.portlet.poll.views.MainView

2004.01.19 23:57:01.979 1 org.apache.jetspeed.portlet.PortletLog debug Servlet.Engine.Transports : 0
  com.ibm.sample.portlet.poll.portlet.PollPortlet.service() dispatching to com.ibm.sample.portlet.poll.views.InitialConfigureView

2004.01.19 23:57:06.516 1 org.apache.jetspeed.portlet.PortletLog debug Servlet.Engine.Transports : 0
  com.ibm.sample.portlet.poll.portlet.PollPortlet.actionPerformed() dispatching to com.ibm.sample.portlet.poll.actions.ConfigPg2Action

2004.01.19 23:57:06.606 1 org.apache.jetspeed.portlet.PortletLog debug Servlet.Engine.Transports : 0
  com.ibm.sample.portlet.poll.portlet.PollPortlet.service() dispatching to com.ibm.sample.portlet.poll.views.ConfigurePg2View

2004.01.19 23:57:13.145 1 org.apache.jetspeed.portlet.PortletLog debug Servlet.Engine.Transports : 2
  com.ibm.sample.portlet.poll.portlet.PollPortlet.actionPerformed() dispatching to com.ibm.sample.portlet.poll.actions.ConfigPg3Action

2004.01.19 23:57:13.225 1 org.apache.jetspeed.portlet.PortletLog debug Servlet.Engine.Transports : 2
  com.ibm.sample.portlet.poll.portlet.PollPortlet.service() dispatching to com.ibm.sample.portlet.poll.views.ConfigurePg3View

2004.01.19 23:57:27.255 1 org.apache.jetspeed.portlet.PortletLog debug Servlet.Engine.Transports : 1
  com.ibm.sample.portlet.poll.portlet.PollPortlet.actionPerformed() dispatching to com.ibm.sample.portlet.poll.actions.ConfigAddChoiceAction

2004.01.19 23:57:27.295 1 org.apache.jetspeed.portlet.PortletLog debug Servlet.Engine.Transports : 1
  com.ibm.sample.portlet.poll.portlet.PollPortlet.service() dispatching to com.ibm.sample.portlet.poll.views.ConfigurePg3View

2004.01.19 23:57:31.972 1 org.apache.jetspeed.portlet.PortletLog debug Servlet.Engine.Transports : 1
  com.ibm.sample.portlet.poll.portlet.PollPortlet.actionPerformed() dispatching to com.ibm.sample.portlet.poll.actions.ConfigAddChoiceAction

2004.01.19 23:57:31.992 1 org.apache.jetspeed.portlet.PortletLog debug Servlet.Engine.Transports : 1
  com.ibm.sample.portlet.poll.portlet.PollPortlet.service() dispatching to com.ibm.sample.portlet.poll.views.ConfigurePg3View

2004.01.19 23:57:32.984 1 org.apache.jetspeed.portlet.PortletLog debug Servlet.Engine.Transports : 1
  com.ibm.sample.portlet.poll.portlet.PollPortlet.actionPerformed() dispatching to com.ibm.sample.portlet.poll.actions.ConfigSaveAction

2004.01.19 23:57:33.144 1 org.apache.jetspeed.portlet.PortletLog debug Servlet.Engine.Transports : 1
  com.ibm.sample.portlet.poll.portlet.PollPortlet.service() dispatching to com.ibm.sample.portlet.poll.views.MainView
```

Figure 17-6 Portlet trace messages.

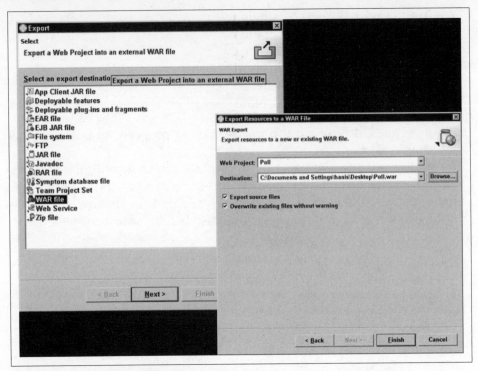

Figure 17-7   Exporting a WAR file.

Generating a Deployable WAR File

Generating a deployable WAR file in Studio using the portal toolkit is very easy. Since the portlet project is consistent with the expected contents of a Web archive file we simply need to export the project to a WAR file. That file can then be installed in WebSphere Portal.

For our Poll portlet simply right-click the `Poll` project in the Project Navigator view and select Export (see Figure 17-7). You can install this portlet application in Portal using the Install administrative portlet.

Deploying Using the Install Administrative Portlet

You can deploy the portlet application WAR file into Portal using the Install administrative portlet. Log in to portal as a user with administrative privilege (is a member of `wpsadmins`) and navigate to the Install pages by first selecting the Administration page, then the Portlets page, and finally the Install page.

The Install page contains a single portlet, the Install portlet. From this portlet you specify the location of the WAR file on your local file system and then execute the install function. The portlet application will be installed in portal. Typcially, the next administrative steps are to add portlet or portlets that were installed with that portlet application to a portlet page and assign resource permissions if required. Note that the Manage Portlet Applications portlet can be used to update an existing portlet application. This updates the portlets defined in the WAR file while preserving the portlet resource permissions and their page associations.

Deploying Using XML Configuration Interface

You can also deploy the portlet application using the XML configuration interface. The XML configuration interface is a command line portal configuration utility that uses an XML input file for configuration information and action requests. A stand-alone utility reads the XML source file and executes against a portal server through an HTTP connection.

Along with deploying portlet applications you can use this utility to back up and restore complete portal configurations, copy parts of a configuration to another portal, install additional resources on a portal, and perform recurring administrative tasks through a programmable interface.

See the current Portal Information Center for a definition of the structure of the XML file, the XML schema, and examples of common function (including deploying a portlet). If for any reason the administrative portlets to deploy portlets or manage access control become unavailable, it is very helpful to keep this utility in mind as it can provide critical function to resolve problems with portlets that you typically rely on to manage the portal environment.

Developing the Poll Portlet with JSR 168 API

In this next section we will discuss the changes needed to your Poll portlet implementation to use the JSR 168 API. A general discussion of the differences in the programming interface was described in Chapter 14. In the remaining section of this chapter we will apply that understanding to the portlet we just created using the IBM Portlet API.

Again we will start our portlet development using the Portal Toolkit in WebSphere Studio. We will be using the Studio wizard to create a new portlet application project to set up the correct class path defined for the JSR168 API, to create the base deployment descriptors, and to define our project directory structure.

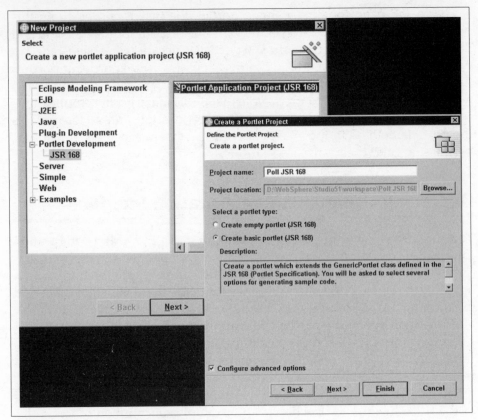

Figure 17-8 Create New Project.

Create the Poll Project

Using Studio 5.1 with the Portal Toolkit 5.02 (or later combination) select File ⇨ New ⇨ Project from the toolbar. From the New Project page that opens (see Figure 17-8), expand Portlet Development in the left pane and select JSR 168. In the right pane select Portlet Application Project (JSR 168) and select Next.

In the next page enter the project name **Poll JSR 168** and select Create Basic Portlet (JSR 168). Then select Configure Advanced Options and select Next.

In the J2EE Settings page (see Figure 17-9) accept the default settings and select Next.

In the Portlet Settings page select Change Code Generation Options to specify the poll portlet class name and the package name that is the same as the portlet you created using the IBM Portlet API. Then we can just copy that code into this project and make changes to the portlet classes without

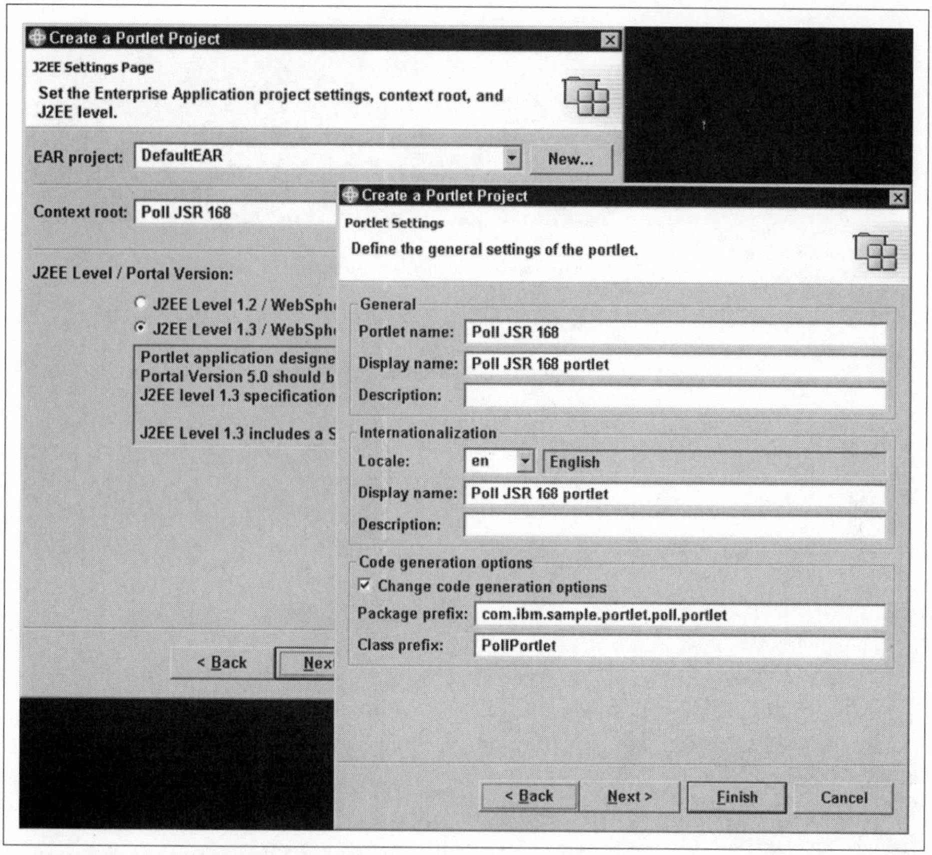

Figure 17-9   J2EE (left) and Portlet Settings (right) pages.

changing the deployment descriptor. The sample code provided specifies the *Package prefix* as com.ibm.sample.portlet.poll.portlet and the *Class prefix* as PollPortlet. Select Next.

In the Action and Preferences page (see Figure 17-10) deselect Add Form Sample and select Next. In the Miscellaneous page select Add Edit Mode and Add Configure Mode to see an example of the portlet implementation for processing of a standard mode (edit) and a custom mode (configure). Select Finish, completing the wizard and creating the project.

Generated Portlet Code

Next you will inspect the generated portlet code. The deployment descriptors are a key part of the generated portlet project.

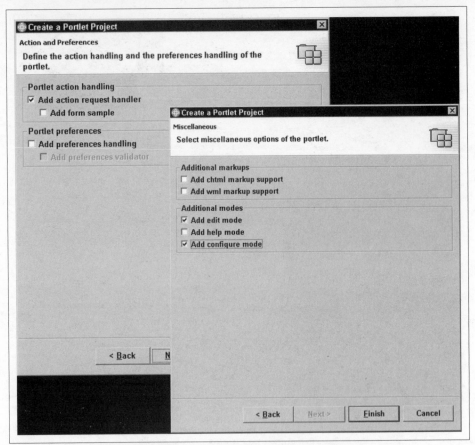

Figure 17-10 Action and Preferences (left) and Miscellaneous (right) pages.

Deployment Descriptors

The portlet and Web deployment descriptors are generated when the wizard completes. In a previous chapter we discussed the differences in the deployment descriptors between both APIs. Here we see the differences in these files.

Notice that with the JSR 168 API the portlet class is no longer defined in the Web descriptor `<servlet-class>` element. Instead it is defined in the portlet descriptor `<portlet-class>` element. The Web descriptor now simply has the welcome file list and a tag lib definition.

Also in the portlet descriptor you see the definition for *configure* custom portlet mode. You should update this file to include the portlet preferences (the portlet settings from the previous API) in the `<portlet-preferences>` element. The `<resource-bundle>` element should also be updated to reference the correct path and filename of the bundle from the previous project that you will import.

```xml
<?xml version="1.0" encoding="UTF-8"?>
<portlet-app xmlns="http://java.sun.com/xml/ns/portlet/portlet-app_1_0.xsd"
  version="1.0" xmlns:xsi="http://www.w3.org/2001/XMLSchema-instance"
  xsi:schemaLocation="http://java.sun.com/xml/ns/portlet/portlet-app_1_0.xsd
  http://java.sun.com/xml/ns/portlet/portlet-app_1_0.xsd">
  <portlet>
    <portlet-name>Poll JSR</portlet-name>
    <display-name>Poll JSR portlet</display-name>
    <display-name xml:lang="en">Poll JSR portlet</display-name>
    <portlet-class>com.ibm.sample.portlet.poll.portlet.PollPortlet</portlet-class>
    <init-param>
      <name>wps.markup</name>
      <value>html</value>
    </init-param>
    <expiration-cache>0</expiration-cache>
    <supports>
      <mime-type>text/html</mime-type>
      <portlet-mode>view</portlet-mode>
      <portlet-mode>edit</portlet-mode>
      <portlet-mode>config</portlet-mode>
    </supports>
    <supported-locale>en</supported-locale>
    <resource-bundle>nls.polling</resource-bundle>
    <portlet-info>
      <title>Poll JSR portlet</title>
    </portlet-info>
    <portlet-preferences>
      <preference>
        <name>persist_type</name>
        <value> </value>
      </preference>
      <preference>
        <name>datasource</name>
        <value> </value>
      </preference>
      <preference>
        <name>pollName</name>
        <value> </value>
      </preference>
    </portlet-preferences>
  </portlet>
  <custom-portlet-mode>
    <portlet-mode>config</portlet-mode>
  </custom-portlet-mode>
</portlet-app>
```

Poll Portlet Class

Review the generated `PollPortlet` class. The first obvious difference between this class and the IBM Portlet API version is that the portlet API objects are imported from the `javax.portlet.*` package. Those classes are resolved in the `portlet.jar` file that has been added to the build class path by the portlet application creation wizard. The portlet creation wizard also includes the `portlet-api.jar`, `wpsportlets.jar`, and `wps.jar` in the build path. You should remove the `portlet-api.jar` and `wpsportlets.jar` from the build path to help ensure you are not including any IBM Portlet API references. The `wps.jar` file includes the `org.apache.pluto.tags.*` classes which are needed for the custom JSP tags defined in the `std-portlet.tld` tag library.

The next noticeable difference is in the `PollPortlet` class definition: `public class PollPortlet extends GenericPortlet`. The portlet class extends `javax.portlet.GenericPortlet` and does not implement `ActionListener`. The JSR 168 API also implements two-phase processing, an action phase and a render phase. But the API defines two different URLs to reference the portlet, an `ActionURL` and a `RenderURL` instead of an event notification and listener mechanism. If the portlet is invoked using the `ActionURL` then the portlet's `processAction` method is called first. Also notice that this method is passed an `ActionRequest` object and an `ActionResponse` object. For render phase processing the `doView`, `doEdit`, `doHelp`, and `doConfigure` methods are passed a `RenderRequest` object and a `RenderResponse` object. The request and response objects are different between the processing phases.

In render phase processing notice that the `do` methods get invoked from the `doDispatch` method instead of the `service` method as in the previous API. The `GenericPortlet` implementation of the `doDispatch` method simply determines the current portlet mode and invokes the appropriate `do` method.

```
protected  void doDispatch(RenderRequest request,
    RenderResponse response)
    throws PortletException, IOException {
  WindowState state = request.getWindowState();
  if(!state.equals(WindowState.MINIMIZED)) {
  PortletMode mode = request.getPortletMode();
  if(mode.equals(PortletMode.VIEW))
    doView(request, response);
  else
  if(mode.equals(PortletMode.EDIT))
    doEdit(request, response);
  else
  if(mode.equals(PortletMode.HELP))
```

```
      doHelp(request, response);
   else
      throw new PortletException("unknown portlet mode: " + mode);
   }
}
```

However, the base implementation does not support a configure mode. The API allows portal vendors to support additional portlet modes as custom modes. The custom mode must be defined in the portlet deployment descriptor and then can be invoked by overriding the doDispatch method as shown in our generated PollPortlet code.

```
protected void doDispatch(RenderRequest request, RenderResponse
response) throws PortletException, IOException {
   if( !WindowState.MINIMIZED.equals(request.getWindowState()) ){
      PortletMode mode = request.getPortletMode();
      if( CUSTOM_CONFIG_MODE.equals(mode) ) {
         doCustomConfigure(request, response);
         return;
      }
   }
   super.doDispatch(request, response);
}
```

Modifying the Poll Project Source

We will work through the changes needed to convert our existing Poll Portlet to use the JSR 168 API. To do that we will copy the existing portlet code into this new project, preserving only the generated Web and portlet deployment descriptors. The generated source code, JSPs, and resource bundle along with their packages and folders should be deleted from the new project.

After deleting these files, use Copy and Paste in Studio to copy the Java Source packages and their contents and the WebContent images and jsp folders from the Poll project to the Poll JSR 168 project. You should have previously removed the portlet-api.jar and wpsportlets.jar from the project build path. As a result, you will see a number of errors in the new project after the copying completes.

PollPortlet

First change the PollPortlet class definition to extend GenericPortlet and remove "implements ActionListener." If you have an init method, then that method signature has changed and so it now throws a PortletException instead of an UnavailableException.

The `actionPerformed` method is replaced by a `processAction` method. The `processAction` method takes `ActionRequest` and `ActionResponse` parameters instead of an `Event` parameter. With no `Event` object available, the event processing is controlled by request parameters put on the `ActionURL` as opposed to an action name available from the `Event` object. All methods invoked from either `processAction` or `actionPerformed` must be updated to take an `ActionRequest` object instead of `PortletRequest`.

```
/**
 * Process an action request
 */
public void processAction(ActionRequest request,
    ActionResponse response)
    throws PortletException, IOException {

  // Get the action handler class and dispatch
  String actionClassName = request.getParameter(ACTION);
  Action action = ActionClassManager.getAction(actionClassName);

  // Dispatch to that class event handler
  PortletContext
  portletContext=getPortletConfig().getPortletContext();
  action.actionPerformed(request, portletContext);
  action.setView(request);
}
```

The `PollPortlet` service method must be replaced with a `doDispatch` method. The `doDispatch` method for our portlet simply gets the `View` class for the current portlet mode and dispatches to it.

```
/**
 * Dispatch to render View class for the current mode.
 * The View class name was set in the Action phase or
 * is the initial View for the current portlet mode.
 */
protected void doDispatch(RenderRequest request,
    RenderResponse response)
    throws PortletException, IOException {

  View nextView = ViewClassManager.getView(request);
  PortletContext portletContext=getPortletConfig().getPortletContext();
  nextView.performView(request, response, portletContext);
}
```

The `ViewClassManager getInitialView` method must then change to handle the custom configure mode. A new `PortletMode` instance is defined for the "config" mode defined by the portal vendor.

```
PortletMode CUSTOM_CONFIG_MODE = new PortletMode("config");
```

Then the current mode can be retrieved from the `RenderRequest` object and checked against this mode to determine the appropriate `View` class.

```
if (CUSTOM_CONFIG_MODE.equals(request.getPortletMode())) {}
```

Action Classes

In general, the only change needed for the `Action` classes is the `action-Performed` method changes to the `ActionRequest` object. One difference we also need to consider is the portlet mode during action phase processing. With the IBM Portlet API a mode change occurs after the action processing. With the JSR 168 API the mode change occurs during the action processing. So, our portlet code needs to take this into consideration when the View is set for the current mode in the action phase. The only issue is during a mode change when we would normally remove the mode-specific View reference from session. With the new API, since the mode has already changed we remove View references for all modes from session.

The use of `PortletSettings` and `PortletData` must be changed to use `PortletPreferences`. Like the `PortletSettings` and `Portlet-Data` objects the `PortletPreferences` object is available from the request object. You use the `setValue` and `getValue` methods to access the preference attributes and the store method to save them.

Model Objects

There are no additional changes needed for our model objects. Likewise, the persistence classes and utility classes require no changes.

View Classes

An additional change (beyond referencing `RenderRequest` and `Render-Response` and changes to use `PortletPreferences`) is the invocation of the JSP.

Prior to rendering output to the response, either writing directly to the response `PrintWriter` or through a JSP, the response content type must be explicitly set. If it is not, you will get the following exception:

```
Nested Exception is java.lang.IllegalStateException: No content
type set.
```

JSPs are invoked from the `RequestDispatcher` instead of from the `portletContext`. So, an example JSP invocation is

```
response.setContentType(request.getResponseContentType());
portletContext.getRequestDispatcher(EDIT_JSP).include(request,response);
```

User Identifier

The API to retrieve the user profile information is quite a bit different between the APIs. The Poll portlet uses the id of the user to uniquely register a vote and to determine if the user has already voted. This function is implemented in the `VoteAction` action class and `MainView` state class, respectively. The IBM Portlet API returns the user identifier from the `User` object:

```
String user = request.getUser().getUserID();
```

The JSR 168 API returns the user identifier from the `java.security.Principle` object:

```
Principal principal = request.getUserPrincipal();
String user = principal.getName();
```

Note that WebSphere Applicaton Server security must be enabled for the `Principal` object to be created. If security is not enabled then the `getUserPrinciple` method will return null. By default for an LDAP configuration the `getName()` method will return the UID attribute.

Therefore, change the code in both classes to return the user name using the `Principle` object, making sure to check for a null object and return a meaningful error message if security is not enabled. The following code snippet assumes that the appropriate error message is defined in the resource bundle.

```
Principal principal = request. getUserPrincipal();
if (principal == null) {
    ResourceBundle bundle = ResourceBundle.getBundle("nls.polling",
        request.getLocale());
    throw new PollMessageException
        (bundle.getString("exception.security"));
}
String userName = principal.getName();
```

JSPs

The JSP must also change to use the new tag library. Instead of the `portlet.tld` tag library that was available with the IBM Portlet API, the `std-portlet.tld` is provided with the JSR 168 API implementation. This library contains the following tags:

```
- <portlet:defineObjects/> initialize RenderRequest,
RenderResponse, and PortletConfig objects support for use within the JSP
- <portlet:actionURL/> create a URL to invoke the processAction method
in the portlet.
```

- <portlet:renderURL/> create a URL to invoke the doDispatch method
in the portlet.
- <portlet:namespace/> provide the encoded namespace of the portlet.

For example, to generate a URL for the portlet specifying an action you would use the following tag:

```
<portlet:actionURL>
    <portlet:param name="action" value="anActionClassName"/>
</portlet:actionURL>
```

Summary

This chapter reviewed the interactive test environment of WebSphere Studio using the Poll portlet you developed in the previous chapter. You learned how to configure the test server and how to use the debugging environment using a local Portal test environment.

In the second part of the chapter you modified that Poll portlet to use the JSR 168 API instead of the IBM Portlet API used in its initial development. The needed changes were reviewed.

## CHAPTER 18

Struts Portlet Framework

This chapter discusses the implementation of a portlet using Struts Portlet Framework. Struts is an Apache Jakarta project providing an open-source framework for building Web applications. WebSphere Portal provides Struts Portlet Framework that supports the deployment of Struts applications as portlets.

Like you did for the JSR 168 API portlet implementation, you will convert the Poll portlet developed using the IBM Portlet API for using Struts Portlet Framework.

After the implementation process has been discussed, various approaches to portlet development will be discussed, with recommendations given on when each approach is appropriate.

Creating the New Project

We initially designed and implemented the Poll portlet separating action event processing from our controller function and maintained clearly separated model and view classes. Because of this design our transition of this code to the struts framework will be very straightforward.

The first step in creating a portlet using Struts Portlet Framework is to import the `PortalStrutsBlank.war` file into your project. In WebSphere Portal V5.0 you will find the `PortalStrutsBlank.war` file in the `<portal_root>\dev\struts\StrutsPortlet` directory. Importing this war file adds the Struts jar files for both Jakarta Struts and IBM's Struts Portlet Framework to the project lib directory. Again, we will use WebSphere Studio for this development. The specific steps shown here are based on WebSphere Studio 5.1.0 with Portal Toolkit version 5.0.2. Follow these steps to create the base project:

1. Import Struts Portlet Framework into a new project. To do so, follow these steps:

   a. Select File ➪ Import ➪ AR file from the Studio menu bar.

   b. In the Import page navigate to the `PortalStrutsBlank.war` file and select New for Project.

   c. In the New Web Project page, enter **Poll Struts** for Project Name and select Finish to create the project.

   d. Select Finish from the WAR file page to complete the import (see Figure 18-1).

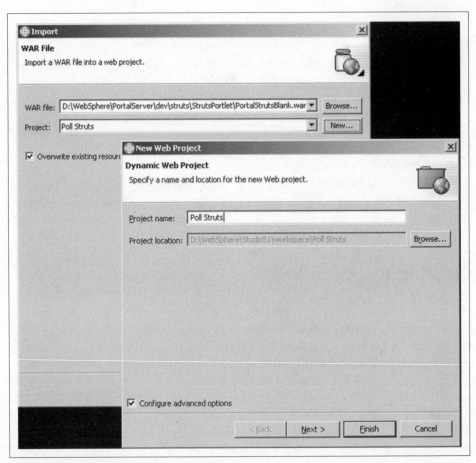

Figure 18-1 Importing the Struts Portlet Framework.

NOTE After the import completes if you get the following error *Attribute "bundle" must be declared for element type "field,"* in the `validation.xml` file, then remove the attribute from this file.

2. Add the portal jar files to the project build classpath. To do so, perform the following steps:

   a. Open the properties on the newly created project by right-clicking the project in the Navigator pane.

   b. Select Properties from the pop-up menu.

   c. Select Java Build Path and then the Libraries tab.

   d. Select Add Variable, then select WPS_V5_PLUGINDIR in the New Variable classpath entry, and click Extend. Select `portlet-api.jar` and select OK.

   e. Select Add Variable, then select WPS_V5_PLUGINDIR in the New Variable classpath entry, and click Extend. Select `wps.jar` and select OK.

   f. Select Add Variable, then select WPS_V5_PLUGINDIR in the New Variable classpath entry, and click Extend. Select `wpsportlets.jar` and select OK.

   g. Select Add Variable, then select WAS_50_PLUGINDIR in the New Variable classpath entry, and click Extend. Expand the lib directory, select `dynacache.jar` and select OK.

   h. Select OK to save the property changes.

3. Change the newly created project to J2EE 1.3. To do so, follow these steps:

   a. Open the properties on the newly created project by right-clicking the project in the Navigator pane.

   b. Select Properties from the pop-up menu.

   c. Select Web and then change J2EE Level to 1.3.

   d. Click OK to save the change.

4. Add `portlet.tld` to the tag lib folder in the new project. To do so, follow these steps:

   a. Right-click the `tld` folder in the project.

   b. Select Import and then File System.

   c. On the File System page browse to find the `<wp-root>\shared\app\WEB-INF\tld` directory and select OK. Highlight (do not click the check box of) tld, in the right pane.

    d. Click the check box for `portlet.tld`.

    e. Finally, click Finish.

5. If you see a warning that states "Web context root should start with slash(/) character for portlet application debugging" open the properties on the newly created project by right-clicking the project in the Navigator pane. Then select Properties from the pop-up menu. Select Web and then add a / to the Context Root.

6. Add the JavaServer Pages Standard Tag Libraries. Add `standard.jar` and `jstl.jar` to the portlet project's lib folder (`WebContent\WEB-INF\lib`). These tag libraries are used to retrieve language-specific text from resource bundles based on the user's locale. The tag libraries are open-source code available from Jakarta at (`http://jakarta.apache.org/`).

Web Deployment Descriptor

A default Web deployment descriptor is provided with the Portal Struts Framework. You need to update it for the Poll portlet. Edit the `web.xml` file and change the `<display-name>` element to a name for this portlet such as *Poll Struts*. The `ID` attribute of the servlet element must be unique in your deployed Web application. Change this value to a unique string such as the Poll Portlet class name, `com.ibm.sample.portlet.poll.portlet.PollPortlet`. Change the `<servlet-class>` element to the portlet class name, `com.ibm.sample.portlet.poll.portlet.PollPortlet`.

Struts Portlet Framework takes advantage of struts module support to provide both mode and device (markup) differentiation for the Struts configuration. When using modules, an application's configuration information and directory structure are separated by module. Therefore, instead of a single `struts-config.xml` file for the application, you have multiple control files within separate directory structure, identified by module-relative portions of the application URI. The search path is used to determine the module and `struts-config.xml` file to use. It also determines the base directory for locating JSPs.

Add the following initialization parameter to set the search path to take markup name and mode into consideration when searching for modules.

```
<init-param>
<param-name>ModuleSearchPath</param-name>
<param-value>markupName, mode</param-value>
</init-param>
```

You will need to create two modules for this application, one for edit mode and one for configure mode. The view mode is configured through the base struts configuration. The two modules are defined as init parameters in the form: `/config/<device>/<mode>`. The value associated with each of these parameters specifies the name and location of the struts configuration file.

```
<init-param>
  <param-name>config/html/configure</param-name>
  <param-value>/WEB-INF/html/configure/struts-config.xml</param-value>
</init-param>
<init-param>
  <param-name>config/html/edit</param-name>
  <param-value>/WEB-INF/html/edit/struts-config.xml</param-value>
</init-param>
```

Finally, update the welcome file list. The Struts Portlet Framework lets you specify the initial view for each device/mode combination. This is specified through the welcome file list. The default welcome file list only provides a welcome file specification for the view mode.

```
<welcome-file-list>
  <welcome-file>index.jsp</welcome-file>
  <welcome-file>html/edit/index.jsp</welcome-file>
  <welcome-file>html/configure/index.jsp</welcome-file>
</welcome-file-list>
```

Portlet Deployment Descriptor

The portlet deployment descriptor must also be updated. The changes to both descriptors as well as the build path are necessary since we created a Web project during the WAR file import. Previously, we created a portlet application project using the Creation Wizard from the portal toolkit. Part of that process created complete deployment descriptors and set the correct build path.

Edit the `portlet.xml` file and make the following changes.

- Change the `uid` attribute of the `<portlet-app>` element to a unique identifier such as *"com.ibm.sample.portlet.poll .portlet.PollPortlet:1"*
- Change the `<portlet-app-name>` element to a meaningful name such as *Poll (Struts) Application.*
- Change the `href` attribute of the `<portlet>` element to reference the servlet id that you specified in the Web deployment descriptor appended after *"WEB-INF/web.xml"*.
- Change the `<portlet-name>` element to a meaningful name such as *Poll (Struts).*

- Add markup elements for configure and edit modes as well as the default view mode.
- Change the `uid` attribute of the `<concrete-portlet-app>` element to a unique identifier such as `com.ibm.sample.portlet` `.poll.portlet.PollPortlet:1.1`.
- Change both the `<portlet-app-name>` element and the `<portlet-name>` element for the concrete portlet application to meaningful names such as *Poll (Struts) Applications* and *Poll (Struts)*.
- Finally, specify meaningful values for the language-specific attributes for title, short title, description, and key words.

```xml
<?xml version="1.0" encoding="UTF-8"?>
<!DOCTYPE portlet-app-def PUBLIC "-//IBM//DTD Portlet Application
1.1//EN" "portlet_1.1.dtd">
<portlet-app-def>
  <portlet-app
uid="com.ibm.sample.portlet.poll.portlet.PollPortlet:1"
    major-version="1" minor-version="0">
    <portlet-app-name>Poll (Struts) Application</portlet-app-name>
    <portlet id="Portlet_1"
      href="WEB-
INF/web.xml#com.ibm.sample.portlet.poll.portlet.PollPortlet"
      major-version="1" minor-version="0">
      <portlet-name>Struts Blank</portlet-name>
      <cache>
        <expires>0</expires>
        <shared>NO</shared>
      </cache>
      <allows>
        <maximized/>
        <minimized/>
      </allows>
            <supports>
                <markup name="html">
                  <view />
                  <configure />
                  <edit />
                </markup>
            </supports>
    </portlet>
  </portlet-app>
  <concrete-portlet-app
uid="com.ibm.sample.portlet.poll.portlet.PollPortlet:1.1">
    <portlet-app-name>Poll (Struts) Application</portlet-app-name>
    <concrete-portlet href="#Portlet_1">
      <portlet-name>Poll (Struts)</portlet-name>
      <default-locale>en</default-locale>
```

```
<language locale="en">
  <title>Poll (Struts)</title>
  <title-short>Poll (Struts)</title-short>
  <description>
    Poll portlet using the struts portlet framework
  </description>
  <keywords>Poll, Struts</keywords>
</language>
      <config-param>
        <param-name>FilterChain</param-name>
        <param-value>StrutsTranscoding</param-value>
      </config-param>
    </concrete-portlet>
  </concrete-portlet-app>
</portlet-app-def>
```

Struts Configuration Files

The struts configuration file (`struts-config.xml`) contains the application definitions that the struts framework uses for control, navigation, and configuration settings, including form beans that are needed. The module initialization parameters defined in the deployment descriptor specified two module-specific struts configuration files. Along with the base struts configuration file that is located in the `WebContent/WEB-INF` directory, you need to create two new `struts-config.xml` files: one in the `WebContent /WEB-INF/html/configure` directory for configure mode and one in the `WebContent/WEB-INF/html/edit` directory for edit mode.

The struts configuration definitions map fairly well to our existing Poll portlet. Our implementation already has Action classes that provide the application function that is expected by the struts Action classes. The class definition and method signature will change somewhat but for the most part the implementation of these classes remains the same. With the exception of changes needed for portlet URL addressability, we do not need to change the existing JSPs. In general, the View classes were associated with Actions and simply invoked the appropriate JSP. In the struts configuration the JSPs are defined and in cases associated with actions. Our Poll portlet used form data beans for user input in configure mode and the struts implementation defines the form data beans as well.

Struts Configuration in Portlet View Mode

The portlet edit, view, and help modes are mapped to struts modules. The portlet view mode is controlled from the base struts configuration. You will need to change the `struts-config.xml` file in the `WebContent/WEB-INF` directory to handle the view mode actions.

The view mode configuration requires two actions, one to display the poll and one to register a user's vote. Two JSPs are used by the portlet in view mode, one to render the poll question and answer choices (allowing the user to vote) and one to render the poll results. A poll bean is also used in this configuration.

We have also created a simple JSP to display information when an exception is encountered. The main view action, as well as the exception JSP, is globally defined since they could get invoked from other Actions in the portlet. For example, when you return from edit or configure mode you want to invoke the main view action to render the view page. The following listing shows the struts configuration.

```xml
<?xml version="1.0" encoding="ISO-8859-1" ?>
<!DOCTYPE struts-config PUBLIC
  "-//Apache Software Foundation//DTD Struts Configuration 1.1//EN"
  "http://jakarta.apache.org/struts/dtds/struts-config_1_1.dtd">
<struts-config>
  <!-- ========== Form Bean Definitions ========== -->
  <form-beans>
    <form-bean name="pollBean"
      type="com.ibm.sample.portlet.poll.beans.PollBean" />
  </form-beans>
  <!-- ======== Global Forward Definitions ========== -->
  <global-forwards>
    <forward name="mainview" path="/mainview.do" />
    <forward name="exception" path="/exception.jsp" />
  </global-forwards>
  <!-- ======== Action Mapping Definitions ========== -->
  <action-mappings>
    <action path="/mainview"
      type="com.ibm.sample.portlet.poll.actions.ViewAction"
      name="pollBean" scope="request" validate="false">
      <forward name="question" path="/viewQuestion.jsp" />
      <forward name="results" path="/viewResults.jsp" />
    </action>
    <action path="/vote"
      type="com.ibm.sample.portlet.poll.actions.VoteAction"
      name="pollBean" scope="request" validate="false">
      <forward name="results" path="/viewResults.jsp" />
    </action>
  </action-mappings>
  <!--========== Controller Configuration ========== -->
  <controller
  processorClass="com.ibm.wps.portlets.struts.WpsRequestProcessor">
  </controller>
  <!-- ========== Message Resources Definitions ===== -->
  <message-resources parameter="nls.polling" />
```

```
    <!-- ========== Plug Ins Configuration === ==== -->
  <plug-in className="org.apache.struts.validator.ValidatorPlugIn">
      <set-property
      property="pathnames"
      value="/WEB-INF/validator-rules.xml,/WEB-INF/validation.xml" />
    </plug-in>
</struts-config>
```

Struts Configuration in Portlet Edit Mode

The edit mode configuration is very simple. The portlet edit mode is a single page that allows the user to select a color scheme for the poll result graph. Therefore, your struts configuration will only need to contain an action to save the user preference and the JSP to render the selection page. There is no action needed to render the selection page since the creation of this page does not need any prior application logic processing or bean creation. An edit data form bean is also defined for the user input form.

```
<?xml version="1.0" encoding="ISO-8859-1" ?>
<!DOCTYPE struts-config PUBLIC
    "-//Apache Software Foundation//DTD Struts Configuration 1.1//EN"
    "http://jakarta.apache.org/struts/dtds/struts-config_1_1.dtd">
<struts-config>
    <form-beans>
      <form-bean name="editFormData"
type="com.ibm.sample.portlet.poll.beans.EditFormData"/>
    </form-beans>
    <action-mappings>
      <action
        path="/editsave"
      type="com.ibm.sample.portlet.poll.actions.EditSaveAction"
      name="editFormData"
      scope="request"
      validate="false" >
      </action>
    </action-mappings>
    <controller
      processorClass="com.ibm.wps.portlets.struts.WpsRequestProcessor">
    </controller>
    <message-resources parameter="nls.polling"/>
</struts-config>
```

Struts Configuration in Portlet Configure Mode

The struts configuration for the portlet configure mode is a bit more complicated. Actions are needed for the creation of each of the three configuration pages, to verify the datasource, to add an answer choice, to delete an answer choice, to save the configuration settings, and to cancel the configuration changes. The configuration data form bean is also defined.

The forward definitions for the JSPs for the first and third configuration pages are defined globally since they are used from multiple actions.

```xml
<?xml version="1.0" encoding="ISO-8859-1" ?>
<!DOCTYPE struts-config PUBLIC
   "-//Apache Software Foundation//DTD Struts Configuration 1.1//EN"
   "http://jakarta.apache.org/struts/dtds/struts-config_1_1.dtd">
<struts-config>
  <form-beans>
    <form-bean
      name="configureForm"
      type="com.ibm.sample.portlet.poll.beans.ConfigureFormData"/>
  </form-beans>
  <global-forwards>
   <forward name="configure" path="/configure.do" />
   <forward name="configure_pg1" path="/configure_pg1.jsp" />
   <forward name="configure_pg3" path="/configure_pg3.jsp"/>
  </global-forwards>
  <action-mappings>
    <action path="/configure"
      type="com.ibm.sample.portlet.poll.actions.ConfigPg1Action"
      name="configureForm" scope="request"
      validate="false">
    </action>
    <action path="/configure2"
      type="com.ibm.sample.portlet.poll.actions.ConfigPg2Action"
      name="configureForm" scope="request"
      validate="false">
      <forward
        name="configure_pg2"
        path="/configure_pg2.jsp"/>
    </action>
    <action path="/configure3"
      type="com.ibm.sample.portlet.poll.actions.ConfigPg3Action"
      name="configureForm" scope="request"
      validate="false" >
    </action>
    <action path="/configure_verify"
   type="com.ibm.sample.portlet.poll.actions.ConfigVerifyDatasourceAction"
      name="configureForm" scope="request"
      validate="false" >
    </action>
    <action path="/configure_cancel"
      type="com.ibm.sample.portlet.poll.actions.CancelAction"
      name="configureForm" scope="request"
      validate="false" >
    </action>
    <action path="/configure_save"
```

```
         type="com.ibm.sample.portlet.poll.actions.ConfigSaveAction"
         name="configureForm" scope="request"
         validate="false" >
      </action>
      <action path="/configure_delete"
         type="com.ibm.sample.portlet.poll.actions
         .ConfigDeleteChoiceAction"
          name="configureForm" scope="request"
          validate="false" >
      </action>
      <action path="/configure_add"
         type="com.ibm.sample.portlet.poll.actions.ConfigAddChoiceAction"
         name="configureForm" scope="request"
         validate="false" >
    </action>
    </action-mappings>
    <controller
      processorClass="com.ibm.wps.portlets.struts.WpsRequestProcessor">
    </controller>
    <message-resources parameter="nls.polling"/>
  </struts-config>
```

Action Classes

Your struts action classes will extend `org.apache.struts.action
.Action` and override the execute method. With a struts portlet imple-
mentation you no longer implement a central controller class such as the
PollPortlet class from the previous implementation. This responsibility is
managed by the struts request processor, which we have configured as
WpsRequestProcessor.

You will define an abstract action class to include common functions that
should occur prior to any action getting invoked. This is the function you
had in the PollPortlet's actionPerformed or service methods.

The `AbstractAction` class then implements the *execute* method and
performs any needed processing before dispatching to the subclass. The
listing below shows the `AbstractAction` class for our struts portlet. Notice that the *execute* method is passed `HttpServletRequest` and
`HttpServletResponse` objects. In order to have access to the portlet API,
you need to get the `PortletRequest` and `PortletResponse` objects
from these.

```
public abstract class AbstractAction extends Action
     implements PollConstants {
  public ActionForward execute(ActionMapping mapping, ActionForm form,
    HttpServletRequest request, HttpServletResponse response)
    throws Exception {
```

```
      try {
        // Check for existing session with logged-in user.
        PortletRequest portletRequest = (PortletRequest) request;
        PortletSession session = portletRequest.getPortletSession(false);
        User user = portletRequest.getUser();
        if (session == null || user == null) {
          ResourceBundle bundle = ResourceBundle.getBundle(BUNDLE,
            portletRequest.getLocale());
          String msg = bundle.getString("exception.login");
          throw new PollMessageException(msg);
        }

        // Invoke the action subclass performAction method
        return performAction(mapping, form, user, request, response);
      }

      catch (Exception e) {
        PortletRequest portletRequest = (PortletRequest) request;
        PortletSession session = portletRequest.getPortletSession();
        session.setAttribute(POLL_EXCEPTION,e);
        return (mapping.findForward("exception"));
      }
    }

    public abstract ActionForward performAction(ActionMapping mapping,
      ActionForm form, User user, HttpServletRequest request,
      HttpServletResponse response) throws Exception;


  }
```

Then the Action classes only need to implement the `performAction` method with the parameters shown previously. Copy the source files from the IBM Portlet API Poll portlet implementation to the Poll Struts project to make the appropriate changes.

First you should modify the abstract action class as shown. Then update the method signature of the Action classes and delete the `setView` methods. You will also need to return an `ActionForward` instance from the `performView` method indicating another action to call or a JSP to render using the definitions in the struts configuration.

For example, the following listing shows the action to generate the first page in the configuration mode. Notice that the session data bean is created and the JSP to render the page is identified through a mapping in the configuration file.

```
public class ConfigPg1Action extends AbstractAction {

  public ActionForward performAction(ActionMapping mapping,
    ActionForm form, User user, HttpServletRequest request,
```

```
      HttpServletResponse response) throws Exception {
    // Get the session data
    PortletRequest portletRequest = (PortletRequest) request;
    SessionData sessionData =
      SessionData.getSessionData(portletRequest);

    if (sessionData == null) {
      // Create a new sessionData instance and add it to session
      sessionData = SessionData.createSessionData(portletRequest);
      // Initialize form data from portlet settings
      ConfigureFormData formData = sessionData.getConfigureFormData();
      PortletSettings portletSettings =
        PortletRequest.getPortletSettings();
      String persistType = portletSettings.getAttribute(PERSIST_TYPE);
      String datasource = portletSettings.getAttribute(DATASOURCE);
      formData.setDatasource(datasource);
      formData.setPersistType(persistType);
    }
    return (mapping.findForward("configure_pg1"));
  }
}
```

The other action classes should be modified in a similar way. However, we will not discuss them in detail here. Note also that there are two additional action classes in the struts implementation, one just shown here to generate the first configuration page and one to generate the view page. The logic for this had been in the view classes in the previous implementation but with the Struts Portlet Framework the rendering phase is simply a JSP invocation without additional application logic.

Remaining Poll Portlet Implementation

Now that the struts configuration files are created and the action classes have been updated, much of the work of getting your Poll portlet to work in the Struts Portlet Framework is handled. Differences do exist in portlet URL addressability that will be examined in more detail shortly, but first you need to move the remaining code from your initial implementation into the Poll struts project and see what further changes are needed.

Data Beans

The only change for the data beans is to extend ActionForm. A new form data bean has also been created for edit mode that just contains the color field. This keeps the struts action processing consistent.

Persistence Classes

There are no changes needed for the persistence classes.

Portlet Controller Classes

Portlet Controller classes include the `PollPortlet` controller class and the helper classes for managing Action classes and View classes (`Action-ClassManager` and `ViewClassManager`). These classes are not needed, since the controller function is handled by the request processor and therefore can be deleted. The `PollConstants` class that holds application constants will continue to be used.

Utilities Classes

There are no changes needed for the Utilities classes.

View Classes

View classes are not needed since the rendering phase is a direct invocation of a JSP. The classes should be deleted.

JSP Differences

Recall the changes to the Web deployment descriptor that you made. The first is the change to the welcome file list and the second is the initialization parameter that determines the search path for the module resources.

The following listing shows the welcome file list. This list is used to specify the initial JSP that is invoked. The list specifies JSP files by device and by portlet mode. The default welcome file is `index.jsp` and is located in the WebContent folder. The initial file for edit mode using HTML markup is also an index.jsp file but that is located in the `WebContent\html\edit` folder. Likewise for configure mode in HTML the `index.jsp` file is located in the `WebContent\hntl\configure` folder.

```
<welcome-file-list>
  <welcome-file>index.jsp</welcome-file>
    <welcome-file>html/edit/index.jsp</welcome-file>
    <welcome-file>html/configure/index.jsp</welcome-file>
</welcome-file-list>
```

You will need to create these three files in the appropriate location. The initial page in configure mode and the page in view mode both require action processing prior to rendering. Since we can't add an action in the welcome file list you need to create an `index.jsp` that does a forward such as (for configure mode)

```
<%@ taglib uri="/tags/struts-logic" prefix="logic" %>
<logic:forward name="configure"/>
```

The edit mode page is a bit different in that it does not need additional processing. There is mostly static information that can be rendered from the JSP without requiring prepared beans or other actions. In this case `index.jsp` will contain that JSP code that we had in the `edit.jsp` prior.

Also recall the init parameter for the module resources search path. It was:

```
<init-param>
  <param-name>ModuleSearchPath</param-name>
  <param-value>markupName, mode</param-value>
</init-param>
```

As a result of this, you need to move the view JSPs (`viewQuestion.jsp` and `viewResults.jsp`) to the WebContent folder. Move the remaining JSPs associated with configure mode to the `WebContent\html\configure` folder.

Portlet URL Addressability

One significant difference in developing struts applications for deployment into the portal environment lies in the structure of portlet URIs. Struts action mappings as well as page object references such as JSPs are defined in terms of paths. However, these struts path references must be made in context of a portlet. Portlets have a specific and expected URI format. Therefore, the additional path information needed by the Struts application must be added to the portlet URI to ensure that the portlet gets properly invoked and that the struts path is also available. The struts tags have been modified in the Struts Portlet Framework to provide this function.

The struts tags have also been extended to support specific portal requirements. For example, consider the JSP that displays the last page in configuration mode. The action on the HTML form tag should be a reference to the action class to save the configuration settings. However, the behavior you want in a portal environment is to save the configuration settings *and* return to view mode. So, you need a form tag to do both, invoke the action class to save the configuration settings and also change modes to the previous mode. Since modes are unique to the portal environment, these standard struts tags do not provide that level of support.

The tag implementation in the Struts Portlet Framework supports this behavior and for this example our tag would be the following.

```
<html:form method="post" action="/configure_save" urlType="return">
```

The `urlType` attribute is introduced. This attribute can take either of the values *"return"* or *"standard."* The form tag generated using the above custom tag uses the portlet URI that handles the return and appends the struts path to reference the *configure save* action.

Generating Portlet URIs

In this portlet, like many others, there is a need to generate URIs in Java code so the URI can be dynamically associated with a form submit. The following listing shows how a URI string can be created in a JSP scriptlet. This URI string is used in the JSP that renders the final page in the portlet configuration mode. This portlet URI invokes the action to add an answer choice to the poll.

```
<%@ page import="com.ibm.wps.struts.common.PortletApiUtils" %>
<%
   PortletApiUtils portletUtils = PortletApiUtils.getInstance();
      if (portletUtils != null) {
        String url = "/configure_add.do";
        url = portletUtils.addModulePrefix(url, request);
        Object portletURI =
          portletUtils.createPortletURIWithStrutsURL(request,
          url);
        String addChoiceURI = portletURI.toString();
      }
%>
```

You also need to generate the URI as a string outside a form tag definition but with a portlet mode return action. The next example shows similar code to generate a portlet URI that returns to the previous mode and also invokes a struts action:

```
<%@ page import="com.ibm.wps.struts.common.PortletApiUtils" %>
<%@ page import="com.ibm.wps.struts.common.PortletURIAttributes" %>
<%
   PortletApiUtils portletUtils = PortletApiUtils.getInstance();
      if (portletUtils != null) {
        String url = "/configure_cancel.do";
        PortletURIAttributes uriAttributes = new PortletURIAttributes();
        uriAttributes.setUriType("return");
        url = portletUtils.addModulePrefix(url, request);
        Object portletURI =
          portletUtils.createPortletURIWithStrutsURL(request,
```

```
          url, uriAttributes);
        String cancelURI = portletURI.toString();
    }
%>
```

Which Implementation Should You Use?

The strategic direction for IBM support in portlet API is clearly JSR 168. However, the IBM portlet API will continue to be supported in future versions of WebSphere Portal. There is no immediate need to migrate existing portlets to the JSR 168 API unless this portlet is required to interoperate with other portals that support JSR 168.

For new portlet development the JSR 168 API should be a first consideration when the functionality it provides is sufficient for the portlets' needs or when the portlet is expected to be published as Web Service for Remote Portlets service. If the portlet needs more functionality than that provided by JSR 168, the IBM portlet API should be used. As of Portal 5.02 the JSR 168 support did not extend to portal services such as ContentAccessService and the CredentialVault service.

Struts is the MVC framework of choice for use in portlet development. As of WebSphere Portal 5.02 Struts Portlet Framework did not yet support JSR 168. As the JSR 168 API implementation progresses to meet all the functional capabilities of the IBM Portlet API and Struts Portlet Framework is extended to support the industry standard portlet API, the clear preference in portlet implementation is the MVC framework of struts. As technologies continue to develop Java Server Faces (JSF) plays a more active role as a key development framework. Integration work is underway to allow struts actions, ActionForms and struts configuration within the JSF environment.

As these technologies continue to develop, we might see support in Struts Portlet Framework in the JSF environment. A new request processor would be needed that could receive JSF events and send them to a struts action within Struts Portlet Framework. However, the direction of struts and JSF and the implementation support through Struts Portlet Framework was not known at the time of writing this chapter.

Summary

This chapter examined the implementation of the example portlet using Struts Portlet Framework. As you did for the JSR 168 API portlet implementation, you took the Poll portlet developed using the IBM Portlet API and converted it to use Struts in the portal environment.

Also discussed was the current state of the portlet APIs, and suggestions were offered why you might choose one or the other. The struts framework insulates you to some degree from the portlet API, but as we have seen when converting the Poll portlet, the API is still exposed and used in the struts implementation.

This chapter completes the discussion on portlet development. The next chapter begins the topic of WebSphere Portal within the enterprise enviornment and starts with a discussion on implementing WebSphere Portal identity manager. The chapter focuses on WebSphere Portal's use of LDAP user registries in the enterprise environment.

WebSphere Portal within the Enterprise Environment

## CHAPTER 19

Implementing Authentication for Large Enterprises

Authentication is the process where users are challenged to identify themselves to gain access to a system. The challenge can be immediate or upon trying to access a protected resource. It is usually encountered by the user as requesting for a user id and password but it can also be authenticating through a biometric device or a digital certificate. Information required for authentication is stored in user registries while information relating to the user's profile and preferences is stored in the user repository.

If you have a few users, WebSphere Portal authentication is pretty simple and easy to configure. However, if yours is a large enterprise with many users accessing the site from both your global intranet and extranet, then this subject gets a lot more complex. In this chapter we are going to discuss issues relating to enterprise identity management for WebSphere Portal.

Enterprise Identity Management

WebSphere Portal performs identity management though Member Manager. When a user authenticates, Member Manager validates the information in both the authentication registry and the member database.

WebSphere Portal supports four types of identity management configurations, as seen in Figure 19-1. The first is where the user registry and profile information for WebSphere Portal and WebSphere Application Server is stored on the same LDAP server, which is usually remote. Member Manager maintains and updates all user information in the LDAP server. The second configuration is where Member Manager uses a look-aside repository (that is, a database) to store user profile attributes not supported in the LDAP.

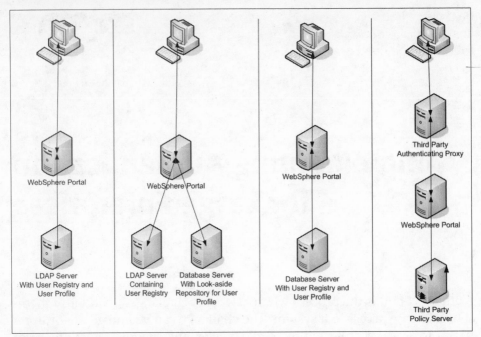

Figure 19-1 Different LDAP configurations.

The split is based on Member Manager configuration XML files. The third identity management configuration is where Member Manager and WebSphere Application Server create and maintain the user identity and profile information in the same database For the third identity management configuration, WebSphere Application Server poses the actual challenge using the data from WebSphere Portal Custom User Registry. For all the configurations, the user registry is shared by both WebSphere Portal and WebSphere Application Server.

The last identity management configuration is using third-party authentication using Trust Association Interceptors. Chapter 20 goes into great detail on this configuration.

LDAP or Database

So the first question you ask yourself when you design the identity management infrastructure is whether to use an LDAP server or an enterprise database. This, of course, leads to the next question: what is LDAP?

LDAP or Lightweight Directory Access Protocol is an open industry standard that defines a standard method for accessing and updating information in a directory. A directory is a database variety that stores typed and ordered information about objects. An LDAP directory is designed for read performance, which means it assumes that the user data will be read far more than it will be changed.

If your company already stores its user registries on an LDAP, then the answer is a "no-brainer." But if it doesn't, then you have to consider the following factors:

1. Does your enterprise have any skill set in configuring and running an LDAP server in production? While some people say that LDAP is simple to install and maintain, this is not true for large directories. It experiences the same operational issues as any database and you need to have the knowledge within your IT area to support it. If they have no experience with an LDAP server but have expertise in DB2 or Oracle, then go with the database.

2. How often is the user data being updated or created versus being read. If the ratio of read to updates for the user data is high, then an LDAP server is well suited. Usually the profile and authentication information such as user ID, password, name, title, address, e-mail, and demographical information does not change that often and is well suited for an LDAP while privilege information such as roles and access control groups can change more frequently and is better suited for a database.

3. Is the management of the users decentralized? LDAP servers usually have a more efficient replication process than databases.

4. Does any of the data have transactional dependencies? That is, if the name and address are being updated, they must both successfully update and if not, they should rollback to their original values. Most LDAP servers do not support transactionality.

5. Do you need to perform sophisticated queries against the directory? LDAP directories use a simple access protocol that cannot match the power of an enterprise database's Structured Query Language for complex update and query functions.

Rules of Thumb for Designing and Maintaining Your LDAP Server

After answering the above questions, you have probably decided that for a large enterprise it is better to go with an LDAP server. So the next steps are as follows:

- Determine Directory Tree by designing the schema and arranging the entries in the tree structure.
- Define the replication and partitioning strategies.
- Create an infrastructure plan.

Designing the Information Model

One of the biggest factors affecting the performance and maintainability of the LDAP server (and thus the Identity Management component of Web-Sphere Portal) is implementation of the information model correctly.

The information model describes how information is stored in an LDAP directory. Information is represented in an LDAP directory by an entry. An entry is equivalent to an object such as employees, servers, and so on. Entries consist of a collection of attributes that contain information about the object. Each attribute has a type and one or more values associated with it. Associated with a type is a syntax that specifies what values can be stored and how a value behaves during searches and other operations. Attributes can also have an alias name that can be used instead of the attribute name. For instance, the common LDAP attribute surname has an alias sn and an LDAP syntax cis associated with it. cis stands for case ignore string, which means case is not significant during comparisons. An attribute can also have a constraint associated with it to limit the number of values or the total size of the value.

The LDAP Schema defines the object classes and attribute types. Object class describes the types of objects each entry can represent and attribute type defines the attributes of each object type, and whether these attributes are optional or mandatory. In order to facilitate interoperability, the schemas have been standardized by Internet Society. Two standards that were adopted by manufacturers are RFC 2252, LDAP (V3); Attribute Syntax Definitions and RFC 2256, A summary of X.500(96) User Schema for use with LDAP V3. For instance in the RFC 2256 standard schema, sn is X.500 surname attribute, which contains the family name of a person. An example of an objectclass is person, which must have the objectclass value on top and either the attribute type surname or commonName and may have the attribute types `userPassword`, `telephoneNumber`, `seeAlso`, and description.

Most of the LDAP servers will have default schema and directory tree layout for the user registries. You should basically not change the structure or elements since this will obviously cause interoperability problems between other directory services and LDAP clients. Definitely do not delete standard schema elements. If you need to add an object class then extend the default schema. Objects added to the LDAP directory should be accessed by more than one user or client. If they are not, then they should be placed in a database.

You need to define who owns the identity management data and who is responsible for keeping it up-to-date. An operations manual should be created that identifies this information. Programs may also need to be created to allow the help desk to administer the data. Insure that there is no inconsistency in the schema; that is, two different attributes with the same data.

If the identity management data is being imported from other sources, develop a strategy for bulk imports and incremental updates. Insure that the data is being imported from the main identity management database and not from another mirror site.

Designing the Directory Information Tree

Data is stored hierarchically in a directory information tree (DIT) over one or more LDAP server(s). The top level of the LDAP directory tree is called the base distinguished name (DN) or a suffix. Each directory record has a unique DN and is read backward through the tree from the individual entry to the top level. The DN is used as a key to the directory record.

For example in Figure 19-2, Ken Chow's entry would be accessed using cn=Ken Chow, ou=Marketing,dc=rigorconsultants,dc=com.

If the DIT is split over multiple servers, then referrals are used to link the servers. This is done by creating an entry of objectClass referral with an attribute ref and assigning the value an LDAP URL, which points to the entry on another LDAP server.

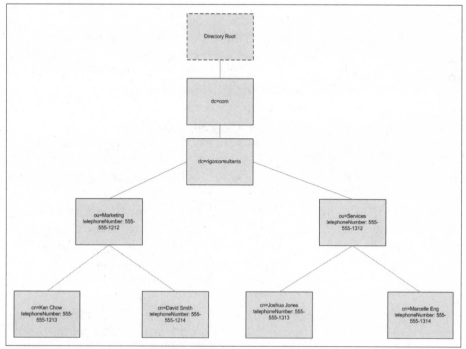

Figure 19-2 A sample directory naming structure.

Given that the LDAP directory is hierarchical, changing the tree is very difficult and should be avoided. Choosing the appropriate naming structure is very important and is usually dictated by the LDAP server. Most LDAP servers base their naming models on either the X.500 methodology or the DNS naming model. The X.500 methodology sets the root of the directory to an organization and has a suffix like o=rigorconsultants, c=us. The DNS model uses the domain name as the suffix like dc=rigorconsultants.com. Microsoft's Active Directory uses the DNS naming model.

When designing the DIT, you have to pay special attention to the branching methodology. If the root branch is based on departments, then a re-org can cause an administrative nightmare. Branching based on geography can restrict sharing organizational information. The branching methodology should be designed to minimize changes to the directory tree. Also make the tree as shallow as possible to maximize search performance. Lastly, consult your security administrator to determine if there are parts of the tree that compliance or organizational rules dictate and that must be physically separated.

Designing the Infrastructure

Identity Management systems for large enterprise must be highly available and able to handle large number of users. LDAP servers support these requirements using partitioning and replication.

Figure 19-3 shows a highly available LDAP server solution. In this solution we have one master server and three slave servers, each with dual network cards. Each server is connected to two separate networks and the connections are bridged together. Read queries are sent to any of the servers while updates, create, and deletes are performed against the master, which replicates the data to the slave servers. If the server fails, client redirection can be done by DNS switchover or using load balancing through the router or the LDAP server. This design eliminates any single point of failure and since writes are infrequent on an LDAP configuration, performance is not impacted.

Scalability issues can be addressed partitioning the directory by geography or some other methodology that accommodated the differences in various network bandwidths and server performances. This also spreads the risk by minimizing the area impacted by a server failure. You can also replicate the LDAP servers to servers closer to the client's geographical location.

Remember that the more complex you make the LDAP infrastructure, the more difficult it is to manage. Try to keep it simple and minimize the input data sources.

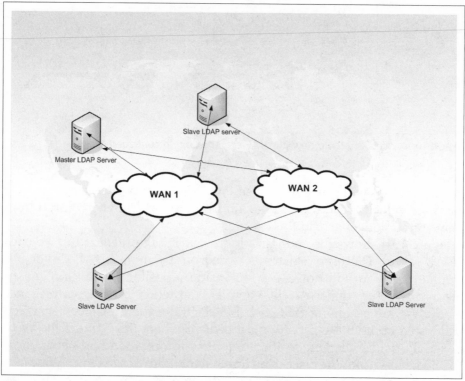

Figure 19-3 A highly available LDAP server configuration.

Implementing WebSphere Portal Enterprise Identity Management

In the previous section we explored the reasons for using an LDAP server for Enterprise Identity Management and discussed the general design issues. Now it is time to leave the theory and deal with the practical aspect. In this section we will explore how to implement Identity Management in WebSphere Portal using the more popular LDAPs:

1. IBM Directory Server V5.1

2. Sun One

3. Microsoft Active Directory

What is conspicuously missing is Domino 6.0. Domino is required if you want to implement collaboration. However, Domino is a lot more than an LDAP server and introducing it in this discussion will cause many

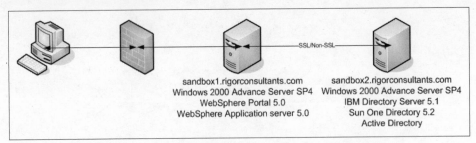

Figure 19-4 WebSphere Portal with LDAP server example configuration.

deviations that will cause us to lose focus on the topic. Instead, you will get more value to read the sections on Domino in WebSphere Portal Info-Center after you have read this chapter.

Figure 19-4 shows the configuration we will be implementing for each LDAP server. The user registry is stored on a remote LDAP server. We assume that you will not use a look-aside repository because it makes the infrastructure unnecessarily complex and tends to have performance issues. We are assuming that each LDAP in question has been installed and tested on both the server and the client where the client is the Web-Sphere Portal server. Due to the amount of information that needs to be covered, we will only be discussing implementation of LDAPs in a Windows 2000 environment. The configuration differences between the Windows 2000 environment and Unix/Linux are minor and are documented in the InfoCenter.

Setting Up Your LDAP Servers

The first step to getting WebSphere Portal working with your LDAP server is to create the Portal Administrator User ID and WebSphere Administrator User ID.

The first directory server we will discuss is IBM Directory Server or Tivoli Directory Server, which comes with WebSphere Portal Extend or Experience. It is built on top of DB2 (tuned for read applications) and WebSphere Application Server. The directory is full function and robust but cannot be considered "light."

There are two methods to create the user ids. The first (recommended) is to modify the LDIF file `portalUsers.ldif` on the first WP CD to conform to your tree structure. LDIF or LDAP Data Interchange Format is a standard format that enables data to be imported and exported between LDAP-based directory servers. The second is to add it using LDAP Directory Web Administrator. If you are going to create the portal administrator user in the LDAP, use the Add Entry function under Directory Management instead of defining it under a Realm using a template. You might find the templates too restrictive especially when you want to associate multiple object classes with the entry.

To create the administrators through an LDIF import, you need to modify the file with your suffix and conform it to your directory tree structure and the naming structure. For IBM Directory we used:

- LDAP suffix is set to dc=rigorconsultants,dc=com
- user prefix is uid
- group prefix is cn=users
- group suffix is cn=groups
- Portal administrator DN is uid=wpsadmin, cn=users, dc=rigorconsultants, dc=com
- Portal administrator group is cn=wpsadmins, cn=groups, dc=rigorconsultants, dc=com of which wpsadmin is a member
- WebSphere Security ID DN is uid=wpsbind, cn=users, dc=rigorconsultants, dc=com

This resulted in the following portalUsers.ldif:

```
version: 1

dn: dc=rigorconsultants,dc=com
objectclass: domain
objectclass: top
# Add lines according to this scheme that correspond to your suffix
dc: rigorconsultants,dc=com
dc: rigorconsultants

dn: cn=users,dc=rigorconsultants,dc=com
objectclass: container
objectclass: top
cn: users

dn: cn=groups,dc=rigorconsultants,dc=com
objectclass: top
objectclass: container
cn: groups

dn: uid=wpsadmin,cn=users,dc=rigorconsultants,dc=com
objectclass: organizationalPerson
objectclass: person
objectclass: top
objectclass: inetOrgPerson
uid: wpsadmin
userpassword: wpsadmin
```

```
sn: admin
givenName: wps
cn: wps admin

dn: uid=wpsbind,cn=users,dc=rigorconsultants,dc=com
objectclass: top
objectclass: person
objectclass: organizationalPerson
objectclass: inetOrgPerson
uid: wpsbind
userpassword: wpsbind
sn: bind
givenName: wps
cn: wps bind

dn: cn=wpsadmins,cn=groups,dc=rigorconsultants,dc=com
objectclass: groupOfUniqueNames
objectclass: top
uniquemember: uid=wpsadmin,cn=users,dc=rigorconsultants,dc=com
cn: wpsadmins
```

To import into IBM Directory Server, stop the directory server

1. Click Start ⇨ Programs ⇨ IBM Directory Server 5.1 ⇨ Directory Configuration.
2. Click Import LDAP, enter the location of the file to import, and click OK. A message will appear that states that you have successfully imported six out of six items or 6 of 6 if your suffix is already defined.
3. Exit and restart your LDAP server.

The next directory server we will look at is Sun One Directory Server formally known as Netscape Directory Server. This is one of the oldest and most popular LDAP directory servers. For Sun One Directory Server 5.2, the process is pretty much similar. The only difference lies in the default naming structure

- group prefix is ou=People
- group suffix is ou=Groups
- Portal administrator DN is uid=wpsadmin, ou=People, dc=rigorconsultants, dc=com
- Portal administrator group is cn=wpsadmins, ou=Groups, dc=rigorconsultants, dc=com of which wpsadmin is a member
- WebSphere Security ID DN is uid=wpsbind, ou=Groups, dc=rigorconsultants, dc=com

Do the following to import into Sun One Directory Server:

1. Start the Sun One Server Console.
2. Under Servers and Application, expand the tree and double-click Directory Server.
3. Go to the Task tab and click Import LDIF.
4. Type **LDIF** file (or browse to it) and click OK.
5. After the data has been imported, go to the Directory tab and validate your directory tree.

The last directory server is the most popular directory server based on market penetration, Microsoft Active Directory. This LDAP server is designed to work very well within a Microsoft environment; however, due to some its propriety features and lack of support for many objectclasses it does not integrate easily to other environments.

To use Active Directory with WebSphere Portal, you must have the Windows 2000 High Encryption Pack, Internet Information Services, and Certificate Services using the standalone root CA option installed. Active Directory requires Secure Sockets Layer (SSL) enabled in order for WebSphere Portal to use it as a user registry (more on this later).

The naming structure that we used with Active Directory is as follows:

- LDAP suffix is set to dc=rigorconsultants,dc=com
- user prefix is cn
- group prefix is cn=users
- group suffix is cn=groups
- Portal administrator DN is cn=wpsadmin, cn=users, dc=rigorconsultants, dc=com
- Portal administrator group is cn=wpsadmins, cn=groups, dc=rigorconsultants, dc=com of which wpsadmin is a member
- WebSphere Security ID DN is cn=wpsbind, cn=users, dc=rigorconsultants, dc=com

Normally you would import the data as an LDIF file using LDIFDE utility. However, the changes to the LDIF are so great that it is easier to add the wpsadmin and wpsbind users and wpsadmins group using the Windows Active Directory Users and Groups administrative tool.

Configuring WebSphere Portal for Your LDAP Server

Now that your LDAP server is all set up, you need to configure WebSphere Portal server to work with it by using the following steps:

1. Ensure that WebSphere security is disabled. If it is not, do the following:

   a. Copy the template security_disable.properties file from `<wps_root>\config\helpers` to `<wps_root>\config`.

   b. Modify the properties based on your values.

   c. Open a command prompt and change the directory to `<wps_root>\config`.

   d. Enter.

   ```
   WPSconfig -DparentProperties "<wps_ root>\config\security_disable" -
   DSaveParentProperties=true
   ```

   e. Upon completion enter **WPSconfig disable-security**.

2. In `<wps_root>\config\helpers`, find the appropriate template and copy it to `<wps_root>\config`. For IBM Directory Server, use `security_ibm_dir_server.properties`, Sun One Directory; use `security_ibm_dir_server.properties`, and Microsoft Active Directory; and `security_active_directory.properties`.

3. In the template, assign the properties values based on Tables 19-1 to 19-3. The values assigned in Table 19-1 are those we used to access each LDAP.

4. Save the file as `ldap.properties`.

5. Ensure that WebSphere Application Server is running but WebSphere Portal has stopped functioning.

Table 19-1 WebSphere Application Server Properties

		PROPERTY VALUE		
PROPERTY	**DESCRIPTION**	**IBM DIRECTORY SERVER 5.1**	**SUN ONE 5.2**	**WINDOWS 2000 ACTIVE DIRECTORY**
WasUserid	The fully qualified name of the WebSphere Application Server security ID with no spaces	uid=wpsbind, cn=users, dc=rigorcon-sultants, dc=com	uid=wpsbind, ou=people, dc=rigorcon-sultants, dc=com	cn=wpsbind, cn=users, dc=rigor-consultants, dc=com
WasPassword	The password for WebSphere Application Server security ID			

Table 19-2 WebSphere Portal Properties Configuration

PROPERTY	DESCRIPTION	PROPERTY VALUE		
		IBM DIRECTORY SERVER 5.1	SUN ONE 5.2	WINDOWS 2000 ACTIVE DIRECTORY
PortalAdminId	The fully qualified name of the WebSphere Portal Administrators with no spaces	uid=wpsadmin, cn=users, dc=rigorconsultants, dc=com	uid=wpsadmin, ou=people, dc=rigorconsultants, dc=com	cn=wpsadmin, cn=users, dc=rigorconsultants, dc=com
PortalAdminShort	Short form of the WebSphere Portal Administrator ID	wpsadmin	wpsadmin	wpsadmin
PortalAdminGroupId	The fully qualified group ID from the group to which the WebSphere Portal Administrator belongs	uid=wpsadmins, cn=groups, dc=rigorconsultants, dc=com	uid=wpsadmins, ou=groups, dc=rigorconsultants, dc=com	cn=wpsadmins, cn=users, dc=rigorconsultants, dc=com
PortalAdminGroupIDShort	The short form of the WebSphere Portal Administrator group ID	wpsadmins	wpsadmins	wpsadmins

Table 19-3 LDAP Properties Configuration

PROPERTY	DESCRIPTION	PROPERTY VALUE		
		IBM DIRECTORY SERVER 5.1	SUN ONE 5.2	WINDOWS 2000 ACTIVE DIRECTORY
LookAside	States whether you are using a look-aside database, which stores attributes that cannot be stored in your LDAP server	false	false	false
LDAPHostName	LDAP server host Name	sandbox2.rigorconsultants.com	sandbox2.rigorconsultants.com	sandbox2.rigorconsultants.com
LDAPPort	The port number that the LDAP server uses	389	389	636
LDAPAdminUid	The LDAP administrator Id	cn=ldsadmin	cn=ldsadmin	cn=ldsadmin
LDAPAdminPwd	The LDAP administrator Id password			
LDAPServerType	Type of LDAP server	IBM_DIRECTORY_SERVER	IPLANET	ACTIVE_DIRECTORY

Parameter	Description			
LDAPBindId	The user Id for LDAP Bind authentication	uid=wpsbind, cn=users, dc=rigorconsultants, dc=com	uid=wpsbind, ou=people, dc=rigorconsultants, dc=com	cn=wpsbind, cn=users, dc=rigorconsultants, dc=com
LDAPSuffix	The LDAP suffix	dc=rigorconsultants, dc=com	dc=rigorconsultants, dc=com	dc=rigorconsultants, dc=com
LdapUserPrefix	User prefix	uid	uid	cn
LDAUserSuffix	User suffix	cn=users	ou=People	cn=users
LDAPGroupPrefix	Group prefix	cn	cn	cn
LDAPGroupSuff Suffix	Group suffix	cn=groups	ou=groups	cn=users
LDAPUserObjectClass	User object class	inOrgPerson	inOrgPerson	user
LDAPGroupObjectClass	Group object class	groupOfUniqueNames	groupOfUniqueNames	group
LDAPGroupMember	The attribute name of the membership attribute of your group objectclass	uniqueMember	uniqueMember	member
LDAPsslEnabled	Is LDAP SSL enabled?	false	false	true

6. In the command prompt (you should still be in the directory <wps_root>\config), enter **WPSconfig - DparentProperties=** "**<wps˙root>\config \ldap.properties**" - **DSaveParentProperties=true**.

7. Test your configuration settings by entering **WPSconfig validate-ldap**. If the test is unsuccessful, recheck your configuration settings.

8. If it is successful, run WPSconfig secure-portal-ldap. If you are using Active Directory or you have enabled SSL, there are a few more steps that will be discussed in the next section. Do not try to implement an SSL configuration (unless you are implementing Active Directory) without getting a non-SSL configuration to work.

9. Validate that your LDAP is properly configured by logging into WebSphere Portal and adding a user under Portal Administration functions. Go to the LDAP Web Administrator and check the new user entry.

Enabling WebSphere Portal to Access Your LDAP Server over SSL

At times you may want information traveling between your WebSphere Portal server and LDAP to be encrypted. For instance if your LDAP servers are spread over multiple geographical locations and are accessed through the Internet, you would want to ensure that sensitive information such as user IDs and passwords is not hijacked, manipulated, or viewed by unauthorized persons. A method to ensure privacy is to enable WebSphere Application Server and WebSphere Portal to access the LDAP server with SSL enabled. Of course, this assumes that you have also enabled SSL between the Web Browser and your Web server.

SSL is a security protocol that supports data encryption, authentication, and data integrity verification. An SSL operation consists of an initiation and a data transfer. At the initiation stage, the client/server and the server try to set up the session and connection state by coming to an agreement on encryption and authentication. Agreement is made once the protocol version is chosen, the encryption algorithm chosen, and both parties have authenticated each other (optional). Upon successful initiation stage, data will be transferred using public-key encryption. Data required for the public-key encryption (including keys) is done through certificates. Certificates need to be created for each component and stored on each counterparts' key database. Certificates can be obtained from a certificate authority (CA) such as Verisign or they can be self-signed. Usually you use self-sign if you have two internal servers communicating with each other as in this instance. Thus to get WAS and WP to access LDAP over SSL, you need the LDAP server certificates in the WAS and WP key storage files. The certificate trust chain can consist of one self-signed certificate or a CA where the CA has confirmed the identity and validity of the certificate.

Setting Up the Server Certificates

Do the following to set up an LDAP server (except Active Directory) over SSL:

1. This step applies to users who need to generate a self-signed certificate. If you are importing a CA certificate (which is in base64-encoded ASCII data and has a .arm extension), skip to step 2.

   a. Execute your security key management utility such as gsk6ikm.

   b. Create a CMS Key Database file or open an existing file and create a new self-signed certificate using X.509 version 3 format and 1024-bit key size. Assign the certificate a label and remember it.

   c. Extract the new self-signed certificate as a certificate file using base64-encoded ASCII data as the data type and save it. The filename can be a filename of your choice but the extension must be .arm.

   d. Configure your LDAP directory with SSL enabled using the CMNS Key Database file contained in the self-signed certificate.

2. Import the certificates to a WAS keystore by doing the following:

   a. Open a command prompt and execute `<was_root>\ikeyman .exe`.

   b. Determine the keystore file by going into the WebSphere Application Server Admin Console, and click Security ⇨ SSL.

   c. Open the keystore file. If it already exists, you will be asked for a password, otherwise you will need to supply it.

   d. Select Signer Certificates from the top drop-down list and click Add.

   e. Select base64-encoded ASCII data as the data type and browse to the certificate file that you exported from your LDAP server.

   f. Enter the certificate label that you assigned in step 1b, and click Save.

3. Next you must import the certificate into WebSphere Portal keystore

   a. Open a command prompt and execute `<was_root>\ikeyman .exe`.

   b. Open the default keystore file `<was_root>\java\jre\lib\ security\cacerts`. The default password is changeit.

   c. Select Signer Certificates in the top drop-down list and click Add.

   d. Select base64-encoded ASCII data as the data type and browse to the certificate file that you exported from your LDAP server.

   e. Enter the certificate label that you assigned in step 1b and click save.

  4. Shut down the non-SSL port (389) if you want to ensure that data exchanged between WAS and WP is confidential.

To configure Active Directory over SSL, you need to first install Active Directory, Internet Information Services, and then WebSphere Application Server. Then perform the following tasks:

  1. Export the root CA certificate:

   a. Open your Web browser and connect to `http://localhost/certsrv`.

   b. Select the task Retrieve the CA Certificate or certificate revocation list and click Next.

   c. Choose the certificate you created and set the format to base 64 encoded. Click Download CA Certificate.

   d. Save the certificate in a file called `certnew.cer`.

   e. Open a command prompt, enter **mmc.exe**, and click File ⇨ Add/Remove Snap-in.

   f. Click Add, choose CA Snap-in, and click OK. Find the root certificate public key and save to a file.

  2. Import the certificate to the WebSphere Application Server keystore:

   a. Open a command prompt and execute `<was_root>\ikeyman.exe`.

   b. Open the default keystore file `<was_root>\java\jre\lib\security\cacerts`. The default password is changeit.

   c. Select Signer Certificates in the top drop-down list and click Add.

   d. Select base64-encoded ASCII data as the data type and browse to the `certnew.cer` file.

   e. Type a name for the certificate and click OK.

Configure WebSphere Portal to Support SSL

To configure WebSphere Portal to use LDAP over SSL (excluding Active Directory) do the following:

1. Ensure that WebSphere Application Server has been configured and is operating with SSL support by selecting Security ⇨ User Registries ⇨ LDAP and ensuring SSL is enabled and the sslconfiguration property file has been correctly entered.

2. Configure WebSphere Portal to use LDAP over SSL by modifying the `<ldapRepository...>` stanza in `<wp_root>/shared/app/wmm/wmm.xml`:

   a. Change the LDAP port number to the SSL port number.

   b. Add the following key/value pairs: java.naming.security.protocol="ssl".

3. Restart WebSphere Portal.

For Active Directory do the following:

1. Ensure that WebSphere Application Server has been configured and is operating with SSL support by selecting Security ⇨ User Registries ⇨ LDAP and ensuring SSL is enabled and the sslconfiguration property file has been correctly entered.

2. Configure WebSphere Portal to use LDAP over SSL by modifying the `<ldapRepository...>` stanza in `<wp_root>/shared/app/wmm/wmm.xml`:

   a. Change the LDAP port number to the SSL port number.

   b. Set wmmmGenerateExtId to false.

   c. Add the following key/value pairs: java.naming.security.protocol="ssl".

3. Remove all occurrences of ibm-appUUIDAux from `wmm.xml`.

4. Enable Active Directory to recognize a short name (as opposed to a fully qualified DN) by selecting Security ⇨ User Registries ⇨ LDAP ⇨ Advanced LDAP Settings in the WebSphere Application Server console and change the user filter from (&(cn=%v)(objectclass=user)) to (&(sAMAccountName=%v)(objectclass=user)).

5. Restart WebSphere Portal.

Mapping of Member Manager Attributes to Your LDAP Attributes

The configuration parameters that are generated by WebSphere Portal installation and WPSconfig are stored in `<wp_root>\shared\app\wmm\wmm.xml`. When you configure WP for LDAP, there is an entry configurationFile

`="<wp_root>/wmm/wmmLDAPServerAttributes_XXX.xml` under the `LDAPRepository` tag in the `wmm.xml` file. This entry refers to an xml that maps the profile attributes to the LDAP object classes and attributes. The last three letters refer to the LDAP directory being mapped. For instance:

- wmmLDAPServerAttributes_IDS contains the maps for IBM Directory Server
- wmmLDAPServerAttributes_SO contains the maps for Sun One Directory
- wmmLDAPServerAttributes_IDS contains the maps for Active Directory

In each file, the names of the various repositories, their Member Managers adapter implementation classes, and the mapping between the Member Manager attribute and the repository are defined. Mapping of the user attributes to the LDAP directory is based on the inetOrgPerson schema. By modifying the `wmmLDAPServerAttributes_XXX` file, you can expose new LDAP attributes to Member Manager.

For instance look at this entry in wmmLDAPServerAttributes_IDS:

```
<attributeMap wmmAttributeName="uid"
                    pluginAttributeName="uid"
                    applicableMemberTypes="Person"
                    requiredMemberTypes="Person"
                    dataType="String"
                    valueLength="256"
                    multiValued="false" />
```

You see that the LDAP attribute (wmmAttrributeName) uid is mapped to the Member Manager attribute (pluginAttributeName) uid where the member type is Person and it is required. The data type is string of length 256 bytes and it cannot have more than one value assigned.

What is more important is that this is the process to define which attributes will be stored in a look-aside database.

Summary

In this chapter we focused in great detail on implementing WebSphere Portal Identity Manager. We specifically focused on using LDAP servers due to their suitability in handling large user registries that are dispersed over multiple locations. In the next chapter we will discuss the logical next topic: implementing WebSphere Portal with Single Sign-on.

## CHAPTER 20

Integrating Security and Identity Management Tools with WebSphere Portal

In this chapter you will learn to integrate security and identity management tools with WebSphere Portal. Because of the complexity involved with security features such as authentication and authorization in environments including many applications and information sources, a new category of products has emerged in the past few years. These products manage repositories of users and their profiles and implement security policies for authenticating and authorizing access based on identifying users and mapping them to static or dynamic roles. These tools allow you to manage a complex entitlement model that spans multiple applications and sources.

Because portals are in many ways the ultimate integrated environment, knowing how to use these tools in the context of WP is increasingly important and many portal initiatives succeed or fail depending on identity management and security. Perhaps the most well-known issue that must be addressed in the context of a portal is that of single sign-on (SSO). A good SSO environment means that once a user has authenticated with the system (and normally this is during the initial log-on to the portal), he or she will not be asked to authenticate again even when they traverse application boundaries. A bad SSO implementation (or no SSO implementation) will constantly ask the user for a user name and a password—every time the user accesses a separate application. Because portals often integrate a large number of back-end applications as portlets, a bad SSO implementation will create a horrendous user experience and can potentially create a usability issue that will cause limited user adoption. This is the basic reason that security and identity management tools have been highly successful in the past few years and the reason that a new category of products has emerged.

Two approaches to SSO can be used. In Chapter 23 we discuss back-end SSO within WP using the Credential Vault. This approach makes use of built-in WP functionality that allows you to store back-end application credentials within WP and associate them with WP users. In this chapter, the focus is the use of external security managers to perform SSO.

Many products address this need for using external security managers to perform SSO. Among them are market-share leaders such as Netegrity SiteMinder and Tivoli Access Manager (TAM). At a conceptual level most of these products provide similar functionality. In this chapter you will learn how to integrate both products into a WP environment. We will not review all functions in both products—from a functional perspective all features described are available in both products. Our choice to provide a description using TAM or SiteMinder is somewhat arbitrary and we will keep this discussion somewhat generic so as not to have to duplicate this description for both products (or others in this category).

Isn't J2EE Security Enough?

The first questions you should be asking yourself are: Why you even need to consider additional security products? and Why are WP and its underlying WAS platform not enough? The answers depend on your portal implementation. If you have a simple portal focused on a single function and are not integrating many applications within the portal or are integrating only J2EE applications developed for WAS, then you might be able to get away with using WAS and WP security. You can use the WAS J2EE security model to manage both authentication and authorization so long as the elements you manage are servlets, EJBs, JSPs, Java clients, and the like. When you also have portlets, the same model can be applied using WP security. These models include the following:

- Declarative security expressed in various deployment descriptors managed by application assemblers or administrators, and
- Programmatic security coded into the application by developers.

In addition, if you need to implement highly specialized security features (such as dynamic roles) you need to delve deep into the underlying JAAS layers. All of these options do not provide you with a full solution when the protected entities are more complex, when the resources are not all running within WP/WAS, and in some cases even when everything is completely within WP/WAS. As an example, WAS has a different model for protecting EJBs than Web applications making the administration process harder. Access control is limited in terms of granularity—forcing you to use either fine-grained method level access control or course-grained package level access control.

These issues have created a category of products focused on identity and security management. With these tools you implement a better and more comprehensive security model that is separate from the underlying WAS/WP platform. Benefits for doing this include the following:

- Support for heterogeneous environments and servers within a single and consistent security model
- Ability to manage virtually any resource
- Central management of security information
- Configurable session management (for example, session time-outs)
- Full support for user provisioning
- Definition of security and access control rules based on users, roles, dynamic roles, and even through rules that match data in a user context with conditions that determine whether the user should have access to a particular resource
- Support for personalized Web and portal content using a consistent rule set regardless of the underlying provider
- Policies and personalization based on IP addresses
- Enhanced security attributes (from an attack perspective)
- Multi-grained security (that is, the ability to define fine-grained access control on some resources and coarse-grained access at the same time)
- Support for SSO (see next section)

Third-Party Authentication and SSO Architectures

SSO Architectures are primarily based on a third-party authentication server that is inserted in your infrastructure as a reverse proxy. Because it serves as a reverse proxy, it intercepts all requests regardless of which server the request is ultimately dispatched to. Because you will have so many applications in a portal environment, the concept of a third-party authentication server says that it makes no sense for any one of these systems and applications to be the main authentication engine; instead, a dedicated authentication server is used to authenticate the user. Once authenticated, the authentication server places the user information in a token that is passed to all systems and applications. These systems look for the information within the token and trust this information. This means that the systems and applications rely on the authentication server and trust the authentication server rather then needing to reauthenticate the user.

In a WP environment, a third-party authentication server is also trusted by WP itself. The mechanism by which this occurs is actually a WAS feature that WP implicitly inherits. Regardless of whether you use SiteMinder or TAM, SSO works through a Trust Association Interceptor (TAI). A TAI is an interface that is part of the WAS security model. It is implemented by a Java class that is installed on WAS (or WP in your case); its task is to validate that the request is legitimate by inspecting agreed upon information that is stored by the authentication server in the request. Once a user is authenticated, the authentication server creates a token; in an HTTP request this information may be placed as specific headers in the request. When the request reaches WP the TAI is invoked. The TAI knows which headers need to be checked and retrieves the correct information from the headers. Because it trusts the authentication server, it applies the appropriate credentials within WP and WP continues as though it is the one who performed the authentication. The TAI should return either a Distinguished Name (DN) or a short name. WP then performs a lookup within the user registry to verify the DN (potentially first converting the short name into a DN if the TAI returns a short name). If the lookup fails, WP will refuse to trust the information and will refuse the request; otherwise, an LTPS token is created and stored as a cookie for subsequent requests within the session.

In order to correctly support user identification and authorization in addition to authentication, both WP and the authentication server must share the same user registry. Specifically, an LDAP server maintaining user information and profiles needs to be registered with both WP and the authentication server.

Once both WP and the security server share the same user registry, you can go one level further than authentication (hence we use the term *security server* here for the first time). Access rights within WP are usually administered using access control lists and are stored within WP's administration database. However, you can also configure an external security manager such as TAM and SiteMinder to protect WP resources. Both TAM and Site-Minder can be used to manage authorization policies for WP resources such as portlets and pages in addition to WAS constructs such as servlets and EJBs. This is mostly based on URL paths and the mapping of URLs to users and roles.

Integrating TAM with WP

In addition to supporting all the features described in the previous section, TAM also supports some WAS-specific security features. WAS supports an IBM proprietary SSO token called Lightweight Third Party Authentication

(LTPA). This is the preferred SSO token method in WAS and therefore in WP. LTPS is naturally also supported by TAM and hence the TAM/WP security integration is very comprehensive.

You should consider using TAM security rather than straightforward WP security for a variety of reasons. First, TAM implements a comprehensive SSO architecture that will cover most if not all of your back-end systems very naturally. In addition, TAM will provide you with a higher level of security for the following reasons:

- TAM includes a secure proxy server (WebSEAL) that has been deployed in very large installations and has proven to be very effective. The WebSEAL proxy acts as an additional security layer within your DMZ, breaking direct access between browsers (and potential attackers) and your core application servers.
- TAM supports multiple authentication schemes including user name/passwords, various forms of certificates, tokens, and biometrics.
- TAM supports cross-domain SSO.
- TAM supports not only WP but also other WebSphere products such as WebSphere Everyplace (see Chapter 24).
- WebSEAL is a layer that can be hardened to a great extent without affecting important platforms such as WP (which would be much harder to lock down and harden).
- TAM can easily be integrated with existing user registries.
- TAM supports rule-based decisions.
- TAM supports full audit capabilities.

Installing TAM Support on WP

The first thing you need to do in order to enable TAM-to-WP integration is to set up the TAM TAI. This TAI is not unique to WP and the installation steps are identical to those you would follow when integrating WAS and TAM. Log in to the WAS Administration Console and click Security ⇨ Authentication Mechanisms ⇨ LTPA. Scroll down, as shown in Figure 20-1, and click Trust Association.

Make sure that trust association is enabled and click Interceptors. Also make sure that your interceptor is defined as `com.ibm.ws.security.web.WebSealTrustAssociationInterceptor`; if it is not, click New and select this class.

Next you need to set up the LDAP settings, including the security server ID, password, host, port, base DN, bind DN, and bind password. Click

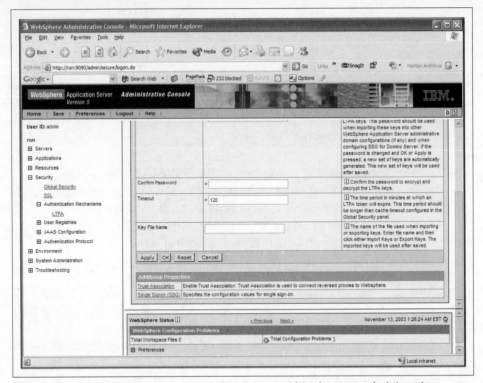

Figure 20-1 Opening the Trust Association Screen within the WAS Administration Console.

Security ⇨ User Registries ⇨ LDAP and enter these values as shown in Figure 20-2. Finally, you will need to restart WAS.

While authentication using TAM is really set up within WAS, authorization via TAM is a WP-specific process and involves WP resources such as portlets and pages. This requires you to configure the connection between WP and TAM by running the following routine from the TAM installation:

```
<TAM_ROOT>/sbin/pdjrtecfg -action config -java_home <WAS_ROOT>/Java/jre
```

Then configure an SSL connection between WAS and TAM, create a key file and a properties file, as well as an agreed-upon user name and groups. To do so, run the following command from your command line:

```
<WAS_ROOT>/Java/jre/bin/java com.tivoli.mts.SvrSslCfg <USER NAME>
<SECURITY MASTER PASSWORD> <PDMGRD HOST> <PDACLD HOST>
```

Next, add the following line to `services.properties`:

```
com.ibm.wps.services.authorization.ExternalAccessControlService =
com.ibm.wps.services.authorization.PDExternalAccessControlServiceImpl
```

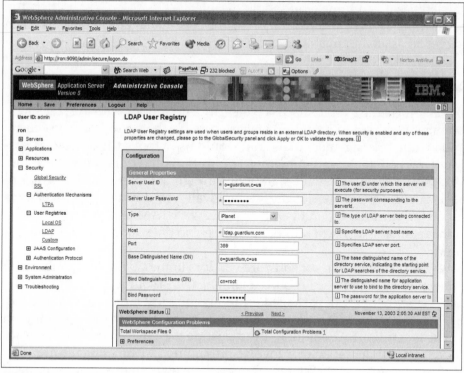

Figure 20-2 Configuring the LDAP User Registry.

Next, edit `externalAccessControlService.properties` within your TAM installation and change the value of `accessControl` to equal `true`.

Next, edit `portallogin.config`. There are two sections called `WpsNewSubject` and `WpsSubjectExists`. In each section you need to add the following line at the end:

```
Com.ibm.websphere.security.auth.module.proxy.WSLoginModuleProxy required
delegate=com.tivoli.mts.PDLoginModule;
```

Restart the portal server and you are done.

Disabling WP User Provisioning and Manipulation

When using an external security manager such as TAM you should also ensure that all user provisioning occurs through TAM. Because TAM is the main security manager all new users must be registered through TAM, and user provisioning directly within WP will create situations in which users have registered and received acknowledgment by WP but when they try to log in they will be denied. Therefore, you must disable WP's user creation capabilities. In addition, you should disable the User Manager portlet. You can do both of these tasks by removing the user management portlets when logged in as an administrator.

Setting Up SSO

Before proceeding on to discuss Netegrity SiteMinder with WP, let's look at some specific (and common) scenarios in which you would use security and identity management tools. You would use a tool such as TAM or Site-Minder when deploying numerous applications and data sources through WP. In this section we will walk you through some specific examples of such a deployment. Specifically, we will walk you through a few scenarios involving the integration of SAP systems with TAM and WP. The discussion is similar in concept (although different in details) when SiteMinder is used.

SAP is one of the largest software vendors in the world and is most well known for its Enterprise Resource Planning (ERP) solution. It maintains the largest market share of packaged solutions and most large corporations run SAP software. In this section we show you two scenarios that are common when integrating SAP solutions in an existing WP environment using TAM. Because such integration may involve presenting SAP functionality through WP and because SAP systems manage their own security, you will need to set up an SSO environment that includes WP and the SAP software—through TAM. This means that in addition to what you already know in terms of WP and TAM, you will have to set up a trust relationship between SAP servers and TAM.

Because the SAP solution set is so broad, an integrated solution can be implemented in many ways and you can choose to use or omit many SAP components. While we cannot cover all options in this section, we will describe two different scenarios that are fairly typical—both in the SAP world as well as in cases in which other suites are being used (for example, PeopleSoft and Siebel) The first scenario describes the integration of the mySAP.com Internet-enabled infrastructure and the second describes the integration of the SAP Enterprise Portal. In both cases the assumption is that you are using a back-end component of SAP such as various SAP R/3 modules (for example, finance and warehousing) or SAP BW (the business information warehouse).

mySAP.com Integration

Before we can show you the steps involved in integrating mySAP.com or the mySAP Workplace, let's review the elements involved in the mySAP.com architecture, and specifically SAP's Internet Transaction Server (ITS).

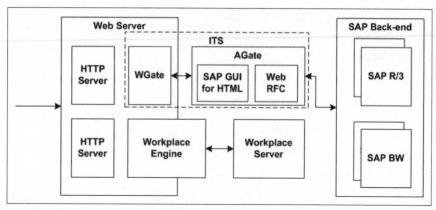

Figure 20-3   mySAP.com Architecture.

Figure 20-3 shows a typical layered scheme of mySAP.com. The back end consists of various application modules within SAP R/3 and SAP BW. In addition to these servers the Workplace Server is a component built on the same infrastructure as the SAP applications and is responsible for SAP application authentication, role administrations, and remote invocations. Because it is built using the same infrastructure (called R/3 Basis), it is able to implement security on behalf of the applications and is the key to SSO.

The infrastructure responsible for creating and delivering Web screens based on the back-end function is ITS. ITS comprises of the WGate and the AGate, the WGate being the interface to the Web server and the AGate being the interface to the SAP back end. Of the two components the AGate does most of the work and is responsible for session management, generating HTML screens from R/3 screens, invoking functional modules from the HTML, managing connections and sessions to the back end, and so on.

From a security perspective, ITS can make use of the internal security services provided within mySAP.com Workplace or can delegate to an external security manager using the Pluggable Authentication Service (PAS)—much like WAS/WP can use its own authentication or use a TAI with a third-party authentication server.

In order to use PAS, you need to establish a trust model between your authentication server (for example, TAM) and mySAP.com. PAS is deployed as a shared library used by the ITS gateway interface. ITS uses PAS to verify the user authentication information generated by TAM. PAS queries TAM and then sends the validated information to the SAP Workplace, which returns a login ticket. This login ticket is then used as the SSO ticket when accessing SAP modules. At a more detailed level the sequence is as follows:

1. User provides credentials, which are forwarded by the Web server to WGate

2. `WGate` sends the credentials to `AGate`

3. `AGate` forwards the credentials to TAM using PAS

4. TAM verifies credentials and replies to PAS

5. PAS passes the user information to the SAP Workplace

6. SAP user information is returned to PAS

7. PAS creates a login ticket and sends it back to the Web browser

8. `WGate` creates a cookie from the login ticket and sends it in the HTTP response

Integrating TAM/WP with `mySAP.com` is done by defining the `mySAP.com` infrastructure within a TAM WebSEAL junction. Follow these steps to configure both TAM and SAP (for more details refer to the `mySAP.com` and the TAM documentation):

1. Create a WebSEAL junction to the `mySAP.com` environment.

2. Add the line `-META=CONTENT` to `webseald.conf`.

3. Set `script-filer` to `yes` in `webseald.conf`.

4. Add entries for filtering URLs to the JMT.

5. Add the line `header=Accept-Encoding` to the filter request headers section in `webseald.conf`.

6. Restart WebSEAL.

7. Copy `sappdssocgi.exe` from the `mySAP.com` installation into the `www/docs/cgi-bin` directory in WebSEAL.

8. Create a secret trusted key named `-sappdsso.key`.

9. Install SAP Secure Network Communications (SNC) on your ITS instance.

10. Stop the ITS Manager if it is running.

11. Copy the `sappdssoauth` shared library to the ITS `programs` directory.

12. Copy `sappdssoauth.srvc` into the ITS services directory.

13. Copy your `mySAP` templates into the ITS `templates` directory.

14. Under TAM's `Policy Director` directory, create an SAP directory with subdirectories for `etc`, `var`, and `bin`.

15. Copy the secret key file generated in step 8 to the `etc` directory.

16. Modify the `login.html` template copied in step 13; replace `WEBSEALSERVERNAME` with the appropriate junction.

SAP Enterprise Portal Integration

Because SAP has so many modules and offerings, it also develops and sells portal solutions. In fact, in many environments SAP Portal is a direct alternative to WP and there are many companies which deploy SAP Portals as its portal even when the content delivered through the portal is not exclusively sourced in SAP software. Still, SAP Portal is primarily used in environments where SAP applications cover a majority of the business functionality deployed in the organization. In environments where this is true and yet portal functionality is still important, it is common to see two portal infrastructures—WP as the overall portal and SAP Portal as a sub-portal. This eliminates some of the pain involved with integrating many SAP applications into WP. More on this topic in Chapter 23.

The SAP Enterprise Portal architecture is shown in Figure 20-4. Much like WP Extend, Enable, and Experience, SAP Enterprise Portals are available as three different offerings:

- SAP Enterprise Information Portal (SEIP)—creating a unified Web interface

- SAP Enterprise Collaboration Portal (SECP)—including all functionality in SEIP and adding personalization, collaboration, categorization, and search capabilities

- SAP Enterprise Unification Portal (SEUP)—including all functionality in SECP with enhanced coordination capabilities and virtual desktop capabilities

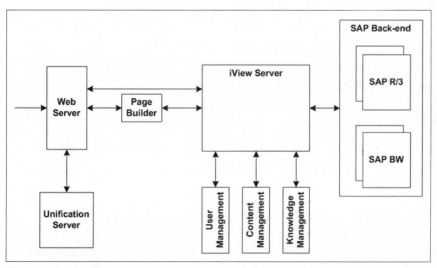

Figure 20-4 SAP Portal architecture.

As any portal, an SAP Enterprise Portal has its own implementation of authentication, authorization, and administration of users. It also has its own implementation of an SSO environment based on a login ticket. However, SAP Portals can externalize authentication and SSO to a third-party product such as TAM and this is the preferred method when an SAP Portal needs to be a part of a larger WP deployment. You can do this in one of two ways. The first involves configuring the SAP Portal to use external authentication by specifying the name of an HTTP header that contains the authenticated user name and creating the appropriate WebSEAL junction. The second is to use a WebSEAL Global Sign-On (GSO) junction, which is configured to pass the user name and password in the form of a Basic Authentication header and configuring the SAP Portal to do normal LDAP lookup. To implement the first option, follow these steps:

1. Ensure that both WebSEAL/WP and the SAP Portal share the same LDAP user registry.

2. Set up a WebSEAL junction for the SAP Portal using the `-c iv_user` option, allowing WebSEAL to pass the user id in the HTTP header.

3. Create a WebSEAL Junction Mapping Table (JMT).

4. Add `IFRAME=REFRESHURL` and `PARAM=VALUE` to `webseald.conf` in the `filter-url` section.

5. Add `TD=ONCLICK` to the `filter-events` section in `webseald.conf`.

6. Add `scheme=hrnp` to the `filter-schemes` section in `webseald.conf`.

7. Add `script-filter=yes` and `rewrite-absolute-with-absolute=yes` to the `script-filtering` section in `webseald.conf`.

8. Log on to the SAP Portal as an administrator.

9. Select System Configuration ⇨ User Management Config ⇨ Authentication Server.

10. Set User Authentication Type to External.

11. Set User Name Header to HTTP_IV_USER.

12. Click Apply.

To implement the second option, follow these steps:

1. Ensure that both WebSEAL/WP and the SAP Portal share the same LDAP user registry.

2. Create a WebSEAL junction for the SAP Portal with the `-v` option.

3. Follow steps 3–9 as described in option 1.

4. Set User Authentication Type to LDAP.

5. Enter the LDAP server information.

6. Click Apply.

Installing SiteMinder Support on WP

When using SiteMinder you have three options:

1. Using SiteMinder as a third-party authentication server

2. Using the SiteMinder Policy Server as an external security manager, or

3. Both

Figure 20-5 shows the different Netegrity components that you may choose to use and how they interact with WAS/WP. You may choose to use Netegrity's authentication server or another authentication server and in either case can still use the Policy Server. The SiteMinder Policy Server allows you to better define and control the security policy and, more specifically, access control on your portal. At a WAS level, the Policy Server interacts with three components (with portlets being managed by the Servlet Agent Controller):

1. The EJB Agent Controller

2. The Servlet Agent Controller

3. The Web Agent Controller

When a protected resource is requested, the appropriate agent validates the request with the SiteMinder Policy Server. As an example, when the

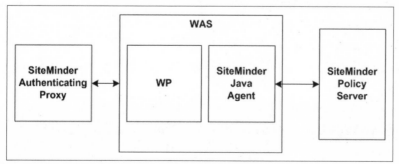

Figure 20-5   Using Netegrity SiteMinder with WP.

resource is an EJB or an invocation of an EJB method, the EJB Agent (which is itself an EJB) communicates with the Policy Server using a set of Java APIs and offers resource protection at the following granularity levels:

- An entire package
- Beans
- Bean methods
- Method signatures

The last granularity type—method signatures—allows you to define protection elements that are based on a combination of method and its parameters, that is, the signature a method may have rather than a unique bean method.

Using SiteMinder as a Third-Party Authentication Server

In order to install SiteMinder as a third-party authentication server you need to install the SiteMinder TAI:

1. Install SiteMinder as a trusted authentication server:
   a. Log in to the WAS Administration Console and click Security ➪ Authentication Mechanisms ➪ LTPA.
   b. Click Trust Association.
   c. Check the Trust Association Enabled check box.
   d. Click Interceptors in the Additional Properties section.
   e. Because SiteMinder is not one of the default authentication servers, you will have to add it. Click New.
   f. Enter the interceptor class name:

      `com.ibm.wps.sso.SiteMinderTrustAssociation Interceptor`

   g. Click Apply.
   h. Click Custom Properties.
   i. Enter custom properties as defined in the SiteMinder installation guide.
   j. Click OK and restart the server.

2. Now that you have completed setting up SiteMinder as a trusted reverse proxy, you can continue to Netegrity-specific configuration:
   a. Install the SiteMinder Java Agent API by adding the JAR files in `<SITEMINDER_ROOT>/sdk/java` to `<WAS_ROOT>/lib` and by

adding the appropriate JNI support library to the PATH variable of the Java VM (for example, in Windows the support library is called `smjavaagentapi.dll`). The primary Java class needed is `netegrity.siteminder.javaagent.AgentAPI`, which can be used to enforce access control by connecting to the Policy Server. The Java Agent API insulates you from the implementation details within the Policy Server and supports full session management, automatic encryption key rollover, and real-time policy updates. All Java-based SiteMinder agents make use of the Java Agent API, and custom agents built using the Java Agent API can participate with standard SiteMinder agents within an SSO environment.

b. Set the `validateSessions` parameter to `true` within `siteminder.properties`.

c. Follow the instructions in the Netegrity Policy Server Management manual to define a Web Agent in the SiteMinder Administration Console. This agent is required to establish a trust association between WAS and SiteMinder and allows the TAI to validate the sessions with the Policy Server.

d. Set the `com.ibm.wps.sso.SiteMinderTrustAssociation` as the class name for the interceptor TAI.

3. Finally, set the following configuration parameters:

```
com.ibm.websphere.security.trustassociation.enabled=true
com.ibm.websphere.security.trustassociation.types=Netegrity
com.ibm.websphere.security.trustassociation.interceptor=
com.ibm.wps.sso.SiteMinderTrustAssociationInterceptor
com.ibm.websphere.security.trustassociation.config=siteminder
```

Using SiteMinder as an External Security Manager

Installing SiteMinder as an external security manager is a little more involved. There are two primary steps involved: installing SiteMinder and modifying WP to delegate policy decisions to SiteMinder. Installing SiteMinder as an external security manager involves the following steps (these steps are for Windows; refer to the Netegrity Policy Server Installation Guide for other platforms):

1. Run the Policy Server setup program `nete-ps-5.5-win32.exe`.

2. Click Next twice and accept the license agreement. Click Next.

3. When asked for the Web servers to configure for use with Policy Server, select the Web server being used by WP.

4. When asked for a JRE for the Policy Server, make sure you give it a JRE 1.3.1—if your currently installed JRE is not version 1.3.1 download a new one and install it.

5. Choose a destination for the installation and click Next.

6. Enter an encryption key and reconfirm it. Remember to record this key for future use. Click Next.

7. If you do not want to configure hardware keys, click Next. If you do, refer to the Netegrity Policy Server Installation Guide.

8. Enter and confirm an administrator password and record this password for future use. Click Next.

9. If you want to configure an SNMP agent at this time refer to the Netegrity Policy Server Installation Guide.

10. Review the settings and click Next if all is correct. When copying is done click Finish to reboot your system.

Modifying WP to use SiteMinder as an external security manager involves setting the following configuration properties:

In `externalacecsscontrolservice.properties`:

```
accesscontrol.domainname=WPS Portal Server
accesscontrol.accountingport=44441
accesscontrol.authport=44442
accesscontrol.aznport=44443
accesscontrol.maxtimeout=5400
accesscontrol.idletimeout=3600
accesscontrol.syncaudit=false
accesscontrol.ipaddress=<your IP>
accesscontrol.scheme=Basic
accesscontrol.agentname=agent
accesscontrol.agentsecret=<Your secret/password>
accesscontrol.admin=siteminder
accesscontrol.password=<Your password>
accesscontrol.userdir=<Your LDAP server>
accesscontrol.public_access_mode=1
accesscontrol.anonymousid=anonymous
accesscontrol.anyauthuser=anyauth
```

In `services.properties`:

```
com.ibm.wps.services.authorization.ExternalAccessControlService=com.ibm.
wps.services.authorization.SiteminderExternlAccessControlImpl
```

In `portlalogin.cfg` add the following to `WpsNewSubject`:

```
com.ibm.websphere.security.auth.module.proxy.WSLoginModuleProxy required
delegate=com.tivoli.mts.SiteMinderLoginModule;
```

In `portlalogin.cfg` add the following to `WpsSubjectExists`:

```
com.ibm.websphere.security.auth.module.proxy.WSLoginModuleProxy required
delegate=com.tivoli.mts.SiteMinderLoginModule;
```

Add a `callbackheaderslist.properties` file to the portal `app config` directory with the following contents:

```
header.1=sm-serversessionspec
header.2=sm-serversessionid
cookie.1=SMSESSION
```

Summary

Setting up a portal is not a trivial thing, but creating a good portal experience is even harder. In this chapter we introduced you to identity management tools and SSO architectures. We explained when you would choose to use these products and how these tools help you in complex portal environments. We then walked you through a brief overview of how to integrate TAM and SiteMinder with WP; a full account of such integration cannot be accomplished in such a short space and you should refer to the documentation of these respective products. Most importantly, we hope you understand the importance of SSO and the importance of creating a good user experience. The main reason of failed portal projects is low user adoption and the main reason for low user adoption is annoying requests to re-login every time a new application is accessed.

While integrating WP within an SSO environment is crucial for large portal projects that serve a large population of users, setting up scaleable and fault-tolerant portal environments is just as important. In fact, you should view this as a prerequisite—after all, if the server is down it really doesn't matter how good of a user experience it could have provided if it were up. In the next chapter we will show you what it takes to build a WP environment with high-availability attributes and will cover topics such as high-availability strategies, portal clusters, horizontal vs. vertical scaling, and how to deploy portlets into a clustered environment.

## CHAPTER 21

Designing High Availability into Your Portal Server

In today's large corporations, one of the most common requirements is that the portal should be available 24 hours and 7 days. When users want 24 by 7, they are not referring to uptime but rather a lot more. The requirement is that the system should be perceived to be working 100 percent of the time, with response times consistently meeting expectations (usually under 3 seconds), and all transactions executing accurately, completely, timely, and reliably. While much of the IT industry considers this definition a highly available system, most users consider it a basic requirement of a system design.

In this chapter we will discuss the issues in creating a highly available WebSphere Portal and show you how to manage and configure WebSphere Portal within a cluster.

The Challenges of High Availability

At first glance, most people do not understand the complexity of high availability. To understand it, examine a simple WebSphere Portal configuration such as the one shown in Figure 21-1. Typical users would feel happy if you told them that each component would have an uptime of 99 percent. At first glance, this seems pretty good but translates to a downtime of 3.65 days for one component. The problem is that a WebSphere Portal system is made up of many components. In Figure 21-1, a high level of 33 possible points of failure are identified. If each point had a 99 percent uptime, then the cumulative uptime would be .99**33 or 71.77 percent. This means that for approximately 103 days of a year, WebSphere Portal

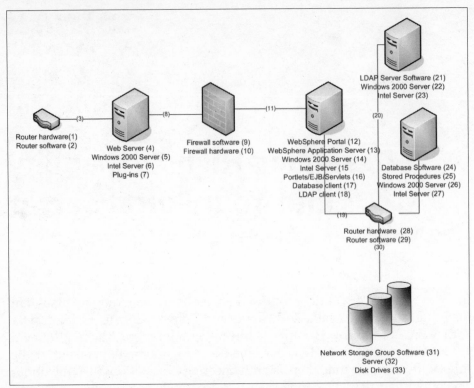

LDAP Server Software (21)
Windows 2000 Server (22)
Intel Server (23)

Router hardware(1)
Router software (2)

Web Server (4)
Windows 2000 Server (5)
Intel Server (6)
Plug-ins (7)

Firewall software (9)
Firewall hardware (10)

WebSphere Portal (12)
WebSphere Application Server (13)
Windows 2000 Server (14)
Intel Server (15
Portlets/EJB/Servlets (16)
Database client (17)
LDAP client (18)

Database Software (24)
Stored Procedures (25)
Windows 2000 Server (26)
Intel Server (27)

Router hardware (28)
Router software (29)
(30)

Network Storage Group Software (31)
Server (32)
Disk Drives (33)

Figure 21-1 Possible WebSphere Portal points of failure.

would be down. It goes without saying that your users would not be happy.

Availability is a metric defined by a user's perception of a system's performance and reliability. It can be calculated as a percentage by the following equation:

```
MTBF/(MTBF+MTTR)
```

where NTGB is the mean time between failures and MTTR is the maximum time to repair or resolve the failure. A WebSphere Portal failure is not just a hardware or software failure but rather anything that prevents the user from performing his or her required function using WebSphere Portal. This includes slow performance, process, and environmental factors. One thing interesting about the equation, which relates to user perception, is that the faster you correct or are perceived to have corrected the problem, the higher the availability. So if problems are shifted to a different system without any interruption in their session, no failure is perceived.

Most IT people believe that high availability can be obtained through hardware redundancy. However, as seen in Figure 21-2, 30 percent of

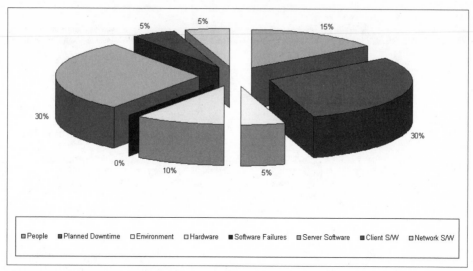

Figure 21-2 Causes of downtime.
Source: IEEE Computer April 1995.

downtime is planned, 10 percent is unplanned hardware downtime, and 40 percent is related to software. This was in 1995. Today with more reliable hardware that is designed to hot pluggable, software failures are increasingly dominating downtime.

Determining a High-Availability Strategy for WebSphere Portal

The most critical decision for you to make is how highly available do you want your WebSphere Portal system to be. The decision should be based on a cost–benefit analysis.

The first step is to determine the impact on your business in dollars and minutes if the system is down. Focus on lost revenue, both in the immediate and distant future. Revenue may be lost in the future due to the impact on customer loyalty and your company's reputation. Also, quantify the impact on employee productivity due to downtime. Look at lost hours, increase in cost due to overtime, and reduced employee efficiency due to poor system performance.

Next calculate the cost of availability. Table 21-1 lists the different levels of cumulative availability. For the first level, 98 percent, determine the cost of implementing availability and multiply it by 10 for each level to get a rough estimate. In other words, level 7 is 60 times more expensive than level 1.

Table 21-1 Availability Levels

LEVEL	PERCENTAGE UPTIME	DOWNTIME/YEAR
1	98%	7.3 days
2	99%	3.65 days
3	99.8%	17 hours, 30 minutes
4	99.9%	8 hours, 45 minutes
5	99.99%	52.5 minutes
6	99.999%	5.25 minutes
7	99.9999%	31.5 seconds

To identify the components that impact availability, you need to look at your process, organization, and technology. Given how little impact hardware has on availability, the largest focus is on the implementation of a well-defined process and the integration of an organization designed to support high availability.

High availability cannot be provided to your WebSphere Portal systems in a vacuum due to the interdependencies on the organization processes, environmental factors, the network, and other systems.

The first step is to get a level set of the state of affairs. A team must be established with representations from development, project management, and infrastructure support to look at system management processes, operations, and the application/infrastructure architecture. The team must also review the system outages and perform a root-cause analysis.

After performing the analysis, the data is used to identify weaknesses in the processes. Processes are examined to reduce the frequency of occurrence of a problem, the duration to fix the problem, and the impact on the complete IT environment. This is done by implementing the following steps:

- Proactive problem prevention that ensures when a problem occurs the root cause is identified and procedures are put in place to ensure it does not recur.

- Effective change management to ensure that only authorized and tested changes are implemented.

- Systems and Applications design is made reliable, scalable, complete, and accurate with features that integrate with the system management infrastructures. All exceptions are detected and are designed to be self-healing or provide automatic recovery. Proper logging is done with well written messages that clearly identify the problem, the module, time, and data that caused the exception.

- Monitoring is proactive so that solutions can be automatically implemented to prevent a problem from occurring.

- Recovery procedures including disaster recovery procedures are automated as much as possible and are documented and regularly tested.

- Situation management procedures are put in place and regularly followed through.

- WebSphere Portal is tested using a formal methodology that covers exception testing, user testing, boundary testing, and load/stress testing. Parallel testing must be done that simulates exactly a worst-case scenario for a production environment. This environment needs to include firewalls configured as they are for production, a similar network (including routers), load/boundary and/or stress test to simulate production, and simulated exceptions to test operation procedure and recovery process.

- The data design is reviewed by the data architects to isolate any corruption or performance issues. Security must also be reviewed to ensure that only authorized applications/users are accessing the data.

- WebSphere Portal system is isolated from other application servers and has sufficiently allocated bandwidth.

- Everything is documented and it is ensured that a process is in place to keep up-to-date. A librarian should be appointed and the documentation should be made public and reviewed regularly.

- Standards need to be in place for each component including operating system (including fix level), WebSphere Portal, hardware, firewalls, application build, routers, and router software. The version and release level should be consistent in each test and production environment and especially if it is a fail-over component. Each component version and release needs to be tested and well mature in the marketplace before being accepted as a standard. They should also be obtained from well-established vendors, thus minimizing the impact of having a nonsupported component.

Processes by themselves do not improve availability. They need to be integrated into the organization to ensure that they are being correctly implemented and those issues are receiving appropriate visibility. Service level agreements need to be established with each department and vendor and metric gathered to ensure that the departments/vendors are meeting their commitments. Regular reporting to upper management of system outages and service level deviation are required. The result of weekly meetings is that for every deviation an action and time factor are required to resolve the issue.

After you address your processes, and your organization, you look at the technological elements associated with WebSphere Portal. Specifically:

- Remove any single point of failure. Look at each component including routers, communication vendors, operating systems, middleware, application servers, applications, disk drives, network cards, servers, portlets, Web servers, databases, and LDAP servers. Single point of failures can be eliminated using hardware redundancy, multiple network cards attached to isolated networks supported by different communication vendors, load balancing, hot fail-over, and clustering. For LDAP servers, look at implementing a master–slave relationship, databases either hot fail-over or parallel databases with data replicated over multiple storages using mirrored disks. Disk redundancy can be implemented with two NAS (network attached storage), each attached to a separate isolated network with storage software that replicates data stored on the master NAS to a slave NAS. Upon failure of the master NAS, the router will redirect to the slave NAS. Keep redundant servers in different locations so they are not impacted by local environmental failures.

- Use only mature software and reliable and serviceable hardware. Most vendors are pressured by the market and their shareholders to release products quickly. Thorough testing is not always performed due to time and cost factors. Sometimes due to number of products that can interact with it, it is not always possible. In mature products, both design and function flaws have been found by the market and usually fixed (or a workaround provided) by the vendor.

- Implement security software to prevent unauthorized access and data corruption.

- Automate the system management as much as possible. Employ operating and server agents and agents for WebSphere Application System. These agents should monitor and perform recovery or performance tuning when a threshold occurs. Also automate the change management process. Integrate the system management process to your help desk.

- Set up a test environment that duplicates your production environment. Ensure that development, test, and production are isolated from each other.

- Reuse well-established configurations. Your staff does not need to learn a system and they are familiar with the issues. The configuration is tested and spare parts are usually available.

■ Over-configure your hardware. Calculate what memory, DASD, and CPU speed you need and multiply by at least 4. It is cheaper to have inefficient software running on faster hardware than tuning the software for the hardware configuration. It is very easy to underestimate capacity needs and costlier to add on when the system is in production. No user ever complained that his or her system was too fast.

■ And now, to drive you nuts, the last and most important point completely contradicts the first point. Consolidate your servers and keep your solution as simple as possible. Complex solutions introduce more failure points and make it more difficult to find the problem. While the time to failure may lengthen with a complex configuration, so also will the time to repair due to the increase in manageability issues.

Implementing a Highly Available WebSphere Portal Solution

So now after reading all this high-level advice on high availability, you must be saying, "Great stuff, but how do I implement a highly available WebSphere Portal?" This section will tell you how. In the paragraphs that follow you will examine two highly available models for WebSphere Portal based on vertical and horizontal scaling. We will discuss their advantages and disadvantages and show you how to implement WebSphere Portal clustering. We are not going to drill down further the process and organizational components because this will require a separate book.

Support for automatic fail-over and load balancing for WebSphere Portal is provided by WebSphere Application Server Network Deployment. It supports the concept of clusters, which enables a logical collection of application server processes to operate logically as a single application server process. If one server within the cluster fails, then the workload is picked up by the other servers.

WebSphere Application Server Network Deployment terminology for a hardware server is a node. A group of nodes under a single administrative node make up a cell. Single point administration for the cell is done by the Deployment Manager, which uses the cell master configuration repository to store the configuration for all nodes in the cell. Each node has an agent that communicates with the Deployment Manager and provides file transfer services, configuration synchronization, and performance monitoring.

You can use three different models for designing your highly available WebSphere Portal: WebSphere Portal using vertical scaling, WebSphere Portal using horizontal scaling, and lastly a hybrid using both horizontal and vertical scaling.

Vertical Scaling with a WebSphere Portal Cluster

Each WebSphere Portal instance has a dedicated JVM. Vertical scaling is basically the implementation of multiple instances of WebSphere Portal on a single node. Figure 21-3 shows a simple example of WebSphere Portal cluster configuration using vertical scaling. Requests first go to a reverse proxy server that sprays the request to an available Web server. The Web server via the plug-in forwards the request to the WebSphere Portal Web containers WebSphere_Portal_1 and WebSphere_Portal_2. Since they are part of a cluster, the node agent will monitor their performances and forward the information to the Deployment Manager and manage the workload if one of the instances goes offline or is busy. Authentication is via the LDAP server, which uses a master–slave relationship to maintain availability. Availability for the database is maintained by using a parallel database. All data is stored on two Network Access Storage systems that mirror each other using storage synchronization software. Each server has two network cards that access two separate networks that are isolated from each other.

Vertical scaling provides many benefits. It enables you to make better use of the CPU since multiple JVMs can more fully utilize the processing power than a single JVM due to JVM's concurrency limitations. It is also easier to maintain and cheaper since you are administrating fewer machines and session management is easier since you can use memory-to-memory session replication.

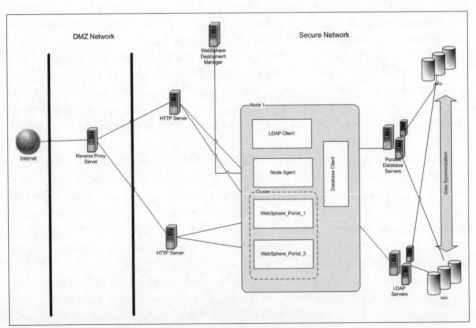

Figure 21-3   WebSphere Portal cluster using vertical scaling.

Of course, the vertical scaling model has certain limitations. It has more single point of failures (LDAP Client, Node Manager, Database Client, hardware, and so on), requires greater memory management, and value decreases significantly as more instances are added.

Horizontal Scaling with a WebSphere Portal Cluster

Horizontal scaling is putting on WebSphere Portal instance per node and then adding the nodes to the cluster. Figure 21-4 shows the previous example using horizontal scaling. As in the previous example, Node Manager monitors the performance of the WebSphere Portal instances; however, this time Deployment Manager receives information from multiple agents.

The benefits of horizontal scaling are numerous. You can isolate the system from various hardware or software failures. Each system can be in different locations, thus isolating you from environmental factors such as a disaster. By creating multiple cells, you can also perform maintenance or test a new version in a production system without interrupting service.

The disadvantages are that it is more costly (more machines, software license), more complicated and thus harder to administrate, and session management is slower and less reliable since it requires database persistence.

The last model combines both vertical and hardware scaling. Each machine runs multiple instances and all the instances are part of a cluster. This, of course, combines the advantages of both vertical and horizontal

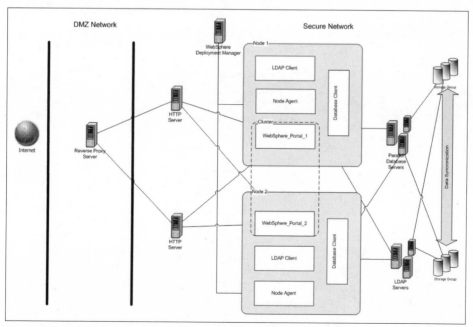

Figure 21-4   WebSphere Portal cluster using horizontal clustering.

clustering so long as you only use a few instances per server. However, it is very costly and complex to administer. This is not a preferred strategy for those who like to keep it simple.

Configuring WebSphere Portal in a Clustered Environment

Now that you understand the advantages and disadvantages of different availability models, the next step is to learn how to implement WebSphere Portal in a clustered environment. Specifically, you will find out how to implement WebSphere Portal using the example infrastructure detailed in Figure 21-5. The infrastructure, which is based on horizontal scaling, has a single IBM HTTP Web Server (sandbox1), which passes requests to two WebSphere Portal Server nodes (sandbox3, sandbox4) that are part of a WebSphere cell. Authentication is performed using IBM Directory Server (sandbox5) and the data is stored remotely on a DB2 server (sandbox6). Another server is used for Deployment Manager (sandbox2). For the purpose of this example, all servers are Windows 2000 Advance Servers; however, any of the WebSphere-supported platforms can be used.

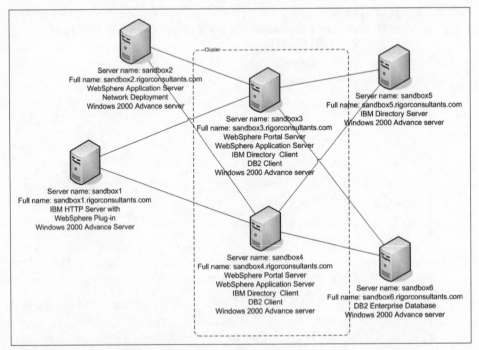

Figure 21-5 WebSphere Portal cluster.

For the purpose of this example, assume the following:

1. You have installed and configured WebSphere Network Deployment 5.0.1 and WebSphere Application server 5.0.1 on `sandbox2.rigorconsultants.com`

2. You have enabled security on Deployment Manager using single sign-on and the authentication server is IBM Directory Server sandbox5. Java 2 security needs to be disabled. Make sure that wpsadmin has been set to an Administrator role in the Deployment Manager Admin console; sandbox2.rigorconsultants.com:9090/admin.

3. IBM Directory Server 5.1 has been installed and configured on sandbox5 and IBM Directory Client is installed on sandbox3 and sandbox4. The latest fixpacks have been installed.

4. DB2 Enterprise 8.1 database has been installed and configured on sandbox6 and the DB2 client is installed on sandbox3 and sandbox4. The latest fixpacks have been installed.

5. IBM HTTP Server 1.3.6 is installed and configured on sandbox1.

6. For both sandbox3 and sandbox4 (which must be done after you set up sandbox1, sandbox2, sandbox5, and sandbox6), you have done the following:

   a. Performed a full installation of WebSphere Portal 5.0. You cannot install WebSphere Portal into an existing cluster environment. If the node is within a cell, you must first remove it, install WebSphere Portal, and then reinstall it.

   b. Configured both WebSphere Portal servers to use the remote Web server sandbox1.

   c. Configured the WP servers to access the remote IBM Directory Server sandbox5 and the remote DB2 server sandbox6.

   d. Configured the tables on the remote database server and exported the data for sandbox4 WebSphere Portal to the DB2 server.

   e. Set up wpsbind and wpsadmin in the LDAP server as administrative users using the definitions specified in the LDIF file.

7. You have validated that each component is working by separately testing each WebSphere Portal server, IBM Directory Server, the DB2 server, and the Network Deployment Manager server.

8. The date and time in Deployment Manager (sandbox2) and the nodes (sandbox3, sandbox4) must be the same or within 5 minutes and must be in the same time zone.

9. WebSphere Network Manager is running on sandbox2 and all the node names are unique in the cell.

10. Server1 and WebSphere Portal are running on sandbox3 and sandbox4.

11. Maximum heap size has been increased to 512 to <was_root>\bin\ addnode.bat and <was_root>\bin\removenode.bat by adding **-Xmx512** to the Java command line.

Adding WebSphere Portal to a Cell

After you have set up your infrastructure, you need to add the WebSphere Portal nodes to the cells by doing the following:

1. Click Start ⇨ Programs ⇨ IBM WebSphere ⇨ Application Server V5.0 ⇨Start the Server.

2. Click Start ⇨ Programs ⇨ IBM WebSphere ⇨ Portal Server V5.0 ⇨Start the Server.

3. Open a command prompt and go to <was_root>\bin and execute addnode sandbox2.rigorconsultants.com 8879 -username wpsbind -password wpsbind -includeapps. The deployment host name is sandbox2.rigorconsultants.com, soup port is 8879, and wpsbind is the Deployment Manager administrator username and password. The -includeapps option is used for the first cell only in order to install the applications into the Deployment Manager cell. Upon completion (which will take some time) you will see the message "node sandbox3 has been successfully federated."

4. Repeat the process for sandbox4 except do no use the -includeapps option in the addnode command.

Remember that when you add a node to a cell, all administration must be done through the Deployment Manager Administration console instead of the Portal Administration console. So you need to remove the Portal Administration console to avoid future problems with the plug-in configuration. Do the following to remove the Portal Administration console:

1. Open the administrative console
   http://sandbox2.rigorconsultants.com:9090/admin

2. Log in as the administrative user **wpsbind**.

3. Expand Applications on the Navigation menu.

4. Click Enterprise Applications.

5. Find WpsAdminconsole application and click Uninstall.

6. Save the changes to the master configuration.

Implementing the WebSphere Portal Cluster

Now that WebSphere Portal nodes have been added to the cell, you need to create the cluster. Perform the following tasks:

1. Log in into the Deployment Manager Administrative console `http://sandbox2.rigorconsultants.com:9090/admin` as **wpsbind**.

2. Expand Servers and select Clusters. On the right side is the Create a New Cluster window.

3. Enter the cluster name (we chose **Portal_Cluster**) and check Prefer Local Enabled and Create Replication Domain for this Cluster.

4. Assign a weight that determines how much workload is distributed to that node relative to the other node. We recommend keeping an equal weight or the default value.

5. Click Select an Existing Server to add to this cluster, choose the server WebSphere_Portal from the node sandbox3, and click Next.

6. Enter the name of the next cluster member. We called it **WebSphere_Portal_Sandbox4**.

7. Assign a weight that determines how much workload is distributed to that node relative to the other node. We recommend keeping an equal weight or the default value.

8. Select the node sandbox4 and check Generate Unique HTTP Ports and Create Replication Domain for this cluster. It is imperative that you click Generate Unique HTTP Ports, otherwise there will be conflicts between the original servers and other servers on sandbox4.

9. Click Apply and the cluster member WebSphere_Portal_sandbox4 will appear on the application server list on the bottom of the page.

10. Click Next and the summary window is displayed. Then click Finish.

11. Save the changes to the master configuration.

12. Log in remotely to sandbox3 and sandbox4 and change the application server name to the cluster name so that the portlet deployment can work. Open a command prompt and go to `<wp_root>\shared\app\config\services and edit DeploymentService.properties`. Change the value assigned to `wps.appserver.name` to Portal_Cluster, and save the file.

13. Go back to the Deployment Manager Administrative console, expand Servers, and click Clusters.

14. Select the cluster Portal_Cluster and click Start. Wait for some time.

15. Check if the cluster members have started by expanding Servers, selecting Application Servers, and refreshing the Status view.

The next few steps relate to updating the WebSphere plug-in configuration since the plug-in configuration now resides on the Deployment Manager (sandbox2) instead of the nodes (sandbox3, sandbox4). The HTTP Server host name and port must be added to the host alias list in order for a clustered portal application to be accessible. (Remember, you are still in the Deployment Administrative Console.)

16. Expand Environment and click Virtual Hosts.

17. Select default_host, and click Host Aliases on the Additional Properties table.

18. Click New and add `sandbox1.rigorconsultants.com` (our Web Server) for the Host Alias and 80 for the Port Number.

19. Save the configuration.

20. Regenerate the plug-in expand Environment, select Update Web Server Plug-in, and click OK.

21. Copy the `plugin-cfg.xml` file located on the `<nd_root>\config\cells` directory to `<was_root>\config\cells` on sandbox1 (our Web server). Edit `plugin-cfg.xml` and change `<nd_root>\etc\plugin-key.kdb` to `<was_root>\etc\plugin-key.kdb`. Also change `<nd_root>\etc\plugin-key.sth` to `<was_root>\etc\plugin-key.sth`. Save the files.

These last steps are to enable dynamic caching. Dynamic caching improves performance by caching the output of dynamic servlets and Java Server Pages. However, it is also required for clustered portal applications because all nodes in a cluster share the same cache information.

22. Expand Servers, click Application Servers, and select WebSphere_Portal.

23. Select Dynamic Cache in the Additional Properties section and select Enable service at server startup.

24. Select Enable cache replication and click on its link. Select the portal cluster name (Portal_Cluster) and the desired application server name as the replicator (WebSphere_Portal).

25. Ensure the runtime mode is Push only and click OK.

26. Save the changes to the master configuration.

27. Go to step 22 and repeat for application server Websphere_Portal_Sandbox4.

Testing Your WebSphere Portal Cluster

Before you perform the next steps, you need to ensure that WebSphere Portal cluster is working. You can do this by testing the fail-over functionality. This is done as follows:

1. Log in into the Deployment Manager Administrative console `http://sandbox2.rigorconsultants.com:9090/admin` as **wpsbind**.
2. Expand Servers and click Clusters.
3. Select the cluster Portal_Cluster and click Start. Wait for some time.
4. Check if the cluster members have started by expanding Servers, selecting Application Servers, and refreshing the Status view.
5. Log in into WebSphere Portal `http://sandbox1.rigorconsultants.com/wps/portal` using **wpsadmin**.
6. Select Administration page. If everything is fine, go back to your home page.
7. Pull the network cable out of a WebSphere Portal Node (sandbox3 or sandbox4).
8. Select the Administration page. It should show up without any problems. Repeat the test except plug-in the network cable and take out the cable from the other node.
9. Select the Administration page again. If it appears then your WebSphere Cluster has been successfully implemented.

Deploying Portlets into a WebSphere Portal Cluster

The next task you have to do to set up Deployment Manager to automatically deploy an installed Portlet to all WebSphere Portals application server in the cluster. Basically, what you do is install a portlet through WebSphere Portal, and Deployment Manager will then synchronize all the other cluster members. The following are the steps to do this:

1. Log into WebSphere Portal `http://sandbox1.rigorconsultants.com/wps/portal` using **wpsadmin**.
2. Go to Administration ⇨Portlets ⇨Install.
3. Browse for the portlet WAR file and Click Next.

4. The portlets included in the WAR file will be displayed. Click Next and then click Install.

5. You will then get a message stating that your portlets were installed but not activated.

6. Open the Deployment Manager Administrative console `http//sandbox2.rigorconsultants.com:9090/admin`. You need to manually synchronize all nodes. You can set the autosynchronization on; however, it is recommended for portlets to still manually resync them.

7. Expand System Administration and select Nodes.

8. Select sandox3 and sandbox4 and click Synchronize.

9. Expand Applications and select Enterprise Applications. Find your portlet and click Start.

10. Log in again into the WebSphere Portal `http://sandbox1` `.rigorconsultants.com/wps/portal` using **wpsadmin**.

11. Go to Administration and click on Portlets icon. Select Manage Applications.

12. To activate the portlet, select the portlet application and then the portlet name and click Activate/Deactivate.

Deploying Themes and Skins into a WebSphere Portal Cluster

Like portlets, you install new theme and skin or modify it, it has to be synchronized with the other Portal Servers. Specifically, you have to export the Portal EAR file from Deployment Manager, update the EAR file with the new or modified theme and skin directories, and import the EAR file back to the Deployment Manager cell. Using the example in Figure 21-6, you would do this by taking the following steps:

1. Log in to sandbox2, open a command prompt, and go to `<nd_root>\bin`.

2. Enter wasdmin -user wpsbind -password wpsbind where wpsbind is the administrator ID and password we set up.

3. Enter AdminApp export wps `c:\temp\wp_old.ear`.

4. Enter **Quit**. Deployment Manager WebSphere Portal EAR will be exported into the file `c:\temp\wp_old.ear`.

5. Create the directory `c:\temp\wp_expand` and expand the `wp_old` `.ear` file by typing the command **EARExpander-ear c:\temp\wp_ld.ear -operationDir c:\temp\wp_expand\ -operation expand**.

6. Copy the new themes to `c:\temp\wp_expand\wps.war` `\themes\<markup>\`.

7. Copy the new skins to `c:\temp\wp_expand\wps.war` `\skins\<markup>\`.

8. Collapse the files back to an EAR file by typing the following command: **EARExpander -ear c:\temp\wp_new.ear -operationDir c:\temp\wp_expand\ -operation collapse**

9. Now you will import the modified EAR back into the Deployment Manager. Enter **wasdmin -user wpsbind -password wpsbind**, where wpsbind is the administrator ID and password you set up.

10. Enter **AdminApp** and install wps `c:\temp\wp_new.ear`. If you are updating EAR then you add the options -update -appname wps. Wait for the message that Application wps has installed successfully.

11. Enter **AdminConfig save**, which saves the changes to the master configuration.

12. Enter Quit.

13. Next you have to add the new skin and theme to the Portal Administration page, by doing the following:

    a. Log on to `http://sandbox1.rigorconsultants.com/ wps/portal` as **wpsadmin**.

    b. Select Administration ⇨ portal User Interface ⇨ Themes and Skins and click Add New Skin.

    c. Enter the Skin name and default locale title.

    d. Enter the skin directory name and click Add New Theme.

    e. Enter the theme name in Theme Name and default locale title and enter theme directory.

    f. Select the desired skins and click OK.

Summary

In this chapter we have touched on some of the challenges in implementing a highly available WebSphere Portal. We have discussed the various availability components that need to be looked at when implementing WebSphere Portal. We also showed how to implement WebSphere Portal in clustered environment.

But if there is one message that you need to get out of this chapter, it is that high availability is very complex and costly. You need to have a good financial reason to put it in place and major commitment from all levels of the organization. In our simple example we identified 33 single point of failures and this did not include organizational, process, or environmental factors. In a real-life organization there are thousands of elements that impact a major system and addressing every one is cost prohibitive. You need to focus on the components that have the largest impact upon failure and are the least costly to fix (otherwise known as the low hanging fruit).

As we showed in the beginning of this chapter, most of the problems that cause outages (or performance degradation that appears as outages) relate to software bugs or configuration errors. If you put a buggy portlet into a cluster, all that will happen is all the nodes will crash at the same time. If you misconfigure your servers, operating system or WebSphere Portal, the cluster will probably fail. Remember that putting WebSphere Portal cluster does not imply that you will get higher availability. It may actually get worse.

The complexity of WebSphere Network Deployment requires a very disciplined and well-run IT shop with defined processes that staff adhere to. If you implement clustering in a haphazard mode, the probability of your application having frequent outages is quite high. Before you implement high availability, you have to first ensure that quality and engineering processes are in place, metrics are collected, and that there is a high-level organizational visibility and accountability.

Do not perform a high-availability implementation if your organization is just giving it lip service or is not prepared to address cultural issues. Instead, just focus on reducing your failure points and providing better diagnostic and automated repair processes.

In the next chapter we will discuss a technology preview that was introduced in WebSphere 5.0.2, Web Service Remote Portlets or WSRP.

WebSphere Portal Support for Web Services and Remote Portlets

Web services have become the preferred method for Internet-based integration and have been adopted by all vendors. This widespread adoption has made Web services a technology that any Web developer needs to understand and use—and portal developers are no exception.

In this chapter you will learn to use Web services with WP. You will see how to make Web service calls from portlets using the various wizards available within WebSphere Studio. We will show you how to discover existing Web services using UDDI registries and how to use them from within portlets you develop and deploy from within your portal. In addition (and perhaps more importantly) you will learn about the Web Services for Remote Portal (WSRP) standard and the concept of portal proxies. Using WSRP support in WP you will see how to publish your portlets for use by other portals and how you can use remote portlets from within your own WP instance. This integration metaphor allows you to bypass all development efforts and use existing portlets (including both the functional layer and the presentation layer) within your portal. You will learn how to enable your portal for WSRP, how to produce remote portlets, and how to use them within a portal.

We think it is important that you understand these two main methods for using Web services within WP. The first method uses core Web service functionality—for example, calls to remote functions that are described by WSDL and that are formatted using SOAP over HTTP. This is the most general-purpose use of Web services and one that can be utilized in every environment. The second, using WSRP, is more limited to remote portlets but allows you to integrate the function as well as the presentation with little or no development effort.

A Quick Review of Web Services and Remote Portlets

A brief review is in order for those who have not recently used Web services. The goal in this section is not to teach you all about Web services but rather to ensure that the concept is well understood by all readers of this chapter.

Web services are functional elements deployed on a node on the network and accessed over the Internet. This description is quite generic and doesn't say too much; what makes such a service endpoint a Web service is the "how," not the "what." Web services are based on a set of standards—specifically the Simple Object Access Protocol (SOAP), the Web Service Description Language (WSDL), and Universal Description Discovery and Integration (UDDI). SOAP is a protocol by which a remote client can invoke the functionality implemented by the Web service. Developers of Web services use WSDL to define the metadata describing the Web service, and remote clients use WSDL to learn what arguments are required for invoking the Web service (as well as other things required to make the remote call). Web service providers use UDDI to publish their Web services, and clients of Web services use UDDI to discover where these Web services, and the metadata describing them, reside. For an overview of SOAP, WSDL, and UDDI see *Executive's Guide to Web Services* by Eric Marks and Mark Werrell and for an in-depth discussion see *Java, XML, and Web Services Bible* by Mike Jasnowski.

SOAP, WSDL, and UDDI form the core of the Web services stack, and Web services are not specially made for portal deployment. Using Web services within the context of portlet development is no different than making use of Web services when developing servlets, JSPs, or any other Java programs. But Web services do not stop with SOAP, WSDL and UDDI—in fact, there are over 100 higher level protocols and definitions within the world of Web services. One of these "extensions" is very much specific to portals and portlets—remote portlets and the Web Services for Report Portlets (WSRP) standard.

WSRP is an OASIS standard that was created to simplify the integration of remote applications and content into portals. OASIS (www.oasis-open.org) is a not-for-profit global consortium that drives the development, convergence, and adoption of e-business standards and is responsible for much of the work in areas such as XML and Web services. The purpose of WSRP is to allow exposing content from third-party portlets in portals with zero programming effort. This is possible because WSRP defines an interface for presentation-oriented Web services rather than basic functional Web services.

WSRP allows a portlet—both its functionality and its presentation—to be packaged as a reusable component using Web service technologies. Web services allow you to take a function, describe and publish it in a standard way,

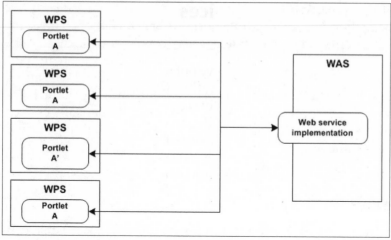

Figure 22-1   Multiple portlets calling a Web service.

and allow others to find and invoke it in a standard way. The inventors of the remote portlet concept have taken a viewpoint of a portlet as a "reusable function." Instead of requiring you to separate your application functionality from the presentation layer, it allows you to embed both function and presentation inside a single reusable component that uses Web service infrastructure such as SOAP and UDDI registries to perform the plumbing.

The difference between using Web services from within a portlet and the use of remote portlets is best exemplified by the implementations shown in Figures 22-1 and 22-2. In Figure 22-1 a portlet makes use of a Web

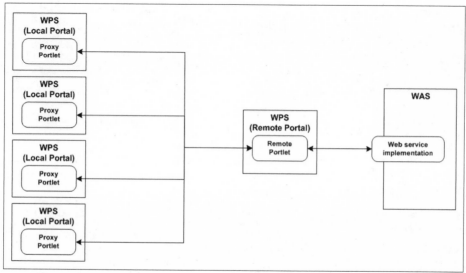

Figure 22-2   Multiple proxy portlets using a single report portlet.

service. While the same Web service implementation can be used by many portlet instances, there are still multiple portlets that can either be the same packaged portlet deployed on multiple portals or, as is more likely, involve separately developed portlets that deliver similar functionality into the portal. In Figure 22-2, a single portlet makes calls to the published Web service and multiple proxy portlets embed this portlet within multiple portals. The proxy portlets in this case are artifacts of WP that are automatically created and that do not need to be developed—saving you work in building portlets that do the same thing anyway.

Using Remote Portlets in WP

WSRP is a relatively new initiative support for WSRP within WP. Version 4x of WebSphere Portal supported Web services and remote portlets through a proprietary IBM implementation. Version 5 of WP still supports this proprietary method but we highly recommend that you do *not* use this method. This implementation is being phased out by IBM and is being replaced by the WSRP-conformant implementation. At the time of writing this chapter, WP did not yet fully support the WSRP specification for production environments; WSRP support within WP 5.0.2 was supplied as a Technology Preview by IBM. However, this implementation is fairly mature and it is likely that by the time you read this chapter and use Web services within your portal, WP will fully support WSRP. Therefore, we will cover only the WSRP support within WP and suggest that if you use remote portlets you use WSRP.

Figure 22-3 shows the full life cycle support provided by WP for remote portlets. Starting off with a portlet, which you wish to make available to other portal servers, the major steps in the life cycle are as follows:

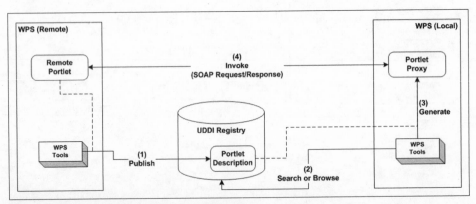

Figure 22-3   Report portlet life cycle with WP.

1. Using WP, you publish your portlet metadata to a UDDI repository. This can be either a private UDDI repository that you have set up or a public repository available on the Web. Throughout the chapter, we will mostly use a public test UDDI repository but we will also discuss about using a private repository.

2. As a portal administrator who wants to embed a certain function packaged as a portlet in your own portal, you use the UDDI browser to search the UDDI registry for available portlets.

3. Once you find the desired remote portlet, you use the Web services manager to create a portlet proxy based on the published portlet. You can then add the portlet to any page(s) on the portal.

4. When the portlet proxy is opened on a portal page, it communicates with the remote portal running on your portal to retrieve not just data but also the entire portlet content. The mechanics of these steps are interesting. The portal server calls the portlet proxy passing it the normal `PortletRequest` and `PortletResponse` objects—for the portal server the portlet proxy is just another portlet. The portlet proxy marshals all arguments into a SOAP request and invokes the remote portal. The remote portal makes use of the information in the request to find the remote portlet and then unmarshals all the information from the original `PortletRequest`. When the response is received by the remote portlet, it is marshaled into a SOAP response and returned to the portlet proxy that returns it to the local portal server.

We now turn to the details of using Web services within WP. While for most part, the chapter focuses on remote portlets, we will start with the most basic scenario—using a regular Web service from within a portlet.

Using Web Services as "Back-End" APIs

There is nothing special about using a Web service call from within a portlet. It merely involves two development tasks: developing the portlet and using the Web service. Because we have already discussed portlet development extensively, our focus in this section will be on how to make use of an existing Web service from your Java program (your portlet code).

Use of a Web service from Java code is supported within WebSphere Studio by the Web Services wizard. The Web Services wizard allows you to use the UDDI explorer to search for a UDDI registry for a Web service, find the service you need and the WSDL file describing the Web services, and then import the WSDL definitions. This import process creates a Java

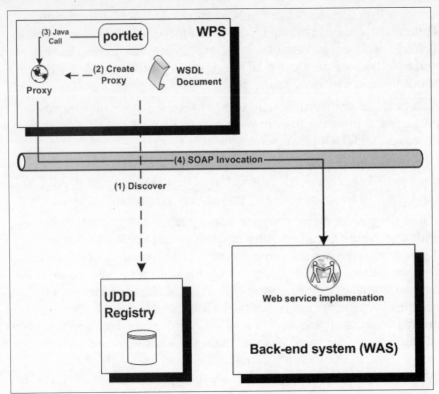

Figure 22-4   Generating and using the Web service proxy from a Java portlet.

proxy object that has the same interface as the object implementing the Web service, allowing you to make calls from within your portlet code to the Java proxy, which then communicates over SOAP to the implementation routine as shown in Figure 22-4.

In the following subsections we walk you through the process shown in Figure 22-4, including registering with a public registry, discovering the Web service, generating the proxy, and invoking the service using the proxy.

Using the IBM UDDI Business Test Registry

UDDI registries allow you to publish businesses and services. Once you publish your Web services to a UDDI registry, they can be discovered and used by potential customers. UDDI registries can be partitioned into private and public registries. A private UDDI registry is one that you can set up and manage yourself. It is usually used to set up a UDDI-based discovery scheme within a company or an organization—an example is the IBM WebSphere UDDI Registry that comes on the CD set of WP. Publishing your

Web service onto a private registry makes it visible only to those who have access to that registry. The IBM UDDI Business Test Registry is a public UDDI registry that can be used to register businesses and services to the public. It is most commonly used to test the publishing and discovering aspects of Web services in a development and test environment.

Before you can publish your Web services to this registry, you will need to set up a user account. Open your browser and navigate to `https://uddi.ibm.com/testregistry/registry.html`. Then click the Get an IBM User ID and Password link. Fill in the registration page; the most important values to remember are the ID and password. Make sure you have the spelling of your e-mail account correct because you will need to receive an activation e-mail.

Once you have a registered user in the IBM UDDI Test Registry, you can proceed to search for a Web service that you would like to use. We will show you how to do this based on a Web service that is already published to the IBM UDDI Business Test Registry as part of the IBM Speed-start Web services program and the Speed-start community. The service we will use is a simple one—merely providing the server clock time or the server on which the Web service is deployed.

Discovering a Web Service

The first thing you need to do is discover the service. Within WebSphere Studio you use the Web services explorer to search a UDDI registry and import Web service definitions. Bring up the Web services explorer by selecting File ➪ Import from the menu bar. This brings up the Import wizard where you need to select Web Service and click the Next button. Check Launch the Web Services Explorer to find a Web service from a UDDI Registry and make sure that the IBM UDDI Test Registry is selected. Click the Finish button to bring up the Web services explorer in import mode. Once you are in the explorer, click the Find tool in the top-right pane. Then select Businesses from the drop-down list and SpeedStartExample as the name of the business you wish to find and press Go, as shown in Figure 22-5.

The results will include the SpeedStartExample registry entry and you can proceed to import WSDL into your WebSphere Studio environment. Click on the business that is retrieved by the search. Expand the query result entry in the UDDI Navigator pane and click SpeedStartExample. Click the Get Services tool in the pane's toolbar. You will see the details for the RemoteServerClock service as shown in Figure 22-6. Click the Get Service Interface tool and then the Import WSDL to Workbench tool. Select a project name and click Go. This imports the WSDL definition into a file within your project from which you can go ahead and generate the Java proxy that will enable you to make the remote call.

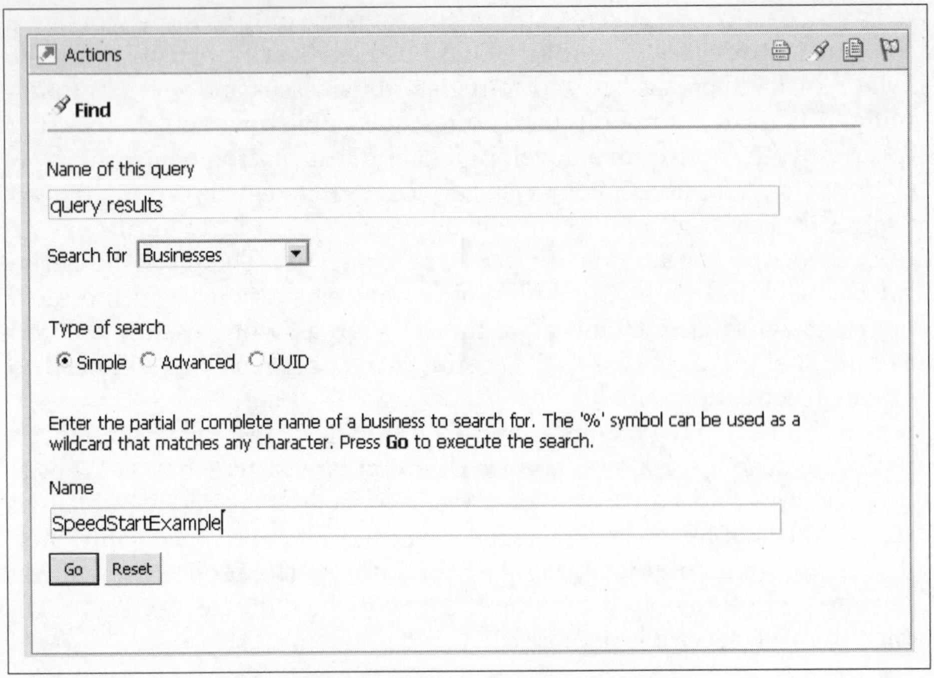

Figure 22-5   Searching for the Web service.

Generating a Java Proxy

To create the proxy, you also use the WebSphere Studio Web Services wizard. Follow these steps:

1. Select File ⇨ New ⇨ Other from the menu bar.
2. Select Web Services in the left pane and Web Service Client from the right pane.
3. Select Java Proxy from the drop-down menu and check Test the Generated Proxy. Click Next.
4. Enter the WSDL binding document.
5. Click Finish.

This will generate a proxy that you can use from your local programs to invoke the service remotely. The wizard also asks you if you want to generate a test application. The test application comprises a set of simple JSPs that provide a simple UI making calls to the proxy and the remote Web service—it is a convenience to allow you to test that everything is functioning correctly.

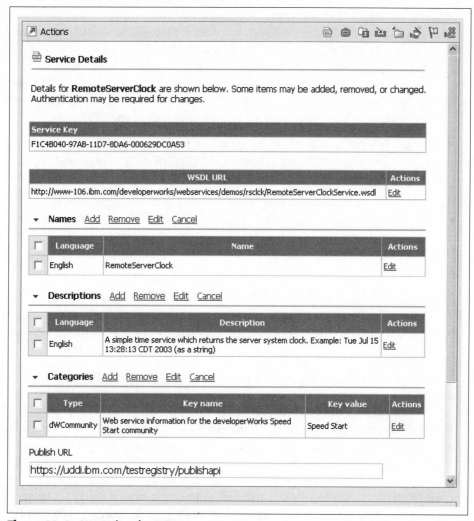

Figure 22-6   Importing the WSDL.

This simple process is all you need to follow in order to make Web service calls from your own portlets. While this is indeed quite simple, remote portlets and WSRP eliminate even this small amount of work.

Using WSRP within WP

WP support for WSRP services is based on producers of content and consumers of content. Producers are portals that implement WSRP services and that offer one or more proxy portlets. These services are used by remote portlets—the consumers. A consumer is a portal that uses WSRP interfaces to incorporate and consume content supplied by producers. The consumer receives markup from the WSRP service and presents it as a native portlet.

In order for this to occur, producers need to provide enough information about the services they provide. This is done through a set of WSRP interfaces that are used by consumers; note that not all of these interfaces are mandated by the WSRP standard for remote portlets to be able to work:

- Service description. A producer *must* provide an interface through which a consumer can interrogate which portlets are available for use. WP supports the service description interface.

- Markup. A producer *must* provide an interface through which a consumer can request markup fragments forming the content of the remote portlet. This interface must support the various states a portlet may be in. WP supports the markup interface.

- Portlet management. A producer *may* allow consumers to manage state of the proxy portlet including its persistent state. WP supports the portlet management interface.

- Registration. A producer *may* provide registration capabilities for use by consumers. WP does not support the registration interface.

In the technology preview provided in version 5.0.2, configuration is done using the XML configuration interface. This is the only tested and supported method or configuration WSRP services at this time.

The XML configuration interface includes updates that are required for configuring WSRP, including a new portal resource type called `wsrp-producer` allowing you to browse and integrate remote portlets using the producer interface. You can also access WSDL documents describing the remote portlets by using another added element: the `wsdl-url` element within the `wsrp-producer` element. The WSDL description itself will be accessed at runtime by using the `http://<host>/WP_ROOT/wsdl/wsrp` URL where WP_ROOT is the root directory of your WP installation. Finally, a new configuration element called `preferences` has been added to the XML configuration interface allowing you to define which user attributes you want transferred in the WSRP communications with the producer. `Preferences` is an extension of the name-value element supporting multivalued names. This allows you to associate one or more child elements with portal resources such as `wsrp-producer`, which is important given that you will typically have many consumers per producer.

In addition to these added elements, some existing resource types have been changed in the XML configuration interface:

- `portlet`. WSRP-based portlets will not reside within your existing WAR files. Therefore, this XML configuration interface element has been changed, allowing you to specify a `handle` attribute and specify that a portlet is being implemented as a remote portlet using a new flag called `provided`.

- `portlet-app`. Similarly, when a portlet application containing multiple portlets is provided from a remote implementation, the application needs to provide a `group-id` attribute corresponding to the `concrete-portlet-app` tag normally found in `portlets.xml`.

WP provides WSRP support for both producers and consumers. On the producer side, WP allows you to take an existing portlet and expose it as a WSRP producer, which can then be used by a remote consumer. On the other side, WP allows you to take existing WSRP services and include them as local portlets within your portal.

Configuring WP for WSRP

Regardless of whether you want to set up producers of WSRP services or consume WSRP services, you first need to enable WSRP within your portal. In order to support both of these functions, you need to perform the following settings in `WP_ROOT/shared/app/config/services/Config Service.properties`:

1. Set `portal.enable.jsr168=true`.
2. Set `portal.enable.wsrp=true`.
3. Restart the portal instance.

In addition to these mandatory settings, there are a few additional configuration settings that may be appropriate for your environment. These include proxy settings and security settings.

In terms of proxy settings you may want to configure a proxy for WSRP. Unfortunately, you cannot specify a proxy for WSRP communication only—this will affect all communications. To do this you need to change the JVM arguments for the WP/WAS instance using `-DproxyHost` and `-DproxyPort`.

In terms of advanced security configuration, you can enable WSRP communications over SSL and you can implement additional security for URLs exposed through WSRP. To enable SSL for WSRP communications, you first need to enable SSL for your WP and WAS instances. Then you need to activate WSRP security by setting `wsrp.security.enabled=true` in `WP-ROOT/shared/app/config/services/ConfigService. properties`.

Controlling security for URLs exposed through WSRP is important because WSRP allows you to use content generated by a remote producer. In such scenarios you have little control over the links provided in the markup and, therefore, where your users may be taken in terms of link navigation. You provide this control by implementing the `WSRPResourceURLFil-terFactory` interface and register your class with WP. This registration is done through the `wsrp.resource.url.filter.factory` property in `WP_ROOT/shared/app/config/services/ConfigService.properties`, which should name the class you create. The interface to be implemented is shown below and is used by consumers as they process resource URLs:

```
package com.ibm.wps.wsrp.Consumer.security;

/**
 * This interface describes a factory that can be used
 * to provide a <code>java.io.Writer</code> and
 * <code>java.io.Reader</code> which are used to encode and decode
 * resource URLs used by the WSRP Consumer. The reader and writer
 * implementation should be symmetric.
 *
 * This provides a plug-point for custom resource URL filters
 * that can, for example, be used to encrypt and decrypt WSRP
 *resource URLs.
 **/
public interface WSRPResourceURLFilterFactory
{
    /**
     * Get the <code>java.io.Writer</code> used to filter the passed
     * Writer. WSRP Resource URLs are written to that Writer.
     * An implementation of this Writer could for example encrypt
written
     * resource URLs. It is important that writing to that Writer does
     * not generate characters that are reserved in URIs. See
     * <a href="http://www.ietf.org/rfc/rfc2396.txt">RFC 2396</a> for a
list
     * of reserved URI characters.
     *
     * @param out The underlying character stream
     * @return A <code>java.io.Writer</code> which can be used to modify
     * WSRP resource URLs written to it.
     **/
    public java.io.Writer getUrlFilterWriter(java.io.Writer out);
    /**
     * Get the Reader used to modify the characters passed to the
Reader.
     * Requested WSRP Resource URLs are read from that Reader.
     * An implementation of this Reader could, for example, decrypt
     * WSRP resource URLs which have been encrypted using the previous
Writer.
     *
     * @param out The underlying character input stream
```

```
      * @return A <code>java.io.Reader</code> which is used to modify
WSRP
      * resource URLs read from it.
      **/
     public java.io.Reader getUrlFilterReader(java.io.Reader in);
}
```

Setting Up WSRP Producers

WSRP producer support within WP includes the entire remote portlet life cycle including adding services, removing services, and exporting portlets. In order to add a WSRP portlet service, use the XML configuration with the following XML:

```
<?xml version="1.0" encoding="UTF-8" ?>
<request type="update" xmlns:xsi="http://www.w3.org/2001/XMLSchema-
instance" xsi:noNamespaceSchemaLocation="PortalConfig_1.2.xsd">
  <portal action="locate">
   <web-app action="locate" active="true" uid="portlet.war.webmod">
    <portlet-app action="update" uid="stdTestsuite.war">
     <portlet action="update" name="TestPortlet1" provided="true" />
    </portlet-app>
   </web-app>
  </portal>
 </request>
```

In order to remove a service, use a similar XML command except for changing the `provided` attribute to `false`:

```
<?xml version="1.0" encoding="UTF-8" ?>
<request type="update" xmlns:xsi="http://www.w3.org/2001/XMLSchema-
instance" xsi:noNamespaceSchemaLocation="PortalConfig_1.2.xsd">
  <portal action="locate">
   <web-app action="locate" active="true" uid="portlet.war.webmod">
    <portlet-app action="update" uid="stdTestsuite.war">
     <portlet action="update" name="TestPortlet1" provided="false" />
    </portlet-app>
   </web-app>
  </portal>
 </request>
```

Finally, to export the WSRP portlets use the XML file provided in `WP_ROOT/doc/xml-samples/ExportAllPortlets.xml` and search for WSRP producers or portlets that have the `provided` attribute set to `true`:

```
<?xml version="1.0" encoding="UTF-8"?>
<request
    xmlns:xsi="http://www.w3.org/2001/XMLSchema-instance"
    xsi:noNamespaceSchemaLocation="PortalConfig_1.2.xsd"
```

```
        type="export">
        <portal action="locate">
            <wsrp-producer objectid="*" action="export"/>
        </portal>
</request>


<?xml version="1.0" encoding="UTF-8"?>
<request
    xmlns:xsi="http://www.w3.org/2001/XMLSchema-instance"
    xsi:noNamespaceSchemaLocation="PortalConfig_1.2.xsd"
    type="export">
    <portal action="locate">
        <portlet provided="true" action="export"/>
    </portal>
</request>
```

Setting Up WSRP Consumers

To set up a consumer you first need to create a producer instance within
WP. This may be a little confusing at first but WP needs to know about
the service definitions or the producer's WSDL definitions in order for a
consumer to be created. To create the producer specification using a WSDL
definition, use the following XML:

```
<?xml version="1.0" encoding="UTF-8"?>
<request type="update" xmlns:xsi="http://www.w3.org/2001/XMLSchema-
instance" xsi:noNamespaceSchemaLocation="PortalConfig_1.2.1.xsd" create-
oids="true">
  <portal action="locate">
    <wsrp-producer action="update" registration-required="false"
uniquename="wps.myProducer">
      <wsdl-url>
        http://hostname/wsdl/wsrp_service.wsdl
      </wsdl-url>
      <localedata locale="en">
        <title>My Producer</title>
      </localedata>
    </wsrp-producer>
  </portal>
</request>
```

Alternatively, you can create the producer using a service description
URL and a markup URL. This is useful when you don't have direct access
to the remote portlet and its WSDL when creating the producer and consumer. You will need the remote portlet to be available at runtime in order
to use it, but you may not need it when you are setting up the consumer. In
this case use the following XML:

```
<?xml version="1.0" encoding="UTF-8" ?>
<request type="update" xmlns:xsi="http://www.w3.org/2001/XMLSchema-
```

```
instance" xsi:noNamespaceSchemaLocation="PortalConfig_1.2.1.xsd" create-
oids="true">
  <portal action="locate">
    <wsrp-producer action="update" uniquename="wps.myProducer">
      <service-description-url>
        http://hostname/wps/WSRPServiceDescriptionService
      </service-description-url>
      <markup-url>
        http://hostname/wps/WSRPBaseService
      </markup-url>
      <localedata locale="en">
        <title>My Producer</title>
      </localedata>
    </wsrp-producer>
  </portal>
</request>
```

Once you create the producer definition, you can go ahead and define the consumer using this producer. In order to do this you need to provide the `handle` and `groupID` for the remote portlet:

```
<?xml version="1.0" encoding="UTF-8"?>
<request type="update" xmlns:xsi="http://www.w3.org/2001/XMLSchema-
instance" xsi:noNamespaceSchemaLocation="PortalConfig_1.2.1.xsd">
  <portal action="locate">
    <wsrp-producer action="locate" uniquename="wps.myProducer">
      <portlet-app action="update" active="true"
groupid="_2_00KJL5N5NE0U0FIA_LT">
        <portlet action="update" active="true" defaultlocale="en"
              handle="_5_00KJL5N5NE0U0FIA_FN" name="WSRP">
          <localedata locale="en">
            <title>WSRP</title>
            <description>Sample WSRP</description>
          </localedata>
          <access-control externalized="false" owner="undefined"
private="false"/>
        </portlet>
      </portlet-app>
    </wsrp-producer>
  </portal>
</request>
```

Once you define the consumer you can use the normal portal administration to add the remote portlets; at this point there is no difference between these WSRP consumers and other local portlets.

By default WP caches producer service descriptions once they have been defined within a consumer. This allows WP to avoid multiple network requests when numerous services are being used. In some cases you might want to disable this caching while troubleshooting WSRP support. To do this set `cacheinstance.wsrp.cache.servicedescription.enabled`

`= false` in `WP_ROOT/shared/app/config/services/Cache Man-agerService. properties`.

Futures

WSRP support in WP 5.0.2 is a technology preview. Future versions of WP will provide more robustness and more functions than the current implementation. Among these added features you should keep in mind that future versions will provide the following support:

- Complete implementation of JSR 168
    - More comprehensive implementation of the OASIS WSRP specification
    - Use of UDDI for discovering WSRP services
- Better tools in addition to the XML interface including administration portlets for WSRP configuration

UDDI and tModelKeys

Now that you understand how Web services are used from within a portal in both a pure Web service scenario as well as in a WSRP scenario, it is time to merge all of these concepts. We mentioned that WSRP is a standard that is layered on top of the core WSRP layers (SOAP, WSDL, and UDDI). This means that all producers of WSRP services use the core Web service layers and that consumers create report portlets by using core UDDI and WSDL features. The key to all this is the tModel.

UDDI allows you to describe Web service not only in business and service terms but also in technical terms. The tModel structure provides the ability to describe the specification to which the Web service adheres to including a description of how the service behaves, what conventions it follows, and what standards the service is compliant with. The tModel represents a set of technical specifications including wire protocols, interchange formats, and sequencing rules.

The tModel is the part of the UDDI framework that allows decoupled software components that need to communicate with each other to adhere to a preagreed specification. Such specifications are not dependent on a particular Web service (in fact, it is the other way around). The designers of such specifications can establish a unique technical identity with a UDDI registry, which can then be used by multiple service publications. Each one is registered with the UDDI registry while referencing the appropriate tModel identifier (`tModelKey`).

This is also true for WSRP and report portlet support within WP. A special tModel defines the technical structure for any Web service that is used as a remote portlet, allowing WP to generate the appropriate portlet proxy based on this specification.

Summary

Web services are becoming the mainstream in terms of system integration. Given that portals are often the main integration platform, you need to be able to use Web services from within your portal. This includes both core Web service integration and WSRP-based integration. Initially, you are more likely to use low-level Web services given that WSRP is still in its infancy. However, WSRP has the benefit that it allows you to reuse a complete function including the presentation layer, as opposed to using just a remote function. While the usage of core of both types of Web services is the same, the mechanics within WP are different. In this chapter we showed you how to perform development and setup in both cases so that you are prepared for all types of Web service integrations.

In the next chapter we will tackle the broader issue of integration. We will show you the various methods and tools that you have at your disposal when integrating applications and content to be delivered through WP. Because portals are becoming the "uber-application" for most organizations, application integration is certainly one of the most important topics you will come across when using WP.

## CHAPTER 23

Integrating External Applications with WebSphere Portal

In this chapter you will learn about the various options you have for integrating external applications using a WebSphere Portal infrastructure. We will describe a number of approaches to achieve such integration and for each one provide you with enough tools to start doing some of the integration work. We will try to keep the discussion at a generic level that is true to all such applications including integration of custom-built and home-grown applications as well as commercial off-the-shelf (COTS) application suites. Because custom applications will involve custom APIs and integration, our examples will focus on integrating packaged business applications such as SAP, PeopleSoft, Siebel, J.D. Edwards, Oracle, and so on.

Why Discuss Integration?

Portals are about integration. A portal is really just an integrator and an aggregator of information and applications. In an enterprise environment, portals are quickly becoming the new "corporate desktop" through which functions related to human resources applications, finance applications, and corporate communications are delivered to all employees. As another example, consumer portals try to be a one-stop-shop for all activities and offer links to many other applications, Web sites, and easy-to-use search engines.

Figure 23-1 is a conceptual depiction of what portals try to accomplish. Some people call this aggregation and others call this unification—but whatever your preference, it is really all about integration of other applications, systems, data stores, and so on. Without robust integration capabilities, a

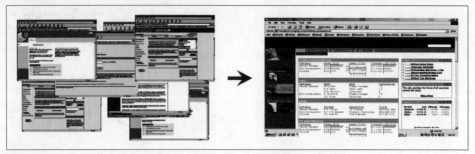

Figure 23-1 Integrated applications delivered through the portal.

portal is just an empty shell that allows you to manage a Web user interface. With many applications integrated into the portal infrastructure, the portal becomes *the* application delivery platform. To exemplify this further, the personalization features of WP would be meaningless without integrated environments. What exactly would you personalize?

Portals deliver Web-based content to a user. Applications generate content that needs to be used by users. Therefore, any portal platform needs to provide good integration tools for allowing you to expose application content through your portal. This is why integration is such a crucial topic for any portal platform and why we devote this chapter to an overview of WebSphere's (and specifically, WP's) integration capabilities. We should mention that integration, and WebSphere integration specifically, is a very broad topic—one on which numerous books can be (and have been) written (for an excellent reference see *Enterprise Integration: An Architecture for Enterprise Application and Systems Integration* by Fred Cummins). Therefore, we do not provide a comprehensive discussion on integration within WebSphere. Instead, we focus on what kind of integration approaches you can use specifically within WP and provide you with tools to help you decide which integration pattern is right for you and how to start such an integration project.

What Options Can You Choose from?

When looking to integrate your applications into the portal, the first thing you need to do is determine which of the many options is most appropriate for your specific case. We will therefore first outline the possibilities you can choose from and provide a simple classification that can help you understand the big picture before delving down into the details. Throughout the rest of this chapter we will provide more details on each of these integration patterns. At the end of the chapter we will summarize with some

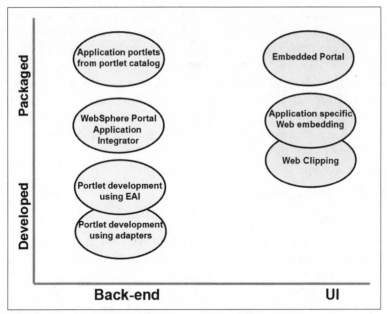

Figure 23-2   Classification of integration patterns within WP.

basic guidelines for choosing the right integration pattern based on some simple characteristics.

As Figure 23-2 shows, we chose to classify the major WP integration patterns based on two dimensions. The first dimension is developed versus packaged. Many of the tools we will show you in this chapter allow you to make calls into enterprise information systems and applications but require that you develop the code that makes these calls and the portlets that display the information returned by these calls. Other integration options include using prepackaged portlets created by IBM or by third parties—portlets that package not only the logic for interfacing with applications but also the presentation layer. It should be clear that such portlets can only exist for applications with a large installed based—greater chances are that there will be no packaged portlets for custom-built and proprietary applications used by your company.

Our classification makes use of a second dimension: back-end versus UI-based integration patterns. In back-end integration patterns, adapters are used by your code to make remote invocations or send messages to the application. This allows you to retrieve information and make changes to the data stored within the application. These patterns are called back-end integration because the application is front-ended by your code. In our context, the application sits in the back-end and is front-ended by portlets deployed on the portal. Because these patterns make use of application adapters, we will sometimes refer to these patterns as adapter-based integration patterns.

UI integration patterns are fairly recent and make use of the fact that Web-based applications use a consistent interaction model between the Web browser and the application server. All these systems make use of HTTP request/response pairs, URLs, and various markup languages such as HTML and WML. This commonality allows WP to introduce a new breed of integration patterns—patterns that make calls on the front-end of the system and script the UI rather than make use of APIs based in the back end. These patterns can often offer you very quick results in terms of exposing existing Web-based applications on your portal.

Which Tools Are Available to You?

The integration patterns described above can broadly be classified into portlet-based integration methods and adapter-based integration methods. Each of these methods is supported by a different set of tools within the WebSphere world. For portlet-based integration, the major tool you will use is the WebSphere Portlet Catalog available on the IBM developer domain (for example, at www7b.software.ibm.com/wsdd/zones/portal/catalog). The catalog includes many portlets that you can download and use—many of which include prepackaged integration options with major application providers such as SAP, PeopleSoft, and Siebel. In addition, a number of special portlets are really integration tools packaged in a way that assists you in exposing other applications as portlets. The most important such tool is the WeSphere Portal Application Integrator.

Adapter-based integration makes use of existing APIs exposed by application providers. Adapters are tools that make use of these APIs and allow you to easily call these APIs from your code. They handle issues such as session handling, calling procedures, and transaction handling so that you don't have to deal with each application provider and its proprietary integration methodology. This makes integration simpler and more consistent and if you master the use of adapters you will find that integrating with one package is not all that different than integrating with another.

Adapter-based integration is based on a different set of tools—a set of tools that is part of the broader family of WebSphere products and not specific to the portal server. An adapter can broadly be classified as Java Connector Architecture (JCA) based or messaging middleware adapters. JCA adapters are deployed on WebSphere Application Server (WAS), in your case on the server that forms the underlying platform for the portal server. The latter category includes adapters used within WebSphere MQ (formerly MQ Series) and adapters used within the CrossWorlds architecture. The actual adapter that you choose will depend on your overall environment and your familiarity with these platforms. In addition to these infrastructures, you will find that WebSphere Studio Application Developer Integration Edition (WSADIE) is a useful tool for developing the integration code.

Developing Portlets Using Adapters

Integration of external applications using adapters appears in the lower left-hand quadrant of our taxonomy shown in Figure 23-2. This integration pattern involves quite a bit of development because it requires two distinct implementation/development tasks. The first involves writing code that makes use of an adapter to connect to the APIs exposed by the external application and the second involves writing the portlets that make use of this information. While both parts of this integration code are written in Java, they are distinct pieces of code and should be viewed in this manner. They could (and probably should) be developed by different individuals or groups and the development involves different tools. Specifically, portlet development can be done in any WebSphere Studio environment that has the portlet toolkit installed while the code interfacing with the external application—(sometimes called an enterprise information system (EIS))— is best done within WebSphere Studio Application Developer Integration Edition (WSADIE). Because we have already discussed portlet development and the portlet toolkit in Chapters 14 through 19, the focus in this section will be on the back-end integration aspects and using WSADIE.

JCA Resource Adapters

While there are many adapters for enterprise systems that can be used, J2EE defines a standard architecture for building adapters: the J2EE Connector Architecture (JCA). The JCA standard provides a mechanism to store and retrieve enterprise data in J2EE and is akin to the standardization provided by JDBC to access relational databases. JCA is relatively new in the J2EE landscape and has already been highly successful in making enterprise integration easier to accomplish.

In order to use JCA you must have a JCA resource adapter. A JCA adapter is specific to an EIS (for example, SAP or PeopleSoft) and is contained in a resource adapter archive (RAR) file composed of the jar files and native libraries necessary to deploy the resource adapter on a J2EE container. JCA adapters interact with a J2EE server and manage things such as connections, transactions, and security. Connection management includes establishing, pooling, and tearing down connections, allowing listeners registered with a connection to receive events, and so on. The underlying protocol an adapter uses to connect to an EIS is outside the scope of the JCA specification.

Transaction management includes support for both distributed transactions providing a mechanism to propagate transactions that originate from inside an application server to an EIS system as well as local transactions existing only on a particular EIS resource. Finally, security allows the application server to connect to an EIS system using security properties defined either at deployment time or at runtime.

JCA resource adapters are available for major packaged applications. As an example, we will continue the discussion of this integration pattern while using the WebSphere Adapter for mySAP.com to connect to a SAP R/3 system. At the time of writing this chapter, this adapter supported SAP R/3 release 3.1H and higher, 4.0B and higher, 4.5A and higher, and 4.6A, 4.6B, and 4.6C. In addition, you should download the WebSphere Adapter for mySAP.com from the IBM Web site; there is no charge involved.

The JCA adapter for SAP provides a standards-based connection architecture for interfacing with SAP systems—and specifically, access to Remote Function Call (RFCs) and Business Application Programming Interfaces (BAPIs). RFC is the protocol used by SAP for remote communication, that is, for communications between two independent SAP systems or for communications between an SAP system and a non-SAP system. Programs using RFCs can either make or receive RFC to or from an SAP system. SAP R/3 systems contain a set of business objects, which are an object-oriented representation of real-world business objects. Examples of business objects are a purchase requisition, a G/L account, or an employee. BAPIs provide a programming interface to such business objects and can be accessed from Java programs using the JCO Java library provided by SAP.

WebSphere Adapter for mySAP.com and WSADIE

WebSphere Studio Application Developer Integration Edition, as its name suggests, packages a large number of tools for helping you with integration tasks. Once you install the WebSphere Adapter for mySAP.com, you can browse BAPIs and RFCs from the SAP Business Object Repository and create Web Service Definition Language (WSDL) representations of the desired function modules. You can then use the WSDL representations to generate Java proxies for BAPIs/RFCs both as Java beans and stateless session EJBs. These beans can be used by your portlets.

Given that you have downloaded the WebSphere Adapter for mySAP.com from the IBM Web site and that you have a working version of an SAP R/3 system, the next thing to do is install the adapter into the appropriate WebSphere Studio environment—in this case into WSADIE. This is important because the JCA adapter not only provides a runtime environment for making the calls to SAP but also includes a tool plugin, which will make using the adapter much easier. Installing the mySAP.com adapter involves running the installation file and then performing the following procedure within WSADIE:

1. Select Import from the File menu.

2. Select RAR file and click Next.

3. Specify the location of the WebSphere Adapter for mySAP.com RAR (`sap.rar`).

4. Check the Standalone connector project box and specify a project name.

5. Click Finish to import the resource adapter.

6. Open the Server Configuration perspective.

7. Create a server instance and a server configuration (EE Test Environment).

8. Expand Server Configurations in the Server Configuration view.

9. Double-click your server configuration.

10. Click the J2C tab and click Add beside the J2C Resource Adapters list in the server settings.

11. Select the name of your resource adapter (specified in step 6) from the Resource Adapter Name drop-down list. Click OK.

12. Click Add beside the J2C Connection Factories pane. On the Create Connection Factory window enter a name, a JNDI name for the connection factory. Click OK.

13. In the Resource Properties pane enter the SAP R/3 connection properties.

14. Close the editor and click Yes to save the changes.

15. Make sure to add the following entry to the PATH environment variable:

```
<WSADIE ROOT>\WORKSPACE_NAME>\<CONNECTOR_PROJECT_NAME>
\connectorModule\windows
```

If the PATH environment did not include this segment then you will have to exit WSADIE and restart it for the changes to take effect.

Your server configuration should look similar to that shown in Figure 23-3. Having finished the installation, you can start using the JCA Tool Plugin to connect to SAP, find the proper BAPIs, build WSDL files to describe the APIs, and generate proxy beans for making the call from your portlets. The JCA Tool Plugin makes use of WSDL to describe an EIS-specific binding and to automatically generate a WSDL definition from the metadata

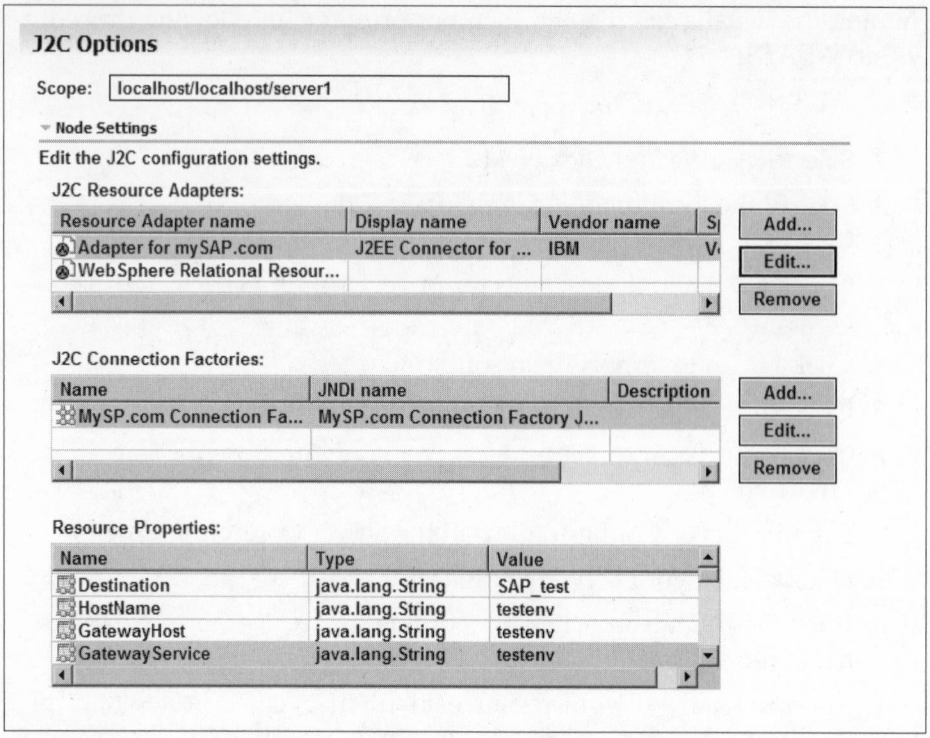

Figure 23-3 Server configuration within WSADIE—node settings.

exposed by the EIS as well as automatically generate a proxy based on this WSDL. This allows you to decouple yourself from the actual EIS and think of the APIs available through the adapter as being similar to Web services—at least in terms of the way they are described.

Describing the Interface Using WSDL

WSDL is perfectly suitable for describing any service (in fact, it is easier to think of it without the "W'—i.e. as Service Definition Language). The authors of the JCA Tool Plugin recognized this fact and made use of WSDL to describe which services are offered by a specific EIS instance and how to access them. Figure 23-4 shows the mapping between WSDL constructs and JCA constructs. The service created by the JCA Tool Plugin (described by the WSDL document) is called an SAP service.

Generating the SAP Service and Using an SAP Proxy

To generate an SAP service you need to follow the steps given below:

1. Open the Service Project wizard by selecting File ⇨ New ⇨ Project.

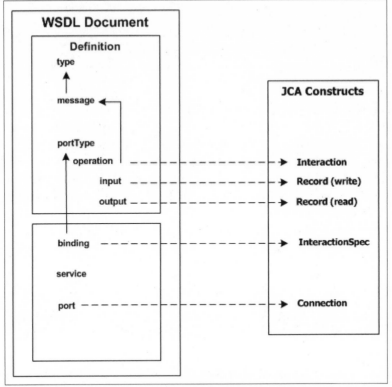

Figure 23-4   Mapping WSDL constructs to JCA constructs.

2. Select Business Integration from the left pane and Service Project from the right pane. Click Next.

3. Enter the project name and click Finish.

4. The Service Provider browser opens with a list of available service providers. Select SAP Services. The Connection Properties page opens.

5. In the "SAP Import" dialog, specify the necessary SAP R/3 connection properties for your SAP instance. For a system without load balancing, the required properties are: `hostName`, `systemNo`, `client`, `userId`, and `language`. Click Continue.

6. In the following page, specify a query string to list the desired BAPIs/RFCs or type in a * for a catch-all query. Click the List Port Types button to establish a connection with the SAL R/3 system and query the available BAPIs/RFCs that match the query string.

7. Select the BAPIs/RFCs for which you want to generate the service definitions by checking the BAPIs/RFCs you want to use. Then click the Add Service button.

8. Accept the default values and click the Finish button; this generates the WSDL representation.

9. Switch back to the Service Provider browser and repeat steps 7 and 8 for each BAPI and RFC you require. The wizard will create two WSDL files for each BAPI/RFC.

WSADIE creates a service interface file, a service binding file, and a schema definition file, all very similar to those generated for a Web service. (See www-106.ibm.com/developerworks/views/webservices/tutorials.jsp for a list of tutorials on Web services and WebSphere Studio.) In addition, WSADIE creates a .ser file with serialized information about the SAP R/3 instance. Note that while there is a service file and a binding file per BAPI/RFC, there is only a single schema file common to all.

Once you have the WSDL definitions, you can use the service binding file to generate a proxy bean called an SAP proxy by invoking the Service Proxy wizard:

1. Right-click on one of the service binding files and select New ⇨ Proxy.

2. Click Next on the first page of the wizard. On the second page of the wizard, select the Command bean option and check the BAPI/RFC. Click Finish to generate the proxy.

3. Repeat steps 1 and 2 for every BAPI/RFC for which you want to generate a proxy.

You can then use the proxy from your portlet code to get access to data from the SAP system. In a runtime environment (after packaging your code and deploying it on an instance of WP/WAS), this will look like Figure 23-5.

If you want to create a stateless session EJB as a wrapper to the BAPI/RFC, make sure you have already created an Enterprise Application project and within this project do the following:

1. Right-click the service binding file for the BAPI/RFC and select New ⇨ Deployment.

2. The WSDL, service, and port type will be filled in from the values stored in the service binding file. Make sure that the EAR, EJB, and Web project values are correct. If you wish to enable the proxy function as a Web service (perhaps to be used later by a remote portlet), select SOAP as the incoming binding type. Click Next.

3. Click Next on the next wizard page leaving the JNDI name as default. Specify the SOAP binding properties and click Next. Specify the SOAP port address and click Finish.

4. By following these steps you have created both an EJB binding file and a SOAP binding file. The deployment descriptor for the EJB

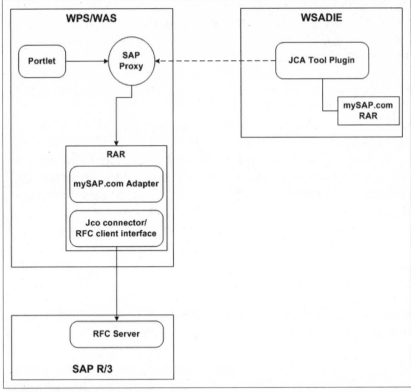

Figure 23-5   Generating and using the SAP proxy.

references the SAP connection factory. In order to bind this resource reference to a physical connection factory, click the J2EE View tab and expand EJB Modules, then right-click EJB and select Open with => EJB Extension Editor. Click the Bindings tab, expand the EJB entry and the service entry, and select ResourceRef.

5. Enter the JNDI name you selected when configuring your environment (for example, eis/SAP). Save your changes; you can now use not only the proxy from your portlet but also the session bean and a SOAP interface from local or remote portlets.

Developing Portlets Using EAI Connectors

Using EAI adapters to connect to external applications is similar to using JCA adapters in that you can view the integration project as comprising two development tasks: developing the code that makes the call using the adapters and developing the portlets that generate the user interface making use of the data and functions exposed through the adapters. The difference between using JCA adapters and using EAI adapters is an architectural one. When you use the JCA adapter your deployment architecture includes WP running on WAS and the external application. (For example, you use the WebSphere Adapter for mySAP.com to create code running on your WAS instance accessing an SAP R/3 system.) When you use an EAI adapter your architecture involves another infrastructure component: the messaging middleware.

There are many EAI products available with adapters for WebSphere and adapters for packaged business applications and it is not within the scope of this chapter to even list all the options, much less explore them. Of these many options there are two options that are part of the WebSphere family of products: specifically, WebSphere MQ and IBM CrossWorlds. WebSphere MQ, or MQSeries as it was formerly called, has been a cornerstone of IBM's integration strategy and is very well integrated with WAS. CrossWorlds was acquired by IBM at the end of 2001 and is thus more loosely integrated; using CrossWorlds for your WP integration is, from a technical standpoint, not that different from using other middleware products such as WebMethods, Vitria, and TIBCO.

WebSphere MQ adapters exist for every major business application suite. These adapters typically transform data from application-specific formats to MQSeries messages (usually in XML format) and rely on the messaging broker—WebSphere MQ Integrator—for routing messages and for transforming between different application-specific message structures. Because WebSphere MQ can be directly called from within code running on WAS, you can use this infrastructure to connect to packaged applications from your integration code, which is called by your portlets.

As an example, the WebSphere MQ adapter for mySAP.com uses MQSeries Adapter offering technology to integrate with SAP systems using RFCs, BAPIs, or IDOCs. RFCs and BAPIs were already defined in the previous section; Intermediate Documents (IDOCs) are features of SAP's Application Linking Enablement and are used for message data interaction with SAP. Regardless of whether you use RFCs, BAPIs, or IDOCs, all messages sent to SAP through the WebSphere MQ adapter conform to the SAP XML message format or need to be converted to this format. The adapter includes a set of inbound and outbound templates used for receiving and generating SAP XML messages and a DTD generator used for producing DTD files that define the SAP XML needed to represent the various SAP interfaces involved in the business transactions. The integration architecture using this MQ component is shown in Figure 23-6.

Using EAI connectors as opposed to JCA adapters means that your architecture must include an additional messaging broker component. You may be wondering why you need this added complication and when you would prefer to use this integration pattern rather than using a JCA adapter.

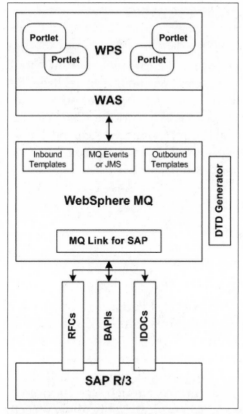

Figure 23-6   Using WebSphere MQ for integrating with SAP.

There are two cases in which you should consider using the EAI integration pattern:

1. You already have an EAI backbone or have decided to invest in an EAI backbone as a strategic decision. In this case you have already made an investment in EAI, you probably have a set of adapters between the applications you use and the EAI backbone, and there is no point in duplicating effort and creating a separate point-to-point integration between your WP infrastructure and your business applications.

2. You need to connect to applications and systems for which there are no mature JCA adapters. MQ Series has been out there for a very long time and there will be more MQ adapters than JCA adapters.

   If neither of these cases applies you will find that JCA adapters are easier to set up, easier to develop, and easier to maintain. Keeping your architecture as simple as it can be is always a good idea.

Using the Portal Application Integrator

The WebSphere Portal Application Integrator (WPAI) allows you to create new portlets that use JCA adapters accessing back-end applications without any programming. You create these portlets from within the portal itself. By selecting business objects available from the Enterprise Application, you can specify which data fields should be displayed in your portlet. The WPAI is available from the IBM WebSphere Portlal Portlet Catalog and can be downloaded from `www-3.ibm.com/services/cwi/portal/_pagr/105/`. It supports the following Enterprise Applications:

- PeopleSoft 7.5 with PeopleTools 7.54
- PeopleSoft HRMS 8.30 with PeopleTools 8.18
- Siebel 7 or higher
- SAP R/3

Note that WPAI includes the RARs for Siebel and PeopleSoft but not for SAP; you will have to download the SAP libraries from `http:service .sap.com` if you want to integrate with an SAP R/3 system. The JCA adapters are prepackaged within the WPAI, which means that you do not have to do development to get access to the information and display it within your portlets. The flip side is that you have much less control on what you can do with the information and can typically only allow object-centric behavior—that is displaying data associated with an object, making modifications to a single object, and so on.

Use of the WPAI involves two stages: downloading from the portlet catalog and installing it on your portal and then setting up the configuration attributes for the specific enterprise system you want to use. For example, if you want to use WPAI to expose a PeopleSoft 8 HRMS system, you should follow these steps:

1. Extract the contents of the WPAI zip file and copy `psjoa.jar` and `pstools.properties` from your PeopleSoft server to a new directory.

2. Deploy the `psft.rar` JCA adapter from the WPAI zip file as a J2C Resource Adapter to your WP/WAS instance.

3. Define a connection factory for the PeopleSoft JCA adapter—right-click J2C Connection Factories in the resource adapter entry and create a new factory using a JNDI name of `eis/psft`. Then click the Connections tab and specify the `hostname`, `portNumber`, and `jarPath` to the PeopleSoft server.

4. Extract `psft8adapter.jar` from `psft.rar` and place it in the `lib` folder under WAS. Restart the server instance.

5. Extract the contents of `wps_ps_portlets.zip`.

6. Start PeopleSoft Application Designer. Select File ⇨ Copy Project from File to create a new project from the extracted files. Call the project `WPS_PS_PORTLETS` and once saved, exit PeopleSoft Application Designer.

7. Log into the PeopleSoft Web application. Select PeopleTools ⇨ Maintain Security ⇨ Use ⇨ Permission Lists to set the permissions for the component interface. Select the Component Interface tab on the permission list to display the panel for adding component interfaces and add all of the imported component interfaces to a permission list. You can use an existing permission list or create a new one.

Now you need to install WPAI into your WP environment. Log into your WP instance using the administrator password and click Administration. Then click Portlets, and then Install. Select the location of the .war file from the WPAI zip file. You will then see the object builders available for installation as shown in Figure 23-7.

You are now ready to use the WPAI within your WP instance to build portlets. As mentioned, WPAI provides an object-centric view to applications and you first have to select which object to use. You can either use existing portlets that come prepackaged with WPAI for the supported

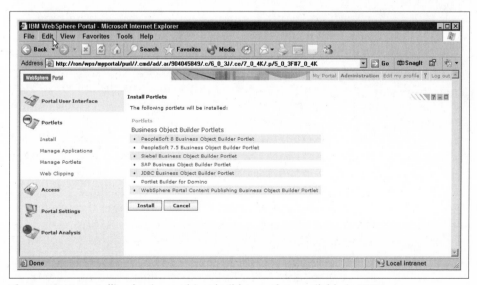

Figure 23-7   Installing business object builder portlets available in WPAI.

enterprise systems or select the Create New Portlet button. You will then be requested to name your portlet and enter the name of your PeopleSoft instance and user credentials. Click Next and then click Create New Business Object. Select the object you need to display within your portlet and define which actions you allow from within your portlet—an action can be search, update, create, and delete. Enter the titles to use when performing these actions within your portlet and click Next.

Once WPAI knows which object your portlet will use, it reads the object metadata using the adapter and presents you with a list of fields. For each field that you want displayed/edited within your portlet, check the appropriate check box, define a user-presentable name to be used as a label, define the field behavior (for example, read only versus editable), and select which field you want to appear on the finder allowing a user to search for objects matching some field criteria. Click Next to complete the creation of your portlet. You can now make this portlet available to your users.

Using the Credential Vault

In the example shown in the previous section, you built a portlet to access objects within PeopleSoft. Note that once you access this portlet at runtime (after adding it to your page), you will first have to enter the username and password to be able to log in to the PeopleSoft instance. Because WPAI front-ends your back-end systems, you need to pass user information to the back-end application. If you do not want this additional login phase, you need to implement back-end single sign-on using the Portal Server Credential Vault (CV). CV consists of vault segments and slots for maintaining the data required to access the back-end system. CV stores secrets such as user ID and password and CV service provides an API for portlets to be able to look up such values (per portal user or per shared secret).

The vault provides a bridge between a physical store and a logical API that is then available to portlets (your code). The API is provided by the `CredentialVaultService` interface, which uses adapters to access the resources themselves. The default adapter that comes packaged with WP uses the portal database to store the resources. You can also use a Tivoli Access Manager (AM) adapter for resources stored in AM and you can build your own adapter by extending the `VaultAdapter` class.

In Chapters 10 and 21 we already dealt with various single sign-on issues and certainly SSO is one of the more important functions supported by portals. Normally when you hear SSO, it is in the context of UI-oriented integration where a Web application is delivered through the portal and you do not want your users to have to log in to the application once they have

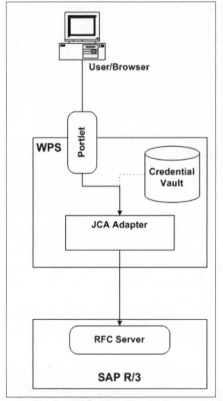

Figure 23-8   Back-end SSO using the CV.

logged into the portal. When using WPAI and adapter-based integration, you will also have to deal with SSO—in this case, back-end SSO.

Back-end SSO means that you will have to make sure that programs running on your WP instance (whether it is code you have developed or whether it is WPAI portlets) use a correct user credential when accessing the back-end system using a JCA adapter, as shown in Figure 23-8. Instead of hard-coding this into your code, you should use Credential Vault—a place to maintain credentials such as those required to access the back-end system.

Credential Vault Segments

CV is one of the built-in portal services within WP providing a mechanism for portlets to be able to map a user identity with stored credentials. The CV is partitioned into vault segments, which are themselves partitioned into vault slots. Slots can be specific to a back-end application (in which case they are shared among many users) or can be specific to a pairing of back-end system and user. In addition, the CV can contain two types of segments: administrator managed and user managed.

Use the WebSphere Portal CV portlet to create a segment within CV as follows:

1. Log in as an administrator and click Administration.

2. Select the Access option and the CV suboption.

3. Click Add a Vault Segment.

4. Enter a vault segment name and click OK as shown in Figure 23-9.

Credential Vault Slots

CV segments contain one or more CV slots. You use slots to store user credentials and portlets access slots within segments to store and retrieve values. A single slot contains a single value and is used either as a single credential for a specific user or as a value that is shared among all users. Slots can be divided into three types:

- System credentials. Shared among all users and portlets and created in administrator-managed CV segments

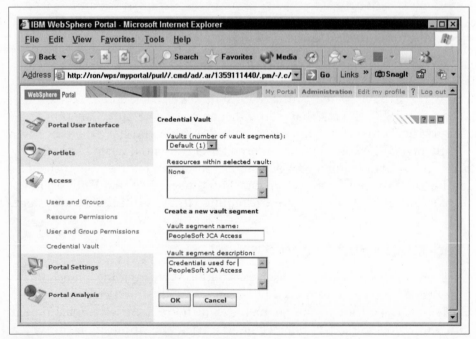

Figure 23-9 Creating a CV segment.

- Shared credentials. Shared among all portlets of a single user; also created in the administrator-managed CV segments
- Private credentials. Private to a combination of user and portlet

Slots are accessed through the CV service as instances of the `CredentialSlotConfig` class. This class stores the metadata associated with the slot as well as a link to the actual resource. Slots can be created programmatically in user-managed segments or using the CV portlet for administrator-managed segments. To create CV slot in an administrator-managed segment, log in as an administrator and follow these steps:

1. Click Administration ⇨ Access ⇨ Credential Vault.
2. Select Add a Vault Slot.
3. Select the vault and the CV segment in which this slot will be created.
4. Enter a unique name for the slot and select a resource to be created (or link the slot to an existing resource).
5. If you are creating a shared slot for all resources, check the Vault slot is shared check box and enter the user ID and password to be used; if there will be a distinct value for each user in WP leave this check box empty.
6. Finally, enter a description and click OK, as shown in Figure 23-10.

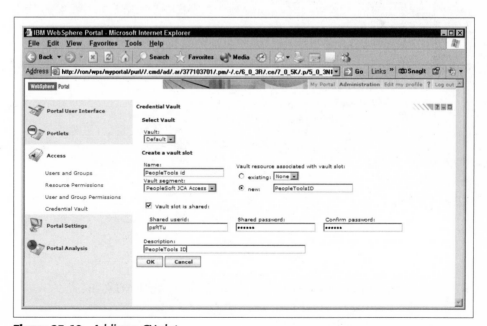

Figure 23-10   Adding a CV slot.

Using the Credential Vault Service API

The CV service provides an API for portlets to access the CV. The API is available from the com.ibm.wps.portletservice.credentialvault. credentials package and allows you to programmatically create slots, create or modify credentials, and access credentials stored in a slot.

In order to use the CV service, you will first need to initialize the CredentialVaultService object:

```
try {
    vaultService =
            (CredentialVaultService)getPortletConfig().getContext().
                        getService(CredentialVaultService.class);
} catch(Exception e){
        e.printStackTrace(System.out);
}
```

Once you have the vault service object, you can create a new private slot and store a value in it as follows:

```
try {
    PortletData data = portletRequest.getData();
    String slotId = "PeopleTools id";
    String resourceName = "PeopleToolsID";
    ObjectID segmentID = vaultService.getDefaultUserVaultSegmentId();
    Map description = new Hashtable();
    Map keywords = new Hashtable();
    int secretType =
        vaultService.SECRET_TYPE_USERID_STRING_PASSWORD_STRING;
    boolean active = true;
    boolean portletPrivate = false;

    CredentialSlotConfig slot =
        vaultService.createSlot(
            resourceName, segmentID, description,
            keywords, secretType, active, portletPrivate,
portletRequest);

    vaultService.setCredentialSecretUserPassword(
            slotId, userID,
            password.toCharArray(),portletRequest);
    } catch(Exception e){
      e.printStackTrace(System.out);
    }
```

To access credentials from a private slot (using portlet data):

```
Map toReturn = new Hashtable();
try {
    String slotId = (String) portletRequest.getData().
```

```
                              getAttribute("PeopleToos id");
        if(slotId == null) return ;

        UserPasswordPassiveCredential credential =
            (UserPasswordPassiveCredential)vaultService.getCredential
               (slotId, "UserPasswordPassive", new HashMap(),
    portletRequest);
        toReturn.put("userid", credential.getUserId());
        toReturn.put("password", String.valueOf(credential.getPassword()));
    } catch(Exception e){
        e.printStackTrace(System.out);

    }
```

Using the WebSphere Portlet Catalog

The next category of integration is the portlet catalog, allowing you to make use of ready-made packages that provide both the portlet and the back-end integration component. This means that you have no development activities, and very little setup is required—making this pattern the easiest to use. The limitation of this pattern is that it can only provide you with the functionality that was implemented and packaged by the provider and this may not be precisely the functionality you need nor will the user interface always be consistent with your look and feel.

Business application portlets are available from the WebSphere Portlet Catalog at `www-3.ibm.com/services/cwi/portal/_pagr/105/`—this site is maintained by IBM. The catalog lists and describes offerings available from IBM and IBM Business Partners. The catalog enables you to search for information that meets specific criteria such as:

- Portlets and portlet builders
- Tools and other applications, which integrate with WP
- Solutions, such as services and value-added offerings

The catalog is organized based on a set of categories and each catalog entry contains information on the function as well as pointers to additional information about the offering. You can either browse the catalog using content lists such as the one shown in Figure 23-11 or search by category. The following are the available categories listed on the catalog (excluding categories that are based on the company creating the portal, language, markup, or market category):

- Collaboration
  - Calendar

← Return to Portlet Catalog front page

Application: Collaboration , Personal Tools

Catalog entry type: Example , Other , Portlet , Service , Tool

Company: 10 Technology , ActiveBuddy , Actuate , Adexa , Agilan , atHoc , Atview , Autonomy , Aztlan Technologies , Baan, an Invensys Company , BackWeb Technologies, Inc. , Bowstreet , Business Objects , Cactus Computers , Cerith , Citrix , Clear Technologies , Cognos , CommercialWare , CONET , CoreMedia , Correlate , Cross Systems , Crystal Decisions , DataGlider Inc. , Dialog , Digital Union , divine , Dossier Solutions , Droplets , EasyAsk , e Biz Portals , Echospace , eDocs , Elevon , Emblaze Systems , Enigma , en technologies , EximSoft Technologies , Factiva , FatWire Software , Financial Times , FirstRain , Grand Horizon , GruppoPro , Hoovers Online , i2 Technologies , IBM , iCore effective , iMarkup Solutions , Information Builders , Inktomi , InQuira , Integra SP , IntellectExchange , Interwoven , ITWorx , J.D. Edwards , Kamoon , Knowmadic , Lowry Technologies , MapInfo , MatrixOne , MobileEconomy , NetSilica , NewsEdge , Nexaweb Technologies , Novgorod State University , OnePage , payBox , Peregrine Systems , Picom Software Systems , Pinnacor , Pironet NDH , Pivia , Presence OnLine , Quiver , Republica , RSA Security , S1 , Sapiens , Satyam Computer Services , Scene7 , SLK Software Services , Sofor , SSA Global Technologies , Stellent , Torry Harris Business Solutions , Tri-Bry IT Solutions , Trilog Group , Verity , Vignette , Wimba , YellowBrix , Zygon Systems

Content: Business , News , Syndicated , Travel

Industry: Cross Industry , Education , Financial , Government , Healthcare , Industrial , Internet Service Provider , Life Sciences , Retail and Wholesale , Telecommunications , Travel and Transportation , Utility and Energy Services

Language: Brazilian Portuguese , Czech , English , French , German , Hebrew , Italian , Japanese , Korean , Polish , Russian , Simplified Chinese , Spanish , Traditional Chinese , Turkish

Miscellaneous: Free Preview , Samples , Unknown classification

Portal Client: Desktop Browser , Pervasive Device , Voice Browser

Portal Server: WP 2.1 , WP V4.1 , WP V4.2 , WP V4.2.1 , WP V5 , WP V5.0.1

Portlet Output Format: cHTML , HTML 3.2 , HTML 4 , VoiceXML 1.0 , WML 1.1 , WML 1.2

Price: Fee , Free , Trial

Software Application: App Collaboration , Business Intelligence , Communications , Content Management , Customer Relationship Management , Data Management , Desktop Applications , Development Tools , Document Management , Enterprise Resource Planning , Knowledge Management , Multimedia , Supply Chain Management , Web-based Applications

Tools: Portlet Generators

← Return to Portlet Catalog front page

Figure 23-11   Browsing for portlets.

- Contacts
- E-mail
- Messaging
- Tasks
- Work areas

- Personal tools

  - Personal bookmarks
  - Personal calculators
  - Personal calendars

- Personal clocks
- Personal contacts
- Personal search
- Personal tasks

- Content

    - Business
    - News
    - Syndicated
    - Travel

- Miscellaneous

    - Samples
    - Free preview
    - Unknown classification

- Tools—Portlet generators

- Software application

    - Business Intelligence
    - App Collaboration
    - Lotus iNotes
    - Lotus Notes
    - Microsoft Exchange
    - Communications
    - Content Management
    - Customer Relationship Management
    - Siebel
    - Data Management
    - DB2
    - Oracle
    - Desktop Applications
    - Development Tools
    - Document Management
    - Enterprise Resource Planning
    - PeopleSoft
    - SAP
    - Knowledge Management
    - Multimedia
    - Supply Chain Management
    - Web-based Applications

The importance of the portlet catalog should not be underestimated. The more comprehensive the catalog is, the easier it will be for you to set up meaningful content within your portal. The goal is therefore to have the catalog constantly evolving and have more and more prepackaged portlets offered through the catalog. Because it is supply and demand that drive companies to develop and offer applications, you should make it a point to always look for portlets using the catalog before you opt to develop your own.

While many of the portlets on the catalog are offered by IBM, some of them package integration with business applications. As an example, one of the most popular portlets offered on the catalog is the SAP Enterprise Integration portlets. These portlets were built by IBM using WPAI and support functions in SAP HR, Finance, Material Management, and more. Because the portlets are built using WPAI, they take a very object-centric (rather than process-centric or function-centric) view and support the following views (by category):

- Finance

    - List customer balances
    - List vendor balances
    - Show credit information of customer
    - List open items of debtor
    - List statements of vendor
    - List payment requests

- Human Resource

    - List employee by cost center
    - List and create appraisals
    - Show detail and rate appraisals
    - List qualifications for person
    - List requirements for position

- Sales Orders:

    - Show details of customer
    - List sales orders
    - Check sales order status

- Material Management

    - Material data
    - Material detail
    - Availability of material

- Cost Center

    - List cost center by controlling area

- Cost center general details

- Cost center activities

To install these portlets within your WP instance, you will first have to install the JCO library for SAP. You then need to create a CV slot named `bofactory.slot` associated with a resource named `sap`. You then need to bring up the portlet in edit mode and enter the SAP username, password, hostname, system number, client, language and connections per user pool.

Web Clipping

Referring back to Figure 23-2, we have dealt with the left-hand side of the chart and have covered the patterns termed as back-end integration patterns. All of these patterns have one thing in common: Under the covers portlets use some form of adapter or connector to access the back-end system. In this section we deal with a different kind of integration—integration that is at a user interface level only.

When you use portlets in the context of front-end integration patterns, the portlets do not interact with the application at an API level. Instead, it makes use of Web screen scraping techniques: activating the application through a set of HTTP requests (URLs) and using the responses in HTML (or another markup language) to display information through the portal—either by embedding the pages as is or 'clipping' parts of the HTML and creating a new page from a subset of the original information. Because all Web applications have an identical request/response interaction paradigm, this integration method is very generic.

In Chapter 9 we showed you how Web Clipping helps you build portlets that consume Web content and filter it to present a partial page of relevant portions of an original page. You do this by using the Web Clipping portlet, which helps you build such Web clippers by specifying the URL of the content to retrieve various attributes that affect how the content is clipped. The portlets created by the Web Clipping portlet are called Web clippers or cliplets. Web Clipping supports advanced features such as security and cookies, to allow you to clip not only simple Internet sites but also advanced Web-based applications.

The advanced features of WP cliplets make clipping a useful tool for application integration within WP. Web clipper options include selecting clipping types, modifying firewall options, setting authentication options, modifying rules for URL rewriting, and setting specific security policies. Of

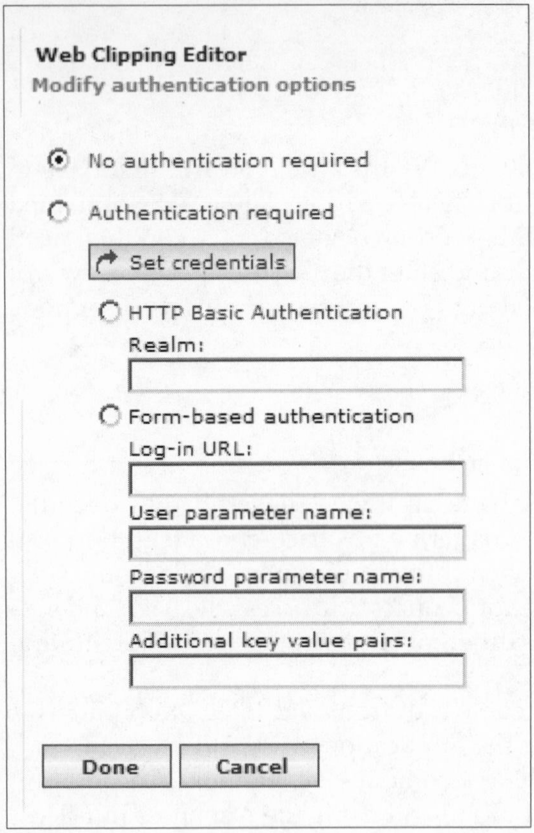

Web Clipping Editor
Modify authentication options

⦿ No authentication required

○ Authentication required

[↱ Set credentials]

○ HTTP Basic Authentication
Realm:
[   ]

○ Form-based authentication
Log-in URL:
[   ]

User parameter name:
[   ]

Password parameter name:
[   ]

Additional key value pairs:
[   ]

[Done] [Cancel]

Figure 23-12 Web Clipping authentication options.

these, the ones that you use most often when integrating with a back-end application are the authentication option and the URL rewriting option.

Web Clipping Authentication Options

In using cliplets you will still have to handle issues of single sign-on. Application content is presented by cliplets because WP opens a connection to the Web or application server and makes an HTTP request. The application needs some way to authenticate this request, and you need to set up the authentication method with which such access will be done. When you click Modify Authentication Options for your cliplet, you can select among various authentication options as shown in Figure 23-12.

Select the Authentication Required option and select HTTP Basic Authentication or Form-Based Authentication. If you select Basic Authentication you need only enter the realm name. Form-Based Authentication is dependent on the form used to log into the application and requires you to

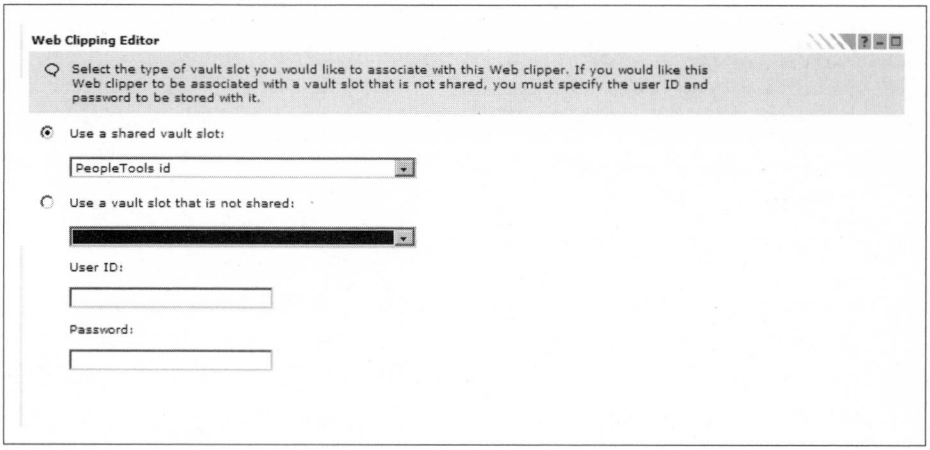

Figure 23-13   Setting the Credentials for Web Clipping authentication.

enter form-specific information—including the URL for the login form and the parameter names within that form where the username and password are entered. You can get these by navigating to the application login form using your browser and viewing the HTML source, looking for the login form and the parameter names. Finally, you need to set the credentials used to perform the login using a CV slot as shown in Figure 23-13. You can use either a shared CV slot or a CV slot that is not shared, in which case you should enter the username and password to be used.

Web Clipping Options for URL Rewriting

You can define the behavior of cliplets in terms of HTML links by using the Web Clipping URL rewriting options. These options control how references are modified when they are part of the cliplet page. Links often need to be modified in order to preserve the portal experience, and the default behavior of URL rewriting involves modifying the links to point at the portal server rather than the original host and ensuring that the page you have navigated to appears within the content area of the portlet.

If you do not want to use the default behavior, you can create a set of rules that affect how URLs are rewritten. When logged in as an administrator, click Administration, then Portlets, and then Web Clipping. Once you have located your cliplet, click Advanced Options and Modify Rules for URL Rewriting. Then check the Use Rules to Exclude URLs from Rewriting Radio button as shown in Figure 23-14. You can then define two sets of URL rules: URLs that will not be modified and, when clicked, will take up the entire browser window. The second set of rules define URLs that will not be

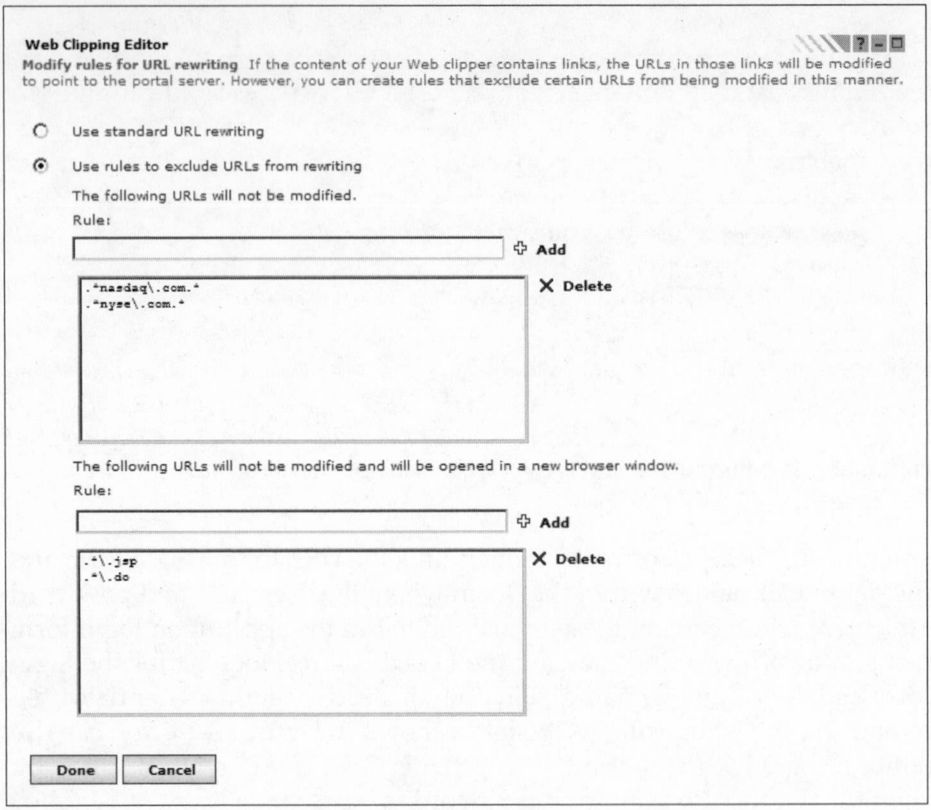

Figure 23-14   Modifying URL rewriting rules.

modified and will be opened in a new window when clicked. In both cases a rule is a Perl expression that defines a pattern. When the cliplet is rendered, the HTML is modified by inspecting each hyperlink and modifying the HREF attribute value based on these rules. If a hyperlink matches a pattern then the rule applies, the URL is not rewritten, and the correct windowing behavior will apply. In Figure 23-14 for example any URL with any host on the `nasdaq.com` or `nyse.com` domain will navigate to take up the browser windows, and any page ending with `.jsp` or `.do` will be opened in a new window.

Application-Specific Web Embedding

Application-specific Web embedding is another type of integration pattern that makes use of HTTP/HTML screen scraping and allows you to deploy existing Web screens directly on your portal without integrating to the back-end system at an API level. What is special about application-specific Web embedding is that because the portlets that perform the integration task know that they only need to interact with a certain application they can make all sorts of assumptions on the application architecture and the way it behaves. Because these portlets do not need to be completely generic, they can do a better job in integrating with the specific application suite involved and they can contain parameters that are specific to the application suite, allowing for better integration with the application.

Two examples of application-specific Web embedding involve the SAPGUI for HTML portlet and the SAP Business Warehouse (BW) integration portlets, both available through the portlet catalog. The SAPGUI for HTML portlet allows you to embed any HTML page created by SAP's Internet Transaction Server (ITS) either as an iframe or as a pop-up window. The SAP BW portlet allows you to embed views from existing SAP BW systems and expose them within your portlet—including functions from opportunity management, personnel administration, and controlling activity-based costing. In this section we focus on SAPGUI for HTML because it is a good example of application-specific Web embedding.

The SAPGUI for HTML portlet is built to use SAP's ITS architecture. As Figure 23-15 shows, a mySAP.com system includes the SAP R/3 application and the SAP workplace middleware. Within SAP workplace, the ITS component serves to create and deliver HTML pages to the browser and serves as the broker between an R/3 system and the Internet. The ITS is placed between the Web server and the R/3 system and comprises two main components: the WGate and the AGate. The WGate resides on the Web server and is the plugin connecting to the application server—the AGate. The AGate controls the communication with the R/3 system and is responsible for session management, mapping R/3 screens or function modules to HTML, connection management, and most importantly the generation of HTML pages.

The SAPGUI for HTML portlet only supports Internet Explorer and has been tested with SAP R/2 version 4.6C. Setting up the portlet merely involves downloading it from the portlet catalog and adding it to your WP environment. You then need to set the following parameters:

- SAPGUIBrowserHost. Host name of the SAP ITS Server. If you do not use port 80 for the connection, you must also specify the port number.

- SAPGUIBrowserPathExtension. URL path where the application is provided by the SAP ITS Server.

- SAPGUIBrowserClient. Client number for the SAP system.

- APGUIBrowserLang. Language settings for SAP ITS server.

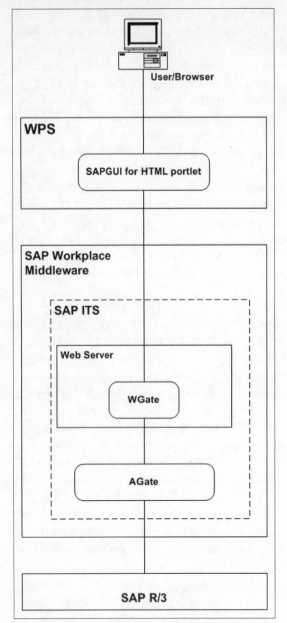

Figure 23-15   Using the SAPGUI for HTML portlet to connect to a SAP ITS system.

- SAPGUIBrowserTxCode. Transaction code for SAP ITS Server.
- SAPGUIBrowserIFrameWidth. Width of the iframe where the HTML page will be shown.
- SAPGUIBrowserIFrameHeight. Height of the iframe where the HTML page will be shown.

■ SAPGUIBrowserDetach. Set to false if you want to view the SAP ITS server's content within a portlet iframe or set to true if you want to pop up a separate window.

Embedding Functional Portals

Functional portals are portals that focus on a certain business domain, set of functions used within the organization, or both. These portals are very common in many organizations and can be managed by a certain business function (for example, an HR portal or a finance portal) or by another organizational entity (for example, a business unit or a geographical unit within the organization). Functional portals can often be deployed quickly, sometimes due to the fact that they are limited in terms of the functions that need to be implemented and sometimes because a single organization is often more effective in making decisions quickly and moving the project further. In addition, many application suite vendors provide a portal that is already integrated with the back-end business function with the intent of making a functional portal very quick to deploy. Examples include SAP portals and the PeopleSoft portal.

Functional portals are popular because they allow an organization to put up their portal quickly. Unfortunately, functional portals often work against the main goal of having an enterprise portal. Referring back to Figure 23-1, many functional portals can create a reality that is not too dissimilar from the left-hand side of that figure. A common enterprise portal (the right-hand side of Figure 23-1) is where most enterprises want to get to.

The last integration pattern addresses a scenario in which an enterprise wants to integrate a number of already existing functional portals. In such a case it is often not desirable to build additional integration directly to the back-end application (that is, circumventing the functional portal). Instead, you can expose the functional portal and the functions deployed on it directly from within your WebSphere Portal.

Embedding functional portals is relatively simple when it comes to integration—and we only mention this pattern here for completeness. The functional portal is accessed by pointing directly to starting-point URLs that reside on the functional portal. In addition, there are two main issues you need to deal with in order to use this integration pattern. The first and most important issue is single sign-on. By this we don't mean using the CV—we mean SSO as presented and described in Chapter 21. In fact, the SSO tool used is really the tool performing the integration. The second issue you will need to deal with involves consistency of the user interface. Because each functional portal may have its own set of styles, skins, and themes (not to mention navigation methods and operational standards), you may need to do quite a bit of look-and-feel standardization.

Summary

In this chapter we walked you through a number of integration patterns. We showed you the abundance of possibilities that are at your disposal and explained what each one entails. We showed you both front-end integration patterns and back-end integration patterns. Front-end integration patterns make use of the fact that the vast majority of applications you will want to integrate into the portal are Web enabled and have an Internet architecture. In these cases you can expose these screens directly within your portal or use sections from the HTML pages and create subsets of information to be exposed through the portal. This allows you to make use of the existing application suites with very little development and with less-than-perfect understanding of the underlying data model and functional semantics forming the core of the application. This type of integration is also useful when you already have a functional portal (for example, HR portal with HR self-service) and are building a larger enterprise portal that needs to provide functional elements as well. In this case you can get integration done very quickly with very little effort. The disadvantages are that you are limited to the functions already exposed through the functional portal and/or the Web-enabled applications, which you have to deal with having a possibly inconsistent user interface look and feel, that you need to handle single sign-on with the external application/portal outside of WP (refer back to Chapter 21 for more on single sign-on) and that you cannot have custom navigation among the existing functions. Even with all these disadvantages, it has been our experience that front-end integration is very effective, relatively easy to perform, and provides good return on investment.

The other category of integration patterns we covered was back-end integration. In these patterns the application suite is accessed through an adapter or connector that retrieves data from the back-end application and uses APIs to perform transactions. Portlets make use of classes that use the adapter to perform all this. Back-end integration provides you with much more control because most application suites have very comprehensive API sets and because (at least in some of these patterns) you are developing your own portlets and can control the user interface and the navigation.

Back-end integration tends to be more complex than front-end integration and tends to require more expertise. On the other hand, it is more stable—APIs and adapters change much less often than user interface and if you use some kind of screen-scraping approach you may be surprised when the back-end application team upgrades their software. Back-end integration also usually means less operational cost because if all users access the application through the portal then you only need to have an API server running and do not require a full Web server environment for the application. Finally, many of the front-end integration portlets have only been tested for specific application versions and are sometimes no more than a proof-of-concept type of solution—be careful to check all the "small print" before you opt to bypass the more comprehensive back-end integration.

In either case, prepackaged solutions mean much less work with a disadvantage of providing you with less control. While back-end integration usually involves more work than front-end integration, prepackaged portlets that may be available on the portlet catalog require by far the least amount of work. Therefore, regardless of whether you choose a back-end or a front-end approach, our suggestion is that you try to use an existing integration solution before you delve into development of new portlets and code and stick with it if you can get most of the functionality you need.

Now that you know about the various methods that are available for integrating applications that may be used by the large user base using your portal, let's turn to the subject of how to support ALL users—regardless of where they access the portal from and what device they use. In the next chapter we address the topic of mobile portals supporting users on-the-go and users using devices other than conventional PCs.

## CHAPTER 24

Supporting Mobile Users

In this chapter you will learn how to use WebSphere Portal to support mobile users. You will see how WP (and products that extend WP) can be used to deploy portlets that provide access using various browsers and microbrowsers commonly used on devices such as Personal Digital Assistants (PDAs) and mobile phones. You will learn how to develop portlets that generate content for such devices and how to deploy Transcoding Technology (TT) that can use existing portlets originally targeting standard browsers to be used from these more limited platforms. You will also learn how to address issues that come up due to the fact that mobile users do not always have a continuous connection back to the server and sometimes need to be able to continue using some portlets in an offline environment.

WebSphere's mobile strategy is centered on the WebSphere Everyplace product family. Parts of this chapter discuss elements of this product family, and predominantly WebSphere Everyplace Access (WEA). WEA is actually a product that includes WP as an embedded component and from a server-centric viewpoint is an extension of WP. We will introduce you to the features directly implemented in WP for allowing you to serve mobile users as well as show you what WEA has to offer as an extension to WP. We will also introduce you to TT allowing you to write portlets that generate content once and have external rules that generate multiple markup types (suited to multiple browsers and devices) from this single portlet presentation. This eliminates the need for multiple portlets that implement the same function but serve different device types. Both WP as well as WEA includes elements of TT and we will review the most important features in TT that can help you deploy multidevice support quickly.

Mobile Users

Most people think of portals in terms of Web pages that are accessed by workstations or laptops used in an office environment and/or from the home. Portals help organize the various applications and data that can be accessed and provide a way to manage the Web desktop.

The reason most people have this large-computer-centric view of portals is that portals, as any computing technology, were initially used primarily by users with a high degree of sophistication when it comes to information technology. However, two trends are making this PC and workstation viewpoint incomplete.

More and more portals serve very large communities—often serving communities that are not necessarily information technology professionals nor have a strong affinity to computers. The second is that today there are a very large number of devices that can access the Internet that are not computers in the classic sense (all these devices have some kind of processor and are technically computers too). These devices include Internet-enabled phones, PDAs, and handhelds. In fact, there are already more such devices being used today than there are PCs and the number of such devices is constantly growing—both in the consumer world and in the business world. This is especially relevant for portal developers. As an example, when large companies decide to build and deploy a large employee portal that will cover all Human Resource functions, the effect can only be achieved through very high utilization levels by employees. This sometimes means that multiple access channels need to be provided to the functionality deployed on the portal.

The direct result of these two trends is the fact that developers of portals and portlets need to address a wide variety of devices that can be used to access content and applications. Different devices have different form factors and different data-entry interfaces. A portlet that creates content that looks good on a laptop may look awful on a mobile phone—in fact, it will probably be unusable. In addition, different devices have data-entry mechanisms. Phones should be used in a way that users are asked to select among various options but should not be forced to key in large amounts of information. Another example includes Symbol Technologies' PDAs that have a barcode reader—in which case data can be entered without any keying in or graffiti-type typing (see Figure 24-1). Symbol has two such product lines—one based on the Palm OS and one on the Pocket PC operating system by Microsoft—both having a barcode scanner. If you have a job that includes delivering packages, you can simply scan a barcode on a label that is attached to the package rather than key in the number, thereby cutting the delivery time as well as errors that will undoubtedly occur if you have to type in the package number.

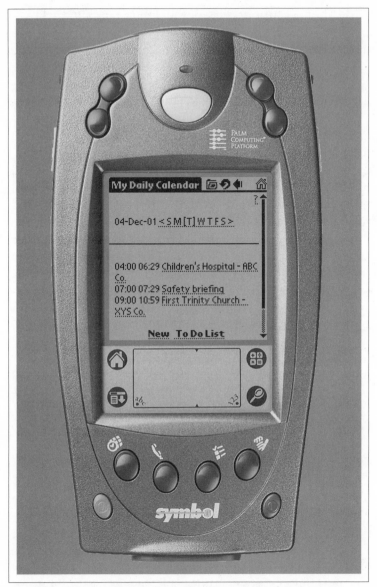

Figure 24-1   Palm OS based Symbol PDA with bar code scanner.

Addressing many devices means carefully thinking not only about the user interface, but also about some technical challenges including the fact that different platforms have different browsers and microbrowsers supporting different languages. For example, both Internet Explorer (IE) on a laptop and Pocket IE on a PDA support HTML but most microbrowsers on mobile phones support the wireless markup language (WML) or an older (and quickly fading) markup language called HDML. In Japan, mobile phones (called i-mode phones) support yet another language called cHTML (compact HTML).

Support for different languages, screen sizes, and input mechanisms are not all you need to worry about. People who use workstations and PCs are normally in an office environment and connected through a high-speed network to the Internet. People who are in the field (such as service technicians) will often need to have access to the portal using a wireless environment—and we don't just mean hot spots in Starbucks shops. Such workers need to have access over true wireless networks that are usually provided by large cellular companies or through private radio networks. These networks tend to be slower and in many parts of the world (for example, the United States) provide spotty service. In order for these workers to be effective, they need to be able to continue to use their data and applications even when the network is down or when coverage is nonexistent (regardless of whether the reason is that there are simply no cell towers in the area or work needs to be performed in a basement of a large building).

To recap, the issues that you should keep in mind when building portals and portlets serving large and mobile communities (and that we will address in this chapter) are as follows:

- Support for multiple presentations for different devices
- Support for both online and offline access
- Support for multiple access networks

Supporting Multiple Markups

Most devices that could be used to access portal functionality have some kind of browser. Such browsers are based on a markup language, examples being HTML, WML, and cHTML. The first thing you need to ensure, therefore, is that your portlets have the right setup for supporting multiple markups.

If you are working within WebSphere Studio Site Developer (WSSD) and have the portlet toolkit installed, you can specify the additional markup support when creating a new portlet application project. Specifically, when you use the wizard for creating such a project click the Next buttons rather than the Finish button; the last wizard panel will allow you to specify additional markup types as shown in Figure 24-2.

Alternatively, if you already have a portlet application project and you want to add additional markup support, double-click the portlet.xml file. This will open the portlet configuration editor. The following steps allow you to add or remove markup supported by your portlet:

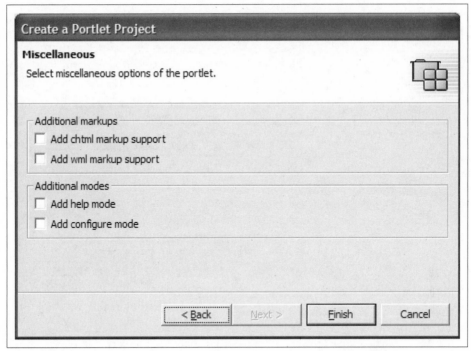

Figure 24-2   Specifying additional markup within the WSSD portlet application project wizard.

1. Select your portlet from within the PortletApplication selection.
2. Scroll down—the fourth section on the right-hand side allows you to add additional markup support. By default you only have HTML support.
3. Click Add and select the markup type as shown in Figure 24-3. Click OK.

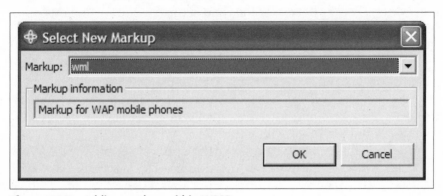

Figure 24-3   Adding markup within WSSD.

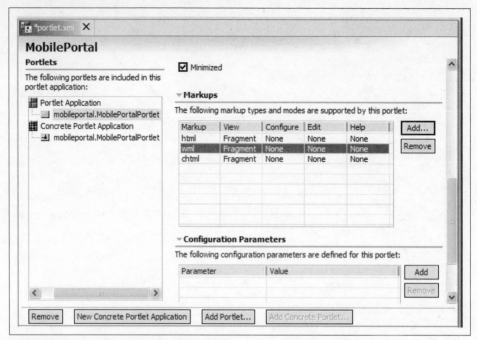

Figure 24-4 Multiple markup support for a portlet application project.

Once you have finished adding the various markup types (for example, as shown in Figure 24-4), save the portlet configuration file.

And finally, if you prefer to edit the portlet.xml file directly, markup is specified within the `supports` tag shown below:

```
<portlet-app
uid="mobileportal.MobilePortalPortlet.50a1bb94df0e00181166c78cbc0d3e57"
major-version="1" minor-version="0">
  <portlet-app-name>MobilePortal application</portlet-app-name>
  <portlet id="mobileportal.MobilePortalPortlet" href="WEB-
INF/web.xml#mobileportal.MobilePortalPortlet" major-version="1" minor-
version="0">
    <portlet-name>MobilePortal portlet</portlet-name>
    <cache>
      <expires>0</expires>
      <shared>no</shared>
    </cache>
    <allows>
      <maximized/>
      <minimized/>
    </allows>
    <supports>
      <markup name="html">
        <view />
```

```
      </markup>
      <markup name="wml">
        <view />
      </markup>
      <markup name="chtml">
        <view />
      </markup>
    </supports>
  </portlet>
</portlet-app>
```

HTML, WML, and cHTML are all supported by default with every installation of WP. There are additional markup types that are supported only through the use of WEA, and within WSSD only when you install the Everyplace Toolkit. In this case additional markups that are provided include the following:

- PDA—a subset of HTML useful for PDA browsing. This markup is also used for offline access with the WEA client.

- VXML—VoiceXML is a markup language that is used to develop and deploy voice-enabled portlets. VXML is supported by many commercial voice servers, and by using VXML markup you can deploy functionality that can be used by making a voice phone call, selecting menu options, and making data-entry commands—all using a normal voice call and pressing your phone keys.

WebSphere Everyplace Access

WEA is a part of the WebSphere Everyplace product line and allows you to deliver content to mobile devices. Interestingly enough, WEA includes an embedded instance of WP. In fact, the main goal of WEA is to extend portal functionality to mobile devices. WEA includes a set of tools as well as portlets for mobile use. From a tool perspective, it includes enhanced transcoding capabilities, synchronization functionality with Microsoft Exchange and Lotus Notes, and support for offline access. From a packaged application perspective, it includes a set of productivity and personal information management portlets.

Supporting Offline Access

In many companies with mobile workforce, there are situations where users have less-than-perfect coverage. If you have a cell phone you must be used to the problems of incomplete coverage. Even if you have good coverage, wireless connections are often considerably slower than landline connections and conventional Internet connections. All this means that supporting a good experience for mobile users often means synchronizing content onto a mobile device, ensuring that the mobile unit is fully functional although it is not connected, and allowing the user to upload actions that were performed on the mobile unit and resynchronize content at a later point in time.

WEA and the WEA client (which needs to be installed on the mobile device) allow you to view, browse, and interact with portal content offline. One of the pages that is created for you by WEA is the offline page. All you need to do per portlet that you want to use offline is make sure that it supports the pda markup and add it to this offline page (incidentally—this means that only HTML-generating portlets can work in an offline mode). The WEA client will then synchronize with WEA and access a special servlet called WebCache that traverses links on the offline page and rewrites the links and pages referenced by the offline page. The rewriting process is done based on a depth parameter that can be configured within WEA and controls how many links will be traversed. As an example, if you have a Web page structure as shown in Figure 24-5 and provide a depth of 4, then the highlighted pages will be offloaded to the mobile unit. To specify the link depth, log in to WEA as an administrator and modify the depth parameter of the offline browsing administration portlet. The default link depth is defined on the WEA Home ⇨ Administration page. A user can also define a user-specific link depth value by navigating to WEA Home ⇨ Configure.

Once you've defined the depth level, you use the WEA client to view the offline page. You need to start the client, configure the access to the WEA server, and synchronize the offline content. As an example, if you are using a PocketPC unit follow these steps:

1. Select Start ⇨ Everyplace Client.
2. Enter your portal name and password.
3. Select My Settings from the drop-down list.
4. Select Network Profiles.
5. Enter the fully qualified name to your WEA server.
6. Select Home from the drop-down list and click the Synchronize icon. This will get the offline portlet content onto your unit.

The offline page supports a perception that you have direct access to the portal at all times. You can navigate between pages and view data. The only difference between offline operation and online access is that when you press Submit in a form, the WEA client will inform you that the submission has been deferred until you resynchronize with the main server. Specifically, you will get the following message:

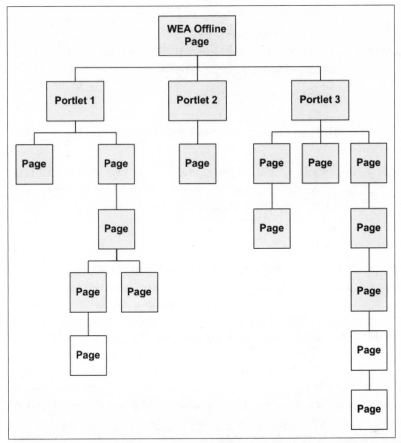

Figure 24-5 Offline synchronization of portlets with a depth of 4 for traversal of links.

Your request is deferred

Due to no active connection now, your request is stored in the database successfully and will be posted by invoking a sync application later.

In addition to the depth parameter, there is one additional WEA configuration step; you need to turn on URI addressability by changing the value of use.requestId to false in

```
<WAS HOME>/lib/app/config/services/ConfigService.properties.
```

Writing portlets that can work offline is nontrivial and requires a different discipline to that you may be used to. When building portlets that will be used in an offline mode you should adhere to the following rules:

1. Always support pda markup.

2. Have only one form per page (this is true for both portlet pages and pages that can be reached from the portlets).

3. Use only POST in your forms; do not use GET.

4. Write code that maintains session in a way that is resilient to duplicate submissions of the form. Synchronization does not guarantee that submissions will occur only once.

5. You can use simple Javascript validations but avoid complex Javascript code.

6. Do not include links within Javascript and do not rely on Javascript navigation.

7. Make sure your pages are well formed. You should verify that all tags are closed correctly as per the XML well-formed-ness rules. You can use tools such as **jtidy** available at `http://lempinen.net/sami /jtidy`.

8. Do not use PortletActions.

9. Avoid dynamic behavior on screen that affects submission parameters (for example, pages that dynamically add to HTML tables for inclusion in a collection; in this case put all options in the table with check boxes used for defining which entries should be added to the collection. Always avoid cascading forms).

Before completing this topic we would like to point out that there are additional packages other than WEA that provide offline portlet capabilities. Probably the best known is AvantGo by Sybase, which can also be used to provide offline portal capabilities. In this case you will be working directly with WP but will need to install an AvantGo server that will be doing the synchronization and caching work.

Supporting Multiple Wireless Environments

When building portals that will be used by mobile users not only do you need to worry about devices, markup, and offline capabilities, but you also address connectivity issues. Wireless networks can be highly complex and diverse and this is a topic that we cannot fully address in this book. Our goal is merely to point out that this is an infrastructure issue you should plan for.

The Internet is an IP-based network and is ubiquitously available from homes and offices throughout the world. This means you do not have to deal with connectivity issues when deploying your portlets and you do not need to think about how users will get access to your portal. For mobile users this is not necessarily true. Different geographies have different networks, some areas have multiple connection types, and others have none. In addition, wireless networks are not always IP-based and some involve highly proprietary radio frequency protocols. The connectivity options include Hot Spots and 802.11b networks, CDPD, GPRS, Mobitex, GSM, CDMA, TDMA, satellite networks, iDEN, TETRA, EDACS, and so on. Each of these networks potentially has its own complexities and peculiarities. Without getting into too much detail, you should distinguish between the following types of wireless networks.

1. IP-based networks that provide you with an "always on" connection. This is the simplest case for you to support because in this case you don't have to do anything special—each mobile unit is perceived to be a node on the Internet and can access your portal in a normal way.

2. Dial-up networks. In these networks you use a phone or another device that acts as a modem. Once setting up a connection through another protocol (for example, PPP or over GSM) you can proceed as though you were connected to the Internet. In this case you will need to use a connection manager that is suited to the network and the devices you are using.

3. All other options have proprietary protocol suites. In these options you will need to either develop a set of adapters using SDKs of the network providers or use a wireless gateway. A wireless gateway abstracts the differences in the networks and provides you with a unified way to access the server regardless of the networks your users will be using. Different wireless gateways have different abstractions. For example, the WebSphere Wireless Gateway (another component within WebSphere Everyplace) abstracts all the networks to an IP network resolving all the complexities. A different example is the Broadbeam Wireless Gateway that creates a queue-based abstraction that allows your client-side applications to place messages that need to be delivered to the portal and have messages come back. The Broadbeam software then takes care of delivering these messages regardless of the underlying networks.

While adding an additional server to the mix certainly complicates your environment (see Figure 24-6), we strongly suggest that if you need to deploy your portlets over non-IP networks you use a gateway architecture. The alternative integration to multiple-carrier SDKs are far more complex.

Transcoding Technology

TT is an enabling technology that allows you to easily deploy portlets that can support different devices. TT implements three methods that transform content based on device information associated with the request.

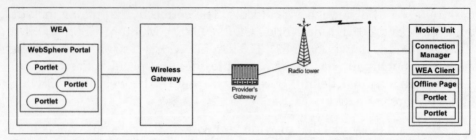

Figure 24-6 High-level architecture view including a wireless gateway and WEA.

TT inspects user agent information that is part of the headers packaged with the request and allows you to provide specific instructions for transforming the original content to a form that is suitable for the device that initiated the request. Elements of TT are available in WP but the full package is only available in WEA and most of the methods detailed in this section relate to the more advanced TT available in WEA.

In order to enable TT in WEA, log in to the portal as an administrator and follow these steps:

1. Select the Portal Administration tab.
2. Select Global Settings.
3. Check the `Enable trancoding of portlet content` check box.
4. Save and exit.

TT offers three ways to transform content, which are as follows:

1. XML style sheets—this method uses style sheets expressed in XSL to define mappings that should be applied before the content is delivered to the user's device.
2. Annotators—this method allows you to associate a set of annotation instructions with generated content. This instruction set allows you to specify (either within the generated content or using an external set of annotators) how the original portlet content should be modified before it is delivered to the user's device.
3. Transcoding plug-ins—a set of generic content modifiers that address common tasks such as conversion from normal HTML to WML.

In addition to the transcoding plug-ins TT has a built-in fragmentation transcoder. Fragmentation is important because many mobile phones have severe limits on storage capacity. As an example, some i-mode phones and gateways have a limit of 2048 bytes per document and some WML phones and gateways have a limit of 2880 bytes. Large documents must be broken

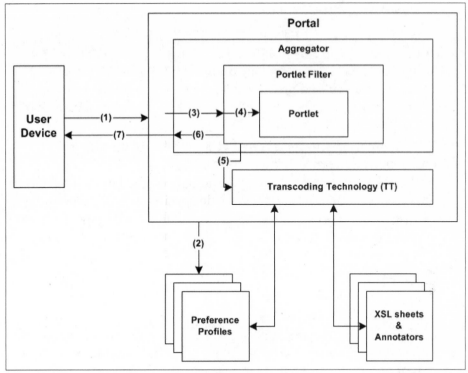

Figure 24-7   Request flow using TT as handled by the portal.

down into multiple documents linked together before they can be delivered to the user device. This function is carried out by the fragmentation transcoder.

Figure 24-7 shows the request handling flow that makes use of TT to adapt generated content. The flow shown in Figure 24-7 includes the following steps:

1. When a request comes in, the portal determines what the user agent is. This value captures which device the user is using.

2. The portal matches the user agent with the preference profiles installed. Preference profiles allow you to specify how to treat documents that will be delivered to different end user devices. You should place your preference files as `.prop` property files in the `<TT_ROOT>/etc/preferences/device` directory and name the files based on the user agent to which they correspond. Selection of the appropriate preference profile is based on the following sequence:

   a. The HTTP header is inspected to see whether it includes a value for `X-IBM-PVC-Device-Type`.

b. The `User-agent` field is checked in the HTTP header.

c. If neither exists, TT uses the default device profile.

d. In addition, you can specify a custom field in the HTTP header that will be used for selecting a user-specific profile (rather than a profile that is based on the device only). To do this, set the `httpUserIdField` value in `<TT_ROOT>/etc/localConfig .prop`.

Commonly used parameters that you can control through the preference profile files include the following:

a. `deviceRule`—defines which user agent this profile will be matched up with. You should include wild cards to cover multiple browsers and microbrowsers rather than have a specific preference profile for every different browser since many browsers and microbrowsers behave similarly.

b. `javaAppletsSupported`—a boolean value specifying whether applets should be stripped out of the content for devices that cannot render Java applets.

c. `javaScriptSupported`—a boolean value specifying whether Javascript code should be stripped out of the content for devices that cannot interpret and run Javascript.

d. `framesSupported`—a boolean values specifying whether the device can support HTML frames.

e. `desiredContentTypes`—a MIME type specifying the content type sent back to the user device.

f. A value for the maximal deck size as used by the fragmentation transcoder. This value defines the maximal size per fragment. As an example, the parameter for WML fragmentation is called `WMLMaximumDeckSize`.

3. The portal calls the aggregator that in turn calls the appropriate portlets. Each such portlet has a portlet filter that is invoked by the aggregator. An appropriate portlet is one that is configured to use TT. In order to configure a TT-enabled portlet you need to set two configuration parameters within your `portlet.xml` file as follows:

```
...
<portlet-app-def>
  ...
  <concrete-portlet-app ... >
    ...
    <concrete-portlet ... >
      ...
```

```
<config-param>
  <param-name>DoTranscoding</param-name>
  <param-value>true</param-value>
</config-param>
<config-param>
  <param-name>FilterChain</param-name>
  <param-value>Transcoding</param-value>
</config-param>
        </concrete-portlet>
      </concrete-portlet-app>
    </portlet-app-def>
```

Alternatively, log in to the portal as an administrator, select Administration ⇨ Portlets ⇨ Manage Portlets, select your portlet, and click Edit Parameters. Then add values for the two parameters as shown in Figure 24-8.

4. The portlet filter calls the portlet to retrieve the content (in the source markup—for example, HTML).

5. The portlet filter then calls the TT runtime sending it the portlet's content. TT uses the information in the profiles as well as style sheets and annotator files to create the new content.

6. The portlet filter returns the content generated by TT as if this is the content generated by the portlet.

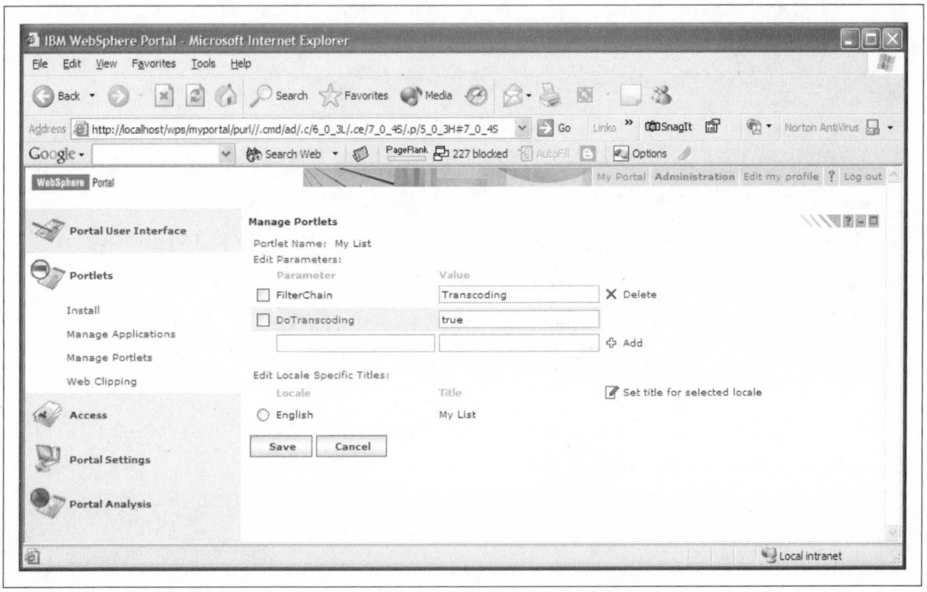

Figure 24-8 Enabling TT for your portlet—adding appropriate parameters.

7. The aggregator returns the aggregated content post-fragmentation (if relevant) and the portlet returns the content to the end user device.

Using XSL for Adapting Content

So long as all content generated by portlets is well-formed XML (and this is a nontrivial assumption that you should pay special attention to), XSL style sheets are a very natural and architecturally elegant solution to generating multiple presentations from a single portlet. In addition, XSL is an industry standard and the use of XSL for mapping one content to another is a common practice, which means that many people will be familiar with this method. There are numerous tools that can help you in doing this right—including the various versions of WebSphere Studio that include an XML editor, an XSL editor, and an XML-to-XML mapping editor.

To use style sheet transcoding you first need to configure the portal for XML processing, which can be done as follows:

1. Edit `<WAS_ROOT>/lib/app/config/services/PortletFilterService.properties` and add entries to allow for transcoding to the various markup types that your portal should support. Look for the last entry in the file starting with `Transcoding.transcodeMarkup` and make sure you use the next available sequence. As an example, for transcoding to WML and cHTML add the following entries:

```
Transcoding.transcodeMarkup.4 = xml->wml
Transcoding.transcodeMarkup.5 = xml->chtml
```

2. Log in to the portal as an administrator and select Administration ⇨ PortalSettings ⇨ Supported Markups. Click Add New Markup and enter the values as shown in Figure 24-9. Click OK.

3. The new markup type will be added as inactive. Select the xml markup and click Activate/Deactivate Selected Markup.

4. Validate your markup types by clicking Show Info; your display should include an active XML markup as shown in Figure 24-10.

Once the portal has been set up for XML transcoding, you need to tell it which style sheet should be used for transcoding each portlet. Specifying a style sheet per portlet can be done in one of the following three ways:

1. Add a `config-param` element within the `concrete-portlet` element in `portlet.xml` and put the style sheet in the WAR file.

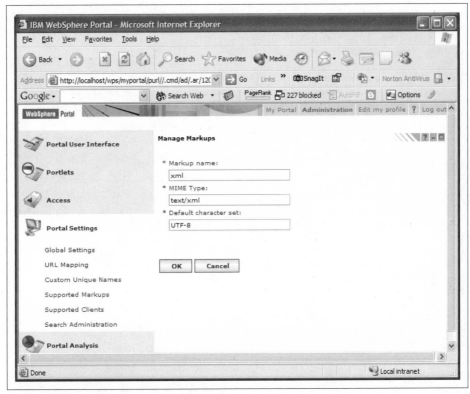

Figure 24-9   Adding support for XML markup for XSL transcoding.

2. Select Administration ⇨Portlets ⇨Manage Portlets, select your portlet and click Edit Parameters. Then add a parameter called `StylesheetFile` with the file name as the value.

3. If you need to transcode XML content into multiple other markup languages and want to separate the XSL transformation instructions into separate style sheets, your portlet can produce XML output with specific transcoding processing instructions. Each such directive includes a condition that defines the location of the style sheet and a category of user agents for which the style sheet should be applied. As an example, to apply one style sheet for all Nokia phones, which is different from a style sheet used for conventional Web browsers, add the following two directives to the code producing your XML content:

```
<xml version="1.0" encoding="ISO-8859-1"?>
<wtp-condition stylesheet="/browsers.xsl" condition="(user-
agent=*Mozilla*)"?>
<?wtp-condition stylesheet="/nokiaPhones.xsl" condition="(user-
agent=*Nokia*)"?>
... The rest of your XML content ...
```

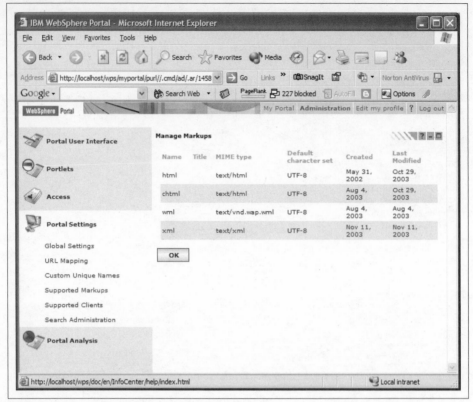

Figure 24-10 Validating active XML markup.

Using Annotators for Adapting Content

The second method to adapt content involves annotators that are TT-specific constructs that can help you transform HTML generated by a portlet. Annotators are important even though they are not a standard technology because XSL sheets are often hard to write while annotators follow a very simple instruction-based mapping metaphor. It is therefore often easier to build an annotator than an XSL sheet. In addition, annotators transform HTML content, which is probably what most of your portlets produce—making them easy to incorporate with your portlet JSPs or classes. You should therefore have both options in your arsenal of techniques.

Annotation instructions come in two flavors: external annotations and internal annotations. External annotations are instructions that are placed in an annotation file (a file with a .ann extension) and comprise two parts—a location and an action. The location is an XPath expression that defines the location at which the action should be applied. The action is an activity such as add or remove and is applied to the fragment of HTML pointed to by the location. Internal annotations have the same functional behavior but are placed directly within your HTML document as small XML fragments within HTML comments. Annotators are applied by TT after your portlet returns its HTML content. At this point TT traverses your document and applies each annotation instruction. This happens before any other TT processing is performed, for example, transcoding to other markup languages. As an example, if you need to create WML based on a subset of your HTML page, you can add annotators that strip out less important information and then use a generic HTML-to-WML transcoder.

External annotations are placed in a `.ann` file. This is an XML file that has an `<annot version="2.0">` element as the root XML element. The file then follows with a series of `description` elements—each one including a location specified by a `target` attribute and a `take-effect` attribute, and an action as an embedded element. For example, to replace a text fragment in the first paragraph in the body of your HTML document, use the following annotation:

```
<?xml version="1.0" encoding="ISO-8859-1"?>
<annot version="2.0">
 <description take-effect="before" target="/HTML[1]/BODY[1]
/P[1]/text">
   <replace>
     <text>Replacement Text</text>
   </replace>
 </description>
 ...
</annot>
```

Internal annotations can be added using any text editor. In addition, internal annotations are supported by the Page Designer Classic tool within WebSphere Studio Application Developer (which you have to install as an add-on). When using Page Designer Classic, point to the HTML fragment to which you want to apply the annotation, and right-click and select Annotation along with the action you want to perform. When adding or modifying a fragment, enter the new fragment in the dialog that opens. To make modifications to a TABLE, select the entry and choose Edit ⇨Attributes from the menu bar. The last tab on the dialog is the Annotation tab.

Each such annotation changes your HTML code; as an example, if you add a `replace` annotation, your HTML code will now include a fragment similar to (we added line breaks to make it clearer) what follows:

```
<!--METADATA type="Annotation" startspan
<?xml version="1.0"?>
  <annot version="2.0">
    <replace>
      <text>Replacement Text</text>
    </replace>
  </annot>-->
```

```
<P>Original Text</P>
<!--METADATA type="Annotation" endspan-->
```

Finally, if you would like an annotation to apply only to certain devices, use a user-agent-based condition. As an example, if you want replacement text to apply only to Nokia phones you can modify the internal annotation as follows:

```
<!--METADATA type="Annotation" startspan
<?xml version="1.0"?>
  <annot version="2.0" condition="!(user-agent=*Nokia*)">
    <replace>
       <text>Replacement Text</text?>
    </replace>
  </annot>-->
<P>Original Text</P>
<!--METADATA type="Annotation" endspan-->
```

The same set of annotators is available regardless of whether you are using internal or external annotations. Annotators supported by TT include the following:

- column—removes a TABLE column located by the XPath expression
- field—modifies a field within the HTML form located by the XPath expression
- insertattribute—inserts an HTML attribute into the element located by the XPath expression
- keep—keeps the HTML fragment located by the XPath expression
- inserthtml—inserts content before the HTML located by the XPath expression
- remove—removes the HTML fragment located by the XPath expression
- replace—replaces the element located by the XPath expression with the specified fragment
- replacewithhtml—similar to replace but the content is always an HTML fragment
- row—removes a TABLE column located by the XPath expression
- splitpoint—specifies a location at which fragmentation should occur. This allows you to control how the fragmentation transcoder (mentioned in the section titled "Transcoding Technology") will break up long documents
- table—used with other annotators such as column and row and affects the heading of the TABLE located by the XPath expression

Transcoding Plug-ins

In addition to the use of TT for generating content for mobile and offline users, WEA provides a set of transcoding plug-ins that can help you prepare portlet content for delivery to mobile units. Plug-ins are generic and handle elements that exist in almost any portlet and hence can often do a lot of work that you would otherwise have to do yourself. Transcoding plug-ins include the following:

- Image transcoding plug-in: this plug-in converts images ensuring that you don't download large images to devices with lower resolution and overslow networks.

- Text transcoding plug-in: this plug-in can convert text fragments (including HTML and XML) from one format to another and can be used to simplify output. For example, it can be used to convert a complex multilevel table to a simple ordered list.

- HTML-to-WML transcoding plug-in: this plug-in converts HTML to WML and can be used to convert existing HTML pages to WML pages without additional custom work on your behalf.

- HTML-to-cHTML transcoding plug-in: similar to cHTML.

Enhanced Portlets

WEA provides not only tools but also packaged applications. These enhanced portlets allow you to support mobile users quickly and with no additional development work. You can support mobile users with out-of-the-box functions on the following devices:

1. Devices with Pocket IE compliant with HTML 3.2 and Javascript support as defined in the Windows CE JS3.0 specification

2. Palm OS devices with Eudora 2.1, the AU Mobile Internet browser and Palm Web Pro Browser 1.0 and higher

3. WML microbrowsers

In terms of the functionality provided, the following portlets are available for use by mobile users:

1. Lotus Notes portlets:
   a. E-mail
   b. Calendar
   c. To-do lists
   d. Contacts

    e. Journal

  2. Microsoft Exchange portlets:

    a. E-mail

    b. Tasks

    c. Contacts

    d. Notes

  3. Reminder portlet

  4. World Clock portlet

  5. QuickLinks portlet

  6. Internet Mailbox portlet

  7. Banner AD portlet

  8. Image Viewer portlet

The Application Integrator Portlet

In Chapter 23 we discussed the Application Integrator portlet that allows you to portalize functions implemented within back-end application suites from vendors such as SAP, PeopleSoft, and Siebel. One of the useful features of Application Integrator is that it can also work with pocket-PC-based PDAs. More specifically, you can use Application Integrator to deliver applications to Pocket IE running on a Pocket PC 2000 or a Pocket PC 2002 environment—but you will need WEA version 4.3 or higher. If you also want these functions to be available in an offline mode, you will need to install the WEA client version 4.2.1 or higher.

When using Application Integrator there are some additional settings that you need to specify in order for the back-end functionality to be available on mobile devices. More specifically, remember the following:

1. Choose the markup type from the Select Markup to Configure pull-down list in the Object Builder page.

2. Install the WEA client on all PDAs and RIM devices—Application Integrator supports offline usage for applications once the client is installed.

3. Make sure the clipping portlet is installed—Application Integrator makes use of clippers to create the offline content and deliver it to the mobile unit.

Summary

People are mobile—they have always been mobile. For developers, viewing a user as someone using a full-blown PC connected through a fast connection to the Internet has always been a convenience. But this viewpoint is quickly becoming obsolete—and more so for portal and portlet developers. If you are part of a large-scale WP rollout, there is a good chance that sooner or later you will have to service people on the move using mobile phones, PDA, wireless-enabled laptops, or Blackberry devices. If so, remember that WP and WEA allow you to provide comprehensive support to your users.

From a rollout perspective you can handle many issues relating to multiple devices and markup within WP—and if this covers all of your requirements then your environment can be kept much simpler. If on the other hand you need complex transcoding then you need to introduce WEA into the mix and use its advanced TT capabilities. If you can stay with simple transcoding but need offline operations, then you can either choose WEA or another caching solution such as AvantGo by Sybase or MCP by ViryaNet. Finally, if the networks through which your functionality will be accessed include non-IP networks, then you need to introduce a gateway such as WebSphere Wireless Gateway or a third-party gateway such as the Broadbeam gateway or integrate proprietary SDKs that are usually provided by the network provider.

Index